Acceptance and Mindfulness-Based Approaches to Anxiety

SERIES IN ANXIETY AND RELATED DISORDERS

Series Editor: **Martin M. Antony**, *Anxiety Treatment and Research Centre, St. Joseph's Hospital, Hamilton, Ontario, Canada*

ACCEPTANCE AND MINDFULNESS-BASED APPROACHES TO ANXIETY
Conceptualization and Treatment
Edited by Susan M. Orsillo and Lizabeth Roemer

CONCEPTS AND CONTROVERSIES IN OBSESSIVE-COMPULSIVE DISORDER
Edited by Jonathan S. Abramowitz and Arthur C. Houts

SOCIAL ANXIETY AND SOCIAL PHOBIA IN YOUTH
Characteristics, Assessment, and Psychological Treatment
Christopher A. Kearney

A Continuation Order Plan is available for this series. A continuation order will bring delivery of each new volume immediately upon publication. Volumes are billed only upon actual shipment. For further information please contact the publisher.

Acceptance and Mindfulness-Based Approaches to Anxiety
Conceptualization and Treatment

Edited by

Susan M. Orsillo
Suffolk University
Boston, Massachusetts

and

Lizabeth Roemer
University of Massachusetts
Boston, Massachusetts

 Springer

Library of Congress Control Number: 2005925980

ISBN-10: 0-387-25988-0   e-ISBN 0-387-25898-9   Printed on acid-free paper
ISBN-13: 978-0387-25988-8

Printed in the United States of America.   (SBA/BP)

9 8 7 6 5 4 3

springer.com

CONTRIBUTORS

Sonja V. Batten, VA Maryland Health Care System and University of Maryland School of Medicine, Baltimore, Maryland, USA

John T. Blackledge, University of Nevada, Reno, Nevada, USA

Jennifer Block-Lerner, Department of Psychology, Skidmore College, Saratoga Springs, New York, USA

Jeffrey Brantley, Duke Center for Integrative Medicine, Duke University Medical Center, Durham, North Carolina, USA

LeeAnn Cardaciotto, Drexel University, Philadelphia, Pennsylvania, USA

Lisa W. Coyne, Brown University, Providence, Rhode Island, USA

Jill Ehrenreich, Boston University, Boston, Massachusetts, USA

Matthew T. Feldner, University of Vermont, Burlington, Vermont, USA

Kim L. Gratz, McLean Hospital and Harvard Medical School, Belmont, Massachusetts

Laurie A. Greco, Vanderbilt University Medical Center, Nashville, Tennessee, USA

Scott E. Hannan, The Institute of Living/Hartford Hospital, Hartford, Conecticut, USA

Steven C. Hayes, Department of Psychology, University of Nevada, Reno, Nevada, USA

James D. Herbert, Drexel University, Philadelphia, Pennsylvania, USA

Darren W. Holowka, University of Massachusetts, Boston, Massachusetts, USA

Maria Karekla, University at Albany, State University of New York, Albany, New York, USA

Ellen W. Leen-Feldner, University of Vermont, Burlington, Vermont, USA

Jill T. Levitt, New York, New York, USA

Akihiko Masuda, Department of Psychology, University of Nevada, Reno, Nevada, USA

Douglas S. Mennin, Yale University, New Haven, Connecticut, USA

Susan Orsillo, Suffolk University, Boston, Massachusetts, USA

Lizabeth Roemer, University of Massachusetts, Boston, Massachusetts, USA

Kristalyn Salters-Pedneault, Boston VA Healthcare System and Boston University School of Medicine, Boston, Massachusetts, USA

David F. Tolin, The Institute of Living/Hartford Hospital, Hartford, Conecticut, USA

Matthew T. Tull, Boston VA Healthcare System and Boston University School of Medicine, Boston, Massachusetts, USA

Michael P. Twohig, Department of Psychology, University of Nevada, Reno, Nevada, USA

Alethea A. Varra, Department of Psychology, University of Nevada, Reno, Nevada, USA

Amy W. Wagner, University of Washington, Seattle, Washington, USA

Robyn D. Walser, VA Palo Alto Health Care System, National Center for PTSD, Palo Alto, California, USA

Andrew R. Yartz, University of Vermont, Burlington, Vermont, USA

Michael J. Zvolensky, University of Vermont, Burlington, Vermont, USA

PREFACE

Fear and anxiety are natural, human responses to the threats we encounter, perceive, or anticipate. The uncertainties inherent in our lives on a personal and global level almost inevitably give rise to feelings of anxiety. Most of us experience bodily responses (e.g., muscle tension, rapid heart beat), cognitive responses (e.g., anticipating something unfortunate happening in our future), and behavioral responses (e.g., choosing not to do something because it may make us uncomfortable) that signal the presence of anxiety from time to time. However, for some, these anxious responses become severe and pervasive, causing intense distress and/or severely restricting or impinging on quality of life.

Anxiety disorders constitute the most prevalent class of mental health problems in the United States (Narrow, Rae, Robins, & Regier, 2002) and are associated with significant disruptions in functioning (Leon, Portera, & Weissman, 1995) and substantial health care costs (for both medical and psychological treatment, Greenberg et al., 1999). Fortunately, efficacious psychosocial (cognitive-behavioral) treatments have been developed for the anxiety disorders (see Barlow, 2002, for extensive reviews), so that many individuals are able to successfully address their spiraling anxiety and habitual avoidance patterns and learn new ways of responding to actual and perceived threats. However, not all clients accept or respond to these interventions, demonstrating a need for further treatment innovation in order to maximize the beneficial impact of our psychosocial interventions.

The last decade has seen an explosion of interest in acceptance- and mindfulness-based approaches within the cognitive-behavioral tradition.

These approaches, drawn in part from experiential (e.g., Rogers, 1961; Greenberg, 2002) and Buddhist (e.g., Kabat-Zinn, 1990; Nhat Hanh, 1992) traditions, but grounded in behavioral theory (e.g., Hayes, Barnes-Holmes, & Roche, 2001; Linehan, 1993), emphasize the way that efforts to control our internal experiences might in fact exacerbate them. They suggest that cultivating an open, expansive, compassionate, present-moment awareness might facilitate adaptive functioning and reduce distress associated with living in the past or the future. Within these perspectives, fear and anxiety will naturally arise, as will other painful emotional experiences. However, by bringing gentle awareness to these experiences, and recognizing their transience, we can allow these experiences to inform us, but not to control us and interfere with our lives.

These acceptance-based behavioral therapies have begun to accrue promising data supporting their efficacy in both experimental and treatment settings. Their applicability to and utility for anxiety disorders is supported both empirically and theoretically. It may be that integration of these approaches provides the enhanced efficacy that is needed to broaden our impact on this significant mental health problem.

In this volume, for the first time, clinicians and clinical researchers specializing in anxiety disorders come together to present perspectives on the utility of this integration. In the first part of the book, "Integrating Acceptance and Mindfulness and Existing Psychological Traditions," we, along with Darren W. Holowka, begin with a conceptual and practical overview of how acceptance-based approaches complement and expand existing cognitive-behavioral theories and therapies, emphasizing both the commonalities and distinctions in these approaches. Doug Mennin then highlights the way that an emotion perspective (based on emotion theory and research, as well as experiential therapy traditions) can inform and enhance acceptance-based behavioral treatments for anxiety disorders.

In the second part, "General Approaches to Assessment and Treatment," Jenn Block-Lerner, Kristi Salters-Pedneault, and Matt Tull provide an extensive review of conceptual and operational definitions of mindfulness and acceptance that provides an important basis for work in this area. The next three chapters provide examples of how existing acceptance-based therapies can be directly applied to the anxiety disorders. First, Mike Twohig, Akihiko Masada, Alethea Varra, and Steve Hayes review acceptance and commitment therapy (ACT) and its application to anxiety. Then Jeff Brantley provides an overview of mindfulness-based stress reduction (MBSR) as it applies to anxiety disorders. Finally, Kim Gratz, Matt Tull, and Amy Wagner discuss the ways that mindfulness skills from dialectical behavior therapy (DBT) might be applied to treat individuals with anxiety disorders.

In the third part, "Specific Populations," experts within each specific disorder (or population) present an overview of each disorder and the current status of treatments for it, an acceptance-based conceptual model specific to the disorder, and practical suggestions for integrating acceptance and mindfulness into treatments for the disorder. Jill Levitt and Maria Karakela begin with a discussion of panic disorder, sharing some interesting and innovative pilot work aimed at enhancing Panic Control Treatment with acceptance strategies. James Herbert and LeeAnn Cardaciotto introduce an acceptance-based model of social anxiety disorder. The next two chapters discuss ways in which an acceptance based approach may be relevant to the two most treatment resistant anxiety disorders. First, we present our model of generalized anxiety disorder and we share some preliminary data from a randomized control trial examining the potential efficacy of an acceptance-based approach. Sonja Batten, Sue Orsillo, and Robyn Walser discuss how acceptance-based approaches might be applied particularly to treating complex posttraumatic stress disorder. Scott Hannan and Dave Tolin review obsessive–compulsive disorder (OCD) and address the ways in which acceptance-based approaches might supplement exposure and response prevention in the treatment of OCD. Finally, Laurie Greco, John Blackledge, Lisa Coyne, and Jill Ehrenreich discuss some of the unique challenges and applications associated with acceptance-based strategies for treating children with anxiety disorders.

Although there has been an explosion of interest in acceptance-based approaches in the past decade, much more research is needed to explicate the precise mechanisms underlying these approaches. In the final part, "Future Directions," Mike Zvolensky, Matt Feldner, Ellen Leen-Feldner, and Andrew Yartz place this recent work in the larger context of emotion regulation and anxiety, provide an overview of basic research on these processes, and offer suggestions for a research agenda aimed at furthering our understanding of experiential avoidance, acceptance, and mindfulness. Together, these contributions provide an excellent overview of the current status of research and clinical thinking in this burgeoning area, which we hope will stimulate further innovation and inquiry into the utility of these approaches.

Preparation of this book was supported in part by National Institute of Mental Health Grant MH63208 to the editors.

For us, this book is a product of years of professional and personal development that has been influenced by far more people than could possibly be named in this forum. We are extremely grateful to Marty Antony, the series editor, for encouraging us to do the book and consistently supporting our work over the years. We have been supported and inspired by many clinical psychologists in these areas, most notably Tom Borkovec, Steve Hayes, Kelly Wilson, Zindel Segal, Mark Williams, John Teasdale, Dave Barlow, Brett Litz, Doug Mennin, and Amy Wagner; their influences are evident in our work. We also wish to acknowledge the influence of Buddhist and other nonpsychologist writers, particularly Jon Kabat-Zinn, Thich Nhat Hanh, Pema Chodron, and Sharon Salzberg. All of the contributing authors in this volume have also enhanced our work; we are very grateful for the chapters they have provided here and for their ongoing contributions to the field. We are particularly grateful to the graduate students and post-doctoral fellows who have worked with us throughout the years. Our work has been profoundly shaped and enhanced by their enthusiasm, insight, and efforts, and we look forward to their continued contributions to the field. We also thank the clients who have courageously shared their struggles and their wisdom with us. Finally, we offer unending gratitude to our friends and loved ones, who help us stay in contact with what matters. In particular, Sue thanks her husband Paul for his sustaining love and unrelenting support.... We would like to dedicate this book to the children in our lives, Sarah, Sam, Josh, and Sophia, for encouraging us to bring beginner's mind to the present moment.

Susan M. Orsillo
Lizabeth Roemer

REFERENCES

Barlow, D. H. (Ed.). (2002). *Anxiety and its disorders: The nature and treatment of anxiety and panic* (2nd ed.). New York: Guilford.

Greenberg, L. S. (2002). *Emotion-focused therapy: Coaching clients to work through their feelings*. Washington, DC: American Psychological Associations.

Greenberg, P. E., Sisitsky, T., Kessler, R.C., Finkelstein, S. N., Berndt, E. R., Davidson, J. R. T., et al. (1999). The economic burden of the anxiety disorders in the 1990s. *Journal of Clinical Psychiatry, 60*, 427–435.

Hayes, S. C., Barnes-Holmes, D., & Roche, B. (Eds.). (2001). *Relational frame theory: A post-Skinnerian account of human language and cognition*. New York: Plenum.

Kabat-Zinn, J. (1990). *Full catastrophe living: Using the wisdom of your body and mind to face stress, pain and illness.* New York: Delacorte.

Leon, A. C., Portera, L., & Weissman, M. M. (1995). The social costs of anxiety disorders. *British Journal of Psychiatry, 166*(Suppl 27), 19–22.

Linehan, M. M. (1993). *Cognitive-behavioral treatment of borderline personality disorder.* New York: Guilford.

Narrow, W. E., Rae, D. S., Robins, L. N., & Regier, D. A. (2002). Revised prevalence based estimates of mental disorders in the United States: Using a clinical significance criterion to reconcile 2 surveys' estimates. *Archives of General Psychiatry, 59,* 115–123.

Nhat Hanh, T. (1992). *Peace is every step: The path of mindfulness in everyday life.* New York: Bantam Books.

Rogers, C. R. (1961). *On becoming a person: A therapist's view of psychotherapy.* Boston: Houghton Mifflin Company.

CONTENTS

III. SPECIFIC POPULATIONS

IV. FUTURE DIRECTIONS

PART I

INTEGRATING ACCEPTANCE AND MINDFULNESS AND EXISTING PSYCHOLOGICAL TRADITIONS

ACCEPTANCE-BASED BEHAVIORAL THERAPIES FOR ANXIETY

USING ACCEPTANCE AND MINDFULNESS TO ENHANCE TRADITIONAL COGNITIVE–BEHAVIORAL APPROACHES

Susan M. Orsillo, Lizabeth Roemer, and Darren W. Holowka

The ubiquity of anxiety to the human existence is obvious in the poetry, philosophical essays, religious tomes, and clinical/empirical literature of our society. From the standpoint of existential philosophy, anxiety is seen as a natural, multifaceted response to both the freedom and the responsibility associated with making daily choices about how to live one's life. However, from a traditional mental health perspective, the universally human experience of anxiety can prompt a cascade of responses that signal the presence of a psychological disorder. Specifically, significant distress may emerge as a secondary response to fear and anxiety and impairment in important domains of life functioning can occur as an individual attempts to avoid situations that elicit fear and anxiety.

Anxiety disorders are in fact the most commonly experienced class of mental health problems in the United States (Narrow, Rae, Robins, & Regier, 2002), with a conservative estimate of the 1-year prevalence for any disorder of 13.1% for adults aged 18–54. Moreover, many anxiety disorders are associated with a chronic course (e.g., Hirschfeld, 1996; Kessler, Sonnega, Bromet, Hughes, & Nelson, 1995; Noyes et al., 1992) and diminished quality of life as evidenced by higher rates of financial dependence, unemployment (e.g., Leon, Portera, & Weissman, 1995), poorer quality of life (Massion, Warshaw, & Keller, 1993), and increased risk for completed suicide (Allgulander, 1994).

Given the chronic course and deleterious associated features of the anxiety disorders, it is no surprise that individuals in our society spend billions of dollars each year seeking medical and psychological treatments aimed at reducing or eliminating their anxiety (Barlow, 2002). The annual cost of anxiety disorders in the United States in 1990 was estimated to be approximately $42.3 billion or $1,542 per individual with the vast majority of the cost deriving from nonpsychiatric (54%), psychiatric (31%), and pharmacological (2%) treatment (Greenberg et al., 1999). The average health care costs for individuals with anxiety disorders are double those of patients without those disorders even after adjusting for medical comorbidity (Simon, Ormel, Von Korff, & Barlow, 1995).

A BRIEF OVERVIEW OF THE EFFICACY OF COGNITIVE–BEHAVIORAL THERAPY FOR ANXIETY DISORDERS

Fortunately, psychotherapy development and research has been particularly fruitful across the anxiety disorders, with evidence emerging for the efficacy of cognitive–behavioral approaches for each individual disorder (see Barlow, 2002, for disorder-specific, detailed reviews). Recent meta-analyses confirm that cognitive–behavioral treatments (CBTs) for panic disorder (Gould, Otto, & Pollack, 1995), obsessive–compulsive disorder (OCD; Eddy, Dutra, Bradley, & Westen, 2004), generalized anxiety disorder (GAD; Borkovec & Ruscio, 2001), and posttraumatic stress disorder (PTSD; Bradley, Greene, Russ, Dutra, & Westen, 2005) are associated with recovery from, or improvement in, anxiety symptoms.

Despite these promising findings, much more work is needed to translate the gains achieved in the randomized clinical trials (RCTs) to widespread clinical success in reducing the significant distress and life interference associated with anxiety among clients who seek relief from primary care clinicians and mental health providers in the community. The meta-analyses of the effectiveness of RCTs on CBT for anxiety conducted to date highlight the significant average reductions in anxiety symptoms from pre- to posttreatment among clients who present for and accept randomization in clinical trials. Yet, they do not uniformly account for clients who refuse randomization (or treatment), those who are excluded on the basis of the severity or complexity of their presentation, those who fail to complete treatment, and those who fail to respond.

Moreover, outcome may be defined much more narrowly in RCTs than it is in clinical practice. RCTs tend to rely too heavily on measures of symptom reduction as the primary indices of treatment success, ignoring the more salient, but difficult to measure, potential impact of treatment on quality of life. Further, many clients who are categorized as treatment responders continue to experience substantial residual symptoms and associated impairment (e.g., Bradley et al., 2005). More extensive data addressing the stability and maintenance of treatment gains are needed (e.g., Bradley et al., 2005; Eddy et al., 2004), as well as studies that measure or report on the number of participants who seek additional treatment following their participation in the clinical trial (Barlow, 2002).

Anxiety researchers have recently recognized the importance of addressing these fundamental issues in clinical research and a number of studies are currently underway that are aimed at increasing the acceptability and effectiveness of treatments for the anxiety disorders. Borkovec and Castonguay (1998) persuasively argue that treatment development, innovation, and refinement will be most powerful when it is driven by programmatic research aimed at increasing our knowledge of the nature of the psychological problem being treated and the potential underlying processes associated with change. Thus, understanding the function of symptoms associated with anxiety disorders as well as the mechanisms associated with treatment response will likely yield more powerful and sustaining treatment approaches. The goal of this chapter is to describe how acceptance-based behavioral approaches may be particularly well suited to enhance existing CBTs for anxiety, as these approaches specifically target many of the perceived shortcomings of CBT discussed above (for a more extensive discussion of how acceptance-based conceptualizations correspond to and enhance behavioral and cognitive models of anxiety disorders, see Orsillo, Roemer, Block-Lerner, & Tull, 2004). In this chapter, we will briefly describe this new branch of behavior therapy and present the conceptual framework for understanding anxiety disorders from the theoretical perspective that underlies this form of treatment. Further, we will provide practical guidelines for how acceptance-based methods can be used to enhance traditional cognitive–behavioral approaches to anxiety disorder treatment. However, before we describe acceptance-based conceptualizations of anxiety, we will briefly overview current cognitive–behavioral conceptualizations of anxiety.

COGNITIVE AND BEHAVIORAL CONCEPTUALIZATIONS OF ANXIETY AND PROPOSED MECHANISMS OF CHANGE

EARLY BEHAVIORAL AND COGNITIVE MODELS

Early theories on the development and treatment of anxiety disorders generally suggested that fear develops through traumatic conditioning (e.g., Marks, 1969; Wolpe, 1958), is maintained operantly through avoidance learning (Mowrer, 1947), and is reduced through extinction or the decrease in a learned response due to repeated, nonreinforced exposure to a conditioned stimulus (CS). Although these theories provided a fundamental basis for behavioral theory and therapy, a number of criticisms were levied against this early model of learning, including the limited evidence for the role of direct traumatic conditioning in the development of most fears and phobias (Lazarus, 1984) and the evidence for reduction in fear when avoidant responses are not prevented (Rachman, Craske, Tallman, & Solyom, 1986).

Interest in cognitive processes as potential causes of psychopathology and mechanisms of change in the treatment of anxiety disorders led to a vigorous effort to develop cognitive alternatives to previously established behavioral principles, particularly as a way to extend the explanatory power of behavioral theories (James, 1993). Generally, cognitive models of psychopathology assume that an individual's schemas, which include belief systems, expectancies, and assumptions, assert a strong influence on both mood and behavior by influencing how information is perceived, encoded, and recalled (Beck, 1993). Anxiety disorders are thought to be caused and maintained in part by a disturbance in information processing that leads to an overestimation of danger or perceived threat and an associated underestimation of personal ability to cope (Beck, Emery, & Greenberg, 1985). For instance, Clark (1986, 1988, 1996) proposed that catastrophic misinterpretations of somatic sensations are primary in the development and maintenance of panic disorder. Similarly, beliefs that one might behave in an inept and unacceptable manner and that such behavior would have tremendous social cost are proposed to causal factors in social phobia (Clark & Wells, 1995).

Despite the popularity of the cognitive models of psychopathology, the constructs at its foundation remain vague and difficult to operationalize and measure. Cognitive researchers have yet to demonstrate how irrational cognitions are acquired, who acquires them, and how they can be measured independent of anxiety or panic (Bouton, Mineka, & Barlow, 2001). The assumption that particular cognitions, such as "people are judging me," are irrational may be inaccurate, particularly in the light of a rich tradition of social psychological research demonstrating social perception and bias (Hughes, 2002). The basic premise of cognitive–behavioral theory, that cognition predicts behavior, has yet to be convincingly supported. Longitudinal studies have confirmed that "dysfunctional attitudes" wax and wane over time with symptoms (Persons & Miranda, 1992); the association between cognitions and emotions is bidirectional (e.g., Nolen-Hoeksema, Girgus, & Seligman, 1986; Wells & Matthews, 1994); and responses (such as panic attacks) occur without the presence of detectable cognitions (e.g., Kenardy & Taylor, 1999). Most concerning is the fact that cognitive therapy has failed to achieve its intended impact. Cognitive therapy is not uniquely associated with changes in cognition (Arntz, 2002; McManus, Clark, & Hackmann, 2000; Westling & Öst, 1995), there is little evidence for long-lasting overall superiority of cognitive treatments (Booth & Rachman, 1992; Craske, Glover, & DeCola, 1995; Fava et al., 1994; Foa et al., 1999; Gould, Buckminster, Pollack, Otto, & Yap, 1997; Lovell, Marks, Noshirvani, Thrasher, & Livanou, 2001; Marks, Lovell, Noshirvani, Livanou, & Thrasher, 1998; Tarrier et al., 1999), and changes in dysfunctional attitudes do not appear to mediate changes in depression and anxiety in CBT (Burns & Spangler, 2001).

CONTEMPORARY MODELS OF LEARNING AND COGNITION

Contemporary conditioning models move beyond simple stimulus–response relations and postulate more complex models in which responses (both cognitive and emotional) can become cues in and of themselves, prompting efforts at avoidance and escape (e.g., Foa & Kozak, 1986; Lang, 1985). For instance, interoceptive conditioning, a process by which low-level somatic sensations of anxiety or arousal may become conditioned stimuli associated with higher levels of anxiety or arousal, has been proposed to be critically important in the development of panic disorder (Bouton et al., 2001; Goldstein & Chambless, 1978; Razran, 1961) and interoceptive exposure has demonstrated efficacy in the treatment of panic disorder (e.g., Gould et al., 1995). Similarly, anxiety sensitivity, or the fear of anxiety-related symptoms (Reiss, 1991), and fear of other emotional states (Williams, Chambless, & Ahrens, 1997) have been identified as prominent factors in the development of anxiety disorders, and anxiety sensitivity has recently been demonstrated to be a mechanism of change in CBT of panic disorder (Smits, Powers, Cho, & Telch, 2004). Thought action fusion, or the belief that thoughts can directly influence external events (e.g., "If I imagine my son being hit by a car, it will happen") and that having neg-atively evaluated intrusive thoughts (e.g., "I want to stab my children") is morally equivalent to carrying out a prohibited action, has been im-plicated in the development and maintenance of OCD (Shafran, Thordar-son, & Rachman, 1996) as have metacognitive beliefs concerning the need to control thoughts (Gwilliam, Wells, & Cartwright-Hatton, 2004). These models suggest that reactions (both cognitive and emotional) to one's own internal experiences (thoughts, feelings, bodily sensations) may underlie the development and/or maintenance of anxiety disorders.

Finally, there is growing recognition of the importance of contextual features or "meaning" in learning models. Bouton et al. (2001) review a body of research examining the role of the context during extinction tri-als in the reemergence of fear following extinction. Contextual stimuli are thought to include both external cues in the environment and internal cues, such as drug and mood states and even the passage of time. The cumu-lative research suggests that extinction does not generalize well between contexts, which has significant implications for improving the efficacy of exposure therapy as a treatment for anxiety disorders. For instance, there is mounting evidence that extinction does not reflect a destruction of the stimulus–response relationship. Instead, new learning is proposed to oc-cur in which the stimulus becomes an ambiguous signal that may elicit different reactions depending on the context (Bouton, 2002).

Although modern learning theory provides one of the best prevail-ing empirically based explanations for the development and treatment of anxiety, this theory is also not without its shortcomings. Moreover, al-though this theory offers a relatively nice account for the development of panic disorder, the application to other anxiety disorders, particularly those with complex cognitive rather than somatic involvement, such as GAD, remains unstudied. Further, critical gaps remain in the translation from animal research to clinical application. For instance, in the typical conditioning paradigm animals have no learning history with the stimu-lus that is conditioned to elicit fear. Once the extinction process is engaged, the CS becomes an ambiguous stimulus, its fear-eliciting properties de-pendent on the context. This new ambiguity may explain why the initial fear conditioning is mostly resistant to context, whereas extinction is more context specific (Bouton, 2002). However, humans rarely develop anxiety disorders to a CS to which they have never been exposed. Thus, the CS is likely ambiguous from the initial fear acquiring experience, which may have implications for its endurance and treatment, deserving further study. Finally, and most critically, learning models based on nonhumans may be less useful in areas in which language and cognition dominate (Hayes, Barnes-Holmes, & Roche, 2001).

Concurrent with the development and elaboration of learning theory models of the development and treatment of anxiety disorders, cognitive models have also evolved. In response to many of the shortcomings of traditional *content*-focused cognitive–behavioral approaches to psychotherapy, a number of theories and techniques now focus on cognitive *processes*, particularly the narrowing of attention toward threat (a prominent feature of the anxiety disorders; see Barlow, 2002, for reviews). For instance, Wells and Matthews (1994) developed the Self-Regulatory Executive Function (S-REF) model of psychological disorders that causally links psychological disturbances to a syndrome of cognitive–attentional responses characterized by self-focused attention or "online" processing of negative self-beliefs, worry/rumination, threat monitoring, resource limitation, and maladaptive coping. From this model, a key component of CBT is presumed to be the direct modification of cognitive processes, particularly attention. Interventions aimed at this goal have preliminarily been applied to the treatment of panic disorder (Wells, 1990), social phobia (Wells & Papageorgiou, 1998; Wells, White, & Carter, 1997), and PTSD (Wells & Sembi, 2004). This emphasis on process rather than content is similar to the shift in emphasis that characterizes approaches that have been described as the "third wave" of behavioral and cognitive therapies (Hayes, 2005).

THE THIRD WAVE OF BEHAVIOR THERAPY

Hayes (2005) has described the possible emergence of a third wave of behavioral and cognitive therapies, such as acceptance and commitment therapy (ACT; Hayes, Strosahl, & Wilson, 1999), dialectical behavior therapy (DBT; Linehan, 1993a, 1993b), functional analytic psychotherapy (FAP; Kohlenberg & Tsai, 1991), integrative behavioral couples therapy (IPBCT; Jacobson & Christensen, 1995), and mindfulness-based cognitive therapy (MBCT; Segal, Williams, & Teasdale, 2002), that build on traditional cognitive and behavioral approaches, but differ in some potentially critical ways.

From Hayes' (2005) perspective, the first wave of behavior therapy, in its emphasis on the importance of scientifically derived theoretical principles and clinical methods, overlooked some of the clinical richness inherent in psychoanalytic and humanistic approaches to therapy. The second wave of behavior therapy, marked by the cognitive therapy movement, involved a renewed interest in the role of internal experiences, such as thoughts and feelings. Specific cognitive patterns were identified for particular patient populations, and the prevailing model was that the detection and correction of irrational thoughts would lead to improved mental health. However, as noted above, there is a growing literature demonstrating significant shortcomings in both cognitive models of anxiety and the unique and specific efficacy of clinical techniques aimed at changing cognitions. Further, widespread changes and developments in the basic philosophy of science suggest a movement from mechanistic to more contexualistic viewpoints (Hayes, 2005).

Hayes (2005) described a number of uniting features of the separate therapy approaches described as third wave therapies. Consistent with traditional cognitive–behavioral approaches, these interventions are grounded in theory and committed to empirical evaluation of their associated basic principles, processes, and outcomes (Hayes, 2005). For instance, the conceptualization of psychopathology and the methods and techniques of ACT are derived from relational frame theory (RFT; Hayes et al., 2001), a functional, contextual theory of language and cognition that underlies an ongoing program of basic research. Experimental research aimed at exploring one potential mechanism of change in ACT, acceptance, is rapidly accruing (Campbell-Sills, Barlow, Brown, & Hofmann, 2005; Eifert & Heffner, 2003; Feldner, Zvolensky, Eifert, & Spira, 2003; Levitt, Brown, Orsillo, & Barlow, 2004). MBCT is supported by basic experimental and mediational research on metacognitive awareness, a cognitive set in which thoughts and feelings are seen passing events in the mind rather than as inherent aspects of the self- and/or accurate reflections of reality (Teasdale et al., 2002). Further, evidence for the efficacy and effectiveness of these approaches is steadily growing (e.g., Bach & Hayes, 2002; Gifford et al., 2004; Hayes, Masuda, Bissett, Luoma, & Gueffero, 2004; Orsillo, Roemer, & Barlow, 2003; Teasdale et al., 2000).

However, in addition to focusing on behavioral change as an outcome, these therapies emphasize contextual and experiential change methods that alter the function of psychological events without directly intervening with their form or frequency (Hayes, 2005). Clinically, this approach has been described as encompassing the dialectic of acceptance and change (Linehan, 1993a). Overall, third wave therapies broaden the focus of outcome from symptom reduction to the development of generally applicable skills aimed at significantly improving quality of life. Finally, third wave approaches underscore the ubiquitous nature of the processes thought to underlie psychopathology, and the assumption is that therapists as humans struggle with many of the same core issues as their clients.

In our own work in this area, we have come to use the term *acceptance-based behavior therapy* to describe the shared approach to treatment that characterizes these therapies. We use the term acceptance-based behavioral therapy to encompass the dual emphasis in these approaches on the importance of accepting or allowing the presence of internal experiences (as an alternative response to the judgmental and avoidant reactions to these experiences that are characteristic of individuals with anxiety and other disorders) while developing behavioral repertoires that are broad, flexible, effective, and values driven (to counteract the rigid, restricted, and avoidant behavioral patterns that are typical of individuals with anxiety disorders). Within this broader category, we include our own integration of many of the underlying principles and techniques derived from these third wave therapies into traditional cognitive–behavioral therapy for anxiety (Orsillo et al., 2003; Roemer & Orsillo, 2005; Roemer, Salters-Pedneault, & Orsillo, in press). Although we have been testing the efficacy of our approach with individuals with GAD (see Roemer & Orsillo, 2005), we use a similar approach with clients with diverse clinical presentations.

CONCEPTUALIZING PSYCHOPATHOLOGY AS EXPERIENTIAL AVOIDANCE

Although mounting evidence suggests that therapies teaching skills of acceptance and mindfulness are effective in reducing psychopathology (e.g., Baer, 2003; Hayes et al., 2004), a careful formulation as to how these approaches specifically address psychopathology is critical (Teasdale, Segal, & Williams, 2003). Although theorists from other traditions have certainly emphasized the importance of acceptance in psychotherapy (e.g., Greenberg & Safran, 1987; Rogers, 1961), we will focus here on behavioral and cognitive–behavioral models. A particularly useful and well-elaborated account comes from Steve Hayes and his colleagues. Hayes, Wilson, Gifford, Follette, and Stosahl (1996) convincingly argued that experiential avoidance, defined as mental and behavioral strategies aimed at changing the form or frequency of one's current internal experience (e.g., thoughts, emotions, images, physiological sensations), contributes to the development and maintenance of many forms of psychopathology. From this perspective, anxiety disorders develop when individuals engage in cognitive and behavioral strategies aimed at reducing or eliminating anxiety-related internal experiences. Most obviously, individuals may severely restrict their behavior with the goal of avoiding certain anxiety-related stimuli and/or environments that are likely to elicit anxiety. As this avoidance or escape behavior increases and generalizes, increasingly more subtle behavioral changes will likely occur that further diminish quality of life. Cognitive strategies, such as efforts to suppress certain internal experiences, distract attention away from them, or actively change their content, are also viewed as methods of experiential avoidance that may contribute to the development and maintenance of anxiety disorders.

If experiential avoidance underlies many forms of psychopathology, particularly anxiety disorders, it is useful to consider how this response develops, how it is maintained, and of course, how to address it in therapy. Clinical researchers have provided theoretical and empirical accounts for both universal factors that may influence experiential avoidance, as well as individual differences that may play a role. Although a number of explanations have been offered at different levels of analysis, at a very general level, several factors seem to contribute to experiential avoidance. Certain internal experiences including feelings (e.g., anxiety, fear, sadness), thoughts ("I am no good"), and bodily sensations (heart racing, face blushing) are judged to be pathological, threatening, or impairing, which triggers escape and avoidance responses. This judgment or appraisal process derives from two main sources. First, through a process of learning described in more detail below, internal experiences are capable of eliciting painful psychological responses that would normally trigger behavioral escape or avoidance. In other words, *imagining* an encounter with a threatening stimulus elicits the same distress that an actual encounter would elicit. Given that escape or avoidance is an innate response to pain, internal experiences can come to elicit these responses. Second, because our society supports the idea that happiness is best achieved through the avoidance of pain, and that internal attempts to suppress or avoid pain are useful, experiential avoidance is learned from and encouraged by multiple sources in an individual's life.

RFT (Hayes et al., 2001) provides one account for why individuals may come to avoid their internal experiences. According to RFT, relational learning, which occurs under arbitrary contextual control, is the core of language and cognition. Although a full explanation of RFT is beyond the scope of this chapter, in short, RFT describes the processes and contexts by which stimuli that have never been directly associated or trained can become related and how those relations can also transform stimulus functions among related stimuli. As humans, we continuously derive relations among events, words, feelings, experiences, and images as we engage with our environment, interact with others, think, observe, and reason. Relational learning is reinforced and maintained both by our verbal community (e.g., humans reinforce one another for verbally describing the learning process of relating two stimuli) and by the instrumental value of understanding stimulus relations in that this level of understanding is often associated with an increased ability to control certain situations or events.

There are, however, also a number of unfortunate consequences of relational learning. Because of the rapid, complex, and continuous nature of relational learning, innumerable cues can elicit psychological pain (for instance, thoughts of a recently deceased spouse can be elicited by a song, a particular restaurant, a feeling of sadness, a beautiful sunset) making it virtually impossible to take some behavioral action that will successfully lead to the complete avoidance of pain (Hayes, 2005). When individuals are unable to avoid emotional pain through behavioral action, they often engage in internal strategies aimed at reducing or escaping this discomfort. Yet there is growing evidence that deliberate attempts to internally suppress painful experiences such as thoughts and emotions may paradoxically increase the associated distress in certain contexts (e.g., Gross & Levenson, 1997; Purdon, 1999; Roemer & Borkovec, 1994; Wegner, 1994).

Another clinically relevant byproduct of relational framing is what Hayes and his colleagues have termed cognitive fusion (Hayes et al., 1999). From a clinical perspective, cognitive fusion is the process by which humans become indistinguishable from their transient internal experiences (e.g., thoughts, emotions, bodily sensations, and images). If a woman with PTSD experiences a flashback of her rape, that flashback is not experienced as simply an image or a memory. Through the process of relational learning, the image takes on the stimulus function of the event itself. The flashback elicits a fear and avoidance reaction as if the rape is occurring once again. Similarly, to someone struggling with social phobia, experiencing the thought "I am a failure" can be as potent as experiencing a socially threatening event.

There are a number of features of relational learning that highlight its critical role in psychopathology. Relational learning is proposed to occur at a rapid rate with continuing deeper and further complexity and elaboration (Hayes, 2005), relational networks are highly resistant to "unlearning" even in the face of contradictory training (Wilson & Hayes, 1996), and behavior governed by relational networks is highly insensitive to shifting environmental contingencies (Hayes, Brownstein, Zettle, Rosenfarb, & Korn, 1986). From a clinical perspective, this model suggests that cognitive fusion will be associated with prolonged and chronic psychological distress and rigidity in behavioral responding.

Teasdale and colleagues (2002) implicate a process similar to that of cognitive fusion in their work on the prevention of relapse in depression. Specifically, they highlight metacognitive awareness, or the processing of experiencing negatively perceived thoughts and feelings from a decentered perspective, as the mechanism of change in psychotherapy. Decentering is defined as changing the way one relates to one's internal experience from a stance of personally identifying with one's thoughts and feelings to one of cultivating a wider context of awareness in which thoughts and feelings are seen as transient events that are differentiated from "self" or "reality" (e.g., Teasdale et al., 2002).

The universal and naturally occurring processes of relational learning and experiential escape and avoidance are amplified by cultural forces that suggest that control over internal experiences is not only possible, but highly desirable (Hayes et al., 1999). Purposefully exerting control over one's behavior and environment is often associated with successful problem resolution. In other words, if a chair is broken, there are a number of concrete, controlled behavioral actions that can be directed toward successfully fixing the chair. It is reasonable to expect that a rule that works and is strongly reinforced in one domain could be applied more generally in other domains. Also, control efforts directed toward internal experiences are sometimes successful; for example, focused breathing and relaxation strategies can reduce one's perception of pain or feelings of anxiety in the short term. Attempting to control all of one's negative thoughts, feelings, bodily sensations, and images through will power and determination is an action that is highly regarded and reinforced in our culture, despite the limited success and paradoxical rise in distress often associated with this strategy.

Further, individuals may have unique experiences that make them particularly vulnerable to problems with experiential avoidance. Temperamental differences in behavioral inhibition (e.g., Kagan, 1989) or neuroticism (Eysenck, 1967, 1981) may influence the frequency and intensity with which anxiety is experienced, potentially attenuating an individual's tolerance for the experience of anxiety. Linehan (1993a) discussed a similar concept regarding individual differences in emotional vulnerability, including sensitivity to emotional stimuli, emotional intensity, and slowed return to baseline following the elicitation of an emotion. On the other hand, environmental characteristics such as repeated interactions with those who invalidate one's internal experience may also contribute to the development of an experientially avoidant style (Linehan, 1993a).

In summary, models of anxiety developed from modern learning, cognitive, and relational frame theories converge on several key points. Complex learning that involves the development of associations among internal experiences such as thoughts, emotions, and physiological sensations is thought to play a critical role in the development and maintenance of anxiety disorders (e.g., Bouton et al., 2001; Foa & Kozak, 1986; Goldstein & Chambless, 1978; Hayes et al., 2001). Reactions to those internal experiences such as judgment, fusion, fear, and avoidance are associated with increased distress and impairment in functioning (Gwilliam et al., 2004; Hayes et al., 1999; Reiss, 1991; Shafran et al., 1996; Teasdale et al., 2002; Williams et al., 1997). One perspective on how existing treatments for the anxiety disorders may be enhanced by this cumulative knowledge is reflected in the acceptance-based behavior therapies, which are directly aimed at decreasing reactivity to and attempts at avoidance of internal experiences, while simultaneously expanding behavioral repertoires.

INTEGRATING ACCEPTANCE INTO TRADITIONAL CBT FOR ANXIETY

Acceptance-based behavior therapies for anxiety disorders can be thought of as involving three main goals that may complement and enhance traditional cognitive–behavioral approaches to these disorders. Given that anxiety is associated with a restricted focus of attention toward threat-related cues (both internal and external), often one main goal of treatment is to expand the client's awareness of his or her experience. In addition to the traditional CBT emphasis on increasing awareness of situational cues, and cognitive, emotional, and behavioral responses, clients can be taught and encouraged to observe their emotional responses with increased clarity, to observe the function of their internal experiences, to become more aware of actions that they take, internally and externally, aimed at controlling internal experiences such as anxiety and anxiety-related thoughts, and to more keenly observe the consequences associated with those actions.

A second goal of these approaches to treatment is to encourage a radical shift from a judgmental and controlling stance toward one's internal experiences to a compassionate, accepting stance. It is likely that traditional CBT approaches also accomplish this by increasing clients' awareness and understanding of their responses and highlighting the way that many of their negative thoughts about their own reactions are not supported by evidence. However, acceptance-based approaches make this shift an explicit emphasis of therapy and are careful to avoid strategies that might inadvertently fuel negative reactivity toward and judgment of one's internal experiences (such as labeling one's thoughts "irrational"). A variety of clinical methods can be employed to help clients develop the sense of a transcendent, consistent self, an observing self, that is separate from the myriad of transient thoughts, feelings, and bodily sensations that are experienced on a moment-to-moment basis, and to promote a compassionate stance toward these internal experiences.

A final, and most basic goal of acceptance-based behavior therapies, is to increase the quality of the client's life. Therapy is aimed at decreasing the intense distress associated with the client's internal experience. However, more importantly, when someone is struggling with an anxiety disorder, behavior is typically driven largely by avoidance. Thus, acceptance-based behavioral approaches encourage choice and flexibility. Clients are urged to engage in activities that reflect their personal values, to actively participate and engage with important people in their life, and to choose actions that will be effective in helping them pursue their goals. This is of course similar to the traditional behavior therapy focus on behavior change, although here an explicit emphasis is on those changes that will enrich a client's life.

A number of traditional cognitive–behavioral methods, as well as new methods drawn from acceptance-based approaches, can be used to facilitate these three primary goals of treatment. In this next section, we will describe a few of the ways in which acceptance-based methods can be integrated into traditional cognitive–behavioral therapy.

Setting the Stage for Therapy: Assumptions and the Therapeutic Relationship

Traditional CBT and acceptance-based behavior therapies share a number of assumptions about the therapeutic relationship. From both perspectives, therapist warmth, respect, empathy, and genuineness is critical. Compassion toward the client and all of his or her experiences and actions is explicitly emphasized in acceptance-based behavioral approaches. In an effort to increase the client's compassion toward his or her own internal experience, the therapist is encouraged to validate and actively model genuine compassion throughout treatment, consistently responding to emotional distress, extreme thoughts, and bodily sensations as naturally occurring, universal human responses.

Both CBT and acceptance-based approaches highlight the importance of a collaborative relationship and a client-centered approach to treatment. However, one subtle distinction between the two may be that acceptance-based approaches explicitly highlight the fact that the very processes the client is struggling with (judging and attempting to control internal experiences) are difficult for the therapist as well. Following from this premise, the methods and techniques of these therapies are as relevant to the therapists as they are to the clients. To illustrate this point in therapy, we will often use the "Two Mountain" metaphor from ACT to explain why it is that the therapist is often able to offer a new perspective on the client's current struggle (which is likened to climbing a mountain). The therapist is not resting comfortably at the peak, having successfully mastered the climb. Instead, the therapist is able, from a separate mountain, where the therapist is struggling with his or her own climb, to observe the client, directing him or her toward an obscured foothold or promising new path. A common element of the third wave of behavior therapies is this often "radically nonhierarchical" perspective on treatment (Hayes, 2005).

Functional analytic psychotherapy (FAP; Kohlenberg & Tsai, 1991) is a third wave or acceptance-based behavioral approach that specifically focuses on the therapeutic relationship. A guiding principle of FAP is that the therapist–client relationship provides a rich social environment with incredible potential to elicit and change, through naturally occurring reinforcement, instances of the client's problem behaviors as they occur within the therapy session. Therapists are encouraged to practice awareness of clinically relevant behaviors (CRBs) that emerge within session. For instance, when working with a client with social phobia, who reports difficulties engaging in his or her interpersonal relationships, the therapist would notice CRBs such as diverted eye contact or the use of nervous laughter as a distancing strategy and use the opportunity of their occurrence as a therapist–client relationship learning opportunity (Kohlenberg et al., 2004). Therapists might respond by self-disclosing their personal reaction to the client's behavior. Similarly, if the client were to try out a new behavior in sessions, such as opening up more in the presence of the therapist and making direct eye contact, an engaged and attentive therapist would respond, perhaps by amplifying his or her positive responses toward the client, using natural reinforcement to support the client's behavior. This use of relational reinforcement using natural instead of arbitrary responses is also a core aspect of DBT (Robins, Schmidt, & Linehan, 2004).

THE GOALS OF TREATMENT

A significant feature of third wave or acceptance-based therapies is the focus on the construction of flexible, effective, behavioral repertoires over the elimination of narrowly defined symptoms (Hayes, 2005). The implicit goal of CBT for anxiety disorders is to produce clinically significant changes that will improve the client's overall quality of life. However, with the advent of brief, targeted therapies specifically aimed at reducing levels of anxiety and behavioral avoidance, increased quality of life as a therapeutic target has been largely ignored. Acceptance-based models of psychotherapy explicitly change that focus of treatment in at least two very important ways.

In our own clinical work, heavily influenced by ACT, during the informed consent process, we collaboratively develop treatment goals with our clients aimed at increasing the quantity and quality of activities that they value. Our first line of intervention is to deeply explore with our clients the way in which they perceive that their anxiety is interfering in their relationships with family, friends, and romantic partners; their occupational or educational functioning; and in their pursuit of recreational activities. Outside of session writing activities, based on the values assignments from ACT (Hayes et al., 1999; Wilson & Murrell, 2004) and emotional processing paradigms described by Pennebaker (1993), invite clients to deeply process their thoughts and feelings related to this topic as they write for 20 minutes three times over the course of a week. In subsequent sessions, clients are asked to engage in similar exercises that involve describing in vivid detail the ways they would like to be in each of the valued domains described above (e.g., how open and intimate they want to be with the important people in their lives, what characteristics about their occupation are important to them), exploring potential barriers to value-consistent action, and connecting with their deepest thoughts and feelings related to not acting consistently in accordance with those stated values.

The second major difference between goal-setting in traditional cognitive–behavioral therapy and acceptance-based approaches is that acceptance-based approaches aim to promote the development of skills and repertoires that can be broadly applied (Hayes, 2005). For instance, acceptance-based treatments for anxiety disorders target experiential avoidance of the full range of emotions and encourage a willingness stance toward all internal experiences. Mindfulness is offered as a way of being in the world, not merely as a method of anxiety reduction.

Although the explicit focus of acceptance-based therapy is improved quality of life, a reduction in psychological distress is obviously an important goal of treatment. From an acceptance standpoint, a distinction is made between the pain that is part of being human and the chronic intense distress that the client is currently experiencing as a result of his or her anxiety disorder and the vicious cycle of labeling and judging experiences, experiential avoidance, and behavioral restriction. Acceptance is not a resignation that one must learn to live with the chronic, intense distress of an anxiety disorder. Nonetheless, the goal of acceptance-based behavior therapy is not to eliminate the basic emotions of fear, sadness, anger, and disgust from the client's experience. Self-doubt, thoughts about one's inadequacy, painful memories of past experiences, and fears about future events will not be completely erased as a result of treatment. Instead, the goal of treatment is to normalize these human experiences, to reduce the internal struggle and distress associated with having them, and to encourage the client not to engage in behaviors aimed only at changing those thoughts and feelings, but to meaningfully engage in life with them present.

PSYCHOEDUCATION

In ours and others' acceptance-based approaches (e.g., Linehan, 1993b; Segal et al., 2002), psychoeducation, a mainstay of traditional CBT, is also a key component of acceptance-based behavior therapies. Drawing from existing treatment models, in order to help our clients better understand their experience of fear and anxiety, we describe the adaptive function of anxiety, the fight or flight response, and the cognitive, behavioral, and physiological components of anxiety. We share our model of anxiety with the client, our conceptualization of specific difficulties, and the rationale for our treatment plan. However, there are some important distinguishing features of an acceptance-based approach to treating anxiety that are worth noting.

First, the content of psychoeducation in these approaches is likely to be somewhat expanded and differentiated from traditional cognitive–behavioral approaches. For instance, when working with clients with anxiety disorders, in early sessions we broadly discuss the function of emotions (borrowing from Linehan, 1993b) as signaling the importance of particular events, communicating salient information to others, narrowing our attention toward important cues, and preparing us to take action (see Mennin, 2005, for a more extensive discussion of the role of emotion in acceptance-based approaches). We draw an analogy between physical and emotional pain. Neither is experienced as a pleasant sensation, but both are critical to our survival. Drawing from and expanding on behavioral models, we also describe the relationship between emotion and behavior, highlighting the fact that emotions are linked with action tendencies (e.g., I may experience the urge to escape or avoid when I experience the feeling of anxiety), but that they do not control behavior (I can stay in a situation when I am anxious). Further, we describe examples of situations in which the prevailing emotion may be associated with a behavior that is inconsistent with what is important to us. For example, I (SO) might find giving a clinical workshop to a large audience threatening, and I may experience an urge to escape or avoid, both because I am hard-wired to be sensitive to social rejection and because my performance in the workshop is something that matters to me. However, a meaningful part of my professional identity is sharing what I do clinically with other mental health professionals so that methods I think are important are widely disseminated. From an acceptance standpoint, it makes sense that such an important experience increases my anxiety, and produces an urge to avoid.

Often clients readily accept and understand from an objective standpoint the material presented on the function of emotion. Yet, they have a more difficult time reconciling that model with their own internal experience, which is often characterized by intense, lingering, complicated emotional distress. Through psychoeducation, drawing from the ACT perspective of "clean" and "dirty" emotions, therapists can describe the process by which emotional responses, and other internal events, can become complex and muddied. For instance, we often highlight the fact that in addition to having acute, specific emotional responses to actual events that occur in our environment, humans are able to experience emotional responses to a wide variety of cues related to imagined future events and our recollection of past events. We discuss the processes by which we come to judge and evaluate our emotions and other internal events and the inevitable urge toward experiential control and avoidance. We present information about the innately human processes and the pervasive societal forces that support efforts at internal control and we discuss the potential limits and paradoxical effects of such control efforts.

Finally, drawing from ACT, therapists can introduce an alternative to the clients' current approach to solving their problems with anxiety. Specifically, they can propose an alternative approach that involves adopting an acceptance or willingness stance toward one's internal experiences and focusing control efforts toward behavior that is in the service of increasing valued action. Toward this end, therapists may introduce the concept of mindfulness (e.g., Linehan, 1993b; Segal et al., 2002), as described more fully below.

This brief overview provides some distinction about the psychoeducational material that may be presented in an acceptance-based behavioral therapy for anxiety disorders. The methods for providing this information are also important to note. Didactic presentation of material with accompanying handouts and subsequent discussion is typically only one small component of treatment. These approaches all emphasize that the "proof" of the model lies in its utility or workability from the client's own experience (e.g., Hayes et al., 1999). Working from this perspective requires that the therapist be particularly cautious so as not to argue with or attempt to persuade the client to embrace a particular perspective.

A core characteristic of acceptance-based behavioral approaches is the use of experiential clinical methods. Paradox, metaphors, poems, stories, and experiential exercises, including mindfulness practice, are heavily favored over the logical, rational Socratic method of teaching that often characterizes traditional CBT. For instance, several metaphors derived from ACT can be used to experientially demonstrate the limits of attempts at internal control. Clients can be asked to consider their ability to banish their thoughts and images of a vividly described warm jelly doughnut or slice of chocolate cake. They can be asked the likelihood of being able to internally suppress physiological symptoms of anxiety while attached to a sensitive polygraph machine that will explode at the first detection of anxiety symptoms. Segal and colleagues (2002) emphasize the importance of having clients experience mindfulness through exercises, rather than trying to rationally explain what it is. Drawing from their approach, we use poems such as *The Guest House* (see Block-Lerner, Salters-Pedneault, & Tull, 2005) to evoke the possibility of remaining open to the full range of one's internal experiences.

SELF-MONITORING AND OBSERVATION: TRAINING IN MINDFULNESS AND ENHANCEMENT OF COGNITIVE DEFUSION

Both CBT and experiential avoidance models acknowledge the important role of narrowed attention to threat cues in the development and maintenance of anxiety disorders. Treatment from both perspectives involves facilitating the client's awareness of and differentiation of particular internal events. Clients are encouraged to notice, and typically monitor using written records, individual thoughts, particular emotions, and specific physiological reactions that are elicited by different events and cues over the course of their daily lives. Both approaches also encourage clients to broaden the scope of their attention beyond an exclusive focus on internal experiences and perceived threat cues. In traditional CBT, this broadened attention is typically used to dispute or disprove the client's prevailing irrational thoughts about their anxiety and its consequences or to modify perseverative self-focused attention (Wells, 2000). Acceptance-based approaches promote a broadening of awareness that increases contact with present moment contingencies, as opposed to more rigid, rule-governed (e.g., Hayes et al., 1999) patterns of responding that are not based in current circumstances (Borkovec, 2002; Kabat-Zinn, 1994). This broadened awareness, and increased responsivity, is hoped to reinforce and support more flexible, effective, and values-driven behavioral responding. Additionally, continued observation of internal experiences as transient events that are separate from one's sense of self promotes cognitive defusion, which should reduce a client's urgency to engage in experiential avoidance.

A potentially unique feature of an acceptance-based approach to observation or self-monitoring is the assumption that many clients have not practiced this form of observation and that, since for most clients their natural instinct will be toward experiential avoidance, simply assigning the task of self-monitoring may not be sufficient. Thus, in our work, we use a progressive series of mindfulness exercises specifically aimed at developing and sharpening observation skills. Mindfulness involves practicing changing the focus of attention, first purposefully focusing on a particular event (such as the act of breathing, or thoughts as they arise in one's mind), and then expanding attention to capture a broader context. Mindful attention involves paying attention to the present moment. Although we are often pulled toward thoughts and images about the past and the future, through mindfulness practice we can learn to acknowledge the presence of such "tugs" on our attention and to repeatedly turn our attention toward the present moment.

Moreover, acceptance-based approaches emphasize a particular quality of attention or observation that has been described most explicitly in definitions of mindfulness (Kabat-Zinn, 1994; Linehan, 1993b; Segal et al., 2002). Mindful attention involves cultivating a compassionate, nonjudgmental, and accepting response to one's observation of events in the present moment. Clients are encouraged to observe internal and external experiences with an openness and curiosity, to use a "beginner's mind" to see things as they are, rather than as one believes them to be.

Psychoeducation sets the stage for compassion toward one's internal experience by offering a model by which clients can begin to understand the origin and function of certain internal experiences and the ubiquitous nature of human suffering. Yet the work of therapy is experientially applying this abstract principle to clients' personal struggles with anxiety. We use a series of formal mindfulness exercises, sequentially ordered to build specific skills to enhance this quality of awareness with our clients. Formal mindfulness exercises are practiced in sessions and clients are asked to continue the practice between sessions. In addition, clients are encouraged to engage in informal mindfulness practice by bringing a present-focused, compassionate, single-minded focus to a variety of daily activities, such as driving, eating, doing household chores, listening to music, and interacting with others (Nhat Hanh, 1992).

Two formal mindfulness exercises we use are derived from techniques used commonly in traditional CBT—diaphragmatic breathing and progressive muscle relaxation. However, the focus of these exercises is not to control or change one's experience of anxiety (and, in fact, some research suggests that the use breathing retraining with exposure therapy may actually decrease the efficacy of exposure (Schmidt et al., 2000) likely because it could be conceptualized as teaching avoidance (Barlow, 2002). Instead, we encourage clients to focus on their experience of breathing (and tension) to fully notice the sensations involved, and then to make a subtle change and observe what happens (i.e., to let go of the tension in their shoulders). We use a mindfulness of sounds exercise (Segal et al., 2002) to allow clients to notice how difficult it is to focus on the tonal quality of sounds and to notice how quickly our minds label (e.g., siren) and judge (e.g., bad) them. After significant practice, clients are encouraged to begin to observe their emotions and thoughts, for instance by imaginally placing each thought on a leaf on a stream (e.g. Hayes et al., 1999) on a conveyer belt or on a cloud in the sky (Linehan, 1993b), and to bring a compassion and openness to these experiences. Again, the ultimate goal is for clients to change the relationship they have with their internal experiences such that thoughts, feelings, and sensations are seen as transient natural events rather than threatening reflections of their psychopathology that must be suppressed or eliminated. As these skills are developed through formal practice in and outside of sessions, clients can be encouraged to apply them in their daily lives, thus strengthening their ability to accept, rather than react to, their own reactions and engage fully in their lives.

Exercises and clinical methods derived from ACT (Hayes et al., 1999) are also useful in promoting self-observation and cognitive defusion. For instance, therapists might adopt a number of verbal conventions in sessions, and ask their clients to use them as well, such as describing experiences exactly as they are. So rather than saying "I can't do that," clients can say, "I'm having the thought that I can't do that" and "I am depressed" can be more accurately stated as, "I am having feelings of sadness and the thought that I am not good." Particularly relevant to clients with anxiety disorders, we ask our clients to consider substituting the word "but" for "and" to see if it provides a more accurate description of events. Rather than saying, "I want to go to the mall with my daughter, but I am anxious," the client would be encouraged toward "I want to go to the mall with my daughter and I have having some feelings of anxiety."

COGNITIVE THERAPY

Acceptance-based and cognitive approaches are similar in that they both acknowledge the role of life experiences (learning or programming) in contributing to the content of thoughts and experiences commonly associated with anxiety disorders. However, they differ radically in the presumed role of cognitions in the development and treatment of the disorders. As discussed earlier, a cognitive model of anxiety assumes that cognitions (or schemata) are at least partially causal in the development of anxiety disorders. In contrast, acceptance-based (and more traditional) behavioral approaches view cognitions as responses or symptoms associated with an anxiety disorder.

The techniques of cognitive therapy can be divided into three main components: (a) self-monitoring, or the identification and labeling of thoughts; (b) logical analysis, which involves restructuring or changing the content of a dysfunctional cognition through verbal examination, questioning, challenging, and reasoning; and (c) hypothesis testing, or the evaluation of the validity of dysfunctional cognition through the design and implementation of behavioral experiments (Jarrett & Nelson, 1987). As noted above, the first step of self-monitoring and observation integrates well with acceptance-based approaches.

The integration of acceptance-based approaches with the logical analysis of cognitive restructuring is more problematic, although there is some evidence for this integration with some third wave approaches (e.g., Kohlenberg et al., 2004; Segal et al., 2002). It is important to note that logical analysis can be further divided into a number of techniques that differ significantly from one another in form and function. For instance, some forms of logical analysis involve changing the content of a presumably irrational thought such as "I will die if I have a panic attack" through Socratic questioning such as "What is the probability you will die from a panic attack? How many panic attacks have you had before? Have the consequences been deadly?" In contrast, other techniques that fall into the category of logical analysis are focused more on contextual change. For instance, a client who thinks "I can't write when I am feeling anxious" may be encouraged to consider that he or she can engage in the process of writing while experiencing feelings of anxiety. Also, some approaches to cognitive restructuring emphasize promoting flexibility (e.g., "How many ways are there to see this?," Borkovec & Sharpless, 2004, p. 223) or decentering (e.g., providing a list of cognitive distortions to help clients notice them and decenter from them if they arise; Segal et al., 2002) rather than encouraging clients to replace one thought with another. These latter approaches appear more congruent with an acceptance-based behavioral emphasis, although not all acceptance-based approaches use them (e.g., Hayes et al., 1999; Roemer & Orsillo, 2005).

Although traditional cognitive therapy aimed at content change can conflict with the explicit emphasis on acceptance of internal experiences in acceptance-based behavior therapies, methods that focus on changing one's *relationship to* one's thoughts and feelings and viewing thoughts as thoughts rather than as reality can be effectively integrated with other acceptance-based strategies (Hayes et al., 1999; Segal et al., 2002; Teasdale et al., 2002).

EXPOSURE THERAPY

Exposure therapy is one of the most effective components of CBT for particularly for treating panic disorder (e.g., Gould et al., 1995), specific phobias (Antony & Barlow, 2002), OCD (Abramowitz, 1997), social anxiety disorder (Gould et al., 1997), and PTSD (Foa, Keane, & Friedman, 2000). Yet, despite the demonstrated efficacy of this approach, relatively few clients receive this treatment in clinical practice (e.g., Cook, Schnurr, & Foa, 2004; Goisman et al. 1993). Although some of the barriers to dissemination may be due to misconceptions about exposure therapy on the part of the client and the therapist (Cook et al., 2004), there is some evidence that exposure therapy is less effective with more severe (e.g., Barlow, 2002) and emotionally avoidant (Foa, Riggs, Massie, & Yarczower, 1995; Jaycox, Foa, & Morral, 1998) clients. Acceptance-based approaches may enhance the effect of exposure therapy by directly addressing existing concerns about clients' unwillingness to engage in exposure, the complexities of exposure with comorbid conditions, and the reduced utility of this approach with highly avoidant clients.

As it is traditionally delivered, exposure therapy typically involves the development of a fear and avoidance hierarchy of anxiety-eliciting situations and the prescription of a systematic and progressive program of exposure to those situations. Depending on the form of the exposure, the anxiety-eliciting situations can involve internal experiences such as images (imaginal exposure), psychophysiological sensations such as increased heart rate or body temperature (interoceptive exposure), or, in the case of in-vivo exposure, external objects (e.g., spiders, needles) and situations (giving a speech, walking into a mall). Although behavioral models have begun to identify emotions themselves as potential conditioned stimuli (e.g., Goldstein & Chambless, 1978; Williams et al., 1997), it has been less common to include such emotional responses as specific targets of exposure in CBT. Although the hierarchy construction is a collaborative process between the therapist and the client, situations are chosen primarily on the basis of their ability to elicit fear and avoidance. Although the true mechanism of change in exposure has yet to be fully explicated (Rachman, 1991; Steketee & Barlow, 2002), the prevailing rationale for exposure is extinction; repeated exposures to a feared stimulus paired with the blocking of escape and avoidance behaviors will ultimately lead to reduced fear.

Experiential avoidance is a key target in acceptance-based behavioral therapies, rendering exposure therapy a highly complementary therapeutic method. However, although the methods of exposure therapy used in acceptance-based therapies and CBT can be topographically similar, the rationale and goal are different in what may be particularly important ways. Acceptance-based therapies (most notably ACT and approaches that integrate it) explicitly connect exposure to increasing quality of life. Clients are encouraged to identify valued directions in their lives and to commit to actions that are consistent with these values. It is acknowledged that these actions will inevitably bring up painful thoughts, feelings, images, and sensations and urges to avoid. Engaging in behavioral or "exposure" assignments is directed at reducing avoidance, but not extinguishing internal responses (although it is acknowledged that extinction may occur). Engagement in the actions themselves is seen as inherently valuable.

As a practical example, using a CBT framework, individuals with social anxiety disorder may be encouraged to ask an acquaintance at work out to lunch because such an action is associated with fear and avoidance. The client would be encouraged to remain in the anxiety-provoking situation, meeting specific behavioral goals (rather than emotional goals such as feeling comfortable), without distracting or avoiding. Often clients develop alternative statements they can use in the situation to represent the cognitive-restructuring work they have been doing in sessions. The model suggests that within sessions habituation will occur, although clients are typically told that anxiety will not always decrease. In our clinical practice, we would encourage our clients, using the extensive values exercises described above, to deeply explore what is meaningful about connecting intimately with others. We would validate and humanize the anxiety and anxiety-related thoughts elicited by taking such as risky action, use mindfulness and defusion methods to encourage the client to view those internal experiences as tolerable transient events, and encourage the client to commit to a values-consistent action (such as asking a co-worker to lunch). During the interaction, the client would be encouraged to use mindfulness skills to stay in the moment, to engage and actively participate in the interaction, while having compassion for any anxiety that arises.

Although this approach is not inconsistent with traditional CBT, there are a number of subtle differences that may increase the efficacy and acceptability of what is a powerful component of CBT. Acceptance-based approaches include a number of specific clinical methods (psychoeducation, acceptance, mindfulness, cognitive defusion) directly aimed at decreasing experiential avoidance and increasing willingness which may increase the acceptability of this approach to highly avoidant clients who may decline traditional exposure. Additionally, explicitly connecting approach or exposure with values may increase the willingness of a previously reluctant client to experience private events, since the purpose and benefit of doing so may be more obvious and salient than in traditional behavioral approaches. This emphasis on clinically significant change may address a major shortcoming of many RCTs in that the operationalization of clinical significance, if done at all, is often done a priori using outcome measures that may or may not represent the client's ability to function better in some palpable way (Kazdin, 1998).

Acceptance-enhanced exposure therapy may be conducted in two distinct ways. As described in many of the chapters in this book, systematic exposure therapy can be conducted very similarly to how it is conducted in CBT, with an altered rationale and goal, following a number of sessions using other acceptance-based strategies to decrease experiential avoidance.

Alternatively, exposure may be conducted in a less systematic and artificially derived manner with natural opportunities for "exposures" occurring within and between sessions as clients begin to engage in more valued actions.

Experimental research documenting the relevance of an acceptance rationale in the treatment of anxiety disorders has begun accumulating. Eifert and Heffner (2003) compared the impact of a brief acceptance intervention to breathing retraining on self-reported distress, physiological responding, and behavior of students who engaged in a CO_2 challenge. Although the groups did not differ in the physiological responses they demonstrated, those in the acceptance condition reported less intense fear and were more willing to engage in future aversive interoceptive tasks. Levitt and colleagues (2004) conducted a similar study with participants diagnosed with panic disorder and also found that while physiological response to the CO_2 challenge was similar across groups, clients in the acceptance group reported less anxiety and a greater willingness to participate in a second challenge than did clients who engaged in a suppression or neutral condition.

Although the generalizability of these experimental findings to clinical practice is unknown, the results of these studies do provide some support for continued examination of the potential integration of acceptance into exposure therapy for the anxiety disorders. Throughout this volume, there are a number of chapters that specifically describe how acceptance-based approaches might be used to enhance exposure therapy.

CONCLUSIONS

There has been an explosion of theoretical, empirical, and practical interest in acceptance-based behavioral approaches to treating psychological disorders in general, and anxiety disorders in particular, in recent years. We have provided a brief overview of how these approaches complement and extend existing cognitive–behavioral approaches to understanding and treating the anxiety disorders. Although initial studies are promising, more research is needed to determine the efficacy and effectiveness of these approaches, along with the optimal forms of intervention and integration, and the underlying mechanisms of therapeutic change. We hope this chapter provides a useful introduction for researchers and clinicians interested in continuing and expanding this important work, which we hope will serve to further enhance our interventions for these chronic and impairing disorders.

REFERENCES

Abramowitz, J. S. (1997). Effectiveness of psychological and pharmacological treatments for obsessive–compulsive disorder: A quantitative review. *Journal of Consulting and Clinical Psychology, 65*, 44–52

Allgulander, C. (1994). Suicide and mortality patterns in anxiety neurosis and depressive neurosis. *Archives of General Psychiatry, 51*, 708–712.

Antony, M., & Barlow, D. H. (2002). Specific phobias. In D. H. Barlow (Ed.), *Anxiety and its disorders: The nature and treatment of anxiety and panic* (2nd ed., pp. 380–417). New York: Guilford.

Arntz, A. (2002). Cognitive therapy versus interoceptive exposure as treatment of panic disorder without agoraphobia. *Behaviour Research and Therapy, 40*, 325–341.

Bach, P., & Hayes, S. C. (2002). The use of acceptance and commitment therapy to prevent the rehospitalization of psychotic patients: A randomized controlled trial. *Journal of Consulting and Clinical Psychology, 70*, 1129–1139.

Baer, R. A. (2003). Mindfulness training as a clinical intervention: A conceptual and empirical review. *Clinical Psychology: Science and Practice, 10*, 125–143.

Barlow, D. H. (Ed.). (2002). *Anxiety and its disorders: The nature and treatment of anxiety and panic* (2nd ed.). New York: Guilford.

Beck, A. T. (1993). Cognitive therapy: Nature and relation to behavior therapy. *Journal of Psychotherapy Practice and Research, 2*, 345–356.

Beck, A.T., Emery, G., & Greenberg, R. L. (1985). *Anxiety disorders and phobias*. New York: Basic Books.

Block-Lerner, J., Salters-Pedneault, K., & Tull, M. T. (2005). Assessing mindfulness and experiential acceptance: Attempts to capture inherently elusive phenomena. In S. M. Orsillo & L. Roemer (Eds.), *Acceptance and mindfulness-based approaches to anxiety: Conceptualization and treatment* (pp. 71–99). New York: Springer.

Booth, R., & Rachman, S. (1992). The reduction of claustrophobia: I. *Behaviour Research and Therapy, 30*, 207–221.

Borkovec, T. D. (2002). Life in the future versus life in the present. *Clinical Psychology: Science and Practice, 9*, 76–80.

Borkovec. T. D., & Castonguay, L. G. (1998). What is the scientific meaning of empirically supported therapy? *Journal of Consulting and Clinical Psychology, 66*, 136–142.

Borkovec, T. D., & Ruscio, A. M. (2001). Psychotherapy for generalized anxiety disorder. *Journal of Clinical Psychiatry, 62*(Suppl 11), 37–42.

Borkovec, T. D., & Sharpless, B. (2004). Cognitive behavioral therapy for generalized anxiety disorder: Living in the present. In S. Hayes, M. Linehan, & V. Follette (Eds.), *Mindfulness and acceptance: Expanding the cognitive–behavioral tradition* (pp. 209–242). New York: Guilford.

Bouton, M. E. (2002). Context, ambiguity, and unlearning: Sources of relapse after behavioral extinction. *Biological Psychiatry, 52*, 976–986.

Bouton, M. E., Mineka, S., & Barlow, D. H. (2001). A modern learning theory perspective on the etiology of panic disorder. *Psychological Review, 108*, 4–32.

Bradley, R., Greene, J., Russ, E., Dutra, L., & Westen, D. (2005). A multidimensional meta-analysis of psychotherapy for PTSD. *American Journal of Psychiatry, 162*, 214–227.

Burns, D. D., & Spangler, D. L. (2001). Do changes in dysfunctional attitudes mediate changes in depression and anxiety in cognitive behavioral therapy? *Behavior Therapy, 32*, 337–369.

Campbell-Sills, L., Barlow, D. H., Brown, T. A., & Hofmann, S. G. (2005). *Effects of suppression and acceptance on emotional responses of individuals with anxiety and mood disorders*. Manuscript under review.

Clark, D. M. (1986). A cognitive approach to panic. *Behaviour Research and Therapy, 24*, 461–470.

Clark, D. M. (1988). A cognitive model of panic attacks. In S. Rachman & J. D. Maser (Eds.),*Panic: Psychological perspectives* (pp. 71–89). Hillside, NJ: Erlbaum.

Clark, D. M. (1996). Panic disorder: From theory to therapy. In P. M. Salkovskis (Ed.), *Frontiers of cognitive therapy* (pp. 318–344). New York: Guilford Press.

Clark, D. M., & Wells, A. (1995). A cognitive model of social phobia. In R.G. Heimberg, M.R. Liebowitz, D. A. Hope, & F. R. Schneier (Eds.), *Social phobia: Diagnosis, assessment and treatment* (pp. 69–93). New York: Guilford.

Cook, J. M., Schnurr, P. P., & Foa, E. B. (2004). Bridging the gap between posttraumatic stress disorder research and clinical practice: The example of exposure therapy. *Psychotherapy: Theory, Research, Practice, Training, 41*, 374–387.

Craske, M. G., Glover, D., & DeCola, J. (1995). Predicted versus unpredicted panic attacks: Acute versus general distress. *Journal of Abnormal Psychology, 104*, 214–223.

Eddy, K. T., Dutra, L., Bradley, R., & Westen, D. (2004). A multidimensional meta-analysis of psychotherapy and pharmacotherapy for obsessive–compulsive disorder. *Clinical Psychology Review, 24*, 1011–1030.

Eifert, G. H., & Heffner, M. (2003). The effects of acceptance versus control contexts on avoidance of panic-related symptoms. *Journal of Behavior Therapy and Experimental Psychiatry, 34*, 293–312.

Eysenck, H. J. (Ed.). (1967). *The biological basis of personality*. Springfield, IL; Charles C. Thomas.

Eysenck, H. J. (1981). *A model for personality*. New York: Springer.

Fava, M., Bless, E., Otto, M. W., Pava, J. A., et al. (1994). Dysfunctional attitudes in major depression: Changes with pharmacotherapy. *Journal of Nervous and Mental Disease, 182*, 45–49.

Feldner, M. T., Zvolensky, M. J., Eifert, G. H., & Spira, A. P. (2003). Emotional avoidance: An experimental test of individual differences and response suppression using biological challenge. *Behaviour Research and Therapy, 41*, 403–411.

Foa, E. B., Dancu, C. V., Hembree, E. A., Jaycox, L. H., Meadows, E. A., & Street, G. P. (1999). A comparison of exposure therapy, stress inoculation training, and their combination for reducing posttraumatic stress disorder in female assault victims. *Journal of Consulting and Clinical Psychology, 67*, 194–200.

Foa, E. B., Keane, T. M., & Friedman, M. J. (Eds.). (2000). *Effective treatments for PTSD: Practice guidelines from the International Society for Traumatic Stress Studies.* New York: Guilford.

Foa, E. B., & Kozak, M. J. (1986). Emotional processing of fear: Exposure to corrective information. *Psychological Bulletin, 99*, 20–35.

Foa, E. B., Riggs, D. S., Massie, E. D., & Yarczower, M. (1995). The impact of fear activation and anger on the efficacy of exposure treatment for posttraumatic stress disorder. *Behavior Therapy, 26*, 487–499.

Gifford, E. V., Kohlenberg, B. S., Hayes, S. C., Antonuccio, D. O., Piasecki, M., Rasmussen-Hall, M. L., et al. (2004). Acceptance-based treatment for smoking cessation. *Behavior Therapy, 35*, 689–705.

Goisman, R. M., Rogers. M. P., Steketee, G. S., Warshaw, M. G., Cuneo, P., & Keller, M. B. (1993). Utilization of behavioral methods in a multicenter anxiety disorders study. *Journal of Clinical Psychiatry. 54*, 213–218.

Goldstein, A. J., & Chambless, D. L. (1978). A reanalysis of agoraphobia. *Behavior Therapy, 9*, 47–59.

Gould, R. A., Buckminster, S., Pollack, M. H., Otto, M. W., & Yap, L. (1997). Cognitive behavioral and pharmacological treatment for social phobia: A meta-analysis. *Clinical Psychology: Science and Practice, 4*, 291–306.

Gould, R. A., Otto, M. W., & Pollack, M. H. (1995). A meta-analysis of treatment outcome for panic disorder. *Clinical Psychology Review, 15*, 819–844.

Greenberg, L. S., & Safran, J. D. (1987). *Emotion in psychotherapy: Affect, cognition, and the process of change.* New York: Guilford.

Greenberg, P. E., Sisitsky, T., Kessler, R. C., Finkelstein, S. N., Berndt, E. R., Davidson, J. R. T., et al. (1999). The economic burden of the anxiety disorders in the 1990s. *Journal of Clinical Psychiatry, 60*, 427–435.

Gross, J. J., & Levenson, R. W. (1997). Hiding feelings: The acute effects of inhibiting negative and positive emotion. *Journal of Abnormal Psychology, 106*, 95–103.

Gwilliam, P., Wells, A., & Cartwright-Hatton, S. (2004). Does meta-cognition or responsibility predict obsessive–compulsive symptoms: A test of the metacognitive model. *Clinical Psychology and Psychotherapy, 11*, 137–144.

Hayes, S. C. (2005). Acceptance and commitment therapy, relational frame theory, and the third wave of behavioral and cognitive therapies. *Behavior Therapy, 35*, 639–665.

Hayes, S. C., Barnes-Holmes, D., & Roche, B. (Eds.). (2001). *Relational frame theory: A post-Skinnerian account of human language and cognition.* New York: Plenum.

Hayes, S. C., Brownstein, A. J., Zettle, R. D., Rosenfarb, I., & Korn, Z. (1986). Rule-governed behavior and sensitivity to changing consequences of responding. *Journal of the Experimental Analysis of Behavior, 45*, 237–256.

Hayes, S. C., Masuda, A., Bissett, R., Luoma, J., & Gueffero, L. F. (2004). DBT, FAP, and ACT: How empirically oriented are the new behavior therapy technologies? *Behavior Therapy, 35*, 35–54.

Hayes, S. C., Strosahl, K. D., & Wilson, K. G. (1999). *Acceptance and commitment therapy: An experiential approach to behavior change.* New York: Guilford.

Hayes, S. C., Wilson, K. G., Gifford, E. V., Follette, V. M., & Strosahl, K. (1996). Experiential avoidance and behavioral disorders: A functional dimensional approach to diagnosis and treatment. *Journal of Consulting and Clinical Psychology, 64,* 1152–1168.

Hirschfeld, R. M. A. (1996). Placebo response in the treatment of panic disorder. *Bulletin of the Menninger Clinic, 60,* A76–A86.

Hughes, I. (2002). A cognitive therapy model of social anxiety problems: Potential limits on its effectiveness? *Psychology and Psychotherapy: Theory, Research and Practice, 75,* 411–435.

Jacobson, N. S., & Christensen, A. (1995). *Integrative couple therapy: Promoting acceptance and change.* New York: Norton.

James, J. E. (1993). Cognitive–behavioural theory: An alternative conception. *Australian Psychologist, 28,* 151–155.

Jarrett, R. B., & Nelson, R. O. (1987). Mechanisms of change in cognitive therapy of depression. *Behavior Therapy, 18,* 227–241.

Jaycox, L. H., Foa, E. B., & Morral, A. R. (1998). Influence of emotional engagement and habituation on exposure therapy for PTSD. *Journal of Consulting and Clinical Psychology, 66,* 185–192.

Kabat-Zinn, J. (1994). *Wherever you go there you are.* New York: Hyperion.

Kagan, J. (1989). Temperamental contributions to social behavior. *American Psychologist, 44,* 668–674.

Kazdin, A. E. (1998). *Research design in clinical psychology.* Needham Heights: Allyn & Bacon.

Kenardy, J., & Taylor, C. B. (1999). Expected versus unexpected panic attacks: A naturalistic prospective study. *Journal of Anxiety Disorders, 13,* 435–445.

Kessler, R. C., Sonnega, A., Bromet, E., Hughes, M., & Nelson, C. (1995). Posttraumatic stress disorder in the National Comorbidity Survey. *Archives of General Psychiatry, 52,* 1048–1060.

Kohlenberg, R. J., Kanter, J. W., Bolling, M., Wexner, R., Parker, C., & Tsai, M. (2004). Functional analytic psychotherapy, cognitive therapy, and acceptance. In S. C. Hayes, V. Follette, & M. M. Linehan (Eds.), *Mindfulness and acceptance: Expanding the cognitive–behavioral tradition* (pp. 96–119). New York: Guilford.

Kohlenberg, R. J., & Tsai, M. (1991). *Functional analytic psychotherapy: Creating intense and curative therapeutic relationships.* New York: Plenum.

Lang, P. J. (1985). The cognitive psychophysiology of emotion: Fear and anxiety. In A. H. Tuma & J. D. Maser (Eds.), *Anxiety and the anxiety disorders* (pp. 131–170). Hillsdale, NJ: Erlbaum.

Lazarus, A. (1984). On the primacy of cognition. *American Psychologist, 39,* 124–129.

Leon, A. C., Portera, L., & Weissman, M. M. (1995). The social costs of anxiety disorders. *British Journal of Psychiatry, 166*(Suppl 27), 19–22.

Levitt, J. T., Brown, T. A., Orsillo, S. M., & Barlow, D. H. (2004). The effects of acceptance versus suppression of emotion on subjective and psychophysiological response to carbon dioxide challenge in patients with panic disorder. *Behavior Therapy, 35,* 747–766.

Linehan, M. M. (1993a). Cognitive behavioral treatment for borderline personality disorder. New York: Guilford

Linehan, M. M. (1993b). Skills training manual for treating borderline personality disorder. New York: Guilford.

Lovell, K., Marks, I. M., Noshirvani, H., Thrasher, S., & Livanou, M. (2001). Do cognitive and exposure treatments improve various PTSD symptoms differently? A randomized controlled trial. *Behavioural and Cognitive Psychotherapy, 29,* 107–112.

Marks, I. (1969). *Fears and phobias.* London: Heinman Medical Books.

Marks, I., Lovell, K., Noshirvani, H., Livanou, M., & Thrasher, S. (1998). Treatment of posttraumatic stress disorder by exposure and/or cognitive restructuring: A controlled study. *Archives of General Psychiatry, 55,* 317–325.

Massion, A., Warshaw, M., & Keller, M. (1993). Quality of life and psychiatric morbidity in panic disorder versus generalized anxiety disorder. *American Journal of Psychiatry, 150,* 600–607.

McManus, F., Clark, D. M., & Hackmann, A. (2000). Specificity of cognitive biases in social phobia and their role in recovery. *Behavioural and Cognitive Psychotherapy, 28,* 201–209.

Mennin, D. S. (2005). Emotion and the acceptance-based approaches to the anxiety disorder. In S. M. Orsillo & L. Roemer (Eds.), *Acceptance and mindfulness-based approaches to anxiety: Conceptualization and treatment* (pp. 37–68). New York: Springer.

Mowrer, O. H. (1947). On the dual nature of learning—A re-interpretation of "conditioning" and "problem-solving." *Harvard Educational Review, 17,* 102–148.

Narrow, W. E., Rae, D. S., Robins, L. N., & Regier, D. A. (2002). Revised prevalence based estimates of mental disorders in the United States: Using a clinical significance criterion to reconcile 2 surveys' estimates. *Archives of General Psychiatry, 59,* 115–123.

Nhat Hanh, T. (1992). *Peace is every step: The path of mindfulness in everyday life.* New York: Bantam Books.

Nolen-Hoeksema, S., Girgus, J. S., & Seligman, M. E. P. (1986). Learned helplessness in children: A longitudinal study of depression, achievement, and attributional style. *Journal of Personality and Social Psychology, 51,* 435–442.

Noyes, R., Woodman, C., Garvey, M. J., Cook, B. L., Suelzer, M., Clancy, J., et al. (1992). Generalized anxiety disorder versus panic disorder: Distinguishing characteristics and patterns of comorbidity. *Journal of Nervous and Mental Disease, 180,* 369–370.

Orsillo, S. M., Roemer, L., & Barlow, D. H. (2003). Integrating acceptance and mindfulness into existing cognitive–behavioral treatment for GAD: A case study. *Cognitive and Behavioral Practice, 10,* 223–230.

Orsillo, S. M., Roemer, L., Block-Lerner, J., & Tull, M. T. (2004). Acceptance, mindfulness, and Cognitive–Behavioral Therapy: Comparisons, contrasts, and application to anxiety. In S. C. Hayes, V. Follette, & M. M. Linehan (Eds.), *Mindfulness and acceptance: Expanding the cognitive–behavioral tradition* (pp. 30–44). New York: Guilford.

Pennebaker, J. W. (1993). Putting stress into words: Health, linguistic, and therapeutic implications. *Behaviour Research and Therapy, 31*, 539–548.

Persons, J. B., & Miranda, J. (1992). Cognitive theories of vulnerability to depression: Reconciling negative evidence. *Cognitive Therapy and Research, 16*, 485–502.

Purdon, C. (1999). Thought suppression and psychopathology. *Behaviour Research and Therapy, 37*, 1029–1054.

Rachman, S. J. (1991). Neo-conditioning and the classical theory of fear acquisition. *Clinical Psychology Review, 11*, 155–173.

Rachman, S. J., Craske, M. G., Tallman, K., & Solyom, C. (1986). Does escape behavior strengthen agoraphobic avoidance?: A replication. *Behavior Therapy, 17*, 366–384.

Razran, G. (1961). The observable unconscious and the inferable conscious in current Soviet psychophysiology: Interoceptive conditioning, semantic conditioning, and the orienting reflex. *Psychological Review, 68*, 81–147.

Reiss, S. (1991). Expectancy theory of fear, anxiety and panic. *Clinical Psychology Review, 11*, 141–153.

Robins, C. J., Schmidt, H., & Linehan, M. M. (2004). Dialectical behavior therapy: Synthesizing radical acceptance with skillful means. In S. C. Hayes, V. Follette, & M. M. Linehan (Eds.), *Mindfulness and acceptance: Expanding the cognitive–behavioral tradition* (pp. 30–44). New York: Guilford.

Roemer, L., & Borkovec, T. D. (1993). Worry: Unwanted cognitive experience that controls unwanted somatic experience. In D. M. Wegner & J. Pennebaker (Eds.), *Handbook of mental control* (pp. 220–238). Englewood Cliffs, NJ: Prentice-Hall.

Roemer, L., & Orsillo, S. M. (2005). An acceptance based behavior therapy for generalized anxiety disorder. In S. M. Orsillo & L. Roemer (Eds.), *Acceptance and mindfulness-based approaches to anxiety: Conceptualization and treatment* (pp. 213–240). New York: Springer.

Roemer, L., Salters-Pedneault, K., & Orsillo, S. M. (in press). Incorporating mindfulness and acceptance-based strategies in the treatment of generalized anxiety disorder. In. R. Baer (Ed.), *Mindfulness-based interventions: A clinician's guide.* New York: Elsevier.

Rogers, C. R. (1961). *On becoming a person: A therapist's view of psychotherapy.* Boston: Houghton Mifflin.

Schmidt, N. B., Wollaway-Bickel, K., Trakowski, J., Santiago, H., Storey, J., Koselka, M., et al. (2000). Dismantling cognitive–behavioral treatment for panic disorder. Questioning the utility of breathing retraining. *Journal of Consulting and Clinical Psychology, 68*, 417–424.

Segal, Z. V., Williams, J. M., & Teasdale, J. D. (2002). *Mindfulness-based cognitive therapy for depression: A new approach to preventing relapse.* New York: Guilford.

Shafran, R., Thordarson, D., & Rachman, S. (1996). Thought action fusion in obsessive compulsive disorder. *Journal of Anxiety Disorders, 5,* 379–391.

Simon, G., Oreml, J., Von Korff, M., & Barlow, W. (1995). Health care costs associated with depressive and anxiety disorders in primary care. *American Journal of Psychiatry, 152,* 352–357.

Smits, J. A. J., Powers, M. B., Cho, Y., & Telch, M. J. (2004). Mechanism of change in cognitive–behavioral treatment of panic disorder: Evidence for the fear or fear mediational hypothesis. *Journal of Consulting and Clinical Psychology, 72,* 646–652.

Steketee, G. S., & Barlow, D. H. (2002). Obsessive–compulsive disorder. In D.H. Barlow (Ed.), *Anxiety and its disorders: The nature and treatment of anxiety and panic* (2nd ed., pp. 516–551). New York: Guilford.

Tarrier, N., Pilgrim, H., Sommerfield, C., Faragher, B., Reynolds, M., Graham, E., et al. (1999). A randomized trial of cognitive therapy and imaginal exposure in the treatment of chronic posttraumatic stress disorder. *Journal of Consulting and Clinical Psychology, 67,* 13–18.

Teasdale, J. D., Moore, R. G., Hayhurst, H., Pope, M., Williams, S., & Segal, Z. V. (2002). Metacognitive awareness and prevention of relapse in depression: Empirical evidence. *Journal of Consulting and Clinical Psychology, 70,* 275–287.

Teasdale, J. D., Segal, Z. V., Williams, J. M. G. (2003). Mindfulness training and problem formulation. *Clinical Psychology: Science and Practice, 10,* 157–160.

Wegner, D. M. (1994). Ironic processes of mental control. *Psychological Review, 101,* 34–52.

Wells, A. (1990). Panic disorder in association with relaxation-induced-anxiety: An attentional training approach to treatment. *Behavior Therapy, 21,* 273–280.

Wells, A. (2000). *Emotional disorders and metacognition: Innovative cognitive therapy.* New York. Wiley.

Wells, A., & Matthews, G. (1994). *Attention and emotion: A clinical perspective.* Hilldale, NJ: Erlbaum.

Wells, A., & Papageorgiou, C. (1998). Social phobia: Effects of external attention on anxiety, negative beliefs, and perspective taking. *Behavior Therapy, 29,* 357–370.

Wells, A., & Sembi, S. (2004). Metacognitive therapy for PTSD: A preliminary investigation of a new brief treatment. *Journal of Behavior Therapy and Experimental Psychiatry, 35,* 307–318.

Wells, A., White, J., & Carter, K. (1997). Attention training: Effects on anxiety and beliefs in panic and social phobia. *Clinical Psychology and Psychotherapy, 4,* 226–232.

Westling, B. E., & Öst, L. (1995). Cognitive bias in panic disorder patients and changes after cognitive–behavioral treatments. *Behaviour Research and Therapy, 33,* 585–588.

Williams, K. E., Chambless, D. L., & Ahrens, A. (1997). Are emotions frightening? An extension of the fear of fear construct. *Behaviour Research and Therapy, 35,* 239–248.

Wilson, K. G., & Hayes, S. C. (1996). Resurgence of derived stimulus relations. *Journal of the Experimental Analysis of Behavior, 66,* 267–281.

Wilson, K. G., & Murrell, A. R. (2004). Values-centered interventions: Setting a course for behavioral treatment. In S. Hayes, M. Linehan, & V. Follette (Eds.), *Mindfulness and acceptance: Expanding the cognitive–behavioral tradition* (pp. 120–151). New York: Guilford.

Wolpe, J. (1958). *Psychotherapy by reciprocal inhibition.* Stanford, CA: Stanford University Press.

Chapter 2

EMOTION AND THE ACCEPTANCE-BASED APPROACHES TO THE ANXIETY DISORDERS

Douglas S. Mennin

Recent years have seen an eruption of interest and subsequent research on what are now being termed, acceptance-based behavioral treatments (Orsillo, Roemer, & Holowka, 2005). Approaches such as dialectical behavior therapy (DBT; Linehan, 1993a), acceptance and commitment therapy (ACT; S. C. Hayes, Strosahl, & Wilson, 1999), and mindfulness-based cognitive therapy (MBCT; Segal, Williams, & Teasdale, 2002) have expanded the boundaries of the cognitive-behavioral paradigm considerably. These approaches have offered novel solutions to vexing problems (e.g., relapse, poor outcome in functionality, and life satisfaction) in personality disorders (Linehan, 1993a), depression (Segal et al. 2002), and, particularly, anxiety disorders (Eifert & Forsyth, 2005; S. C. Hayes et al., 1999; Roemer & Orsillo, 2005). Cognitive–behavioral approaches to the anxiety disorders have historically demonstrated considerable efficacy (see Chambless & Gillis, 1993), but it has become increasingly clear that for more complex, chronic, and refractory presentations of these conditions, further intervention may be required to instill a lasting sense of change, functionality, and life satisfaction (Newman, 2000).

A significant common thread in the acceptance-based approaches may be the notion that a flexible approach to one's experiences brings with it a sense of health and well-being, even when sometimes those experiences are painful. Indeed, the unwillingness to stay in contact with certain aspects of experience (i.e., *experiential avoidance*; Hayes et al., 1999) and rigidity and pejorative judgment in responses to these experiences (as opposed to a state of *mindfulness*; Kabat-Zinn, 1990) have been proposed to be key factors in the maintenance of emotional dysfunction. Implicit in the acceptance-based conceptualizations of health and disorder is the notion that experiences characterized by strong emotions often challenge an individual's sense of efficacy in responding to internal and external stimuli (as would be expected by life's challenges). However, psychopathology occurs when individuals further their problems by attempting to avoid this emotional pain.

Thus, emotion is not purely detrimental in these approaches and is often seen as an important aspect of effective, healthy functioning. This inclusion of emotion factors in both the understanding of psychological disorders and the process of treatment is novel and contrasts with traditional cognitive-behavioral approaches, which often downplayed the role of emotion factors in functionality (Greenberg & Safran, 1987). Although slower to emerge in the clinical psychological literature, the importance of emotion has been embraced within numerous fields of psychology, including development (e.g., Eisenberg, Fabes, Guthrie, & Reiser, 2000), cognition (e.g., Gray, in press), social interaction (e.g., Lopes, Brackett, Nezlek, Schütz, Sellin, & Salovey, 2004), abilities and expertise (e.g., Mayer, Caruso, & Salovey, 1999), and neurobiological function (e.g., LeDoux, 1995).

These investigators have drawn from emotion theory (see Ekman & Davidson, 1994, for a discussion), which holds that emotions are not solely disruptive entities that impede functioning and success. Rather, these theorists define emotion as adaptive, goal-defining aspects of experience that help aid in decision making concerning movement toward or away from particular actions or plans (e.g., Frijda, 1986). In addition, the manner in which individuals are able to manage emotional experience to conform adaptively to a given context may also be important to mental health (Gross & Muñoz, 1995).

Although acceptance-based approaches have incorporated emotions in their conceptualizations of health and well-being, the functional value of emotions and the role of regulation are not always explicitly stated (but see Linehan, 1993b). Further, the evocation of emotion within the therapeutic context is also not consistently incorporated. In contrast, experiential therapies based on the historical traditions of client-centered, gestalt, and existential therapies have explicitly incorporated a functional view of emotions and the need for their evocation as a central component of their interventions (see Greenberg & Van Balen, 1998). However, these approaches have traditionally not been as committed to empiricism. More recently (e.g., Greenberg, 2002), the experiential paradigm has strengthened connections to basic and applied research endeavors and is more focused on matching particular interventions to specific problem areas. As a result, these experiential approaches may have increasing relevance for acceptance-based approaches to the anxiety disorders.

Acceptance-based behavioral approaches may be further enhanced by their explicit incorporation of emotion theory, basic research on emotions, attention to the role of emotions in psychopathology, and emotion-focused interventions that effectively elicit emotional states capable of being addressed within a therapeutic context. This chapter aims to (1) illustrate the relevance of basic research on emotion to clinical psychological endeavors; (2) argue for the importance of examining different facets of disruption and dysregulation in emotions as central factors in the anxiety disorders; and (3) review how the traditions of cognitive-behavioral and experiential orientations have evolved into the increasingly congruent approaches of acceptance-based behavioral approaches and emotion-focused therapy, respectively; and (4) demonstrate how this convergence, lessons from basic affective sciences and the nexus between emotions and psychopathology can inform acceptance-based behavioral treatments for anxiety disorders.

EMOTIONS AND THEIR REGULATION

Conceptual and biological theories underlying basic affective sciences argue that emotion is not a passive entity but, rather, an integral component of activating, shaping, and processing experience. It both contributes to and is affected by cognitive and behavioral systems. Contemporary approaches suggest that the key to the functions of emotion may lie in its adaptive value. Frijda (1986) argues that emotions are cues for readiness for action that work to establish, maintain, or disrupt a relationship with particular internal and external environments that signify importance to the person. This is not a drive-like response but, instead, represents a stimulus-sensitive behavioral potential to act (Greenberg, 2002).

Emotion serves an information function to notify individuals of the relevance of their concerns, needs, or goals in a given moment. In this manner, motivation and personal goal attainment are essential aspects of the function of emotions. Goals can be both innate (e.g., attachment, self-protection) and learned (e.g., specific beliefs about how to obtain relatedness or financial security) in origin (Greenberg & Safran, 1987). As a result of these conceptualizations, some theorists have argued that emotional and motivational systems should be viewed as unitary (e.g., Lang, Bradley, & Cuthbert, 1998). In the moment, emotions can give immediate salience to goals such that a given course of action can be deemed appropriate. In addition, emotions can give the motivational force to translate this potential for action into movement (Greenberg & Safran, 1987). Efran, Lukens, and Lukens (1990) explain that, because emotion serves this function, it is in a continuous but changing state at all times. One may feel "emotional" at a given time but emotion systems are constantly present, responding to environmental and internally generated cues.

Emotions are also adaptive because they serve a communication function. Facial expressions are clear indicators of emotional experience (Ekman, 1993). The expression of emotion, especially in facial expression, may aid individuals in understanding their own emotions (Ekman, 1993). In addition, research has supported the role of emotions as social signals (Campos, Mumme, Kermoian, & Campos, 1994). Expression of emotion has also been found to be tension relieving (Pennebaker, 1993) and essential to emotional and physical health (Kennedy-Moore & Watson, 1999). Pennebaker and colleagues have shown the ameliorative effects of emotional disclosure on autonomic nervous system activity, immune functioning, and physical and emotional health (e.g., Pennebaker, 1993). Campos and colleagues (1994) have also illustrated the importance of conceptualizing emotion in a relational context. They explain that emotions can provide signals for others to maintain or change their behavior.

Frijda (1986, p. 401) explains that "people not only have emotions, they also handle them." Emotion regulation, as a field of study, examines how individuals influence, control, experience, and express their emotions (Gross, 1998). Related constructs such as *mood regulation* (Parkinson, Totterdell, Briner, & Reynolds, 1996) and *affect regulation* (G. J. Taylor, Bagby, Parker, & Alexander 1997; Westen, Muderrisoglu, Fowler, Shedler, & Koren, 1997) encompass similar definitions (but see Ekman & Davidson, 1994, for a discussion of the differences between emotion, affect, and mood). Emotion regulation was first addressed in the developmental literature (e.g., Campos et al, 1994) but has also been examined in adults (e.g., Gross, 1998). More recently, investigators in both the developmental and adulthood emotion regulation fields have jointly presented this construct in a life-span perspective (e.g., Levenson & Izard, 1999).

Historically, the term *emotion regulation* has often been construed as denoting the reduction or control of emotion. However, more contemporary definitions of emotion regulation recognize that many control efforts are dysregulatory and that the allowance and accentuation of emotion can also be regulatory. Thompson (1990) has stressed the importance of not only restraint of emotion but also its maintenance and enhancement. Needs to diminish emotional arousal in order to work effectively or contain one's anger in a public setting are aspects of emotion regulation. However, investigators have more recently argued for the importance of accentuating both *positive and negative* emotional experiences to gain a greater understanding of motivation and goal pursuit (see Bonnano, 2001). For example, a person who is feeling "numb" may listen to a sad piece of music to help identify his or her feelings and become "unstuck." In addition, communication with others is often encouraged when one feels negatively in order to "work through" these emotions. It may also be more adaptive when one is in a "bad mood" with no clear precipitant to not attempt to control this experience but rather to allow its presence and let emotional experiences shift more naturally as a regulatory action. This broader view of emotion regulation as incorporating the allowance and benefit of emotional experience is quite consistent with acceptance-based approaches.

Effective regulation of emotions can involve regulation of emotions by an external regulator *or* the regulation of an external source *by* emotion (Dodge and Garber, 1991). Essential to the definition of emotion regulation is that activity in a given response domain may serve to magnify or modulate activation in another response domain. From this notion, it may be assumed that emotion regulation is both regulated by and is a regulator of other processes such as cognition. Cicchetti, Ackerman, and Izard (1995) have stressed that a central component of emotion regulation is the inter-coordination of the emotions and cognitive systems. Gross (1998), citing Solomon (1976), likens emotion regulation to a harmonious relationship between reason and the passions. In this manner, cognition about emotion is essential to the regulation of emotion. However, emotional regulation also describes the ability for the cognitive system to gain information from the emotion system (Cicchetti et al., 1995).

Recent explorations of the biological underpinnings of emotion have illustrated the need for such a view (e.g., Damasio, 1994; Davidson, Jackson, & Kalin, 2000; LeDoux, 1996). This research has shown a relational interdependence of emotion and cognition through depiction of multiple connections between limbic cortices and the neocortex. These connections include pathways originating in the thalamus and extending to the amygdala that may demonstrate early processing to signal emotional response. In addition, the amygdala has pathways to the neocortex, which suggests that emotional responses can signal higher order cognitive processing as well as modulate sensory activity. Finally, the neocortex has been found to have fibers leading back to the amygdala that could be interpreted as cognitive feedback to further influence the emotional response. Damasio (1994) explains the importance of such cognitive–emotional findings. He states that emotional input provides a unique contribution to reason such that what we consider to be "rationality" could not exist without such an influence.

Recent models of the beneficial role of emotions have stressed that individuals differ in their ability to utilize emotions effectively. Salovey, Mayer, and colleagues (e.g., Mayer, Salovey, Caruso, in press) theorize that people differ in their ability to attend to, process, and act as a result of their emotions, which they have called *emotional intelligence*. Emotional intelligence may be demonstrated at four different levels: (1) perception, appraisal, and expression of emotion; (2) emotion's facilitative effect on thinking; (3) understanding and analyzing emotions/employing emotional knowledge; and (4) reflective regulation of emotions to promote emotional and intellectual growth. Thus, someone who is able to recognize emotion experiences, understand their meaning, utilize their informational value, and manage this experience according to contextual demands would be expected to respond more effectively to life's demands. Research supports the benefits of emotional intelligence and implicates the fourth regulatory factor as being central to functional outcome (e.g., Lopes et al., 2004).

FUNCTIONAL EMOTIONS AND THE ANXIETY DISORDERS

If high levels of emotion regulation are associated with productivity and positive emotional health, then low levels of emotion regulation should have the converse effect. Cicchetti et al. (1995) divide emotional regulation problems into two categories. The first involves difficulties in modulation of emotional experience and/or expression; the second involves frequent or automatic attempts to control or suppress emotional experience or expression. In the first scenario, the person experiences emotions with great intensity but is unable to adequately modulate the experience (e.g., self-soothe, inhibit emotional expression). In the second scenario, the person engages in control strategies in an effort to prevent emotion from being experienced. One way in which this may occur is that the person may attend to cognitive information at the expense of emotional experience. By decreasing attention to emotional experience, emotion is avoided or blunted, thereby reducing ability to benefit from its possible information value. Thus, modulation of emotion can be effective in certain contexts but not all forms of management are adaptive (e.g., attempts to control, constrain, or suppress emotion in order to avoid this experience). Berenbaum, Raghavan, Le, Vernon, and Gomez (2003) propose a similar dichotomy in their discussion of two emotional regulation disturbances, which they term *emotional hyperreactivity* and *hyporeactivity*. These characteristics of emotional dysregulation can be conceptualized as the antitheses of emotional intelligence.

The relationship of emotional deficits and dysregulation with psychopathology has received increasing attention (e.g., Berenbaum et al., 2003; Gross & Muñoz, 1995; Kring & Bachorowski, 1999). However, little is known regarding the specific nature of the maladaptive emotional experiences that may underlie these disorders. My colleagues and I (for an introduction to this perspective, see Mennin, Heimberg, Turk, & Fresco, 2002; Mennin, Heimberg, Turk, & Carmin, 2004) have developed an emotion dysregulation model of anxiety and mood disorders. In this model, emotion disruption and dysregulation may be reflected in (1) heightened intensity of emotions; (2) poor understanding of emotions; (3) negative reactivity to one's emotional state (e.g., fear of emotion); and (4) maladaptive emotional management responses.

In a multisample factor analytic study, we have obtained a solution that confirms these four factors from a number of commonly used measures of emotional ability and dysfunction (Holaway, Mennin, Fresco, & Heimberg, 2004). Exploratory and confirmatory factor analytic methods corroborated this four-factor model. Further, these four factors correspond quite well as antitheses to the emotional intelligence abilities described by Salovey and colleagues (Mayer et al., in press) above. Moreover, these four factors were found to have unique patterns of prediction to generalized anxiety disorder (GAD), social anxiety disorder (SAD), and depression. All psychopathologies showed a relationship with at least one of the components of the model but only GAD demonstrated a relationship with all four factors (Holaway et al., 2004). Similarly, a composite variable encompassing these four factors has been found to contribute to the prediction of GAD beyond the predictive contributions of worry, anxiety, and depression (Mennin, Heimberg, Turk, & Fresco, in press).

Following the theoretical approaches of Thompson (1990) and Gross (1998), Rottenberg and Gross (2003) caution that, when looking at the relationship between emotion dysregulation and psychopathology, investigators need to recognize that regulation occurs dynamically throughout different points in the emotion-generative process. As such, it may be that the four factors of the emotion dysregulation model are related in a rapid temporal manner. Although the temporal relationship among these factors has not yet been substantiated by research, one might hypothesize that individuals with certain anxiety disorders may frequently experience strong negative affect and have emotional reactions that occur intensely, easily, and quickly (i.e., heightened emotional intensity). These individuals may react strongly to situations that are not evocative to most other people. A number of anxiety psychopathologies may also involve a difficulty in identifying primary emotions such as anger, sadness, fear, disgust, and joy and instead experience their emotions as undifferentiated, confusing, and overwhelming (i.e., poor understanding of emotions), particularly when these individuals are in the midst of an intense emotional state. Given strong emotional responses and a poor understanding of them, anxious individuals may experience emotions as aversive and become anxious when they occur (i.e., negative reactivity to emotions). Associated reactions may include rigid hypervigilance or avoidance of threatening information and activation of negative beliefs about emotions. Finally, given this aversive state, individuals with anxiety disorders might attempt to manage their emotional responses. However, these individuals may have difficulty knowing when or how to enhance or diminish their emotional experience in a manner that is appropriate to the environmental context (i.e., maladaptive emotional management). For instance, one may need to contain one's feelings of inadequacy due to a co-worker's comments during a business meeting but in a different context, such as a romantic relationship, discussion of feeling hurt may be beneficial.

Specific findings in the anxiety disorders support aspects of this emotion dysregulation model, although the temporal unfolding described above has not been examined yet. Mennin and colleagues (in press, Studies 1 & 2) found that individuals with GAD rated their emotional experiences as significantly more intense than other individuals. This factor appears to be more specific to GAD as it has differentiated individuals with GAD from those with other anxiety disorders such as SAD (Turk, Heimberg, Luterek, Mennin, & Fresco, 2005) and obsessive compulsive disorder (OCD; Holaway & Heimberg, 2003).

Consistent with the notion in the model that individuals with anxiety disorders have poor understanding of their emotions, individuals with either GAD or SAD have reported more difficulty than control participants in identifying, describing, and clarifying the motivational content of emotions than controls (Mennin et al., in press; Studies 1 & 2; Turk et al., 2005). Further, individuals with GAD who underwent a negative mood induction had more difficulty understanding their reactions to their resultant emotional state than controls (Mennin et al., in press; Study 3). Deficits in emotional understanding have also been reported in a number of other anxiety disorders such as panic disorder (Parker, Taylor, Bagby, & Acklin, 1993) and childhood sexual abuse-related posttraumatic stress disorder (PTSD; Cloitre, Scarvalone, & Difede, 1997). Understanding one's emotions predicts active coping and positive attributions (Gohm & Clore, 2002). In addition, firefighter trainees who reported greater clarity of their emotions were more able to effectively manage a series of live-fire exercises (evidenced by clearer thinking and fewer instances of "blanking out") than those with lower levels of clarity (Gohm, Baumann, & Sniezek, 2001). Finally, Feldman-Barrett, Gross, Conner Christensen, and Benvenuto (2001) found that individuals were more likely to effectively regulate their intense emotional experiences when they could differentiate the emotions being experienced.

The third component of this emotion regulation model, that individuals with anxiety disorders may react negatively to their emotions with fear and anxiety, has been demonstrated in a number of studies. Leahy (2002) found that both depression and anxiety were associated with viewing one's emotions as incomprehensible, uncontrollable, different than others' emotions, and characterized by guilt. However, whereas depression was more associated with expectations of long mood duration, anxiety was more likely to be associated with lack of acceptance of emotions. Chambless and colleagues have extended the construct of anxiety sensitivity (see S. Taylor, 1999, for a review) to address not only fear of anxiety but also a more generalized tendency to fear emotions (including fear of anxiety, sadness, anger, and positive emotions) and have associated this reactivity to emotions to panic (Williams, Chambless, & Ahrens, 1997; Berg, Shapiro, Chambless, & Ahrens, 1998). Individuals with GAD have also reported greater fear of anxiety, sadness, anger, and positive emotions than controls, and fear of sadness and anxiety made unique contributions to the detection of GAD (Mennin et al., in press; Studies 1 & 2). Persons with GAD also reported greater fear of sadness than persons with SAD (Turk et al., 2005), and fear of negative emotions was significantly and uniquely associated with severity of GAD, controlling for degree of worry (Roemer, Salters, Raffa, & Orsillo, 2005). Further, negative reactivity to one's emotions, measured 3 months after the events of September 11, 2001, mediated the relationship between GAD (measured September 10, 2001) and increases in anxiety/mood symptoms and functional impairment 1 year later in young adults directly exposed to the World Trade Center collapse (Farach, Mennin, Smith, & Mandelbaum, 2005).

The final component of the emotion regulation model involves maladaptive regulatory responses including both difficulties in managing emotional experiences and the usage of control strategies to avoid emotions (Cicchetti et al., 1995). Individuals with GAD have difficulty soothing themselves following a negative mood. In particular, they demonstrated lower trait (Mennin et al., in press; Studies 1 & 2) and state levels (following an experimental mood induction; Mennin et al., in press; Study 3) of returning negative moods to a euthymic baseline state than controls. There are numerous strategies for managing emotional experiences (Parkinson et al., 1996), with some being more adaptive to a given context and some inevitably leading to greater dysfunction. Given their high level of emotional intensity, difficulty understanding, and reactivity to emotions, individuals with GAD, if unable to soothe negative moods, may turn to a number of maladaptive methods for managing aversively perceived emotional experiences.

Maladaptive management is likely not specific to GAD, however. Indeed, individuals with SAD endorsed a similar level of poor ability to manage emotions as did individuals with GAD (Turk et al., 2005). Future research will be necessary to determine if there are specific microbehavioral differences that may distinguish disorders even though poor emotional management is likely to be a general factor in many forms of psychopathology.

More work is clearly necessary to determine exactly how these factors relate to each other. They may occur in the temporal manner hypothesized by this emotion dysregulation model. However, it is likely also possible that poor management of emotions increases emotional intensity. Indeed, attempts to suppress or avoid emotions have been found to increase emotional intensity (e.g., Gross & Levenson, 1997). One compelling study (Lynch, Robins, Morse, & MorKrause, 2001) has examined the relationship between heightened emotional intensity and dysregulation in both clinical and nonclinical samples. In particular, these investigators examined affect intensity and emotional inhibition (in particular, maladaptive management strategies of thought and expressive suppression) in distress levels (i.e., hopelessness and depressive symptoms). Using structural equation modeling, emotional inhibition was found to mediate the relationship between affect intensity and psychological distress in both samples. The authors concluded that emotional inhibition may be a particularly negative management strategy that leads to dysfunction, especially when emotions are experienced intensely. This study provides an elegant example of how dysfunctional emotional processes may begin at one point of a spectrum (i.e., intense emotional experience) but lead to another point (i.e., inhibition of emotion). Likely, this is a feedback loop and causes subsequent increases in intensity, as well. From this viewpoint, dysregulation arises from a lack of homeostasis rather than dysfunction in one particular component in isolation from other processes. This conceptualization of dysregulation is quite consistent with an acceptance-based approach that would implicate control efforts as leading to increases in the unpleasant intensification of anxiety and other emotions.

EVOLVING THERAPEUTIC APPROACHES TO EMOTION

A functional account of emotions and their regulation may also have implications for treatment. The evolution of traditional behavioral and cognitive approaches to acceptance-based models represents a unique period in clinical psychology for not only the incorporation of a more central role for emotion but also for the integration of other intervention approaches that have traditionally comprised emotion elements. This section reviews the historical development of views of emotion from the more traditional cognitive-behavioral approaches to the acceptance-based behavioral approaches. Further, experiential interventions are reviewed as this treatment paradigm has typically utilized functional viewpoints of emotion and has more recently been developed in a manner that is increasingly congruent with behavioral approaches.

Acceptance-based models that stress the importance of the allowance of emotional experience may be further strengthened by the explicit incorporation of the functional role of emotions, the view of acceptance as congruent with a regulatory approach (utilizing a wider view of regulation including elevating, diminishing, and allowing emotions), and the need for in session evocation of emotion to focus on phenomenologically relevant emotional patterns that are difficult to address through typical verbal methods. To this end, an integrative approach is suggested that can be incorporated into acceptance-based approaches and an example of such a treatment for anxiety disorders is provided.

Traditional Cognitive–Behavioral Perspective

Cognitive–behavioral conceptualizations have historically underplayed the importance of emotion variables (Greenberg & Safran, 1987; Samoilov & Goldfried, 2000). In addition, cognitive-behavioral treatments have also been found to be characterized by less emotional activation within sessions (e.g., Goldfried, Castonguay, Hayes, Drozd, & Shapiro, 1997). The marginalization of emotion in this approach has its origins in the early behaviorist tradition. Behaviorists originally sought to understand human behavior solely through the examination of observable data. Watson and Skinner considered emotions to be disruptive biological responses and inaccessible to observation and control (Samoilov & Greenberg, 2000). As such, the subjective nature of emotional experience was a troublesome topic of study for early behaviorists, and inquiry into the phenomenon of emotions was clearly disparaged (Pritchard, 1976).

Skinner (1953) directly attacks the notion of emotion as a causal entity in *Science and Human Behavior* within a chapter on emotion that includes a heading entitled "Emotions are not causes." He states that "'emotions' are excellent examples of the fictional causes to which we commonly attribute behavior" (p. 160). As a result of this belief, Skinner sought to redefine emotion in an operant conditioning framework. Holland and Skinner (1961) argued that mental disorders arise as a result of environmental events that serve to reinforce maladaptive actions. Certain external operants, Skinner argued, were more likely to increase the probability of emission of "emotional" behavior. Power and Dalgleish (1997) point out the circularity in this view of emotion. They give the example of a person afraid of a bear. They explain that Skinner's theory would require that a fearful event involving a bear be present for the person to be afraid. However, they question how the bear can be considered a fearful stimulus. They state that "Skinner must resort to saying that it is a fearful event because it gives rise to fear and therein lies the circularity of the Skinnerian theory of emotions" (p. 36). Furthermore, Lyons (1980) points out that some emotions do not typically exhibit external operant properties (e.g., grief).

Following early theorizing, some behaviorists began to argue for the importance of emotions. The noted behaviorist, Mowrer (1960) stated, "The emotions are of quite extraordinary importance in the total economy of living organisms and do not deserve being put into opposition with 'intelligence.' The emotions are, it seems, themselves a high order of intelligence" (p. 308). Other behavioral theorists attempted to combine learning theory with notions of drive that included emotional phenomena (e.g., Dollard & Miller, 1950). These positions were often criticized for incorporating psychoanalytic concepts into a learning framework. However, some behavior theorists did eventually incorporate internal processes into their formulations (Bandura, 1971). The resulting theories were an attempt to bring the concept of mind back into psychological science such that subjective experience would, once again, become an acceptable object of inquiry.

The "cognitive revolution" in clinical psychology was a response to the rapid growth of information processing research that began in the late 1950s (e.g., Neisser, 1967). The information processing framework emphasized cognitive phenomena through delineation of an information processing system. Emotional phenomena were explicitly de-emphasized in cognitive science due to the complexity and subtlety involved in the fuzzy category of emotion (Gardner, 1985). Classical cognitive therapy (e.g., Beck, Emery, & Greenberg, 1985) has approached emotion as a byproduct of cognition. Affect is viewed only as an *outcome* of cognitive activity. As a result, emotion is often relegated to dependent variable status in cognitive-behavioral research examining emotional dysfunction (Greenberg & Safran, 1987). Fancher (1995) argues that cognitively oriented theorists do not ignore emotion. Rather, he explains that cognitions in cognitive-behavioral practice are only examined as they relate to emotional phenomena. So, in this sense, emotion is essential to a cognitive-behavioral approach.

In foundational cognitive-behavioral approaches to the anxiety disorders, anxiety as an emotion was clearly seen as integral to the disorder but rarely was characterized beyond a dysfunctional effect of other phenomena (e.g., behavior or cognitions) and usually characterized by autonomic or "physiological" components (e.g., rapid heart beat, shortness of breath). Early models of emotional processing viewed anxiety in strictly disruptive terms with mental health being defined as the reduction of this emotion (Rachman, 1980). Foa and Kozak (1986), in their seminal article on emotion processing, extended the cognitive-behavioral definition of emotions, stating the importance of eliciting emotional arousal and its associated meaning elements while confronting feared stimuli. This viewpoint emphasized the importance of emotional experience but did not explicitly discuss functional aspects of emotion. Although many cognitive-behavioral interventions for anxiety disorders discuss the adaptive value of emotions in psychoeducational components early in treatment, the active ingredients of treatment often still characterize emotion in disruptive terms. Further, other emotions besides anxiety are not typically considered to be integral to understanding and treating anxiety disorders.

Although some investigators have questioned examining factors beyond cognition (e.g., Alloy, 1991), emotion in cognitive-behavioral theory has recently been increasingly brought to the forefront. Barlow (2002) has developed a perspective on anxiety and mood disorders that is based on emotion theory. He explains that these disorders are primarily *emotional disorders* and, as such, involve dysfunction in emotional processes, not limited solely to anxiety or fear. He cites a number of empirical investigations that have examined the hierarchical structure of anxiety and mood pathology. Investigators such as Clark and Watson (1991), Brown, Chorpita, and Barlow (1998), and Zinbarg and Barlow (1996) have shown that a higher order factor of negative affect is common to anxiety and mood symptomatology. Further, behavioral accounts of anxiety disorders have also begun to incorporate the importance of emotions as automatic, interoceptive cues to fear (Bouton, Mineka, & Barlow, 2001). Friman, Hayes, and Wilson (1998) have argued that anxiety and emotions, in general, as concepts should not be avoided by radical behavior analytic theorists solely because of difficulties in operational definition. Rather, they need to be studied as they are central to the experience of humans but, according to a modern behavioral framework, need to be understood as they relate to our actions to master, control, or accentuate these internal events rather than as instigating entities in themselves.

Acceptance-Based Behavioral Perspectives

A number of recent cognitive and behavioral interventions have begun to emphasize emotional phenomena. Acceptance-based behavioral approaches have been at the forefront of this movement (Cordova,

Jacobson, & Christensen, 1998; S. C. Hayes et al., 1999; Kohlenberg & Tsai, 1991; Linehan, 1993a; Segal et al., 2002). These approaches share a focus on the allowance of emotional experiences, even those that are negative or painful. DBT (Linehan, 1993a), MBCT (Segal et al., 2002), and ACT (S. C. Hayes et al., 1999) are some of the most popular acceptance-based approaches and have clear implications for the anxiety disorders. Indeed, treatments that integrate these different acceptance-based approaches have demonstrated initial efficacy for GAD (Roemer & Orsillo, 2005).

DBT has been widely accepted and is considered a first-line treatment for borderline personality disorder. The treatment involves both group-based skills training and individual sessions wherein these skills are applied to address patient's ongoing conflicts. Following an orientation phase that involves education about the disorder and building the therapeutic relationship, there are four stages to DBT intervention. The first stage targets crisis-oriented and other problematic behaviors such as suicidal acts, parasuicidal behaviors, and substance use. This stage also involves behavioral management skills training that focus on mindfulness, distress tolerance, emotion regulation, and interpersonal effectiveness. The second stage encourages the patient to utilize these skills during exposure exercises aimed at confronting difficult and traumatic life experiences. The third stage involves patients learning life skills to improve employment, living, and relational aspects of their lives. The final stage focuses on a process level concerning the value in accepting personal struggles and managing them, when necessary (in order to encourage the patient to continue to use these skills after treatment).

Anxiety disorders would be expected to be relevant to a DBT framework given that components of the treatment target worry and anxious responding (see Gratz, Tull, & Wagner, 2005, for a discussion of how DBT mindfulness skills might be applied to the treatment of anxiety disorders). However, it is unclear how efficacious this package would be for individuals with anxiety disorders who do not have severe personality psychopathology. DBT has demonstrated efficacy in individuals with individuals with borderline personality disorder, suicidal and parasuicidal behaviors (including but not limited to those with borderline personality disorder), and, more recently, eating disorders (S. C. Hayes, Masuda, Bissett, Luoma, & Guerrero, in press). As a package, DBT has not yet demonstrated efficacy for the anxiety disorders. However, elements of DBT have been incorporated with success into treatments for GAD (Roemer & Orsillo, 2005) and PTSD (Cloitre, Koenen, Cohen, & Han, 2002).

Linehan (1993a, 1993b) was one of the first investigators to incorporate a functional viewpoint of emotions (beyond just fear) into a cognitive-behavioral treatment package. Her model of borderline personality disorder emphasizes the joint roles of a heritable tendency to react intensely to environmental stimuli coupled with an invalidating context. This developmental environmental influence typically involves dismissive, punitive, critical, or neglectful reactions to strong emotional displays. These early emotional experiences are often already quite intense and painful and the disavowal of this experience by caregivers often leads these individuals to pursue stronger means of communicating or controlling these emotions. Linehan argues that borderline personality disorder then develops as a result of this invalidated reactivity to one's own emotional experience, which, in turn, generates a number of maladaptive methods for managing emotions that serve to reinforce this emotional intensity.

DBT incorporates a functional emotional approach involving both acceptance elements that illustrate the adaptive importance of emotions and change elements that highlight the importance of emotion management (Linehan, 1993a, 1993b). A central component of DBT is the inclusion of interventions meant to increase identification, understanding, and management of emotions, especially those that may become disruptive. This is accomplished particularly through the emotion regulation modules of the treatment. Patients learn to understand what compels them to use these poor methods of controlling their emotions and, instead, learn more functional ways to approach and manage their emotional experience. An adaptive view of emotions is also reflected in the mindfulness component (i.e., flexible reactions to one's internal experiences), the distress tolerance component (i.e., importance of allowing painful reactions), and the interpersonal component (i.e., understanding how needs get expressed within a relational context). Given that emotion regulation components have recently been further emphasized in DBT (see McMain, Korma, & Dimeff, 2001) and that the package is currently being update to incorporate recent advances in emotion research (Linehan, 2004), it is likely that this intervention will be quite relevant to improving treatments for the anxiety disorders.

Mindfulness interventions have also been incorporated into a number of acceptance-based behavioral treatments including DBT (Linehan, 1993b) and MBCT (Segal et al., 2002). Mindfulness refers to a process of purposeful, flexible, nonjudgmental awareness of the present moment (Kabat-Zinn, 1990). Mindfulness is derived from a spiritual, Buddhist tradition (Nhat Hahn, 1976) but has been adapted for western usage. Kabat-Zinn (1990) has derived an approach to mental and physical distress using mindfulness. Mindfulness-based stress reduction (MBSR) includes a formalized meditation practice component to aid individuals in remaining in a present oriented, nonjudgmental state. Acceptance-based behavioral approaches have built upon Kabat-Zinn's foundational contributions, retaining much of the same conceptual framework. Some approaches also retained a for-malized meditation component (i.e., daily sitting meditation process, e.g., Segal et al., 2002); whereas others incorporate more flexible applications of mindfulness practice (Linehan, 1993b; Roemer & Orsillo, 2005). Mind-fulness has been applied to a number of conditions including borderline personality disorder (Linehan, 1993a), depression (Segal et al., 2002), and substance disorders (Marlatt, 1994). Mindfulness interventions have demonstrated efficacy for anxiety disorders in both purer formats (Kabat-Zinn et al., 1992) and as a component of an acceptance-based behavioral treatment for GAD (Roemer & Orsillo, 2005).

It is currently unclear as to what mechanisms are involved in mind-fulness or how this process specifically relates to psychopathology (S. C. Hayes, 2002). However, a number of mindfulness-based interventions en-courage an attendance to internal experiences including emotions (Baer, 2003). When "mindful," one is able to step back, gain perspective, and allow current feelings or permit feelings to emerge. Although focus has largely been on the allowance aspects of the mindfulness process, emo-tions are often an integral aspect of this emergent experience. Bishop and colleagues (2004) have argued that mindfulness involves a "decentered" stance toward emotions such that one is able to create distance with the emotional experience, decrease emotional reactivity, and promote a more rapid return to baseline quiescence. Emotions, even negative and painful ones, are seen as important aspects of experience and, thus, should be al-lowed and noticed. In MBCT, Segal and colleagues (2002) devote a part of their fifth session to reading and discussing *The Guest House* (see Block-Lerner, Salters-Pedneault, & Tull, 2005), a poem by the 13th-century Sufi poet, Rumi, which stresses the importance of welcoming unwanted feel-ings. However, the functional and informational value of emotions is not explicitly stressed. The key element is the allowance of their rise and pas-sage without attempts to avoid or control this experience (Segal et al., 2002).

Roemer and Orsillo (2003) state that inherent in the mindfulness pro-cess are emotion-regulating properties. Distress may not be decreased (and is sometimes increased) by mindfulness but through the component pro-cesses of decentering and nonjudgementalness, emotions are seen in a greater context and are, thus, more able to be recovered from. A. M. Hayes and Feldman (2004) argue that mindfulness interventions can be quite consistent with an emotion regulatory framework. They suggest that mind-fulness may provide a balance of extreme emotional responses such as avoidance (i.e., overregulation) or overengagement (i.e., underregulation), such that one is able to have greater clarity in the meaning of his or her emotions. In addition, they argue that mindfulness can be used not only to notice and allow a broader experience of emotions but also to transform destructive emotions. They view this process as similar to exposure in that one needs to allow emotional experiences, even distressing arousal, in order to generate greater meaning and restore a more balanced emotional state. These authors review preliminary evidence that mindfulness has been found to be associated with clarity of feelings and perceived ability to repair one's mood, both essential precursors to effective emotion regulation. However, given that a functional view of emotions is not explicitly delineated in mindfulness practices, one would expect some distinction between this construct and emotion variables. Indeed, a recent investigation demonstrates that a broad range of emotion regulation deficits show a unique relationship with GAD beyond mindfulness deficits (Salters-Pedneault, Roemer, & Mennin, 2005).

In addition to DBT and other mindfulness-based approaches, another acceptance-based approach that has gained popularity is ACT developed by S. C. Hayes and colleagues (1999). The premise of psychopathology in ACT lies in the unwillingness to allow internal experiences including, but not limited to, emotions (as well as thoughts, memories, and sensations). These internal events are constrained, suppressed, and avoided and it is this inability to allow this experience that is considered to be where psychopathologies such as anxiety disorders arise. This dysfunctional process has been termed *experiential avoidance* and is the primary target of ACT interventions. These interventions aim to reduce emotional avoidance by facilitating the process of *acceptance*, which refers to allowance of your internal experience without trying to alter or change it (S. C. Hayes et al., 1999). However, this engagement of experience is not an end itself but rather is theorized to allow greater flexibility to both internal and external possibilities and to promote behavioral action in accordance with one's values (S. C. Hayes et al., 1999). In this sense, as its name suggests, ACT encourages both actions that promote acceptance but also actions that promote change. This is similar to Linehan's emphasis on the dialectic between acceptance and change. This change is typically in a behavioral form (as thoughts and feelings are not responsive to mental command, as per ACT theory) and involves incremental acts toward valued goals (S. C. Hayes et al., in press).

ACT has been applied to myriad of psychopathologies (see S. C. Hayes et al., in press). Avoidant properties of anxiety are central to the conceptualizations of psychopathology in ACT. As such, it is not surprising that the treatment has been applied to a number of anxiety disorders in its complete form (see Eifert & Forsyth, 2005; Orsillo, Roemer, Block-Lerner, LeJeune, & Herbert, 2004; Twohig, Masuda, Varra, & Hayes, 2005) and as a component of other acceptance-based approaches (Roemer & Orsillo,

2005). These treatments have shown promise (e.g., Block & Wulfert, 2002; Orsillo, Roemer, & Barlow, 2003; but randomized controlled trial data are not yet published).

The view of emotions in ACT is based, in part, on the radical behavioral approaches mentioned in the previous section (Friman et al., 1998). Similar to mindfulness approaches, emotions are not directly considered functional entities that hold informational value but are still thought to be an integral aspect of adaptive experience. As such, emotions are not seen as purely disruptive nor are they diminished in ACT (in contrast to traditional cognitive-behavioral approaches; S. C. Hayes et al., 1999). Psychopathology, in this approach, does not arise from emotions but rather from our attempts to avoid the experience of these emotions (and other internal events). As such, effective living characterized by acceptance of emotional experiences is the goal of ACT rather than explicit regulation of emotions (either to diminish or amplify; Blackledge & Hayes, 2001; S. C. Hayes et al., 1999). A. M. Hayes and Feldman (2004), however, have argued that experiential acceptance can be considered as a form of emotion regulation in that it affects change in the qualities of emotional experience, which may facilitate valued action (see Zvolensky, Feldner, Leen-Feldner & Yartz, 2005, for further discussion of acceptance and mindfulness within an emotion regulation framework). In contrast to a focus on emotions directly, assessment of emotional experiences as markers of experiential avoidance or acceptance is encouraged in ACT. S. C. Hayes and colleagues (1999) and Orsillo, Roemer, Block-Lerner, and Tull (2004) have distinguished between "clean" or "clear" emotions and "dirty" or "muddied" emotions. The former types of emotions refer to initial emotional responses to a stimulus. In contrast, the latter types of emotions refer to emotions that overlay clearer emotions because we try to avoid them or because they are clouded by insomnia, perseverative thought (e.g., worry, rumination), or a conditioned response due to associations with past experience. This conceptualization is quite similar to the notion of primary and secondary distinctions outlined in Greenberg's (2002) model of emotions in psychotherapy (reviewed in the following section).

The emphasis on experiential acceptance in ACT may appear to be in conflict with models that suggest that regulation of emotions should include management or alteration of emotional experience. Within ACT, clients are encouraged not to *require* that their emotional experience changes in order to do the things that matter to them, and they are helped to see how, in their own experience, efforts at experiential control have been ineffective. However, accepting responses toward one's emotions may in fact serve to modulate them (perhaps by minimizing "dirty" emotions), as noted by A. M. Hayes and Feldman (2004). Linehan (1993a) notes the importance of seeing the dialectic between acceptance and change, rather than engaging exclusively in one versus the other.

EXPERIENTIAL PERSPECTIVE

Experiential approaches have historically viewed humans in dynamic, interrelated terms incorporating the importance of emotion in adaptive functioning. *Experiential therapy* is an umbrella term for modern approaches rooted in humanistic, gestalt, and existential traditions. Following a rise in interest in these orientations in the 1960s and 1970s, mainstream attention to these approaches diminished. However, the emergence of contemporary treatments (e.g., Greenberg, 2002) has revitalized an interest in these experiential orientations. These treatments are novel as they base their approaches not only on these historical traditions but also on basic research on emotion and affective neuroscience.

Greenberg and colleagues (Watson, Greenberg, & Lietaer, 1998; Greenberg & Van Balen, 1998) have reviewed the contributions of client-centered humanistic, gestalt, and existential traditions in the shaping of modern experiential therapy. The role of emotions figures prominently in the original formulations of these orientations. Carl Roger's client-centered approach was groundbreaking in its primary focus on the phenomenological experience of the client. The ability of the therapist to engage this experience of the client in an empathic, nonjudgmental manner and reflect this back to the client was considered by Rogers to be the essential component of client-centered therapy. Rogers considered dysfunction to arise from an unwillingness to remain aware of all aspects of experiences, particularly those that have growth potential (Rogers, 1959). Rogers believed that an important aspect of this awareness was the allowance of a full range of potential emotions that may be involved in that experience. Rogers argued that clients change from therapy as a function of their ability to become more aware of the emotional reactions in their experience, to accept them, and to understand their importance in engaging in experiences congruent with their needs.

Gestalt therapy, developed by Fritz Perls, historically has also explicitly focused on emotional processes in its approach to therapeutic change. Central to this orientation is the notion that life experiences are not static but are, rather, evolving continuously. Further, one's ability to engage this unfolding of experience and create meaning from it is directly related to his or her ability to function effectively (Watson et al., 1998). In gestalt therapy, exercises are used to generate a focus upon the present moment experience of needs, feelings, sensations, and motor behaviors. From this awareness of experience, clients are able to create meaning of this experience, become more active in determining where they would like these experiences to progress toward, and become more tolerant of when these goals are unable to be realized. Insight into what is impeding their ability to gain this awareness and action related to their emotions occurs through a process of discovery rather than interpretation. Rather than discussing challenges to experiencing at an intellectual level, exercises are conducted in which clients enact conflicts in self or dialogues with others with whom they have unresolved feelings (Watson et al., 1998).

Acceptance of emotional experience as an integral aspect of living is inherent in the tradition of existential approaches (e.g., May, 1977). In existential theory, individuals are conflicted with the knowledge of death, isolation, freedom, and meaninglessness (Watson et al., 1998). Health is seen as the ability to accept the anxiety that accompanies the knowledge of these negative forces and to not resort to trying to ignore, suppress, or control this reality of the finitude of experience. Yalom (1980) stresses the importance of immediate affective experience, especially within the therapeutic context, in assisting clients to accept all aspects of experience and to create meaning, even in the face of uncertainty.

Contemporary experiential approaches build upon the foundational views of emotions inherent in client-centered, gestalt, and existential traditions. Gendlin (1996), in his focusing-oriented psychotherapy, has stressed the importance of awareness of the immediate affective experience, especially as it relates to bodily sensations. Gendlin argues that the *felt sense* of bodily sensations provides individuals with an implicit knowledge of our reactions to both internal and external events. In this treatment, individuals learn to identify these sensations and gain a better understanding about their implicit meanings. Greenberg (2002) has developed emotion-focused therapy, which he considers a "process-experiential therapy," because it focuses on the temporal unfolding of an emotional episode and all of its constituent components. Greenberg draws heavily from the empathic tone of client-centered therapy and the experiential exercises of gestalt therapy.

The goal of emotion-focused therapy is to bring emotions and their associated motivational elements into active awareness (Watson et al., 1998). Using modified gestalt procedures, emotions are enacted within session to address concerns related to unexpressed relational conflicts and conflicts between aspects of self or experience (Greenberg, Rice, & Elliott, 1996). However, not every emotion is considered functional or is the target of experience encouraging interventions. Greenberg distinguishes among types of emotion to determine core emotional reactions (which he terms *primary emotions*; these can be adaptive or maladaptive), which are secondary reactions (which he terms *secondary emotions*; these are largely maladaptive), and which are only evoked strategically to gain a desired outcome (which he terms *instrumental emotions*; these are often manipulative).

Primary adaptive emotional reactions refer to biologically adaptive emotional responses that provide information about action tendencies, associated meanings and motivation for behavior (Greenberg, 2002). These responses include what have been termed the *basic emotions* such as fear, joy, anger, and sadness (Plutchik, 1990). Adaptive primary emotions are integral to understanding our goals and making decisions and, hence, their exploration is encouraged in Greenberg's treatment. This is accomplished through acceptance of emotional experiences, adaptive utilization of this experience to create meaning, and the transformation of maladaptive emotional states to more productive ones that aid in effective decision making and adaptive action engagement (Greenberg, 2002).

Although the experiential traditions have incorporated fundamental views of emotion since their inception, many of the historical foundations of the experiential approach were originally empirically untested and unconnected to other literatures on the process of emotion, disorder, and interpersonal relations. However, this has changed considerably in contemporary experiential therapy. First, Greenberg has developed his approach largely from basic findings concerning the functional role of emotions and their neurobiological substrates. The investigators have shown through a number of studies that depth of experiencing emotions in session is related to positive therapeutic outcome (see Whelton, 2004). Recently, in line with current trends in emotion research, Greenberg (2002) has begun to stress not only the experience of emotions but also the need for their management and regulation. Finally, experiential traditions originally eschewed the concept of disorder. However, recently, experiential therapists have delineated their approaches to specific disorder populations such as depression (Pos, Greenberg, Goldman, & Korman, 2003) and anxiety disorders (Wolfe & Sigl, 1998), thus increasing ability to determine specificity of different experiential therapeutic processes for different forms of psychopathological conditions.

INTEGRATIVE PERSPECTIVE

Taken together, there appears to be a convergence between the developing cognitive-behavioral and experiential paradigms. A number of acceptance-based behavioral approaches have included a functional viewpoint of emotions (e.g., Linehan, 1993b; Roemer & Orsillo, 2005) or have incorporated a regulatory framework (e.g., A. M. Hayes, Beevers, Feldman, Laurenceau, & Perlman, in press; Linehan, 1993b). Further, the foundations of acceptance in some of these approaches are reported to have, in part, been derived from Greenberg's experiential approach (S. C. Hayes et al., 1999; Linehan, 1993b). Greenberg (2002) has also stressed the importance of behaviorally oriented acceptance and mindfulness practices.

Given both this convergence in orientations and the findings that individuals with anxiety disorders have a number of deficits in emotional functioning, incorporation of principles of basic affective sciences, emotion regulatory frameworks, and modern experiential interventions into acceptance-based behavioral approaches to anxiety disorders may be beneficial. If emotion responses impart motivational information, then allowance of this experience is important not only because suppression or control are problematic but also because attending to emotional information may be essential for effective, valued actions. As such, acceptance-based behavioral interventions might, in addition to encouraging acceptance of emotional experience, also encourage individuals to attend to possible adaptive emotional elements that are present. Further, explicit evocation exercises from the experiential tradition may also be beneficial to increasing the salience of emotions within session. Finally, incorporating a regulatory framework may improve acceptance-based approaches by including interventions that not only encourage the acceptance of emotions but change elements when either modulation or accentuation of emotion experience is necessary according to a given context.

Thus, core acceptance and mindfulness techniques could be altered to include these more emotion-focused processes. For instance, during mindfulness exercises, compassionate understanding of one's emotions may become an important focal point. From this understanding, a client may learn more about what motivations and values are involved in the experience and through the flexibility engendered by the mindfulness exercise, she or he may become more able to choose actions congruent with these emotional needs. Conversely, experiential interventions could directly utilize mindfulness and acceptance strategies. By decreasing judgmental and inflexible emotional responses, clients can learn more from emotion eliciting exercises and utilize them to their fullest potential. Finally, an acceptance-based approach might also be supplemented by the training of regulation skills that involve strategies that promote both quiescence (e.g., calming and soothing) and accentuating emotional experience (e.g., Linehan, 1993b).

My colleagues and I have developed an approach to treating GAD that integrates elements of acceptance-based behavioral approaches with emotion focused and regulatory elements. Emotion regulation therapy (ERT; also see Huppert & Alley, 2005; Newman, Castonguay, Borkovec, & Molnar, 2004; Roemer & Orsillo, 2005, for other approaches that incorporate emotion elements in treating GAD) is based on our model of emotion dysregulation in psychopathology (see Mennin et al. 2002, 2003). Despite its association with significant impairment and life dissatisfaction (e.g., Stein & Heimberg, 2004) and increased health care costs and utilization (e.g., Blazer, Hughes, & George, 1991), GAD remains an understudied (Dugas, 2000), misunderstood (Persons, Mennin, & Tucker, 2001), and treatment-resistant (Borkovec & Ruscio, 2001) disorder.

The goals of ERT are for individuals to become better able to (1) identify, differentiate, and describe their emotions, even in their most intense form; (2) increase both acceptance of affective experience and ability to adaptively manage emotions when necessary; (3) decrease use of emotional avoidance strategies (e.g., worry); and (4) increase ability to utilize emotional information in identifying needs, making decisions, guiding thinking, motivating behavior, and managing interpersonal relationships and other contextual demands. Achievement of these therapeutic goals should equip clients with the ability to effectively increase or decrease their attendance to emotional experience as is necessary to attain desired outcomes, tolerate distress and properly adapt to life's inevitable challenges.

ERT integrates components of emotion-focused treatments into a cognitive-behavioral framework. In particular, skills training elements related to awareness of bodily reactions, acceptance, and adaptive regulation of emotions are included in ERT. Berenbaum and colleagues (2003) recommend the use of skills training for individuals with deficits in emotional understanding, especially before the use of exposure techniques with anxious individuals. Indeed, other treatments have demonstrated the efficacy and utility of providing skills training in emotion regulation to increase patients' ability to engage a later exposure component (Cloitre et al., 2002; Linehan, 1993b). In addition, emotion-focused techniques from the experiential tradition (Greenberg, 2002) are utilized for the purpose of in-session emotion evocation. Some techniques are also drawn from the burgeoning area of emotion-focused brief psychodynamic therapy (see Fosha, 2000; McCullough et al., 2003). These are included largely to examine how one's emotions and emotional management styles affect relationships and are affected by them.

Taken together, ERT addresses cognitive factors (e.g., beliefs about threat and security), emotional factors (e.g., avoidance and management of emotional experience), and contextual factors (e.g., patterns of relating to others and the environment) that may contribute to maladaptive responses. Initial sessions of ERT (Phase I) focus on psychoeducation about the disorder, functional patterns of worry and emotions in past and current situations, and self-monitoring of worry and/or anxiety episodes. The following sessions focus on the development of somatic awareness and emotion regulation skills (Phase II). Phase III comprises the most essential and intensive sessions of the treatment as they focus on the application of skills during exposure to emotionally evocative themes. The final sessions focus on terminating the therapeutic relationship, relapse prevention, and future goals (Phase IV).

Formalized outcome data for ERT are not yet available. Given that ERT is still currently under development and will likely be altered from its current form as lessons are learned from its ongoing implementation, it is unclear how this type of integrative approach will fare for GAD or other anxiety disorders. Some evidence is available that an integrative, acceptance-based behavioral approach that incorporates acceptance techniques, experiential techniques, and an emotion regulatory framework is effective for treating depression (A. M. Hayes et al., in press). However, further research is clearly necessary to determine whether an explicit emotion focus and integration of emotion-focused interventions is beneficial to the acceptance-based behavioral approaches.

CONCLUSIONS

Integrative, emotion-focused interventions might further our ability to use acceptance-based behavioral approaches to treat refractory anxiety disorders. A treatment that focuses on improving emotion regulation deficits may also help to enhance client's overall sense of well-being and life quality. However, the efficacy of integrative approaches such as ERT will need to be empirically evaluated, particularly in comparison to existing interventions. In particular, it will be important to determine when and if interventions aimed at changing emotional functioning are warranted. Another important goal of future research in this area will be to study the process of change in acceptance- and emotion-based treatments of anxiety disorders. For instance, it will be important to determine if therapeutic change (i.e., symptom reduction, improvements in functioning and quality of life) occurs as a function of increases in specific emotional acceptance or regulation abilities such as comfort with emotional experience, emotional acceptance, ability to self-soothe, and ability to use emotional information in decision making and action. These questions can only be answered through an examination of both treatment outcome and process.

On a more general level, the understanding of emotions and their management may provide a common language for understanding psychopathological phenomena and treatment process. Functional viewpoints of emotions appear to be providing a unique bridge between historically divergent areas of clinical psychology. Even 10 years ago, it would be unlikely for cognitive-behavioral clinicians to discuss emotional phenomena as being an integral part of adaptive life experience. The acceptance-based approaches have widened the scope of cognitive-behavioral intervention. The advances made by these treatments as well as integration of basic affective science and experiential techniques are likely to provide us with a greater ability to treat anxiety disorders, even in their most chronic, complex, and treatment resistant forms.

REFERENCES

Alloy, L. B. (1991). Depression and anxiety: Disorders of emotion or cognition? *Psychological Inquiry, 2,* 72–74.

Baer, R. A. (2003). Mindfulness training as clinical intervention: A conceptual and empirical review. *Clinical Psychology: Science and Practice, 10,* 125–143.

Bandura, A. (1971). Analysis of modeling processes. In A. Bandura (Ed.), *Psychological modeling* (pp. 1–62). Chicago: Aldine-Atherton.

Barlow, D. H. (2002). *Anxiety and its disorders* (2nd ed.). New York: Guilford.

Beck, A. T., Emery, G., & Greenberg, R. L. (1985). *Anxiety disorders and phobias: A cognitive perspective.* New York: Basic Books.

Berenbaum, H., Raghavan, C., Le, H.-N., Vernon, L. L., & Gomez, J. J. (2003). A taxonomy of emotional disturbances. *Clinical Psychology: Science & Practice, 10,* 206–226.

Berg, C. Z., Shapiro, N., Chambless, D., & Ahrens. A. (1998). Are emotions frightening? II: An analogue study of fear of emotion, interpersonal conflict, and panic onset. *Behaviour Research and Therapy, 36,* 3–15.

Bishop, S. R., Laue, M., Shapiro, S., Carlson, L., Anderson, N. D., Carmody, J., et al. (2004). Mindfulness: A proposed operational definition. *Clinical Psychology: Science & Practice, 11,* 230–241.

Blackledge, J. T., & Hayes, S. C. (2001). Emotion regulation in acceptance and commitment therapy. *Journal of Clinical Psychology, 57,* 243–255.

Blazer, D. G., Hughes, D., & George, L. K. (1991). Generalized anxiety disorder. In L. N. Robins & D. A. Regier (Eds.), *Psychiatric disorders in America: The Epidemiological Catchment Area Study* (pp. 180–203). New York: Free Press.

Block, J., & Wulfert, E. (2002, May). Acceptance or change of private experiences: A comparative analysis in college students with a fear of public speaking. In R. Zettle (Chair), *Acceptance and commitment therapy.* Symposium presented at the annual meeting of the Association for Behavior Analysis, Toronto, Ontario.

Block-Lerner, Salters-Pedneault, K., & Tull, M. T. (2005). Assessing mindfulness and experiential acceptance: Attempts to capture inherently elusive phenomena. In S. M. Orsillo & L. Roemer (Eds.), *Acceptance and mindfulness-based approaches to anxiety: Conceptualization and treatment* (pp. 71–129). New York: Springer.

Bonnano, G. (2001). Self-regulation of emotions. In T.J. Mayne & G. Bonnano (Eds.), *Emotions: Current issues and future directions* (pp. 251–285). New York: Guilford.

Borkovec, T. D., & Ruscio, A. M. (2001). Psychotherapy for generalized anxiety disorder. *Journal of Clinical Psychiatry, 62,* 37–42.

Bouton, M. E., Mineka, S., & Barlow, D. H. (2001). A modern learning theory perspective on the etiology of panic disorder. *Psychological Review, 108,* 2–32.

Brown, T. A., Chorpita, B. F., & Barlow, D. H. (1998). Structural relationships among dimensions of the DSM-IV anxiety and mood disorders and dimensions of negative affect, positive affect, and autonomic arousal. *Journal of Abnormal Psychology, 107,* 179–192.

Campos, J. J., Mumme, D. L., Kermoian, R., & Campos, R. G. (1994). A functionalist perspective on the nature of emotion. *Monographs of the Society for Research in Child Development, 59,* 284–303.

Chambless, D. L., & Gillis, M. M. (1993). Cognitive therapy of anxiety disorders. *Journal of Consulting and Clinical Psychology, 61,* 248–260.

Cicchetti, D., Ackerman, B. P., & Izard, C. E. (1995). Emotions and emotion regulation in developmental psychopathology. *Development & Psychopathology, 7*(1), 1–10.

Clark, L. A., & Watson, D. (1991). Tripartite model of anxiety and depression: Psychometric evidence and taxonomic implications. *Journal of Abnormal Psychology, 100,* 316–336.

Cloitre, M., Scarvalone, P., & Difede, J. (1997). Posttraumatic stress disorder, self and interpersonal dysfunction among sexually revictimized women. *Journal of Traumatic Stress, 10,* 435–450.

Cloitre, M., Koenen, K. C., Cohen, L. R., & Han, H. (2002). Skills training in affective and interpersonal regulation followed by exposure: A phase-based treatment for PTSD related to childhood abuse. *Journal of Consulting and Clinical Psychology, 70,* 1067–1074.

Cordova, J. V., Jacobson, N. S., & Christensen, A. (1998). Acceptance versus change interventions in behavioral couple therapy: Impact on couples' in-session communication. *Journal of Marital and Family Therapy, 24,* 437–455.

Davidson, R. J., Jackson, D. C., & Kalin, N. H. (2000). Emotion, plasticity, context. and regulation: Perspectives from affective neuroscience. *Psychological Bulletin, 126,* 890–909.

Damasio, A. R. (1994). *Descartes' error: Emotion, reason, and the human brain.* New York: Avon.

Dodge, K. A., & Garber, J. (1991). Domains of emotion regulation. In J. Garber & K. A. Dodge (Eds.), *The development of emotion regulation and dysregulation* (pp. 3–14). Cambridge, England: Cambridge University Press.

Dollard, J., & Miller, N. E. (1950). *Personality and psychotherapy.* New York: McGraw-Hill.

Dugas, M. J. (2000). Generalized anxiety disorder publications: So where do we stand? *Journal of Anxiety Disorders, 14,* 31–40.

Efran, J. S., Lukens, M. D., & Lukens, R. J. (1990). *Language, structure, and change.* New York: Norton.

Ekman, P. (1993). Facial expression and emotion. *American Psychologist, 48,* 384–392.

Ekman, P., & Davidson, R. J. (Eds.). (1994). *The nature of emotion: Fundamental questions.* New York: Oxford University Press.

Eifert, G. H., & Forsyth, J. P. (2005). *Acceptance and Commitment Therapy for anxiety disorders: A practitioner's treatment guide to using mindfulness, acceptance, and values-based behavior change strategies.* Oakland, CA: New Harbinger.

Eisenberg, N., Fabes, R. A., Guthrie, I. K., & Reiser, M. (2000). Dispositional emotionality and regulation: Their role in predicting quality of social functioning. *Journal of Personality and Social Psychology, 78,* 136–157.

Fancher, R. T. (1995). *Cultures of healing: Correcting the image of American mental health care.* New York: Freeman.

Farach, F. J., Mennin, D. S., Smith, R. L., Mandelbaum, M. G. (2005). *The impact of pretrauma GAD and posttrauma negative emotional reactivity on the long-term outcome of young adults directly exposed to the September 11 World Trade Center Attacks.* Manuscript submitted for publication.

Feldman-Barrett, L., Gross, J. J., Conner Christensen, T., & Benvenuto, M. (2001). Knowing what you're feeling and knowing what to do about it: Mapping the relation between emotion differentiation and emotion regulation. *Cognition and Emotion, 15,* 713–724.

Foa, E. B., & Kozak, M. J. (1986). Emotional processing of fear: Exposure to corrective information. *Psychological Bulletin, 99,* 20–35.

Fosha, D. (2000). *The transforming power of affect: A model for accelerated change.* New York: Basic Books.

Frijda, N. H. (1986). *The emotions.* London, England: Cambridge University Press.

Friman, P. C., Hayes, S. C., & Wilson, K. G. (1998). Why behavior analysts should study emotion: The example of anxiety. *Journal of Applied Behavior Analysis, 31,* 137–156.

Gardner, H. (1985). *The mind's new science: A history of the cognitive revolution.* New York: Basic Books.

Gendlin, E. T. (1996). *Focusing-oriented psychotherapy: A manual of the experiential method.* New York: Guilford.

Gohm, C. L., & Clore, G. L. (2002). Four latent traits of emotional experience and their involvement in well-being, coping, and attributional style. *Cognition and Emotion, 16,* 495–518.

Gohm, C. L., Baumann, M. R., & Sniezek, J. A. (2001). Personality in extreme situations: Thinking (or not) under acute stress. *Journal of Research in Personality, 35,* 388–399.

Goldfried, M. R., Castonguay, L. G., Hayes, A. M., Drozd, J. F., & Shapiro, D. A. (1997). A comparative analysis of the therapeutic focus in cognitive-behavioral and psychodynamic-interpersonal sessions. *Journal of Consulting & Clinical Psychology, 65,* 740–748.

Gratz, K. L., Tull, M. T., & Wagner, A. W. (2005). Applying DBT mindfulness skills to the treatment of clients with anxiety disorders. In S. M. Orsillo & L. Roemer (Eds.), *Acceptance- and mindfulness-based approaches to anxiety: Conceptualization and treatment* (pp. 147–161). New York: Springer

Gray, J. R. (2004). Integration of emotion and cognitive control. *Current Directions in Psychological Science, 13,* 46–48.

Greenberg, L. S. (2002). *Emotion-focused therapy: Coaching clients to work through their feelings.* Washington, DC: American Psychological Association.

Greenberg, L. S., Rice, L. N., & Elliott, R. K. (1996). *Facilitating emotional change: The moment-by-moment process.* New York: Guilford.

Greenberg, L. S., & Van Balen, R. (1998). The theory of experience-centered therapies. In L. S. Greenberg, J. C. Watson, & G. Lietaer (Eds.), *Handbook of experiential therapy* (pp. 28–57). New York: Guilford.

Greenberg, L. S., & Safran, J. D. (1987). *Emotion in psychotherapy: Affect, cognition, and the process of change.* New York: Guilford.

Gross, J. J. (1998). The emerging field of emotion regulation: An integrative review. *Review of General Psychology, 2,* 271–299.

Gross, J. J., & Levenson, R. W. (1997). Hiding feelings: The acute effects of inhibiting negative and positive emotion. *Journal of Abnormal Psychology, 106,* 95–103.

Gross, J. J., & Muñoz, R. F. (1995). Emotion regulation and mental health. *Clinical Psychology: Science & Practice, 2,* 151–164.

Nhat Hahn, T. (1976). *The miracle of mindfulness.* Boston: Beacon Press.

Hayes, A. M., Beevers, C., Feldman, G., Laurenceau, J. P., & Perlman, C. (2005). Preliminary outcome of an integrated depression treatment and wellness promotion program. *Positive Psychology (Special Issue). International Journal of Behavioral Medicine, 12,* 111–122.

Hayes, A. M., & Feldman, G. (2004). Clarifying the construct of mindfulness in the context of emotion regulation and the process of change in therapy. *Clinical Psychology: Science & Practice, 11,* 255–262.

Hayes, S. C. (2002). Acceptance, mindfulness, and science. *Clinical Psychology: Science & Practice, 9,* 101–106.

Hayes, S. C., Masuda, A., Bissett, R., Luoma, J., & Guerrero, L. F. (in press). DBT, FAP, and ACT: How empirically oriented are the new behavior therapy technologies? *Behavior Therapy.*

Hayes, S. C., Strosahl, K. D., & Wilson, K. G. (1999). *Acceptance and commitment therapy: An experiential approach to behavior change.* New York: Guilford.

Holaway, R. M., & Heimberg, R. G. (2003, November). *OCD and deficits in emotion regulation: Assessing the link between obsessions and compulsions.* Poster presented at the annual meeting of the Association for Advancement of Behavior Therapy, Boston, MA.

Holaway, R. M., Mennin, D. S., Fresco, D. M., & Heimberg, R. G. (2004, May). *The relationship of four higher order emotion factors to anxiety and mood psychopathology.* Poster presented at the annual meeting of the American Psychological Society, Chicago, IL.

Holland, J. G., & Skinner, B. F. (1961). *The analysis of behavior: A program for self-instruction.* New York: McGraw-Hill.

Huppert, J. D., & Alley, A. C. (2005). The clinical application of emotion research in generalized anxiety disorder: Some proposed procedures. *Cognitive and Behavioral Practice, 11,* 387–392.

Kabat-Zinn, J. (1990). *Full catastrophe living: Using the wisdom of your body and mind to face stress, pain, and illness.* New York: Delta.

Kabat-Zinn, J., Massion, A. O., Kristeller, J., Peterson, L. G., Fletcher, K. E., Pbert, L., et al. (1992). Effectiveness of a meditation-based stress reduction program in the treatment of anxiety disorders. *American Journal of Psychiatry, 149*(7), 936–943.

Kennedy-Moore, E., & Watson, J. C. (1999). *Expressing emotion: Myths, realities, and therapeutic strategies.* New York: Guilford.

Kohlenberg, R. J., & Tsai, M. (1991). *Functional Analytic psychotherapy: Creating intense and curative therapeutic relationships.* New York: Plenum.

Kring, A. M., & Bachorowski, J. (1999). Emotions and psychopathology. *Cognition and Emotion, 13,* 575–599.

Lang, P. J., Bradley, M. M., & Cuthbert, B. N. (1998). Emotion, motivation, and anxiety: Brain mechanisms and psychophysiology. *Biological Psychiatry, 44,* 1248–1263.

Leahy, R. (2002). A model of emotional schemas. *Journal of Cognitive Psychotherapy: An International Quarterly, 9,* 177–192.

LeDoux, J. E. (1996). *The emotional brain: The mysterious underpinnings of emotional life.* New York: Simon & Schuster.

Levenson, R. W., & Izard, C. (1999, June). *Emotion regulation across the life-span.* Paper presented at the American Psychological Society, Denver, CO.

Linehan, M. M. (1993a). *Cognitive–behavioral treatment of borderline personality disorder.* New York: Guilford.

Linehan, M. M. (1993b). *Skills training manual for treating borderline personality disorder.* New York: Guilford.

Linehan, M. M. (2004). Discussant. In M. Z. Rosenthal (Chair), *Using translational science in studies of emotion regulation and psychopathology.* Panel discussion presented at the annual meeting of the Association for Advancement of Behavior Therapy, New Orleans, LA.

Lopes, P. N., Brackett, M. A., Nezlek, J. B., Schütz, A., Sellin, I., & Salovey, P. (2004). Emotional intelligence and social interaction. *Personality and Social Psychology Bulletin, 30,* 1018–1034.

Lynch, T. R., Robins, C. J., Morse, J. Q., & MorKrause, E. D. (2001). A mediational model relating affect intensity, emotion inhibition, and psychological distress. *Behavior Therapy, 32,* 519–536.

Lyons, W. (1980). *Emotion.* Cambridge, England: Cambridge University Press.

Marlatt, G. A. (1994). Addiction, mindfulness, & acceptance. In S. C. Hayes, N. S. Jacobson, V. M. Follette, & M. J. Dougher (Eds.), *Mindfulness and acceptance: Expanding the cognitive-behavioral tradition.* Reno, NV: Context Press.

May, R. (1977). *The meaning of anxiety.* New York: Norton.

Mayer, J. D., Caruso, D., & Salovey, P. (1999). Emotional intelligence meets traditional standards for an intelligence. *Intelligence, 27,* 267–298.

Mayer, J. D., Salovey, P., & Caruso, D. (2004). Emotional intelligence: Theory, findings, and implications. *Psychological Inquiry, 15,* 197–215.

McCullough, L., Kuhn, N., Andrews, S., Kaplan, A., Wolf, J., & Hurley, C. L. (2003). *Treating affect phobia: A manual for short-term dynamic psychotherapy*. New York: Guilford.

McMain, S., Korma, L. M., & Dimeff, L. (2001). Dialectical behavior therapy and treatment of emotion dysregulation. *Journal of Clinical Psychology, 57*, 183–196.

Mennin, D. S., Heimberg, R. G., Turk, C. L., & Fresco, D. M. (2002). Applying an emotion regulation framework to integrative approaches to generalized anxiety disorder. *Clinical Psychology: Science and Practice, 9*, 85–90.

Mennin, D. S., Heimberg, R. G., Turk, C. L., & Fresco, D. M. (in press). Preliminary evidence for an emotion dysregulation model of generalized anxiety disorder. *Behaviour Research, & Therapy*.

Mennin, D. S., Turk, C. L., Heimberg, R. G., & Carmin, C. N. (2004). Focusing on the regulation of emotion: A new direction for conceptualizing and treating generalized anxiety disorder. In M. A. Reinecke & D. A. Clark (Eds.), *Cognitive therapy over the lifespan: Evidence and practice* (pp. 60–89). New York: Cambridge University Press.

Mowrer, O. H. (1960). *Learning theory and behaviour*. New York: Wiley.

Neisser, U. (1967). *Cognitive psychology*. New York: Appleton-Century-Crofts.

Newman, M. G. (2000). Recommendations for a cost-offset model of psychotherapy allocation using generalized anxiety disorder as an example. *Journal of Consulting and Clinical Psychology, 68*, 549–555.

Newman, M. G., Castonguay, L. G., Borkovec, T. D., & Molnar, C. (2004). Integrative therapy for generalized anxiety disorder. In R. G. Heimberg, C. L. Turk, & D. S. Mennin (Eds.), *Generalized anxiety disorder: Advances in research and practice* (pp. 320–350). New York: Guilford.

Orsillo, S. M., Roemer, L., & Barlow, D. H. (2003). Integrating acceptance and mindfulness into existing cognitive-behavioral treatment for GAD: A case study. *Cognitive and Behavioral Practice, 10*, 223–230.

Orsillo, S. M., Roemer, L., Block-Lerner, J., LeJeune, C., & Herbert, J. D. (2004). ACT with anxiety disorders. In S. C. Hayes & K. Strosahl (Eds.), *A practical guide to acceptance and commitment therapy* (pp. 103–132). New York: Springer.

Orsillo, S. M., Roemer, L., Block-Lerner, J., & Tull, M. T. (2004). Acceptance, mindfulness, and cognitive-behavioral therapy: Comparisons, contrasts, and application to anxiety. In S. C. Hayes, V. Follette, & M. M. Linehan (Eds.), *Mindfulness and acceptance: Expanding the cognitive-behavioral tradition*. New York: Guilford.

Orsillo, S. M., Roemer, L., & Holowka, D. W. (2005). Acceptance-based behavioral therapies for anxiety: Using acceptance and mindfulness to enhance traditional cognitive-behavioral approaches. In S. M. Orsillo & L. Roemer (Eds.), *Acceptance and mindfulness-based approaches to anxiety: Conceptualization and treatment* (pp. 3–35). New York: Springer.

Parker, J. D., Taylor, G. J., Bagby, R. M., & Acklin, M. W. (1993). Alexithymia in panic disorder and simple phobia: A comparative study. *American Journal of Psychiatry, 150*, 1105–1107.

Parkinson, B., Totterdell, P., Briner, R. B., & Reynolds, S. (1996). *Changing moods: The psychology of mood and mood regulation*. London, England: Longman.

Pennebaker, J. W. (1993). Putting stress into words: Health, linguistic, and therapeutic implications. *Behavior Research and Therapy, 31*, 539–548.

Persons, J. B., Mennin, D. S., & Tucker, D. E. (2001). Common misconceptions about the nature and treatment of generalized anxiety disorder. *Psychiatric Annals, 31*, 501–508.

Plutchik, R. (1990). Emotions and psychotherapy: A psychoevolutionary perspective. In R. Plutchik & H. Kellerman (Eds.), *Emotion: Theory, research, and experience* (Vol. 5, pp. 3–41). San Diego, CA: Academic Press.

Pos, A. E., Greenberg, L. S., Goldman, R., & Korman, L. (2003). Emotional processing during experiential treatment. *Journal of Consulting & Clinical Psychology, 71*, 1007–1016.

Power, M., & Dalgleish, T. (1997). *Cognition and emotion: From order to disorder*. East Sussex, England: Psychology Press.

Pritchard, M. S. (1976). On taking emotions seriously: A critique of B. F. Skinner. *Journal for the Theory of Social Behaviour, 6*, 211–232.

Rachman, S. (1980). Emotional processing. *Behaviour Research and Therapy, 18*, 51–60.

Roemer, L., & Orsillo, S. M. (2003). Mindfulness: A promising intervention strategy in need of further study. *Clinical Psychology: Science and Practice, 10*, 172–178.

Roemer, L., & Orsillo, S. M. (2005). An acceptance-based behavior therapy for generalized anxiety disorder. In S. M. Orsillo & L. Roemer (Eds.), *Acceptance and mindfulness-based approaches to anxiety: Conceptualization and treatment* (pp. 213–240). New York: Springer.

Roemer, L., Salters, K., Raffa, S. D., & Orsillo, S. M. (2005). Fear and avoidance of internal experiences in GAD: Preliminary tests of a conceptual model. *Cognitive Therapy and Research, 29*(1), 71–88.

Rogers, C. R. (1959). *Client-centered therapy: Its current practice, implications, and theory*. Boston: Houghton-Mifflin.

Rottenberg, J., & Gross, J. J. (2003). When emotion goes wrong: Realizing the promise of affective science. *Clinical Psychology: Science & Practice, 10*, 227–232.

Salters-Pedneault, K., Roemer, L., & Mennin, D. S. (2005). *Emotion regulation deficits in GAD: Examining specificity beyond symptoms and mindfulness processes*. Manuscript in preparation.

Samoilov, A., & Greenberg, M. R. (2000). Role of emotion in cognitive–behavior therapy. *Clinical Psychology: Science and Practice, 7*, 373–385.

Segal, Z., Williams, J. M. G., & Teasdale, J. D. (2002). *Mindfulness-based cognitive therapy for depression: A new approach to preventing relapse*. New York: Guilford.

Skinner, B. F. (1953). *Science and human behavior*. New York: Free Press.

Solomon, R. C. (1976). *The passions*. New York: Anchor/Doubleday.

Stein, M. B., & Heimberg, R. G. (2004). Well-being and life satisfaction in generalized anxiety disorder: Comparison to major depressive disorder in a community sample. *Journal of Affective Disorders, 79*, 161–166.

Taylor, G. J., Bagby, R. M., Parker, J., & Alexander, D. (1997). *Disorders of affect regulation: Alexithymia in medical and psychiatric illness*. Cambridge, England: Cambridge University Press.

Taylor, S. (Ed.). (1999). *Anxiety sensitivity: Theory, research, and treatment of fear of anxiety*. Mahwah, NJ: Erlbaum.

Thompson, R. A. (1990). Emotion and self-regulation. In R. A. Thompson (Ed.), *Socioemotional development: Nebraska symposium on motivation, 1988* (pp. 367–468). Lincoln, NE: University of Nebraska Press.

Turk, C. L., Heimberg, R. G., Luterek, J. A., Mennin, D. S., & Fresco, D. M. (2005). Delineating emotion regulation deficits in generalized anxiety disorder: A comparison with social anxiety disorder. *Cognitive Therapy and Research, 29*, 89–106.

Twohig, M. P., Masuda, A., Varra, A. A., & Hayes, S. C. (2005). Acceptance and commitment therapy as a treatment for anxiety disorders. In S. M. Orsillo & L. Roemer (Eds.), *Acceptance and mindfulness-based approaches to anxiety: Conceptualization and treatment* (pp. 101–129). New York: Springer.

Watson, J. C., Greenberg, L. S., & Lietaer, G. (1998). The experiential paradigm unfolding: Relationship and experiencing in therapy. In L. S. Greenberg, J. C. Watson, & G. Lietaer (Eds.), *Handbook of experiential therapy* (pp. 3–27). New York: Guilford.

Westen, D., & Harnden-Fischer, J. L. (2001). Personality profiles in eating disorders: Rethinking the distinction between axis I and axis II. *American Journal of Psychiatry, 158*, 547–562.

Westen, D., Muderrisoglu, S., Fowler, C., Shedler, J., & Koren, D. (1997). Affect regulation and affective experience: Individual differences, group differences, and measurement using a Q-sort procedure. *Journal of Consulting and Clinical Psychology, 65*, 429–439.

Whelton, W. J. (2004). Emotional processes in psychotherapy: Evidence across therapeutic modalities. *Clinical Psychology and Psychotherapy, 11*, 58–71.

Williams, K. E., Chambless, D. L., & Ahrens, A. (1997). Are emotions frightening? An extension of the fear of fear construct. *Behaviour Research and Therapy, 35*, 239–248.

Wolfe, B. E., & Sigl, P. (1998). Experiential psychotherapy of the anxiety disorders. In L. S. Greenberg, J. C. Watson, & G. Lietaer (Eds.), *Handbook of experiential psychotherapy* (pp. 272–294). New York: Guilford.

Yalom, I. D. (1980). *Existential psychotherapy*. New York: Basic Books.

Zinbarg, R. E., & Barlow, D. H. (1996). Structure of anxiety and the anxiety disorders: A hierarchical model. *Journal of Abnormal Psychology, 105*, 181–193.

Zvolensky, M. J., Feldner, M. T., Leen-Feldner, E. W., & Yartz, A. R. (2005). Exploring basic processes underlying acceptance and mindfulness. In S. M. Orsillo & L. Roemer (Eds.), *Acceptance and mindfulness-based approaches to anxiety: Conceptualization and treatment* (pp. 325–359). New York: Springer.

PART II

GENERAL APPROACHES TO ASSESSMENT AND TREATMENT

Chapter 3

ASSESSING MINDFULNESS AND EXPERIENTIAL ACCEPTANCE
ATTEMPTS TO CAPTURE INHERENTLY ELUSIVE PHENOMENA

Jennifer Block-Lerner, Kristalyn Salters-Pedneault, and Matthew T. Tull

This being human is a guest house.
Every morning a new arrival.

A joy, a depression, a meanness,
Some momentary awareness comes
as an unexpected visitor.

Welcome and entertain them all!
Even if they're a crowd of sorrows,
who violently sweep your house
empty of its furniture,

still treat each guest honorably.
He may be clearing you out
for some new delight.

The dark thought, the shame, the malice.
Meet them at the door laughing,
And invite them in.
Be grateful for whoever comes,
because each has been sent
as a guide from beyond.

The Guest House, a poem by Rumi (translated by Barks & Moyne, 1997) that has been utilized in mindfulness-based therapeutic approaches (e.g., Roemer & Orsillo, 2002; Segal, Williams, & Teasdale, 2002), conveys the essence of mindfulness and experiential acceptance. Such a "stance" stands in sharp contrast to the approach that many of us take toward our thoughts, feelings, and bodily sensations, particularly those that we label "unwanted." Bringing mindfulness and/or acceptance to our private experiences may fundamentally alter our relationship to these phenomena. How would we know if an individual was willing to "welcome and entertain them all" (Segal, 2003)? What might it look like to "meet them at the door laughing"? How might we measure this critical shift via self-report or experimental designs?

MEASURING THE PROCESSES OF MINDFULNESS AND ACCEPTANCE: THE HEART OF THE MATTER

Baer (2003) provides a thoughtful overview of the literature on the efficacy of mindfulness-based and related approaches. Commentaries on this target article (Dimidjian & Linehan, 2003; S. C. Hayes & Wilson, 2003; Kabat-Zinn, 2003; Roemer & Orsillo, 2003; Teasdale, Segal, & Williams, 2003) highlight the most salient research questions currently facing the field, including those related to mechanisms of action, the importance of considering the broader context from which such interventions have been drawn, and the compatibility/tension between mindfulness as an inherently "nonstriving" process and the often more goal-driven system of psychotherapy. Our capacity to examine these and associated questions hinges on our ability to operationally define such constructs as "mindfulness" and "acceptance" and to develop valid and reliable instruments that capture the psychological stance characterized by these terms. Such attempts have important implications, as interest in studying these phenomena, both in basic research paradigms and in applied settings, has progressively increased in recent years (e.g., S. C. Hayes, Follette, & Linehan, 2004).

MINDFULNESS VERSUS ACCEPTANCE, MINDFULNESS AND ACCEPTANCE, MINDFULNESS OR ACCEPTANCE?

The terms "mindfulness" and "acceptance" are sometimes used interchangeably. This is probably due in part to the fact that there is much overlap between various methods that attempt to facilitate similar processes (e.g., S. C. Hayes & Wilson, 2003). Perhaps the most salient differences between these two constructs at this point are the divergent contexts from which they have been drawn and the "languages" in which they are currently being discussed (S. C. Hayes, 2002a; Orsillo, Roemer, Block-Lerner, & Tull, 2004). At the level of method, meditation techniques (sometimes referred to as "mindfulness" practices; see S. C. Hayes & Shenk, 2004; S. C. Hayes & Wilson, 2003) have an extensive history within Eastern spiritual traditions (most notably Buddhism; see Campos, 2002; Kumar, 2002) and Western contemplative practices. Although these practices have recently been extracted from their spiritual/philosophical context and are starting to be examined empirically, the language in which they are currently spoken about by some within the psychological community, clearly reflects this heritage and/or a "cognitive point of view" (S. C. Hayes & Shenk, 2004, p. 7).

Acceptance, although a component of all schools of psychotherapy to some extent (see S. C. Hayes, 1994, for a book-length discussion), has most recently been brought to the forefront within the context of the functional contextualism tradition. This tradition implies a unique way of looking at and discussing psychological events; the most useful unit of analysis considered the "act in context" (Nelson & Hayes, 1986). Thus, the construct of acceptance, as we conceptualize it here, is frequently discussed in a more precise, technical language than that with which mindfulness is often spoken.

Because of these divergent histories and "languages," we review definitions and operationalizations of each separately. However, there clearly *is* overlap between mindfulness and acceptance at the process level. Although attempts are being made to explicate these areas of overlap and operationally define facets of each construct (e.g., Baer, Smith, & Cochran, 2004; Bishop et al., 2004), the field is probably not yet in a place where we can discuss the assessment of each entirely separately and comprehensively (and perhaps this is not even the most useful goal; see S. C. Hayes & Shenk, 2004). We present several ideas about the relation between these two constructs throughout our discussion; continued attempts to define and assess each should provide valuable information about the interconnection and distinctions between them, as well as related processes and/or traits (e.g., emotional intelligence, emotion regulation).

CAUTIONS

Although defining any construct verbally carries the risk of reifying a process, it seems that we have to be especially cognizant of this potential in the study of mindfulness and acceptance, processes that, by their very nature, are about the present moment. Thus, we must recognize that any attempts to capture the processes of mindfulness and/or acceptance are necessarily limited and involve a "snapshot" at best.

It is perhaps in large part due to this "elusive" nature of acceptance (Haas, 1994, p. 34) and mindfulness that operationalizing these constructs remains a daunting, though important, task. Although there is disagreement among researchers about what research questions should receive priority and what methodology should be used to address such questions, there is clearly consensus that operational definitions of the processes of mindfulness and acceptance are sorely needed (e.g., Bishop, 2002; Dimidjian & Linehan, 2003; S. C. Hayes & Wilson, 2003; Kabat-Zinn, 2003; Roemer & Orsillo, 2003; Teasdale et al., 2003). Researchers also seem to be in agreement that arriving at such operational definitions will not be easy (e.g., Kabat-Zinn, 2003; Roemer & Orsillo, 2003).

As a field, we are attempting to bring what has been referred to as an essential ingredient of spiritual and/or religious traditions (e.g., Marlatt & Kristeller, 1999; Sanderson & Linehan, 1999; Watts, 2000) and of all schools of psychotherapy (e.g., J. R. Martin, 1997) under the scrutiny of scientific analysis. Some maintain that there are essential ingredients of spiritual and/or clinical practices that cannot be conceptualized intellectually or communicated about in common language, let alone held under the lens of Western scientific methods (e.g., Shapiro & Walsh, 2003; Walsh, 1980). These researchers argue for recognition of the reciprocal nature of scientific/intellectual and other (i.e., more experiential) modes of investigation, and strongly suggest that researchers studying this content area be committed to their own personal practice.

In a sense, these recommendations parallel discussions about the extent to which clinicians and others teaching mindfulness-based methods should have their own practice (e.g., Dimidjian, Linehan, Marlatt, & Segal, 2002; Kabat-Zinn, 2003; Teasdale et al., 2003), yet they add another dimension to such discourse. Although one might be tempted to suggest that this debate offers yet another set of empirical questions, these researchers encourage us to examine the very assumption that our methods can address all questions of interest. They suggest that the paradigmatic assumptions of the behavioral sciences may clash with those of the "consciousness disciplines," and that as researchers, if our intellectual understanding is not grounded in an examination of our assumptions (Walsh, 1980) and "direct practice and experience," we may be "blind to our blindness" (Shapiro & Walsh, 2003, p. 107) with regard to the questions we ask, the methods we use, and the ways we interpret our data.

Thus, it is with a great deal of humility that we begin our review of the assessment of mindfulness and acceptance. We start with several proposed definitions of mindfulness, as well as an exploration of various facets of this process, and then review recently proposed conceptualizations of the process of acceptance. In the second half of the chapter, we review existing assessment procedures that tap the constructs of mindfulness and acceptance.

MINDFULNESS

Unraveling Various Uses and Conceptualizations

In addition to the fact that "mindfulness" has been defined in many different ways by various researchers, S. C. Hayes and Wilson (2003) are troubled by the notion that "mindfulness is sometimes treated as a technique, sometimes as a more general method or collection of techniques, sometimes as a psychological process that can produce outcomes, and sometimes as an outcome in and of itself" (p. 161). Ultimately, it is our intention to focus on mindfulness at the level of process. In order to distinguish elements of this process from other uses of the terms, however, a brief discussion of mindfulness at the levels of technique/method and outcome is warranted.

Mindfulness has been transported into the clinical domain within the context of several intervention packages, including mindfulness-based stress reduction (MBSR; e.g., Kabat-Zinn, 1990) and mindfulness-based cognitive therapy (MBCT; e.g., Segal et al. 2002). Dialectical behavior therapy (DBT; e.g., Linehan, 1993a, 1993b) and acceptance and commitment therapy (ACT; e.g., S. C. Hayes, Strosahl, & Wilson, 1999), as well as other treatment packages that have developed from within contemporary behavior analysis, have also been talked about under the rubric of "mindfulness-based interventions" or, as described by Baer (2003), "interventions incorporating mindfulness training." Although all of these approaches do incorporate some form of mindfulness training, to varying degrees (as well as other components that may themselves be active ingredients; e.g., Baer, 2003; Dimidjian & Linehan, 2003; Roemer & Orsillo, 2003), it is unclear whether all of these methods are placed in the same category because of the overlap in technique or due to the fact that all seem to be targeting and/or attempting to facilitate a similar process. S. C. Hayes and Shenk (2004), for example, argue that meditation training offers but one technique that may help change the context in which private events (e.g., thoughts, feelings, bodily sensations) are experienced (ACT's cognitive defusion strategies [e.g., S. C. Hayes, Strosahl, et al., 1999] and Marlatt's, 1994, "urge surfing" offering other relevant examples). Which of these methods best fosters the stance of interest, under what conditions, with which individuals, remain empirical questions. Nonetheless, when we speak of "mindfulness" and "acceptance," we are attempting to do so without reference to the particular method that may facilitate this process.

At the level of outcome, mindfulness training can be discussed in terms of the outcome of a particular method (e.g., decreased anxiety), and sometimes as an outcome of a process (e.g., increases in mindfulness may lead to increased openness to experience and willingness to act in accordance with values). Discussion of outcome measures, as exemplified by the first use above, is beyond the scope of this chapter, as is more general information about the efficacy of methods that incorporate mindfulness training (see Baer, 2003; Craven, 1989; Perez-de-Albeniz & Holmes, 2000, for reviews).

It is with regard to the other aspect of outcome (i.e., outcomes of the process of mindfulness) where the line between process and outcome becomes particularly challenging to draw. To use an example, several researchers (e.g., S. C. Hayes & Shenk, 2004; Wilson & Murrell, 2004) have pointed to an increase in psychological flexibility as an important outcome of mindfulness and acceptance-based methods. Is this flexibility best conceptualized as part of the process itself (e.g., A. M. Hayes & Feldman, 2004) or as an outcome of a more basic process deemed "mindfulness" or "acceptance"? The answer to this question depends, in part, on the purposes of assessment, which relates to the specific research questions of interest. Although we recognize that this distinction may sometimes be artificial and may depend heavily on one's point of view in any given moment, we attempt to tease apart process (i.e., phenomenological correlates of mindfulness and acceptance) and outcome, and emphasize discussion of the former (see Bishop et al., 2003, 2004).

WORKING DEFINITIONS

Kabat-Zinn's (1994, p. 4) often-cited definition refers to mindfulness as "paying attention in a particular way: on purpose, in the present moment, and nonjudgmentally." Probably in part because many of those studying mindfulness-based methods have implicitly or explicitly based their work on MBSR, many other proposed definitions echo that put forth by Kabat-Zinn. For example, Marlatt and Kristeller (1999) refer to mindfulness as "bringing one's complete attention to the present experience on a moment to moment basis" (p. 68). Brown and Ryan (2003) note that mindfulness is "most commonly defined as the state of being attentive to and aware of what is taking place in the present" (p. 822). Baer (2003), after reviewing definitions proposed by Kabat-Zinn, Linehan, and Hanh, among others, concludes, "thus, mindfulness is the nonjudgmental observation of the ongoing stream of internal and external stimuli as they arise" (p. 125). Other researchers' definitions are less consistent with this standard, if only in emphasis or angle (e.g., Langer, 1989; J. R. Martin, 1997; for more details on the relevant aspects of these definitions, see discussion of "deautomatization" and "decentering" below).

FACETS OF MINDFULNESS

There are clearly commonalities and areas of overlap among the various definitions reviewed. And, the variability in definitions may, at least in part, reflect the fact that mindfulness is a multifaceted process (Dimidjian & Linehan, 2003; Roemer & Orsillo, 2003). Researchers are just beginning to identify particular components, speculate about how they fit together, and examine them empirically. Linehan and colleagues' (e.g., Dimidjian & Linehan, 2003; Linehan, 1993a, 1993b) conceptualization of mindfulness may offer a useful starting point in this effort. This model proposes both "what" (i.e., what one does when practicing mindfulness) and "how" (i.e., qualities related to the ways these activities are done) skills of mindfulness. The "what" skills include observing, noticing, bringing awareness; describing, labeling, noting; and participating. These activities should be done (i.e., the "how" skills) nonjudgmentally, with acceptance, allowing; in the present moment, with beginner's mind; and effectively (Dimidjian & Linehan, 2003).

All of the proposed definitions reviewed seem to acknowledge the component of *attention* and/or *awareness* inherent in mindfulness. Although the content of this attention/awareness may differ on the basis of the specific definition (e.g., some conceptualizations emphasize attention to and/or awareness of internal phenomena, whereas others speak more of awareness of external stimuli), and likely the specific practices employed to facilitate this process, all definitions also seem to recognize the *present-moment nature* of this awareness. In fact, it is this facet that plays a significant role in the proposed mechanism of self-management (e.g., Baer, 2003), which involves increased sensitivity to environmental contingencies (e.g., Borkovec, 2002; Breslin, Zack, & McMain, 2002; Orsillo et al., 2004). What is attended to by an individual being "mindful" in any given moment may largely depend on whatever is most salient for that individual at that point. This component is perhaps best captured in the definition proposed by Baer (2003), reviewed above. In fact, instructions for formal insight meditation, perhaps after guiding the practitioner to attend to each domain of experience separately (e.g., sounds, sights, sensations of the breath, thoughts), often include the guideline to "pay attention to whatever arises in any domain of experience."

In addition to the present-moment nature of attention/awareness, many conceptualizations of mindfulness emphasize qualities of this attending (Linehan et al.'s "how" skills) and/or aspects of intention. For example, Kabat-Zinn (1990) identified seven qualities of attending, including nonstriving, nonjudging, acceptance, patience, trust, openness, and letting go. Shapiro and Schwartz (2000) build on Kabat-Zinn's conceptualization, adding the following "affective (heart) qualities": gratitude, gentleness, generosity, empathy, and lovingkindness. Many of these qualities parallel Neff's (2003a, 2003b) articulation of the construct of self-compassion. It is important to note, however, that some (e.g., Bishop et al., 2004) have argued that these qualities are more usefully considered outcomes as opposed to parts of the process.

Segal et al. (2002) describe several facets of mindfulness and related skills that are "to be learned" (pp. 93–94) in MBCT. These skills include concentration (i.e., sustained attention; also emphasized by Bishop, 2002); awareness/mindfulness of thoughts, emotions/feelings, bodily sensations; being in the moment; decentering; acceptance/nonaversion, nonattachment, kindly awareness; letting go; "being" rather than "doing," nongoal attainment; bringing awareness to the manifestation of a problem in the body. Although these are not mutually exclusive, and some do not fit neatly into the "what" or "how" skills of mindfulness, they are relatively consistent with other conceptualizations. Segal et al. also make explicit another key aspect of mindfulness, one that may instead be implied in others' definitions and/or explication of facets. This component, decentering, actually involves many of the other skills described, and has been talked about by Segal et al. as "a more general mode of mind . . . helpful in relating to difficult experiences" (p. 61) as opposed to another technique in the armamentarium of tools to combat depression.

Decentering has been referred to more recently by Teasdale and colleagues as "metacognitive awareness," defined as a cognitive set in which negative thoughts and feelings are viewed and experienced as transient mental events, rather than as the self (Teasdale et al., 2002). Parallels may also be drawn to Deikman's (1982) "observing self," and S. C. Hayes and colleagues' (e.g., S. C. Hayes, 1984; S. C. Hayes, Strosahl, et al., 1999) notion of "self-as-context" alternatively referred to as "the transcendent self" and "that safe place (that) is consciousness itself" (S. C. Hayes, 2002b, p. 61). As a final example, although speaking explicitly of method, Craven (1989) seems to be referring to a key aspect of the process of mindfulness when he refers to the maintenance of a self-observing attitude as a core and defining feature of "all but most advanced" meditation techniques (p. 649).

What exactly does this "decentered" stance involve? J. R. Martin (1997) uses the popular figure/ground illusion (i.e., black and white picture that may be perceived as either a vase or two profiles facing each other) to illustrate two roles of mindfulness practice, both of which relate to decentering. First, Martin suggests that meditation and other mindfulness practices function to help individuals develop awareness into or insight about the existence or nature of alternative perceptions about the world (that the figure may be viewed as either a vase or a set of profiles). Once this awareness is cultivated, the second step involves the realization that "the phenomena contemplated are distinct from the mind contemplating them" (Goleman, 1980, p. 146, as cited in J. R. Martin, 1997). Martin likens this distinction to Safran and Segal's (1990, as cited in J. R. Martin, 1997) discussion of deautomatization and decentering. Deautomatization is described as a process of stepping out of automatic or habitual modes of processing, while decentering involves stepping back from any immediate perspective and perceiving it within a broader, more detached, context of awareness. Baer's (2003) reference to two statements that may be utilized in the cognitive therapy component of MBCT nicely highlights this distinction: "thoughts are not facts" and "I am not my thoughts" (p. 127), the first reflecting a process of deautomatization and the second illustrating the essence of decentering.

Langer's (1989) notion of mindfulness (i.e., "best understood as the process of drawing novel distinctions"; Langer & Moldoveanu, 2000, p. 1) may involve a deautomatization of sorts. Sternberg's (2000) discussion of this construct seems pertinent here. Sternberg describes Langer's mindfulness as involving, in addition to orientation to the present, elements of openness to novelty; alertness to distinction; sensitivity to different contexts; and implicit, if not explicit awareness of multiple perspectives. Although Langer's conceptualization emphasizes the cognitive domain of experience and individuals' relationships with external, as opposed to internal, stimuli, this notion bears a striking similarity to Linehan et al.'s (e.g., Dimidjian & Linehan, 2003) emphasis on "beginner's mind." It seems that deautomatization represents a necessary precondition for decentering, in a similar way that attention may represent a necessary, but not sufficient, condition for the cultivation of mindfulness (the "how" qualities representing other key elements of this stance). Thus, it seems that almost all agree that the process of mindfulness is characterized by attention and/or awareness in the present moment, and that the quality of this attention or awareness is critical. Various specific terms have been proposed to account for this quality of attention, or the "hows" of mindfulness practice; these seem to fall under the broad labels of compassion/acceptance/nonjudgment and decentering.

Although we consider it useful to examine various facets of the process of mindfulness, especially given the current state of the literature, considering each separately has its limitations as well. Likely, a great deal of overlap exists among these components, and it may be that interactive, as opposed to simple additive, models best account for the effects of technologies that attempt to facilitate this process. After introducing their "what" and "how" skills of mindfulness, Dimidjian and Linehan (2003) readily agree that future research should address questions related to the distinctness of each component and whether all essential components are represented. Accordingly, we will review measures that assess mindfulness more holistically, as well as those that attempt to capture only specific components of the process. This review follows a discussion of the construct of acceptance.

EXPERIENTIAL ACCEPTANCE

Clearly an important component of the process of mindfulness is a nonjudgmental, accepting attitude toward one's own experiences. What exactly does acceptance involve? In what situations might it make sense to consider this process, either in conjunction with, or independent from mindfulness?

"Positive" and "Negative" Conceptualizations

A definitional challenge specific to acceptance (although in some ways it applies to mindfulness as well; see A. M. Hayes & Feldman, 2004) involves the notion that acceptance has often been defined "negatively" (i.e., the processes that it does not involve as opposed to those that it does involve). For example, Dougher (1994) notes that acceptance is often defined by what it is not, such as letting go or giving up on the struggle to control or change one's experience. Although defining and operationalizing various constructs including thought suppression (e.g., Wegner & Zanakos, 1994), emotional numbing (e.g., Litz, 1992), and other forms of experiential avoidance (e.g., S. C. Hayes, Wilson, Gifford, Follette, & Strosahl, 1996) may help us arrive at definitions of our terms, it seems that the assumption that the "flip side" or opposite of these processes fully represents acceptance, must at least be examined. Here, the distinction between constructional versus eliminative approaches seems relevant.

Many behavior change methods involve direct attempts to reduce problematic or maladaptive behavior. As an alternative to this "eliminative" approach, Goldiamond (1974, as cited in Delprato, 1981) instead advocated for a constructional approach, defined as an orientation that involves the creation of behavioral repertoires, rather than a reliance on the elimination of such. In addition to general ethical concerns related to eliminative approaches, attempts to change, avoid, or otherwise eliminate processes at the level of private events (i.e., through punishment) often have paradoxical and unwanted effects (e.g., S. C. Hayes et al., 1996; see Purdon, 1999, for a review of the thought suppression literature). Additionally, instructing someone to "not suppress" his or her own thoughts or feelings does not provide much direction. Although discussion of these types of approaches are related to method, as opposed to process, it seems that making an effort to arrive at "positive" definitions of the processes of mindfulness and acceptance may allow us to more clearly explicate the stance that mindfulness-based and related methods are attempting to foster. It is noteworthy that such a constructional approach, versus an eliminative one, parallels the positive psychology movement, which has developed in part as a reaction to the disease model "empire" (e.g., Seligman, 2002).

Working Definitions

Sanderson and Linehan (1999) explicitly acknowledge that at least some forms of acceptance simultaneously involve passive and active processes. These authors point to the root of this term, "kap, " which means "to take, seize, or catch" and contrast these connotations with the commonly used synonym "receiving." They note that relying on this synonym entails an underappreciation for the "positive" aspects of the process of acceptance, including careful observation and openness to experience. Thus, Sanderson and Linehan conclude, "acceptance is the developed capacity to fully embrace whatever is in the present moment" (p. 200). From this perspective, an individual's capacity for acceptance may be enhanced by the process of mindfulness. Although they acknowledge that acceptance involves skills that must be practiced repeatedly, Sanderson and Linehan's definition seems to reflect a trait-like view of this construct. Others emphasize what acceptance "looks like" on a state or moment-to-moment basis.

In the context of discussing the distinction between MBCT (Segal et al., 2002) and traditional cognitive therapy, Baer (2003) notes that an advantage of MBCT is that "a mindful perspective about one's thoughts can be applied to all thoughts" (p. 129; see also Kabat-Zinn's, 1994, discussion of "weaving the parachute") as opposed to only depressogenic cognitions, those that traditional cognitive therapy targets. Acceptance, as considered within the contemporary behavior analytic tradition, has more limited applicability because it is defined functionally; it can only be understood in relation to the context in which it occurs (e.g., S. C. Hayes & Shenk, 2004; Wilson & Murrell, 2004).

S. C. Hayes (1994) states that "psychological acceptance involves experiencing events fully and without defense, as they are and not as they say they are" (p. 30). He goes on to note, "In a more technical sense, it involves making contact with the automatic or direct stimulus functions of events, without acting to reduce or manipulate those functions, and without acting on the basis solely of their derived or verbal functions" (pp. 30–31). Such a technical definition is embedded, generally, within a particular philosophy of science deemed functional contextualism, and more specifically, within a particular view of human suffering (i.e., S. C. Hayes, Strosahl, et al., 1999; also see S. C. Hayes, Barnes-Holmes, & Roche, 2001). From a contextual perspective, the unit of analysis is "the act in context" (Pepper, 1942, as cited in Nelson & Hayes, 1986). Let us begin to examine the contexts in which it makes sense to consider acceptance as an option.

In discussing the functional nature of this definition, Dougher (1994) states that acceptance is only clinically relevant in situations that involve competing contingencies. Dougher offers the example of an individual considering initiating a conversation with someone that he or she finds attractive. Both reinforcing/desirable (i.e., "whatever immediate consequences are inherent in a potentially pleasant social interaction and the possibility of further development of the relationship, intimacy, shared experiences, etc.," p. 39) and punishing/undesirable (i.e., the possibility of experiencing the aversive thoughts and feelings that typically accompany rejection) consequences are operating here. Because people cannot be simultaneously approached and avoided, this situation inherently involves choice and a willingness to act in accordance with one set of contingencies while somehow "managing" the influence of the other set of contingencies.

Dougher (1994) makes it clear that there is no "right" answer with regard to which set of contingencies is the "better" one to act in accordance with; this "comes down to a question of values" (p. 39). In fact, this connection with what is meaningful and important for a given individual is inherent in all conceptualizations of acceptance from within the ACT community. S.C. Hayes, Strosahl, et al. (1999), for example, state, "... acceptance of negative thoughts, memories, emotions, and other private events is legitimate and honorable only to the extent that it serves ends that are valued by the client" (p. 205).

An individual may contact the thoughts and feelings that will inevitably arise in the context of valued action with various levels of an accepting stance. S. C. Hayes (1994) discusses a continuum of acts of acceptance, from resignation/tolerance, to the abandonment of the "change agenda" in some situations, to emotional/social willingness, to deliteralization. This highest level, deliteralization, is defined as "the defusion of the derived relations and functions of events from the direct functions of these events" (p. 31). In other words, individuals acting from a deliteralized stance view their thoughts as thoughts, their feelings as feelings, and their bodily sensations as bodily sensations, rather than essentially seeing "through" these experiences. This notion bears a striking resemblance to the decentering facet of mindfulness, as discussed above. Thus, mindfulness may necessarily involve acts of acceptance in situations that constitute conflict of the sort discussed by Dougher (1994).

Although a detailed discussion of this issue is beyond the scope of the chapter, it is important to recognize that such conflict may be elicited by a multitude of "events." For example, if an individual is engaging in the practice of insight meditation, he or she may become aware of a painful physical sensation. Often our first reaction is to quickly move away from pain. This could take the form of distraction, movement, and/or avoidance of sitting meditation in general. However, the guidelines of insight meditation practice suggest that one should instead remain aware of and open to all experiences, including those that we label as painful. Additionally, if Buddhist teachings on attachment and "clinging" (e.g., Kumar, 2002) as a main source of our ubiquitous suffering ring true, every time that we experience a thought or sensation that we like and want to hold onto, we face similar conflicting contingencies. Thus, in all such moments, humans seem to be presented with choices.

These (inherently functional) conceptualizations of acceptance have significant implications for the assessment of this process. First, existing measures of acceptance and related constructs may be considered according to which "level(s)" of acceptance they target. Second, studying acceptance within one particular domain of experience (e.g., coping with pain) may offer a way to infer function from the form of specific behaviors (e.g., taking medication, continuing to remain active *with* the pain). However, adequately assessing the process of experiential acceptance may necessarily involve eliciting a conflict of sorts. Several recently conducted experimental studies have used a variety of challenge tasks (e.g., carbon dioxide inhalation, cold pressor task) toward this end. Still, we must bear in mind that the same stimuli may elicit varying degrees of conflicting contingencies in different individuals. In cases in which no conflict is present, "acceptance would not be interesting" (Dougher, 1994, p. 39). Relatively, it is imperative that we consider the nature of the competing contingencies in specific studies (particularly in experimental designs); is what is drawing an individual to approach versus avoid a challenge a pull toward action in line with their values or is it based on demand characteristics that may be inherent in our protocols?

MEASURES

We have made an effort, throughout this chapter, to untangle various uses of the terms mindfulness and acceptance. Putting aside questions of method and outcome, what does the *process* of being mindful look like? What does accepting our emotional responses involve? Unfortunately, our methods do not allow us to directly witness someone "nonjudgmentally observing" his or her thoughts and feelings. Or do they? The methods of cognitive neuroscience have brought us to places we had never dreamed of: EEG readings and fMRI images may offer a window through which to view aspects of this process. However, how do we know what we are capturing? We must either rely on method (i.e., "if he is practicing insight meditation, the readings on this PET scanner must equal "mindfulness") or on subjective reports (i.e., "right now I am accepting whatever thoughts and feelings arise") to make this determination. Several research groups are indeed making progress identifying physiological correlates of meditation practice and/or "more enduring changes in baseline brain function" (Davidson et al., 2003, p. 564) as a function of participation in MBSR or other mindfulness-based interventions (see also Dunn, Hartigan, & Mikulas, 1999).

Certainly, examining particular patterns of alpha and theta waves does give us a glimpse into what the processes of mindfulness and/or acceptance might "look like"; such technology may offer valuable tools in the study of mechanisms of change and related research questions. However, it is important to bear in mind that these methods allow us to be privy to but one domain of emotional experience (i.e., physiological reactions). In an attempt to capture the subjective experience of states of mindfulness, other studies have relied more on indirect methods of measurement. Several measures based on self-report have recently been developed and data are accumulating on their reliability and validity. An overview of these instruments appears below.

Our review is not intended to be exhaustive; we emphasize those assessment methods that have received the most empirical attention and/or that fit best with the conceptualizations of these constructs lain out above (we discuss the decentering facet separately, as assessing this component of mindfulness seems to involve unique challenges). We attempt to emphasize subjective correlates of the processes of mindfulness and acceptance themselves (or what may be considered immediate or short-term outcomes); discussion of measures that assess longer term outcomes of mindfulness (e.g., enhanced self-awareness, openness to experience) is beyond the scope of this chapter; the interested reader is referred to Bishop et al. (2004) and Brown and Ryan (2003) for discussion of these related constructs. Unless otherwise indicated, all instruments may be considered trait measures, or assessments of a general tendency toward taking a mindful and/or accepting stance toward experience.

ASSESSMENT BASED ON SELF-REPORT

Assessment of Mindfulness

Freiburg Mindfulness Inventory. The Freiburg Mindfulness Inventory (FMI; Buchheld & Walach, 2002) is a 30-item German-language inventory, which assesses the general factor of "mindfulness," as conceptualized in Vipassana meditation practices. Although factor analyses yielded some evidence for four separate facets of mindfulness (i.e., attention to present moment without personal identification with the experiences at hand; nonjudgments, nonevaluative attitude toward self and others; openness to one's own negative and positive sensations, perceptions, moods states, emotions, and thoughts; and process-oriented, insightful understanding), the authors suggest a general factor construction. Buchheld and Walach report high internal consistency both before and after a variable-length meditation retreat (Cronbach alpha = .093 and .94); the FMI was also shown to be sensitive to changes over the course of this retreat (with significant increases in FMI scores from Time 1 to Time 2).

Although translated, the FMI has not yet been validated in the English language. The authors also caution that this measure may be valid only with populations that have had exposure to mindfulness meditation; the questions may seem ambiguous or confusing to individuals not familiar with these concepts. However, the measure does seem to capture some of the major facets of mindfulness that we have highlighted above, including present-moment process-focused awareness and acceptance/nonjudgment of internal and external stimuli.

Kentucky Inventory of Mindfulness Skills. The Kentucky Inventory of Mindfulness Skills (KIMS; Baer et al., 2004) is a 39-item scale designed to measure distinct facets of mindfulness in broad populations (including those with no previous exposure to meditation or other mindfulness practices). The aspects of mindfulness tapped by this scale were drawn primarily from DBT (thus, this is a skills-based measure) and include "observing," or attending to internal and external stimuli; "describing," or labeling of noticed phenomena; "acting with awareness," or engaging in present-moment activity without distraction; and "accepting (or allowing) without judgment." Internal consistency estimates in both student samples and a clinical sample (adults diagnosed with borderline personality disorder) were adequate to excellent (.76 to .91).

Subscales of the KIMS have demonstrated convergent validity with measures of constructs theoretically related to mindfulness (e.g., emotional intelligence, life satisfaction, and openness) and divergent validity in regard to measures of neuroticism and general symptomatology, alexithymia, experiential avoidance, and dissociation. Additionally, all scales of the KIMS except for the "observe" scale are significantly correlated with the Mindful Attention and Awareness Scale (MAAS; Brown & Ryan, 2003; described below), with the "act with awareness" subscale demonstrating the strongest relationship.

The KIMS appears to be a particular promising measure of mindfulness, especially as it is conceptualized within DBT. The authors note that this scale may not capture some aspects of mindfulness (e.g., "kindly attention" from MBCT; Segal et al., 2002), but drawn as it is from Linehan et al.'s overarching model of mindfulness skills (e.g., Dimidjian & Linehan, 2003), it has considerable overlap with other conceptualizations of mindfulness.

Cognitive and Affective Mindfulness Scale. The Cognitive Affective Mindfulness Scale—Revised (CAMS-R; Feldman, Hayes, Kumar, & Greeson, 2003; also described in A. M. Hayes & Feldman, 2004) is a 12-item measure of "the awareness, attention, present-focus, and acceptance/nonjudgement aspects of the mindfulness construct" designed for use in a variety of populations with or without experience with mindfulness practice. This scale is composed of four factors: attention, awareness, acceptance of internal experiences, and present focus (A. M. Hayes & Feldman, 2004). A preliminary version (the CAMS) proved sensitive to changes in mindfulness over the course of psychotherapy (Kumar, Feldman, & Hayes, 2003, as cited in A. M. Hayes & Feldman, 2004). The current version (the CAMS-R) is still under development, but appears to be a promising assessment tool. It is associated with clarity of emotions, ability to repair mood, and cognitive flexibility, and predicts self-reported depression and anxiety symptoms (A. M. Hayes & Feldman, 2004).

Toronto Mindfulness Scale. The Toronto Mindfulness Scale (TMS; Bishop et al., 2003) is a 10-item measure of the state of mindfulness, as defined by a consensus team of researchers (Bishop et al., 2004). Although the conceptual model upon which the scale was based posited a two-factor model (i.e., intentional self-regulation of attention to facilitate nonjudgmental awareness; an observational stance characterized by curiosity, acceptance, and openness to experience), factor analysis yielded a single factor that reflects both of these elements (coefficient alpha = .76). The TMS was designed to be administered immediately following a meditation session. Bishop et al. report that the measure positively correlates with reflective styles of self-focused attention, openness to experience, and psychological mindedness, and is unrelated to dissociation, ruminative self-awareness, self-consciousness, and social desirability. The TMS was also shown to discriminate between those with and without meditation experience and to be sensitive to change within the context of an MBSR program (although the authors caution against relying on TMS scores at one time point, which may not be representative of participants' general capacity for mindfulness; interestingly, Sternberg, 2000, argues that examining standard deviations vs. mean scores on such measures may be more valuable).

Preliminary data suggest that Bishop et al.'s measure captures both attention and some of the quality of attention facets of mindfulness, as discussed above. However, it is interesting to note that, although the TMS did discriminate between those with and without previous meditation experience, differences between *novice* and *experienced* meditators were not found. Bishop et al. suggest that these findings indicate that the core components of the process of mindfulness (i.e., attention/awareness with an attitude of acceptance, curiosity, and openness) are distinct from outcomes and/or benefits of sustained mindfulness practice over time (e.g., compassion, patience, nonreactivity), and should continue to be studied as such. Additionally, the single factor solution reported by Bishop et al. supports the notion of interconnected, as opposed to independent, facets of mindfulness.

Mindfulness Attention and Awareness Scale. The Mindful Attention and Awareness Scale (MAAS; Brown & Ryan, 2003) is a 15-item scale, which measures a single factor, the "present attention and awareness" component of mindfulness. The authors note that this type of awareness likely varies at both state and trait levels in all individuals, and thus this measure attempts to understand both inter- and intraindividual variations in the frequency of mindful (and mindless) states over time. Brown and Ryan explicitly chose not to assess the "how" and "why" aspects of mindfulness, as they were most interested in examining the relation between attention/awareness and variables related to subjective well-being and did not want their definition of mindfulness confounded with such outcome measures (also see Bishop et al., 2004).

Participants are instructed to rate each item on a 6-point Likert-type scale (1 = *almost always* to 6 = *almost never*). High scores reflect a greater degree of mindfulness, as the items retained through the scale construction exclusively measure aspects of mindlessness (see Brown & Ryan, 2003, for a discussion of this process and the potential advantages of the indirect approach). Adequate internal consistency of the scale was determined across a variety of samples, including five undergraduate, one community, and one national (U.S.) sample (Cronbach's alphas ranging from .80 to .87). Test-retest reliability in a student sample was also good (intraclass correlation coefficient = .81) over a 4-week period. The MAAS has also demonstrated convergent validity with emotional intelligence, clarity of emotional states, ability to repair mood, attention to emotions, and openness to experience, as well as measures of well-being (positive affectivity, life satisfaction, and self-actualization). It is moderately correlated with the Mindfulness/Mindlessness Scale (MMS; Bodner & Langer, 2001, as cited in Brown & Ryan, 2003), an unpublished measure of the tendency to achieve mindful states, as conceptualized by Langer (1989). Finally, MAAS scores were inversely related to neuroticism, anxiety, depression, negative affectivity, health complaints, and somatization.

Thus, the MAAS is an indirect measure of the awareness/present-moment attention facet of mindfulness. Although it addresses only one potential component of mindfulness, it seems to be a promising tool with regard to a subset of research questions.

Measures of decentering. Of the facets of mindfulness discussed, decentering remains of the most challenging to operationalize (e.g., Roemer & Orsillo, 2003). One assessment tool that has been used to attempt to capture this element of an individual's relationship with his or her thoughts and feelings is a measure of believability. For example, Bach and Hayes (2002) asked participants with psychotic symptoms to rate the degree to which they believed in the "truth" of their particular hallucinations and/or delusions. Change in believability ratings was related to lower rehospitalization rates for participants assigned to the ACT (vs. a treatment-as-usual) condition. A similar believability measure was used by Zettle and Hayes (1987).

Believability ratings may be viewed, at least in part, as one way of assessing the process of decentering. Ratings of cognitive flexibility (e.g., Cognitive Flexibility Scale; M. M. Martin & Rubin, 1995) may also offer a useful way to tap into the deautomatization aspect of decentering. Bishop et al. (2004) offer several additional suggestions for capturing this facet that emphasize what they deem the "complexity of cognitive representations," which involves the experience of one's thoughts, feelings, and sensations as "contextual, relativistic, transient, and subjective" (p. 234). Coding procedures utilized by Labouvie-Vief, Chiodo, Goguen, Diehl, and Orwoll (1995) in the examination of self-narratives, as well as Moore, Hayhurst, and Teasdale's (1996) paradigm utilizing autobiographical memory (Measure of Awareness and Coping in Autobiographical Memory [MACAM]), may begin to capture this process.

Moore et al. (1996) developed the MACAM in an effort to operationally define the construct of metacognitive awareness. In this research paradigm, participants are asked to listen to audiotaped vignettes designed to evoke mild states of depression, and are asked to think of a time when they felt similarly. Through semistructured interviews, responses are elicited and coded with regard to the degree of metacognitive awareness at the time of the event, from 1 (minimal discrimination of various negative thoughts and feelings; statements such as "I feel like crap") through 5 (discrimination of self from thoughts and feelings, reached quickly, more clearly, and/or persistently; e.g., "I was able to step back from my feelings of sadness").

Teasdale et al. (2002) demonstrated that metacognitive awareness, as assessed by the MACAM, plays an important role in the development of depression, in depressive relapse, and in treatment response to both cognitive therapy and mindfulness-based cognitive therapy. Although this measure appears to be a promising research tool in the assessment of the decentering facet of mindfulness, several limitations (e.g., limited structure, retrospective bias) suggest that further efforts to develop similar innovative assessment instruments are warranted.

Assessment of Acceptance

Acceptance and Action Questionnaire. The Acceptance and Action Questionnaire (AAQ; S. C. Hayes, Strosahl, et al., 2004) is a 9-item measure that attempts to assess the construct of "experiential avoidance," or attempts to avoid or control aversive internal experiences such as distressing thoughts or feelings (S. C. Hayes et al., 1996). Although the measure directly assesses phenomena such as the tendency to control or avoid distressing internal stimuli, to experience excessive fusion with or negative evaluation of internal stimuli, or to feel unable to act intentionally while experiencing distressing private events, it is included here as an indirect measure of acceptance—a measure of what acceptance/mindfulness are not.

The final 9-item scale assesses a single factor of experiential avoidance. Internal consistency was adequate (Cronbach's alpha = .70) for this scale. Test-retest reliability in an undergraduate population over a 4-month period was .64. The AAQ is significantly correlated with a number of scales that measure types of coping that may be conceptualized as avoidant, including thought suppression, self-deceptive positivity, thought control, and avoidance coping. Although these correlations were significant, they were not particularly strong (most under $r = .04$); the authors note that the AAQ likely measures unique aspects of broad tendencies to experientially avoid (such as wanting to remove painful life experiences), whereas these measures tap-specific forms of avoidance. The AAQ is also significantly related in the expected directions to general psychopathology, physical symptoms, depression, anxiety, work-related stress and well-being, quality of life and life satisfaction, and self-reported posttraumatic symptomatology.

Although the 9-item AAQ represents a first attempt to create a reliable research tool to explore the construct of experiential avoidance, the authors caution that further iterations of this measure are needed; many of the items may seem too complex for individuals not exposed to these constructs, and the low internal consistency of the measure suggests that a multidimensional approach to measurement of experiential avoidance may be warranted (S. C. Hayes, Strosahl, et al., 2004). The development of a second version of the AAQ addressing some of these concerns is currently underway (F. G. Bond, personal communication, June 15, 2004).

Self Compassion Scale. The Self Compassion Scale (SCS; Neff, 2003a) is a 26-item questionnaire designed to measure the three components of Neff's definition of self-compassion:

> (1) extending kindness and understanding to oneself rather than harsh self-criticism and judgment; (2) seeing one's experiences as part of the larger human experience rather than as separating and isolating; and (3) holding one's painful thoughts and feelings in balanced awareness rather than over-identifying with them." (Neff, 2003a, p. 224)

Participants rate SCS items representing six subscales: self-kindness, self-judgment, common humanity, isolation, mindfulness (e.g., items about keeping things in perspective in the face of failure), and overidentification on a 5-point Likert-type scale (1 = *almost never*, 5 = *almost always*) where higher scores suggest greater self-compassion. Internal consistency for the full scale was excellent (Cronbach's alpa = .92). The SCS is negatively correlated with self-criticism, and positively correlated with social connectedness and attention to, clarity of, and ability to repair emotional states. This scale also predicts mental health outcomes such as self-reported depression and anxiety, life satisfaction, and neurotic perfectionism. Although the SCS is not a measure of acceptance per se, it is included here because it seems to tap inherent components of both mindfulness and acceptance.

Chronic Pain Acceptance Questionnnaire. The Chronic Pain Acceptance Questionnaire (CPAQ; Geiser, 1992, as cited in McCracken, 1998) is a 34-item measure of acceptance of pain. Several studies have provided evidence for the internal consistency and validity of this questionnaire as a measure of pain acceptance (see McCracken, 1998; McCracken & Eccleston, 2003). In analyzing the factor structure of the CPAQ, McCracken (1998) found three components of acceptance, including the ability to engage in normal life activities; recognizing that pain may not change; and not needing to avoid or control pain. These facets may be viewed with regard to how they fit within S. C. Hayes' (1994) continuum of acceptance, as discussed above. For example, the latter two components may correspond with S. C. Hayes' notion of "abandonment of the change agenda" in some situations, whereas the first, the ability to engage in normal life activities, bears some similarity to emotional/social willingness.

Measures of Emotion Regulation/Responding

Various conceptualizations of emotion regulation are differentially compatible with our discussion of acceptance. Most extant measures of this construct (e.g., Catanzaro & Mearns', 1990, Generalized Expectancy for Negative Mood Regulation; Gross & John's, 2003, Emotion Regulation Questionnaire) focus on the presence of behaviors that function to alter or change negative emotional states while maintaining positive ones. Speaking of operationalizations of this sort, Blackledge and Hayes (2001) note that the need to regulate emotion implies an unwillingness to have certain internal experiences. Thus, these measures of emotion regulation may actually assess forms of experiential control versus acceptance. The mood repair subscale of the Trait Meta-Mood Scale (TMMS; Salovey, Mayer, Goldman, Turvey, & Palfai, 1995) may also be considered a measure of this form of emotion regulation (however, the other TMMS subscales, attention to feelings and clarity of feelings, may capture processes more consistent with mindfulness and acceptance).

Newer conceptualizations of emotion regulation (e.g., Gratz & Roemer, 2004) emphasize the function of emotion. As such, the ability to experience an emotion without secondary emotional responses (e.g., guilt, shame) is viewed as adaptive and contributing to greater emotion regulation. These researchers developed the Difficulties in Emotion Regulation Scale (DERS), a 36-item measure that assesses deficits in six aspects of emotion regulation (i.e., nonacceptance of emotions, inability to engage in goal-directed behavior when distressed, poor impulse control, nonawareness of emotions, limited access to strategies for regulation, and poor clarity of emotions). Initial studies support the reliability and convergent validity of this measure (Gratz & Roemer, 2004). Many of the constructs captured by the measure overlap with those addressed in this chapter. For example, the emotional nonawareness and poor clarity subscales may capture elements of the experience of mindlessness of emotions, whereas the nonacceptance and goals factors may tap negative evaluation and inability to engage in valued action.

Similarly, the Anxiety Sensitivity Index (ASI; Peterson & Reiss, 1992; also see Taylor & Cox, 1998, for an expanded version) and the Affective Control Scale (ACS; Williams, Chambless, & Ahrens, 1997) assess "fear of fear" and "fear of emotions" (i.e., anger, depression, and positive emotions, as well as anxiety), respectively. More specifically, these instruments measure fear of losing control over the experience of these emotions and/or one's reactions to them. Anxiety sensitivity and fear of emotions more generally are thought to stem from beliefs about the harmful consequences of emotional reactions and have been associated with avoidance and/or escape of negatively evaluated private experiences (e.g., Stewart, Samoluk, & MacDonald, 1999). These constructs may be conceptualized as capturing, at least in part, the nonacceptance of anxiety and/or broader emotional experiences.

ASSESSMENT AT THE OVERT BEHAVIORAL LEVEL

Researchers are also beginning to examine the processes of mindfulness and/or acceptance at the overt behavioral level. For example, Bishop et al. (2004) offer several innovative suggestions for examining processes of attention (e.g., sustained attention; flexibility in attention/shifting) that they consider inherent in mindfulness (also see Valentine & Sweet, 1999). Salters and Roemer (2003) recently examined the impact of various preparations on individuals' sensitivity to environmental contingencies (as opposed to rule-governed behavior) with the Wisconsin Card Sorting Test (Heaton, 1981) and contingency learning paradigms (e.g., S. C. Hayes, Brownstein, Haas, & Greenway, 1986). Such measures may be particularly useful for capturing the present-moment awareness facet of mindfulness. As a present-moment focus is inherent in Langer's conceptualization of mindfulness (i.e., "actively drawing these distinctions keeps us situated in the present," Langer & Moldoveanu, 2000, p. 2), tasks that her research group have used to measure mindfulness (e.g., Langer, 1989; Langer & Moldoveanu, 2000; also see Sternberg, 2000) might also be of value in the assessment of this facet.

Others have examined overt behavioral outcomes in the context of experimental studies that also examine physiological and/or subjective components of emotional reactions. These studies utilized various challenge tasks, including CO_2 inhalation trials (Eifert & Heffner, 2003; Levitt, Brown, Orsillo, & Barlow, 2004), emotionally evocative film clips (Block-Lerner, Plumb, & Orsillo, 2003; Campbell-Sills, Barlow, Brown, & Hoffman, 2004; Tull, Jakupcak, & Roemer, 2005), and a cold pressor task (e.g., S. C. Hayes, Bissett, et al., 1999). Participants are typically given instructions to face these stimuli in a certain way, based on a rationale for that particular strategy. Although it is challenging to come up with tasks that provide an opportunity for values-driven action in the laboratory, assessment of participants' willingness to engage in stressful tasks in the future may be construed as assessing social/emotional willingness (S. C. Hayes, 1994), psychological flexibility (e.g., S. C. Hayes & Shenk, 2004; Wilson & Murrell, 2004), or a more general approach orientation to experience.

CONCLUSION

From the perspective of behavioral assessment, a response to any assessment method is considered a sample of behavior (under a specific set of contingencies) as opposed to a sign of an underlying trait or disposition (Barrios & Hartmann, 1986; Nelson & Hayes, 1986; also see Street, 1994). In order to fully understand a process, it is thus useful to obtain samples of different domains of behavior under various sets of contingencies (i.e., utilizing a variety of modes of assessment). Continuing to develop and validate measures of each domain and examining how they fit together, while continuing to examine our assumptions and acknowledge the potential value of other "ways of knowing," would seem to offer the most useful set of windows into the processes of mindfulness and experiential acceptance. Glimpses into these windows may ultimately not only allow us to witness the process of "meeting them at the door laughing," but more importantly, to use this knowledge to address our most salient research questions. Shedding light on such questions (e.g., related to active ingredients and mechanisms of action of our interventions) has significant implications for the alleviation of human suffering and maximization of human potential.

REFERENCES

Bach, P., & Hayes, S. C. (2002). The use of acceptance and commitment therapy to prevent the rehospitalization of psychotic patients: A randomized controlled trial. *Journal of Consulting and Clinical Psychology, 70,* 1129–1139.

Baer, R. A. (2003). Mindfulness training as a clinical intervention: A conceptual and empirical review. *Clinical Psychology: Science & Practice, 10,* 125–143.

Baer, R. A., Smith, G. T., & Cochran, K. B. (2004). Assessment of mindfulness by self-report: The Kentucky Inventory of Mindfulness Skills. *Assessment, 11,* 191–206.

Barks, C., & Moyne, J. (1997). *The essential Rumi.* San Francisco: Harper.

Barrios, B., & Hartmann, D. P. (1986). The contributions of traditional assessment: Concepts, issues, and methodologies. In R. O. Nelson & S. C. Hayes (Eds.), *Conceptual foundations of behavioral assessment* (pp. 81–110). New York: Guilford.

Bishop, S. R. (2002). What do we really know about mindfulness-based stress reduction? *Psychosomatic Medicine, 64,* 71–84.

Bishop, S. R., Lau, M., Shapiro, S., Carlson, L., Anderson, N. D., Carmody, J., et al. (2004). Mindfulness: A proposed operational definition. *Clinical Psychology: Science and Practice, 11,* 230–241.

Bishop, S. R., Segal, Z. V., Lau, M., Anderson, N. D., Carlson, L., Shapiro, S., et al. (2003). *The Toronto Mindfulness Scale: Development and validation.* Manuscript in preparation.

Blackledge, J. T., & Hayes, S. C. (2001). Emotion regulation in acceptance and commitment therapy. *Journal of Clinical Psychology, 57*, 243–255.

Block-Lerner, J., Plumb, J. C., & Orsillo, S. M. (2003, November). *Facilitating an experientially accepting stance in the laboratory: Can we design manipulations to test mechanisms of change?* Paper presented at the Association for Advancement of Behavior Therapy, Boston, MA.

Borkovec, T. D. (2002). Life in the future versus life in the present. *Clinical Psychology: Science and Practice, 9*, 76–80.

Breslin, C. F., Zack, M., & McMain, S. (2002). An information processing analysis of mindfulness: Implications for relapse prevention in the treatment of substance abuse. *Clinical Psychology: Science and Practice, 9*, 275–299.

Brown, K. W., & Ryan, R. M. (2003). The benefits of being present: Mindfulness and its role in psychological well-being. *Journal of Personality and Social Psychology, 84*, 822–848.

Buchheld, N., & Walach, H. (2002). Mindfulness in Vipassana meditation and psychotherapy: Development of the Freiburg Mindfulness Questionnaire. *Zeitschrift für Klinische Psychologie, Psychiatrie und Psychotherapie, 50*, 153–172.

Cambell-Sills, L., Barlow, D. H., Brown, T. A., & Hoffman, S. G. (2004). *Appraisal and regulation of emotion in anxiety and mood disorders.* Manuscript submitted for publication.

Campos, P. E. (2002). Integrating Buddhist philosophy with cognitive and behavioral practice (Introduction). *Cognitive and Behavioral Practice, 9*, 38–40.

Catanzaro, S. J., & Mearns, J. (1990). Measuring generalized expectancies for negative mood regulation: Initial scale development and implications. *Journal of Personality Assessment, 54*, 546–563.

Craven, J. L. (1989). Meditation and psychotherapy. *Canadian Journal of Psychiatry, 34*, 648–653.

Davidson, R. J., Kabat-Zinn, J., Schumacher, J., Rosenkranz, M., Muller, D., Santorelli, S., et al. (2003). Alterations in brain and immune function produced by mindfulness meditation. *Psychosomatic Medicine, 65*, 564–570.

Deikman, A. J. (1982). *The observing self: Mysticism and psychotherapy.* Boston: Beacon Press.

Delprato, D. J. (1981). The constructional approach to behavioral modification. *Journal of Behavior Therapy and Experimental Psychiatry, 12*, 49–55.

Dimidjian, S., Linehan, M. M., Marlatt, G. A., & Segal, Z. (2002, November). *Mindfulness practice: Clinical application and training.* Clinical roundtable conducted at the annual meeting of the Association for Advancement of Behavior Therapy, Reno, NV.

Dimidjian, S., & Linehan, M. M. (2003). Defining an agenda for future research on the clinical application of mindfulness practice. *Clinical Psychology: Science & Practice, 10*, 166–171.

Dougher, M. J. (1994). The act of acceptance. In S. C. Hayes, N. S. Jacobson, V. M. Follette, & M. J. Dougher (Eds.), *Acceptance and change: Content and context in psychotherapy* (pp. 37–45). Reno, NV: Context Press.

Dunn, B. R., Hartigan, J. A., & Mikulas, W. L. (1999). Concentration and mindfulness meditations: Unique forms of consciousness. *Applied Psychophysiology and Biofeedback, 24,* 147–165.

Eifert, G. H., & Heffner, M. (2003). The effects of acceptance versus control contexts on avoidance of panic-related symptoms. *Journal of Behavior Therapy and Experimental Psychiatry, 34,* 293–312.

Feldman, G. C., Hayes, A. M., Kumar, S. M., & Greeson, J. M. (2003, November). *Clarifying the construct of mindfulness: Relations with emotional avoidance, overengagement, and change with mindfulness training.* Paper presented at the Association for Advancement of Behavior Therapy, Boston, MA.

Gratz, K. L., & Roemer, L. (2004). Multidimensional assessment of emotion regulation and dysregulation: Development, factor structure, and initial validation of the Difficulties in Emotion Regulation Scale. *Journal of Psychopathology and Behavioral Assessment, 26,* 41–54.

Gross, J. J., & John, O. P. (2003). Individual differences in two emotion regulation processes: Implications for affect, relationships, and well-being. *Journal of Personality and Social Psychology, 85,* 348–362.

Haas, J. R. (1994). The elusive nature of acceptance. In S. C. Hayes, N. S. Jacobson, V. M. Follette, & M. J. Dougher (Eds.), *Acceptance and change: Content and context in psychotherapy* (pp. 33–35). Reno, NV: Context Press.

Hayes, A. M., & Feldman, G. (2004). Clarifying the construct of mindfulness in the context of emotion regulation and the process of change in therapy. *Clinical Psychology: Science and Practice, 11,* 255–262.

Hayes, S. C. (1984). Making sense of spirituality. *Behaviorism, 12,* 99–110.

Hayes, S. C. (1994). Content, context, and types of psychological acceptance. In S. C. Hayes, N. S. Jacobson, V. M. Follette, & M. J. Dougher (Eds.), *Acceptance and change: Content and context in psychotherapy* (pp. 13–32). Reno, NV: Context Press.

Hayes, S. C. (2002a). Acceptance, mindfulness, and science. *Clinical Psychology: Science and Practice, 9,* 101–106.

Hayes, S. C. (2002b). Buddhism and acceptance and commitment therapy. *Cognitive and Behavioral Practice, 9,* 58–66.

Hayes, S. C., Barnes-Holmes, D., Roche, B. (Eds.). (2001). *Relational frame theory: A post-Skinnerian account of human language and cognition.* New York: Plenum.

Hayes, S. C., Bissett, R. T., Korn, Z., Zettle, R. D., Rosenfarb, I. S., Cooper, L. D., et al. (1999). The impact of acceptance versus control rationales on pain tolerance. *The Psychological Record, 49,* 33–47.

Hayes, S. C., Brownstein, A. J., Haas, J. R., & Greenway, D. E. (1986). Instructions, multiple schedules, and extinction: Distinguishing rule governed from schedule controlled behavior. *Journal of the Experimental Analysis of Behavior, 46,* 137–147.

Hayes, S. C., Follette, V., & Linehan, M. M. (2004). *Mindfulness and acceptance: Expanding the cognitive–behavioral tradition.* New York: Guilford.

Hayes, S. C., & Shenk, C. (2004). Operationalizing mindfulness without unnecessary attachments. *Clinical Psychology: Science and Practice, 11,* 249–254.

Hayes, S. C., Strosahl, K. D., & Wilson, K. G. (1999). *Acceptance and commitment therapy: An experiential approach to behavior change.* New York: Guilford.

Hayes, S. C., Strosahl, K. D., Wilson, K. G., Bissett, R., T., Pistorello, J., Toarmino, D., et al. (2004). Measuring experiential avoidance: A preliminary test of a working model. *The Psychological Record, 54,* 553–578.

Hayes, S. C., & Wilson, K. G. (2003). Mindfulness: Method and process. *Clinical Psychology: Science & Practice, 10,* 161–165.

Hayes, S. C., Wilson, K. G., Gifford, E. V., Follette, V. M., & Strosahl, K. (1996). Experiential avoidance and behavioral disorders: A functional dimensional approach to diagnosis and treatment. *Journal of Consulting and Clinical Psychology, 64,* 1152–1168.

Heaton, R. K. (1981). *The Wisconsin Card Sort Test.* Lutz, FL: Psychological Assessment Resources.

Kabat-Zinn, J. (1990). *Full catastrophe living: Using the wisdom of your body and mind to face stress, pain, and illness.* New York: Dell Publishing.

Kabat-Zinn, J. (1994). *Wherever you go there you are: Mindfulness meditation in everyday life.* New York: Hyperion.

Kabat-Zinn, J. (2003). Mindfulness-based interventions in context: Past, present, and future. *Clinical Psychology: Science & Practice, 10,* 144–156.

Kumar, S. M. (2002). An introduction to Buddhism for the cognitive–behavioral therapist. *Cognitive and Behavioral Practice, 9,* 40–43.

Labouvie-Vief, G., Chiodo, L. M., Goguen, L. A., Diehl, M., & Orwoll, L. (1995). Representations of self across the life span. *Psychology and Aging, 10,* 404–415.

Langer, E. J. (1989). *Mindfulness.* Cambridge, MA: Perseus Books.

Langer, E. J., & Moldoveanu, M. (2000). The construct of mindfulness. *Journal of Social Issues, 56,* 1–9.

Levitt, J. T., Brown, T. A., Orsillo, S. M., & Barlow, D. H. (2004). The effects of acceptance versus suppression of emotion on subjective and psychophysiological response to carbon dioxide challenge in patients with panic disorder. *Behavior Therapy, 35,* 747–766

Linehan, M. M. (1993a). *Cognitive–behavioral treatment of borderline personality disorder.* New York: Guilford.

Linehan, M. M. (1993b). *Skills training manual for cognitive behavioral treatment of borderline personality disorder.* New York: Guilford.

Litz, B. (1992). Emotional numbing in combat-related posttraumatic stress disorder: A critical review and reformulation. *Clinical Psychology Review, 12,* 417–432.

Marlatt, G. A. (1994). Addiction and acceptance. In S. C. Hayes, N. S. Jacobson, V. M. Follette, & M. J. Dougher (Eds.), *Acceptance and change: Content and context in psychotherapy* (pp. 175–197). Reno, NV: Context Press.

Marlatt, G. A., & Kristeller, J. L. (1999). Mindfulness and meditation. In W. R. Miller (Ed.), *Integrating spirituality into treatment: Resources for practitioners* (pp. 67–84). Washington, DC: American Psychological Association.

Martin, J. R. (1997). Mindfulness: A proposed common factor. *Journal of Psychotherapy Integration, 7,* 291–312.

Martin, M. M., & Rubin, R. B. (1995). A new measure of cognitive flexibility. *Psychological Reports, 76*, 623–626.

McCracken, L. M. (1998). Learning to live with pain: Acceptance of pain predicts adjustment in persons with chronic pain. *Pain, 74*, 21–27.

McCracken, L. M., & Eccleston, C. (2003). Coping or acceptance: What to do about chronic pain? *Pain, 105*, 197–204.

Moore, R. G., Hayhurst, H., & Teasdale, J. D. (1996). *Measure of awareness and coping in autobiographical memory: Instructions for administration and coding.* Unpublished manuscript, Department of Psychiatry, University of Cambridge, Cambridge, United Kingdom.

Neff, K. (2003a). The development and validation of a scale to measure self-compassion. *Self and Identity, 2*, 223–250.

Neff, K. (2003b). Self-compassion: An alternative conceptualization of a healthy attitude toward oneself. *Self and Identity, 2*, 85–102.

Nelson, R. O., & Hayes, S. C. (1986). The nature of behavioral assessment. In R. O. Nelson & S. C. Hayes (Eds.), *Conceptual foundations of behavioral assessment* (pp. 3–41). New York: Guilford.

Orsillo, S. M., Roemer, L., Block-Lerner, J., & Tull, M. T. (2004). Acceptance, mindfulness, and cognitive–behavioral therapy: Comparisons, contrasts, and application to anxiety. In S. C. Hayes, V. Follette, & M. M. Linehan (Eds.), *Mindfulness and acceptance: Expanding the cognitive–behavioral tradition.* New York: Guilford.

Perez-de-Albeniz, A., & Holmes, J. (2000). Meditation: Concepts, effects and uses in therapy. *International Journal of Psychotherapy, 5*, 49–58.

Peterson, R. A., & Reiss, S. (1992). *Anxiety Sensitivity Index manual* (2nd ed.). Worthington, OH: International Diagnostic Systems.

Purdon, C. (1999). Thought suppression and psychopathology. *Behaviour Research and Therapy, 37*, 1029–1054.

Roemer, L., & Orsillo, S. M. (2002). Expanding our conceptualization of and treatment for generalized anxiety disorder: Integrating mindfulness/acceptance-based approaches with existing cognitive–behavioral models (Featured article). *Clinical Psychology: Science and Practice, 9*, 54–68.

Roemer, L., & Orsillo, S. M. (2003). Mindfulness: A promising intervention strategy in need of further study. *Clinical Psychology: Science & Practice, 10*, 172–178.

Salovey, P., Mayer, J. D., Goldman, S. L., Turvey, C., & Palfai, T. P. (1995). Emotional attention, clarity and repair: Exploring emotional intelligence using the trait meta-mood scale. In J. W. Pennebaker (Ed.), *Emotion, disclosure, and health* (pp. 125–154). Washington, DC: APA Books.

Salters, K., & Roemer, L. (2003, November). *Flexibility and sensitivity to current environmental contingencies: Exploring basic processes in experiential acceptance and avoidance.* Paper presented at the Association for Advancement of Behavior Therapy, Boston, MA.

Sanderson, C., & Linehan, M. M. (1999). Acceptance and forgiveness. In W. R. Miller (Ed.), *Integrating spirituality into treatment: Resources for practitioners* (pp. 199–216). Washington, DC: American Psychological Association.

Segal, Z. V. (2003, November). Discussion. In K. Salters and J. Block-Lerner (Chairs), *Mindfulness and acceptance-based behavioral therapies: Methodologies and mechanisms.* Symposium conducted at the Association for Advancement of Behavior Therapy, Boston, MA.

Segal, Z. V., Williams, J. M., & Teasdale, J. D. (2002). *Mindfulness-based cognitive therapy for depression: A new approach to preventing relapse.* New York: Guilford.

Seligman, M. E. P. (2002). Positive psychology, positive prevention, and positive therapy. In C. R. Snyder & S. J. Lopez (Eds.), *Handbook of positive psychology* (pp. 89–105). New York: Oxford University Press.

Shapiro, S. L., & Schwartz, G. E. R. (2000). Intentional systemic mindfulness: An integrative model for self-regulation and health. *Advances in Mind-Body Medicine, 2000, 16,* 128–134.

Shapiro, S. L., & Walsh, R. (2003). An analysis of recent meditation research and suggestions for future directions. *The Humanistic Psychologist, 31,* 86–114.

Sternberg, R. J. (2000). Images of mindfulness. *Journal of Social Issues, 56,* 11–26.

Stewart, S. H., Samoluk, S. B., & MacDonald, A. B. (1999). Anxiety sensitivity and substance use and abuse. In S. Taylor (Ed.), *Anxiety sensitivity: Therapy, research, and treatment of the fear of anxiety* (pp. 287–319). Mahwah, NJ: Erlbaum.

Street, W. R. (1994). Attitude-behavior congruity, mindfulness, and self-focused attention: A behavior-analytic reconstruction. *The Behavior Analyst, 17,* 145–153.

Taylor, S., & Cox, B. J. (1998). An expanded Anxiety Sensitivity Index: Evidence for a hierarchic structure in a clinical sample. *Journal of Anxiety Disorders, 12,* 463–483.

Teasdale, J. D., Moore, R. G., Hayhurst, H., Pope, M., Williams, S., & Segal, Z. V. (2002). Metacognitive awareness and prevention of relapse in depression: Empirical evidence. *Journal of Consulting and Clinical Psychology, 70,* 275–287.

Teasdale, J. D., Segal, Z. V., & Williams, J. M. G. (2003). Mindfulness training and problem formulation. *Clinical Psychology: Science & Practice, 10,* 157–160.

Tull, M. T., Jakupcak, M., & Roemer, L. (2005). *An experimental investigation of the effect of emotional acceptance and suppression on later emotional reactivity and willingness.* Manuscript submitted for publication.

Valentine, E. R., & Sweet, P. L. G. (1999). Meditation and attention: A comparison of the effects of concentrative and mindfulness meditation on sustained attention. *Mental Health, Religion, and Culture, 2,* 59–70.

Walsh, R. (1980). The consciousness disciplines and the behavioral sciences: Questions of comparison and assessment. *American Journal of Psychiatry, 137,* 663–673.

Watts, A. (2000). *What is Zen?* New York: MJF Books.

Wegner, D. M., & Zanakos, S. (1994). Chronic thought suppression. *Journal of Personality, 62,* 615–640.

Wilson, K. G., & Murrell, A. R. (2004). Values-centered interventions: Setting a course for behavioral treatment. In S. C. Hayes, V. Follette, & M. M. Linehan

(Eds.), *Mindfulness and acceptance: Expanding the cognitive–behavioral tradition.* New York: Guilford.

Williams, K. E., Chambless, D. L., & Ahrens, A. (1997). Are emotions frightening? An extension of the fear of fear construct. *Behaviour Research and Therapy, 35,* 239–248.

Zettle, R. D., & Hayes, S. C. (1987). Content and process analysis of cognitive therapy. *Psychological Reports, 61,* 939–953.

Chapter 4

ACCEPTANCE AND COMMITMENT THERAPY AS A TREATMENT FOR ANXIETY DISORDERS

Michael P. Twohig, Akihiko Masuda, Alethea A. Varra, and Steven C. Hayes

Human verbal abilities are a two-edged sword. Language and cognition enable us to solve everyday problems and create a comfortable world. The same processes, however, allow us to constantly evaluate ourselves, to compare ourselves to an unrealistic ideal, to bring our painful past to the present, and to project fearsome futures. Acceptance and commitment therapy (ACT, said as one word, not initials; Hayes, Strosahl, & Wilson, 1999) is a therapeutic approach that focuses on undermining unhealthy uses of human language and cognition, and to channel it into more productive areas. The present chapter will outline the philosophy and basic science behind ACT, present the core components of ACT, illustrate how ACT would be implemented with an anxiety client, and provide empirical support for the use of ACT with anxiety disorders.

ACT PHILOSOPHY: FUNCTIONAL CONTEXTUALISM

ACT is rooted in a pragmatic philosophical position called functional contextualism (Hayes, Hayes, & Reese, 1988; Hayes, Hayes, Reese, & Sarbin, 1993). Although philosophy can seem far removed from therapeutic methods, ACT is thoroughly integrated with its underlying philosophy and being clear about it helps make sense of certain features of ACT. In order to make that clear, and to make this philosophical description less abstract, we will describe the features of functional contextualism and then show how these features affect ACT.

HOLISTIC AND CONTEXTUAL UNITS OF ANALYSIS

In all forms of contextualism, the whole event is primary. This means that division of any event into pieces and component parts is not necessarily assumed to be required, that many ways of "analyzing" an event are acknowledged to be possible depending on your purposes, and that analysis is seen as a method of achieving goals, not as a way of revealing ontological truth.

The whole unit involved is an "ongoing act in context." To understand any action, its history, current context, and purpose must be included or the whole event has been missed. Functional contextualism views psychological events as ongoing actions of a whole organism interacting with historically and situationally defined contexts. Unlike other philosophical perspectives, these contextual features do not assemble the whole unit: they are facets of the whole unit. One does not construct the front and back of a coin and then put them together to form a coin. Rather both the front and back are facets of a whole coin and neither has independent existence.

In the same way, in behavior analysis operants are whole units: they are not assembled from mechanical parts. There is no "stimulus" in a psychological sense that exists independently from responding. A stimulus that does not stimulate is not a stimulus at all. Similarly, there is no response without something being responded to; there is no reinforcement without a response that is reinforced, and so on.

ACT comes from clinical behavior analysis viewed contextualistically and thus has a holistic quality about it. For example, if a client is struggling with a thought, the primary issue will not be whether that thought is true or rational. Rather the issue will be to understand the whole event and the function that thought serves. The therapist will be interested in the conditions under which the thought occurs, what else comes up when the thought occurs (e.g., what bodily sensations, memories, or feelings covary with it), what the person does when the thought occurs, and what this entire pattern of action is in the service of. The issue will not be of one form because that isolated feature is not the whole event. But this entire chain of analysis will also be viewed contextualistically. Because it is assumed that division of an event into pieces is a somewhat arbitrary action that is merely a method of achieving goals (not as a way to find Truth with a capital T), analysis is flexible and indeed optional. A client asking "is that an irrational thought?" will not necessarily be met by a guided analysis of thinking. The ACT clinician might also ask the person just to notice the question, and to notice the pull toward "understanding." The clinician might situate that question in a contextual stream (e.g., "is it like you to want to ask such a question?" or "have you tried to figure out such things in the past? How has that worked?"), including its possible purposes (e.g., "it seems as though you are getting rather literal right now ... what do you think that is in the service of?").

A PRAGMATIC TRUTH CRITERION

Much of psychology is interested in modeling how things work, based on the assumption that events are like elements of a gigantic machine. In this more traditional mechanistic approach, truth is based on the correspondence between models and their predictions (what is usually just called "understanding"). That kind of "truth" need not have demonstrated utility. In contrast, all forms of contextualism are based on the assumption that what is "true" is whatever moves an analyst toward a specified goal (Hayes et al., 1988). This means that truth is local and epistemological, not ontological, and there can be multiple forms of contextualism depending on the a priori goals of the analyst. The goal of functional contextualism is predicting and influencing behavior with precision, scope, and depth. This difference between mechanism and functional contextualism explains many of the differences between behavior analysis and mainstream psychology, such as its environmentalism. Accomplishing the goal of influencing behavior requires successful manipulation of events, and only contextual variables can be manipulated directly.

The importance of a pragmatic truth criterion is easy to spot in ACT. When a client says, "I have been thinking that I am no good," the therapist might reply, "is that thought holding you back from what is important to you?" The ACT therapist would not question the form or content of the thought, but the degree to which it interferes with successful working. Similarly, ACT measures the success of the treatment by the degree to which the client is living a life that he or she value, not on the change of any particular behavior. The impact of prediction-and-influence as unified goals is felt in the great focus on manipulable contexts in the analysis of cognition and emotion that underlies ACT—a topic to which we now turn.

ACT's Basic Theory: Relational Frame Theory

The ACT approach to treating psychopathology is based on a comprehensive contextual theory of the behavioral processes underlying language and cognition called relational frame theory (RFT; for a book length treatment see Hayes, Barnes-Holmes, & Roche, 2001). According to RFT, human beings learn to derive and combine stimulus relations and to bring them under arbitrary contextual control. Basically, although we do respond to stimuli in our environment (both public and private), we do not usually respond to the formal features of the stimuli, but to verbally created stimuli. The manner in which events in our lives relate to each other affects the way we experience the world. When we think, reason, speak with meaning, or listen with understanding, we do so by deriving relations among events—among words and events, words and words, and events and events. From the RFT perspective, our linguistic practice is the process of this relational learning.

There are six key concepts in relational learning from an RFT perspective. First, such relations show mutual entailment. That is, if a person learns in a particular context that A relates in a particular way to B, then this must entail some kind of relation between B and A in that context. For example, if "going to a mall" is said to be more fearful than "going to a class," then we can derive the relation that "going to a class" is less fearful than "going to a mall" without direct training. Second, such relations show combinatorial entailment: if a person learns in a particular context that A relates in a particular way to B, and B relates in a particular way to C, then this must entail some kind of mutual relation between A and C in that context. For example, if public speech is then said to be more fearful than going to a mall, then public speech is also more fearful than going to a class. An important point here is that the individual never needs to experience public speaking to feel great anxiety in that situation; the learning occurred relationally. Third, both of these relational performances are controlled by specific contextual features of the environment, rather than purely the nonarbitrary features of related events. Said another way, how the event is relationally framed is dependent on the context. For example, someone yelling "duck!" at a construction site has a different function than yelling it while duck hunting. The context indicates how the event should be relationally framed. Fourth, this relational context (or "C_{rel}" for short) is initially acquired through multiple exemplar training. Multiple exemplar training involves a very large number of training trials across a variety of situational contexts that specify the response and the stimuli that occasion it. As a result of the many trials, no specific feature alone evokes relational framing. But because relationally framing is trained through multiple exemplar training, much like generalized imitation, the features that evoke how the event should be relationally framed are context dependent.

Fifth, the direct or acquired functions of one event in a relational network can transform the stimulus functions of related events in accord with the underlying relation among them. Transformation of stimulus function is especially relevant to clinical problems. What makes relational framing clinically relevant is that functions (i.e., psychological impact) given to one member of related events tend to alter the function of other members. A person who had acquired the relations described above, for example, might experience the strongest feelings of anxiety in the public-speaking situation, then in the mall, and the least in class. Again, because of multiple stimulus relations and transformation of stimulus function, the person can experience these events as anxiety producing the very first time, because their function is not solely dependent on direct learning. The anxiety can be experienced as a result of relational framing. Finally, the transformation of stimulus functions is controlled by a functional context (or "C_{func}" for short) that is also initially acquired through multiple exemplar training. Basically, the C_{func} indicates how the function of the stimulus will be transformed. The statement "I cannot go to that party because I will pass out from my anxiety," includes cues to transform the function of the party to be highly anxiety producing.

Stated more simply, relating is an operant. What is different about this operant, however, is that it alters other behavioral processes. That is why understanding both verbal/cognitive and direct contingency streams is necessary in understanding human behavior.

RFT currently has about 70 studies that support its basic premise. RFT helps explain why human language and cognition are a two-edged sword and, more importantly, suggests ways to alter these verbal processes to accomplish applied ends. ACT is an extension of these insights. ACT restricts the use of C_{rel} interventions to a few focused instances (e.g., values, or helping clients state what is important to them) because these tend to elaborate relational networks and simultaneously increase the transformation of stimulus functions seen within them. The majority of ACT interventions (e.g., acceptance, defusion, self as context, contact with the present moment) instead are C_{func} interventions. This produces a notable difference between ACT and other forms of empirical clinical interventions. For example, cognitive restructuring constitutes an attempt to change the relation between verbal events (e.g., your anxiety will not kill you). In contrast, observing a thought as just a thought and not reacting to it literally (e.g., as in the mindfulness exercises used in ACT) is aimed at changing the function of the thought, not its form or frequency. As will become apparent later in the chapter, ACT is based on the RFT insight that the relational framing is difficult to stop, but that the functions that relational framing produce may be readily altered.

THEORY OF PSYCHOPATHOLOGY: PSYCHOLOGICAL INFLEXIBILITY

From the ACT perspective, the core clinical problem is that these verbal processes maintain a narrow set of responses in anxiety-producing contexts (Hayes, 2004). When a person struggling with social phobia enters the mall, the anxiety is experienced as overwhelming and dangerous; thus, these processes illuminate a small set of response options (e.g., get out, or freeze). Clients spend great amounts of time and energy avoiding/escaping their anxiety. Our culture clearly trains its members to evaluate anxiety—and many other private events—as "bad," and supports just about any attempt to avoid this feeling.

Unfortunately, deliberate avoidance of anxiety has several undesirable results. First, it increases the functional importance of anxiety-relevant cues. The process of avoiding something reinforces the verbal processes that cause the event to be experienced as aversive. It strengthens those relational frames. Thus, the event will continue to be experienced as aversive and anxiety producing. It gets worse not better. Second, the verbal rule that guides avoidance efforts is related to anxiety and thus evokes it. Following the rule "don't think of anxiety" is fruitless, for example, because in order to follow the rule the stated purpose of the rule must be broken. Third, the verbal rule that guides avoidance efforts relates anxiety to dramatically negative consequences (e.g., loss of control, death, humiliation) but the natural response to such negative events is anxiety and thus the control rule elicits additional anxiety. Fourth, avoidance occurs in most other circumstances because of danger. Thus, avoidance strengthens the anxiety-danger verbal relation and anxiety becomes something to be anxious about. As a result of these verbal processes, the lives of people diagnosed with anxiety disorders tend to become focused on not experiencing anxiety, rather than living a life that is important to them. This extreme narrowing of repertoire is the core of psychopathology from an ACT perspective. The goal of ACT with these clients is not decreasing anxiety, but increasing psychological and behavioral flexibility in contexts where behavior has been limited.

Cognitive Fusion

Throughout development, language becomes the dominant source regulating our behavior. Verbal humans experience the world through verbal relations, rather than directly—as nonverbal animals do. Stimulus functions from relational frames dominate over other sources of behavioral regulation, individuals are less in contact with here-and-now experience and direct contingencies, and are more dominated by verbal rules and evaluations. This process has been termed *cognitive fusion*. There are two major problems of cognitive fusion regarding psychological inflexibility. First, verbal rules (i.e., verbal relations, thoughts) are difficult to challenge, even in the face of contrary evidence. Once they are derived, they never seem to go away (Wilson & Hayes, 1996). We can add to them, but we cannot readily eliminate them all together. Once we develop a thought "I must get rid of my anxiety to be happy," it is unlikely to disappear at least in form. Second, behavior regulated by verbal rules tends to be relatively inflexible (see Hayes, 1989, for a book-length review). Verbal rules tend to restrict the range of our behavior available to make contact with more direct experiences, thus undermining the impact of consequences on actual experiences and strengthening rule-followings. Stated differently, in some contexts, we continue to engage in what our mind tells us to do regardless of its consequence. "Being right" or "being consistent" becomes more important than "being effective."

Experiential Avoidance

Experiential avoidance is based in part on cognitive fusion (see Hayes, Wilson, Gifford, Follette, & Strosahl, 1996). Experiential avoidance is the attempt to fix and control the form, frequency, or situational sensitivity of private events (e.g., thoughts, feelings, bodily sensations, and memories) even when attempts to do so cause psychological harm. Examples of experiential avoidance include the attempt to control and/or eliminate the immediate experience of a difficult private event, which is normally called suppression, and the situational escape from or avoidance of situations that are associated with unwanted psychological experiences. Experiential avoidance in a person diagnosed with obsessive–compulsive disorder (OCD) could involve trying not to think about the obsession, drinking or taking drugs to not feel anxiety, or avoiding situations that elicit the obsession or anxiety.

It intuitively makes sense that attempts to fix and avoid aversive stimulation eliminate immediate suffering, and the elimination of suffering is the achievement of well-being. This notion is also supported in RFT. For example, the statement, "if I get rid of my anxiety then I can life the life I want," is an example of an IF–THEN relation that often occasions behavior aimed at reducing anxiety. If this thought is taken literally, there is only one way to live the life one wants—get rid of the anxiety. This problem-solving strategy works well in most situations in our lives. If someone does not like his or her wardrobe, he or she can purchase new clothes; if the room is too cold one can turn up the heat. But control and problem solving do not work well with our thoughts and feelings, such as anxiety, because these events are often verbally related and the process of relating cannot be stopped. Thus, private events must be addressed in a different way than we address other events in our lives (how exactly is discussed later). Moreover, as noted above, attempts to avoid these private events can even increase the intensity and frequency of suffering. Literatures on thought-suppression and emotion-focused, avoidance strategies capture the paradox of our controlling and avoidance attempts on psychological suffering (Abramowitz, Tolin, & Street, 2001), although this has not been as thoroughly tested with clinical samples (Abramowitz et al., 2001; Purdon, 1999). Nevertheless, because of the insensitive nature of behavior regulated by verbal rules, experiential avoidance continues to be practiced despite its possibly long-term paradoxical effect.

Experiential avoidance is evidenced in the diagnostic criteria of several of the anxiety disorders. For example, agoraphobia involves avoidance of anxiety-provoking situations; phobias involve avoiding feared objects or situations; full-blown OCD includes rituals performed in an attempt to decrease obsessions (American Psychiatric Association, 2000). From the ACT position, it is not the anxiety that is so problematic; it is what one does with the anxiety that is the problem.

PSYCHOLOGICAL FLEXIBILITY: SIX CORE PROCESSES OF ACT

ACT aims to increase psychological flexibility in situations where experiential avoidance is prevalent and keeps the individual from living a vital life. Psychological flexibility is the ability to contact the present moment more fully as a conscious human being, and to change or persist when doing so serves valued ends (Hayes, 2004; Hayes, Strosahl, Bunting, Twohig, & Wilson, 2004). Psychological flexibility is established in ACT through six core processes: acceptance, defusion, self as context, contact with the present moment, values, and committed action (see Figure 1). From the RFT perspective, each of these processes influences our linguistic practice. Some

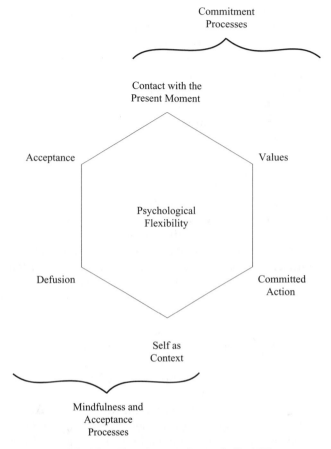

FIGURE 1. The processes that underlie ACT

of these processes undermine the literal and behavior regulatory function of cognition, and others increase the behavioral activation function of cognition. As a whole, these processes are interrelated and influence one another to foster psychological flexibility.

ACCEPTANCE

Given the contextual nature of our private experiences and the paradox of experiential avoidance, ACT provides clients with an alternative approach to them—acceptance. Acceptance should not be confused with tolerance or resignation, both of which are passive and fatalistic. Acceptance involves awareness and the active embrace of private experiences, as they are, not as what they say they are. From a RFT perspective, acceptance is a behavior process of experiencing difficult inner experiences (including bodily sensations, thoughts, unwanted emotions), without acting to reduce or manipulate those functions, and without acting on the basis of the literality of these events. Given its alternative and competing nature in the presence of these events, acceptance process also changes the function of experiential avoidance processes.

Clients diagnosed with anxiety disorders almost always approach treatment with the expectation that the therapist will do something to eliminate or at least significantly reduce their anxiety. This approach is echoed in part by other CBT approaches to treatment that focus on challenging cognitions or controlling and reducing physiological arousal. Acceptance differs from these approaches in that the goal is to allow oneself to have whatever inner experiences are present (including bodily sensations, thoughts, unwanted emotions) without needless defense. Clients are asked to shift their focus from reducing the anxiety to living a valued life.

This approach can be helpful both alone and as a supplement to exposure therapy. One of the strengths of this approach is that the therapist emphasizes to the client that painful experience (even in the form of exposure) is not something seen simply as a means to an end or what the treatment is about. This painful experience is put in the context of the person's broader experience and in the service of their personal goals. Exposure is not simply something the person must make it through to feel better but rather to create more response flexibility. It is an important and noble part of their life and values.

A recent study examined the potential utility of an ACT acceptance intervention for enhancing exposure therapy among clients with panic disorder diagnoses. In this study, physiological arousal, self-reported anxiety, and willingness to participate in a second carbon dioxide inhalation challenge were assessed with participants diagnosed with panic disorder who were randomly assigned to a brief suppression, acceptance, or control condition before engaging in a CO_2 inhalation challenge (Levitt, Brown, Orsillo, & Barlow, 2004). The acceptance intervention was drawn directly from the ACT manual (Hayes, Strosahl, et al., 1999). The groups did not differ in their physiological responses to the challenge; however, clients in the acceptance group reported significantly less anxiety and greater willingness to participate in a second challenge than individuals in the other two groups. Similar results have been shown for pain tolerance (Hayes, Bissett, et al., 1999). Acceptance of private events has also been shown to mediate the impact of ACT in several studies and to differentiate it from other interventions (e.g., Bond & Bunce, 2000; Gifford et al., 2004).

Cognitive Defusion

According to RFT, the problem is not the content of thoughts themselves, but their function that regulates experiential avoidance. Cognitive defusion is the process of undermining the behavior regulatory functions and literal impacts (e.g., believability) of verbally entangled inner events. ACT aims to alter the functions of thoughts by manipulating the verbal context where they occur (Hayes, Strosahl, et al., 1999; Masuda, Hayes, Sackett, & Twohig, 2004). Defusion exercises are C_{func} interventions. Clinically, ACT encourages clients to change their relationship with thoughts and other private experiences and view them as mental events that come and go one after another. Clients learn to see thoughts as thoughts, feelings as feelings, memories as memories, and so on. This is useful because with individuals diagnosed with anxiety disorders there is often a very strong connection between thoughts and emotions and one's ability to interact with the world, as exemplified by the "thought action fusion" experienced with individuals with OCD (Shafran, Thordarson, & Rachman, 1996). Furthermore, from an RFT perspective, cognitive defusion process should increase the likelihood of acceptance behavior and vise versa. In contexts where experiential avoidance occurs, cognitive defusion and acceptance processes assist the person in breaking through the usual avoidance patterns and rules that regulate them.

Evidence for the effectiveness of cognitive defusion comes from several sources. Basic research in the form of a comparison of one ACT defusion exercise with traditional thought control techniques (Masuda et al., 2004) showed that repeating a distressing thought (e.g., "I am stupid") over and over until it lost its meaning immediately reduced the believability and distress of negative self-referential thoughts more so than thought control procedures. Similar results for defusion have been shown in pain tolerance (Gutiérrez, Luciano, Rodríguez, & Fink, 2004). It may also be noteworthy that improvements in cognitive therapy tend to occur most strongly after cognitive distancing occurs but before the disputative components of cognitive therapy begin (Ilardi & Craighead, 1994). Finally, ACT process research has consistently shown that ACT is uniquely effective in decreasing the believability of private events and that these changes help explain the impact of ACT (e.g., Bach & Hayes, 2002; Hayes, Bissett, et al., 2004; Zettle & Hayes, 1986).

Self as Context: A Transcendent Sense of Self

ACT aims to generate and foster a new perspective of self, a transcendent sense of self. A transcendent sense of self is argued in RFT to emerge from the acquisition relational fames involving a particular type of perspective taking, resulting in a sense of "here/now," as opposed to there/then. No matter where and when an individual is, this perspective of self as here-and-now is inherent and unchanged. The great advantage of this sense of self is that self is experienced as an arena in which the content of consciousness is not threatening. Thus, this sense of self is used in ACT to aid in both defusion and acceptance. It is predominantly helpful in undermining a particularly pernicious form of fusion: attachment to the self as verbally constructed, not the self that is experienced in the present moment. Individuals with anxiety problems often begin to talk about their anxiety not as something they experience, but as something that they *are*. This tendency can reduce psychological flexibility. For example, the thought "I am an agoraphobic, and it is because . . . " may box the person into acting in ways that confirm this sense of identity and this analysis. If the events pointed to as reasons do not or cannot change (e.g., if the agoraphobia for instance is thought to have developed as a result of specific childhood experiences) it would show that the analysis is "wrong" if one simply moved ahead. Nothing is actually stopping the person from moving ahead; moving ahead is stopped by the person's own verbal behavior. The person might be right—the traumatic event as a child contributed to his or her struggle with anxiety, but that does not mean that that event or memory must be corrected before one can change his or her behavior. ACT assumes that the person can move ahead just as he or she is, no change in "self" is needed.

Rather than confronting this in the form of challenging this belief's validity, the self as context model encourages individuals to experience themselves in different ways. Anxiety, panic, intrusive thoughts, or worry are things they sometimes have and sometimes do not. They are experiences that are felt, not identifying characteristics.

BEING PRESENT

ACT promotes observation and nonjudgmental description of experiences in the present moment, what has been termed "self as a process of knowing." This helps clients experience change in the world as it is experienced more directly, rather than the world as constructed by our linguistic practice. From the RFT perspective, observation and nonjudgmental description of one's own experience *as it is* requires cognitive defusion and psychological acceptance. Our linguistic practices and resistance to our present experience obscure our experience in the present moment by generating additional verbal behaviors (e.g., rumination). Being present is very similar and contains many of the same principals as several other meditation- and acceptance-based approaches, including mindfulness-based therapies. There is emerging support for the use of these approaches including a study that showed improvements in subjective and objective symptoms of anxiety and panic following an 8-week outpatient group stress reduction intervention based on mindfulness meditation (Miller, Fletcher, & Kabat-Zinn, 1995). These results were maintained at 3-year follow-up including a reduction in the number and severity of panic attacks.

Exposure methods, particularly those that include an interoceptive focus, ask clients to be present with their reactions in the moment without engaging in their typical approaches to avoidance. Data suggest that clients diagnosed with anxiety disorders who are less compliant with this component of traditional cognitive–behavioral therapy benefit less from treatment than do other clients (e.g., Franklin, Abramowitz, Kozak, Levitt, & Foa, 2000; Leung & Heimberg, 1996; Schmidt & Woolaway-Bickel, 2000). Training in staying in contact with the present moment in a broader, more open and more flexible way may establish general skills that are useful in such circumstances.

VALUES

Values are areas of one's life or things that one cares about. Values are different than goals; values can never be achieved, whereas goals can be. For example, a man can value being a great father, but it is something that can never be completely accomplished. Values serve as directions for one's behavior. From the RFT perspective, values may be conceptualized as verbal rules linked to verbally constructed consequences. They are verbal statements that make certain behaviors more appetitive and other behaviors more aversive. This in turn increases certain behaviors that compete with undesirable behaviors, such as avoidance (Hayes, Strosahl, et al., 1999). For example, a person diagnosed with OCD may value being the best parent possible, but spend more time dealing with her obsessions than with her daughter. Thus, for her, clarifying her values to be the best parent possible should make doing her compulsion more aversive and spending time with her daughter more appetitive. This is an example of a C_{rel} intervention. In ACT, clients are challenged to consider what they want their lives to stand for in different life domains such as career family, intimate relationships, friendships, personal growth, health, and spirituality.

Values work can enhance a client's motivation to engage in treatment and provide direction. Values are intimately related to several of the processes addressed thus far. For example, values are an important part of acceptance work as they provide the impetus for change and acceptance. Acceptance can be a difficult and sometimes painful experience, and values puts this suffering and hard work into contexts where it is worth experiencing. Therapists ask their clients to confront anxiety; this is not done just for the sake of it; it is done in the service of the client's values. This may be especially true for exposure work, which can be very difficult for individuals with anxiety.

No component analysis is yet available on this component of ACT, but some clinical trials have so emphasized it that it approaches a component analysis. For example, a small randomized controlled trial by Dahl, Wilson, and Nilsson (2004) showed that a 4-hr ACT intervention with chronic pain that was approximately half values work was notably effective.

COMMITTED ACTION

ACT encourages clients to commit to changes in their behavior. From the RFT perspective, committed action is a constructive behavior pattern that is regulated by values as a verbal antecedent and that is maintained by its consequences that are correspondent with that value. Simply put, commitments in ACT involve defining goals in specific areas along one's valued path, then acting on these goals while acknowledging and accepting psychological barriers. To enhance committed action, ACT intervention tactics vary greatly depending on the individual client and individual problem. One area of committed action that is common to most interventions for anxiety disorders is exposure to anxiety producing stimuli. However, the difference with ACT is that the commitment is tied once again to values and larger life goals and does not simply apply to the actual treatment time and to the reduction of anxiety.

As mentioned above, it is important to note that each of the six specific processes relates to and interacts with the other processes. The first four processes comprise an ACT approach to acceptance and mindfulness; the last four to behavior change and commitment. Some of these relations involve shared functional properties. For example, acceptance and defusion both undermine the literal impact of language processes; self as context and contact with the present moment both involve increasing the raw experience of "here-and-now"; values and committed action both involve building out the practical and effective aspects of language into patterns of behavior change. Therefore, ACT focuses on psychological flexibility by changing the function of ones cognition and language practices in general, in the service of both acceptance and change.

EVIDENCE FOR THE ACT MODEL OF ANXIETY DISORDERS

Outcome research in ACT, reviewed later, provides a crucial form of support for the ACT view of anxiety disorders but several other lines of research not yet mentioned are also supportive. For example, a large number of findings suggest that the ACT model of psychopathology fits with what we know about anxiety disorders. Measures of ACT processes tend to correlate with anxiety. The Acceptance and Action Questionnaire (AAQ; Bond & Bunce, 2003; Hayes, Strosahl, Wilson, et al., 2004), a key measure of experiential avoidance, cognitive fusion, and the resultant inability to take valued actions, is strongly associated with several well know fear and anxiety measures in the .4 to .6 range. These correlations are still significant even after controlling for related concepts such as thought suppression, or for response sets such as social desirability (Hayes, Strosahl, Wilson, et al., 2004). Among childhood sexual trauma survivors, experiential avoidance and emotional expressivity were significantly related to psychological distress. Yet, only experiential avoidance mediated the relationship between being a sexual assault survivor and distress (Marx & Sloan, 2002). High emotional avoiders show particularly strong physiological reactivity to unpleasant stimuli (Sloan, 2004). When presented with carbon dioxide enriched air, high emotional avoiders show more panic symptoms than low avoiders (Karekla, Forsyth, & Kelly, 2004). This same basic process has been shown in specific anxiety disorders. For example, adults suffering from trichotillomania who are high on the AAQ have more frequent and intense urges to pull, less ability to control urges, and more pulling-related distress than persons who are low on the processes thought to be important in an ACT model of psychopathology (Begotka, Woods, & Wetterneck, 2004).

ACT as a Treatment for Anxiety Disorders

As described in the previous sections, the focus of ACT as a treatment for anxiety disorders is not to decrease clients' anxiety, but to help clients live a valued life without regard for anxiety. This is accomplished in ACT through the six core processes: acceptance, defusion, self as context, contact with the present moment, values, and behavioral commitment exercises. The degree to which each core process is stressed varies between disorders and clients. ACT is a functional technology; therefore, these processes can be addressed in any manner that is effective for the client. The following is a general protocol that can be utilized with anxiety disorder clients. This protocol touches on all six of the core ACT processes and is based on Hayes, Strosahl, et al. (1999).

Challenging the Control Agenda

Clients with anxiety disorders almost always come into therapy looking for assistance controlling their anxiety. ACT works under the assumption that control of anxiety is often problematic. ACT uses the client's experiences to present this paradox. This is generally accomplished by discussing (1) what his or her goal has been with regard to anxiety, (2) what he or she has tried to reach these goals, (3) and what strategies have been successful. Clients have tried many things to get rid of anxiety. They will avoid situations that create anxiety such as public places; they will try and talk themselves out of the anxiety such as "I can handle it" or "this will not be so bad, calm down"; they will have tried self help books and other therapists; many will have tried prescription medications, and others will have tried illegal drugs and alcohol to calm themselves.

When asked how well these attempts have worked, there are a variety of answers, but it is quickly obvious that they do not work in the long run. If they did, the client would not need therapy because his or her goals would have been achieved. There are some control strategies that can be immediately successful, such as an individual diagnosed with social phobia leaving the social event, or engaging in the compulsion for the person with OCD. But these "solutions" are usually more of a problem than the anxiety. The pupose here is not to convince the client that anxiety cannot be controlled, but to open the client up to the possibility that what they have been trying to accomplish (i.e., get rid of anxiety) has not been working. Clients will often report feeling like the struggle with anxiety is hopeless and that they do not know what to do at this point. This is good from an ACT perspective because the goal is to help the client become more open to approaching the problem differently. If clients report that they feel as though there is something that they can do to decrease the anxiety, the ACT therapist asks clients to let their experience guide them. For example, a person diagnosed with social phobia might say "if I do it with a lot of confidence, I bet I can pull it off, I am a strong person, I just don't give myself enough credit." The ACT therapist might tell the client to "go home and give that a try and see how well it works."

As the client begins to open up to the possibility that trying to control anxiety has not been working, then the therapist usually introduces a key ACT metaphor that provides a working model for the current situation. An example is the *Man in the Hole* metaphor (Hayes, Strosahl, et al., 1999, p. 101):

> Suppose you are dropped off on a planet, blindfolded, and given nothing but a bag of tools. You do not know this, but the planet is filled with giant craters. Inevitably, as you walk about you fall into one of these holes. After you fall in, you feel around and find there is no way out. You reach into the bag and all you were given is a shovel. So you start digging but you find that no matter how you dig you are not getting out of the hole; it is actually getting larger. Isn't this like your experience? Look at everything you have tried to get rid of the anxiety. Is the hole getting larger? You have probably

secretly come to me with the thought that I have the magical shovel that can get rid of your anxiety. I don't! And even if I, did I wouldn't use it because digging is not a way out of the hole—digging is what makes holes. You can't dig your way out, that just digs you in. If that is the situation maybe we will have to put down the shovel.

The function of the metaphor is to illustrate the client's experience and to open up the possibility that the failure to get rid of the anxiety is a natural result—it is not the client's fault. Hopefully, at this point the client is less attached to the agenda that he or she needs to get rid of anxiety, and a little more open to trying something different.

Control as the Problem

In this phase of ACT as a treatment for anxiety disorders, the therapist continues to challenge the control agenda by illustrating the difficult and paradoxical effects of attempting to control anxiety. This phase usually begins by illustrating why one might be so attached to controlling anxiety:

> Control is a funny thing. It is very useful in some situations but not in all. Control has worked great to allow us to regulate the world around us. If the room is too cold, we can turn up the heat, if we do not look good in our clothes, we can purchase new ones. I would say we can control 95% of the world. But there is the other 5% that we seem to have much more difficulty controlling—the world inside our skin. Does your experience agree with me? The control rules that work in the outside world maybe cannot be applied to the inside world. But we still try.

The following exercises are an experiential way to allow the client to feel the paradoxical effects of control. The *Chocolate Cake Exercise* (Hayes, Strosahl, et al., 1999, p. 124) has to do with our ability to control our thoughts:

> OK. I am going to ask you not to think of something. The thing that I say next, do not think of it. OK, ready? Don't think of *chocolate cake*. Don't think of warm chocolate cake as it is coming out of the oven. There is stream coming off the cake. You put chocolate frosting on the cake; and as you are doing this, the frosting begins to melt. Did you think of it?

Most individuals will think of the chocolate cake. The *Polygraph Exercise* (Hayes, Strosahl, et al., 1999, p.123) illustrates the paradoxical effect of control of feelings. The therapist can say:

> Pretend I have the best polygraph machine that's ever been built. It is state of the art; it can detect even the smallest amount of anxiety. Pretend I hook you up to the machine, and I give you one simple task. *Don't get anxious!* If

you can stay calm for the next minute I will give you one million dollars, and to really motivate you, I put my .44 Magnum to your head. If you get stay calm, you don't get shot and win the money, but if I detect any anxiety on my machine -BAM! OK, ready? Begin! (Wait a couple seconds) What do you think will happen?

These two exercises illustrate the enormous difficulty one often experiences when controlling private events. To further illustrate the difference between what we can control and what we cannot, the therapist can ask the client to not do something in the other 95% (the part outside the skin), such as "don't touch that tissue box." Then say something like, "It is easy not to do that. I have no doubt you could win the million dollars if that was the game. The reason that was easy is because that is in the 95%, whereas not getting anxious with a gun to your head is in the 5%."

To allow the client to experience the problematic impact of attempts to control anxiety, the client can be asked to complete the *Clean vs. Dirty Discomfort Diary* (Hayes, Strosahl, et al., 1999, p. 147). This form, done as homework, has five columns and is completed after situations where the client struggles with anxiety. The first column asks about the experience, the second asks about immediate reactions to the experience, the third asks the client to rate the level of suffering at that point, the fourth asks about the client's reactions to the anxiety, and the fifth asks for the new level of suffering. Most of the time clients find that increases in struggling result in increases in suffering; whereas not struggling has the opposite effect.

Acceptance of Anxiety

After clients have experienced the paradoxical effects of attempts to control their anxiety, they are usually much more willing to try something radically different. Instead of helping the clients figure out a different way to control their anxiety, an ACT therapist proposes figuring out how to live a valued life while having the anxiety. The *Two Scales Metaphor* (Hayes, Strosahl, et al., 1999, p. 133) helps illustrate the issue:

> Pretend there is a scale coming off your right shoulder. It starts at zero and goes up to ten. Let's call this the anxiety scale. And this scale has an associated dial that you have been trying to turn to bring the anxiety down when it is high. But we have discovered that this dial only goes one way—up. What we have been working on, in the last couple sessions, is bringing this other scale, the one over your left shoulder, into focus. This scale is called willingness to have the anxiety. It is just like the anxiety one—it goes from zero to ten. But the difference is that this knob goes both ways. You get to decide how willing you are to feel the anxiety. When the willingness scale is at zero, you are doing whatever you can to get rid of the anxiety. When it is at ten, you

are open to feel the anxiety for what it is. We are going to shift our work from the anxiety scale to the willingness scale. We tried the anxiety one and it has not worked, and probably won't. Being willing is a choice that you can make under any circumstance. I am not going to guarantee that you will not feel anxious if you are willing. But I can guarantee that if you are unwilling, anxiety will usually be high. Willingness does not control anxiety. It allows it to do what it does. Meanwhile if you shift your focus from controlling it to living with it, then you get to decide what your life is about.

Clients will often want to know how to be willing. The therapist must be careful not to give clients rules that they might use to control their anxiety. A safe answer in this situation is to tell the client that willingness is a skill, much like playing a sport. For example, one cannot teach someone how to swim through verbal instruction. The person needs to get in the water and practice and let the natural contingencies shape his or her behavior. Prompts and suggestions can help, but they are not sufficient. Clients need to practice being willing by showing up in the present moment and letting go of control. They will get better at it through practice. Numerous exercises can be used in session to practice willingness. Exposure exercises are particularly helpful. The client can also practice at home, allowing functionality to be their guide.

Self as Context

Acceptance can be difficult when one's thoughts, feelings, and bodily sensations are taken literally. If a person really feels that anxiety will kill them, they are unlikely to be willing to accept its presence. Acceptance of anxiety can be fostered through breaking down the literality of language and uncovering the difference between oneself and ones anxiety. This difference can be described through the *Chessboard* (Hayes, Strosahl, et al., 1999, p. 190) metaphor.

> Pretend we have a chessboard that goes out infinitely in all directions. The board has lots of back and white pieces. It is like normal game of chess where the white ones fight against the black ones. Pretend your thoughts and feelings were these pieces. The anxious thoughts hang out with other anxious thoughts, whereas the comfortable thoughts hang out with other comfortable thoughts. I get the sense that you have been helping the comfortable ones out, trying to get them to beat the anxious ones. There are times when you are riding on the white queen into battle to beat the bad anxiety. But there is a logical problem here. From this posture, huge portions of yourself are your own enemy. From here there are large parts of you that are bad or wrong. And these parts, because this is a level playing field, they can be just as big as you. How can you beat them? Doesn't it seem that the more you fight, the

larger they seem. It is almost like *if you are not willing to have the anxiety then you've got it*. You have been fighting a battle that cannot be won; and this is no way to live.

At this point the therapist should ask the client, "let's say you are not the pieces, then who are you?" The client might think of a variety of answers, but the therapist should lead the client to seeing that he or she could be the board. The advantage of looking at oneself as the board is that the board gives the pieces a place to exist, but the board is not made up of the pieces. The board's existence is not threatened by what happens to the pieces. The board itself is not threatened by the pieces. Experiential and mindfulness exercises are then used to contact this "board level" directly.

DEFUSION

The concept of defusion is core to ACT. Defusion exercises attack the literality of language and support looking at the function of one's thoughts rather than their content. For example, a person diagnosed with social phobia might have the thought "I wanted to go to the party but I was too anxious." An ACT therapist would not discuss whether this thought is "true" or logical, but discuss whether listening to this thought has helped the client live a more vital life. There are many ways by which ACT therapists attack the literality of language. One example is by attacking basic language practices that are supported in our culture. An ACT therapist might respond to the earlier statement by saying,

> Notice that you said, I wanted to go to the party *but* I was too anxious, people often speak that way. Such as if you were driving and came across a large tree that was lying across the road, you might say I would continue down this road *but* there is a tree in my way. You cannot drive down that road with that tree there. I wonder if the same is true with anxiety. Does the anxiety need to be gone before you can go to the party? Can one go to a party while anxious? There are some instances where it might be more accurate and useful to say *and* instead of *but*. Such as, I would like to go to the party *and* I feel anxious. That way you can have the anxiety and go to the party at the same time.

In addition to basic linguistic practices getting in the way of one living a vital life, our linguistic practices often give private events such as anxiety more power than they really deserve. For example, the feeling of being anxious while walking down a dark, dangerous alley is similar to riding on a roller coaster. The main difference is the way we evaluate the two feelings. We will seek out roller coasters, but we will avoid dark alleys. This part of our minds is useful. When one feels anxious in a dark alley, it is likely adaptive to get out of the alley. But there are times when it is not adaptive to respond to that feeling of anxiety, such as the feeling of anxiety a person diagnosed with social phobia feels before going to a party. The *Passengers on the Bus Metaphor* (Hayes, Strosahl, et al., 1999, p. 157) objectifies this process and offers suggestions of how one can respond to anxiety.

> Tell me if your relationship with your anxiety isn't like this. Say you are the driver of this bus, and on this bus are a bunch of passengers. These passengers are your thoughts, feelings, and bodily sensations related to your anxiety. Some of them are mean looking, they are wearing black leather, and they carry knifes and other weapons. When you get to an intersection where they want you to turn, they stand up and yell and threaten you. When they do this, you get anxious and uncomfortable, and you listen. And after a while you build an agreement with them. If you do not scare me and stay hidden I will do pretty much whatever you say. Then one day, you decide that you are not going to listen to them anymore. So, you stop the bus and tell them to get off or you will throw them off. But you notice how scary they are and that you have stopped driving the bus and are dealing with the passengers. They are not willing to leave so you go back to your original plan—they stay quiet and you do what they want. The problem here is that in exchange for the quiet you have given up control of the bus. Now they have 100% control over you. Notice that even thought they say they can destroy you, it has never happened. Thus far, it has all been threats nothing has ever happened. Their threats were enough to control your life.

Another exercise that can help the clients to see their troublesome thoughts in a different context, one where they are less threatening, involves repeating a word over and over (Hayes, Strosahl, et al., 1999; Masuada et al., 2004). This begins with the clients selecting a word or phrase that is very troublesome and gets in the way of them living a valued life. An example would be "my anxiety is too high." The exercise is introduced by saying,

> As a species, language, including thoughts and words, offers us the blessings and the curse of knowledge. The power of language has pros and cons: there is a "light side" and a "dark side." On the positive side, we can influence the environment, and create a comfortable life. On the dark side, we are the only species who worry. The dark side is dominant when we buy into these thoughts and let them guide our lives, especially thoughts about the power of anxiety. We take our thoughts for what they say they are, as representations of reality. You are what they say you are, who you are, and what you can do with your life. However, are you really what they say you are? What if I say that thoughts are simply what they are (thoughts are just thoughts), rather than what they say they are, or you are not what they say you are. It might be difficult for you to understand what I say, so let's do a little exercise.

Next, take the word or phrase that the client stated and ask the client what comes to the clients mind what you say it. For example, say "anxiety" and ask the client what he or she thinks of. The client will think of many things such as "bad or uncomfortable," the client might feel anxious or nervous. This should continue until the client experiences the huge effects the word has. The therapist can then say:

> Now, here is the little exercise. The exercise is a little silly, and you might feel embarrassed doing it, and I am going to do the exercise with you so we can all be silly together. What I am going to ask you to do is to say the word, "anxiety," out loud, over-and-over again and then notice what happens. Are you ready?

This is done for approximately 30 s. Hopefully, during the exercise the client hears the word as a sound and not the word with meaning as in the beginning of the exercise. The therapist can say:

> Did you feel the anxiety during that exercise, or did you just hear a funny sound? If you heard the sound without the anxious feelings and thoughts, note that some of our thoughts that are so troubling are only sounds with meaning attached to them. They are not real, although they act like they are real, and we treat them as though they are real.

These exercises are not the ACT equivalent of cognitive restructuring in traditional cognitive therapy; the function of defusion is to assist the client in seeing that these language practices that make the anxiety feel so daunting are not real. When the client really experiences this, the same verbal statements regarding anxiety that used to guide the clients behavior are not experienced the same, they are more easily accepted for what they are. There are scores of ACT defusion exercises and it is easy to create more spontaneously in session once their nature is well understood.

VALUES

There are multiple functions of the values component of ACT as a treatment for anxiety disorders. Once clients are not behaving with regard to their anxiety, they may be in unfamiliar territory. Values work gives clients direction. One can think of values as a lighthouse on a stormy night. It tells one where to go when one is unsure. Often clients have never thought of just doing the things they value. They have been working on getting rid of the anxiety first. To help point clients in the direction of their values, they can complete the *Values Assessment Form* (Hayes, Strosahl, et al., 1999, p. 224). The form directs the client to write down what they would want in each of the following areas, as if anything is possible: marriage/couples/intimate relations, family relations, friendships/social relations, career/employment, education/personal growth & development, recreation/leisure, spirituality, citizenship, health/physical well-being. After clients have clarified the things that are important to them, they are asked to indicate how important each of these areas are to them and how well they are working toward these values. A short way of getting at one's values is to ask clients what they would like written on their tombstone, and how hard have they been working on that.

A second function of values work in ACT is that it can verbally turn an aversive into appetitive. For example, going to a party may have traditionally been felt as uncomfortable to someone who diagnosed with social phobia, but going to the party to spend time with one's spouse can feel meaningful. It is the same feeling of anxiety, but this verbal change can allow the person to experience the same feeling as something different.

Behavioral Commitment

The final phase of ACT as a treatment for anxiety disorders can look a lot like traditional behavior therapy. Anything can be done in these sessions, although it should be done in an ACT consistent manner. The most common initial commitment component for anxiety disorders is systematic exposure. In ACT, the goal of exposure is response flexibility, not reduction in anxiety. Willingness exercises are structured that involve approaching feared objects, situations, emotions, or sensations while noticing one's thoughts in a defused way. If possible this is done in vivo. Because response flexibility is the goal, often other activities are added during overt exposure, such as telling a joke, deliberately creating anxiety, mindfully noticing bodily sensations, or noticing who in the immediate environment has the worst hairdo (etc.). Topographically, this may look similar to work done in exposure, but the focus of exposure in ACT is different than traditional exposure. The goal in ACT is not to reduce the anxiety or any other private events, but to learn how to live effectively with whatever private events occur.

All behavioral commitment exercises should be based on clients' values. The particular exercises depend on the clients' struggles. If the clients are diagnosed with OCD, the exercises might involve going to areas that occasion their obsessions; if the clients have been diagnosed with panic disorder, it might involve doing exercises that create feeling of a panic attack; an individual diagnosed with social phobia might go to a social event. As therapy progresses, often these begin to include domains that were the more remote goals of therapy (e.g., those that the patient believed would happen naturally after anxiety disappeared). For example, a person diagnosed with agoraphobia might take her daughter on a trip—with anxiety if it showed up.

These exercises are not done to help the client habituate to the anxiety as they are in other treatments. In ACT they are done to help clients change their relationships with their anxiety. Commitment exercises gives clients a chance to see the anxiety for what it is rather than what it says it is, and to move ahead in life now rather than later. ACT clients are often very willing to engage in these types of exercises after going through the earlier components of ACT. Clients will regularly suggest doing increasingly difficult exercises.

OUTCOME DATA ON ACT FOR ANXIETY AND STRESS

ACT has been evaluated as a treatment for a variety of psychological disorders, including psychosis, substance abuse, depression, and social stigmatization (see Hayes, Masuda, Bissett, Luoma, & Guerrero, 2004, for a recent review). The research based on ACT as a treatment for anxiety and stress disorders is small but growing rapidly.

Numerous case studies of ACT as a treatment for anxiety disorders have been published. In one of the first studies on the impact of ACT, Hayes (1987) used ACT as a treatment with 12 individuals with a variety of anxiety disorders, including OCD, agoraphobia with panic attacks, social phobia, and panic disorder. Clinically significant decreases in anxiety were found for all 12 participants. Published case studies have since provided some support for the effectiveness of ACT with a variety of anxiety disorders including posttraumatic stress disorder (Batten & Hayes, 2005; Orsillo & Batten, 2005), panic disorder (Carrascoso, 2000), generalized anxiety disorder (Huerta, Gomez, Molina, & Luciano, 1998), and agoraphobia (Zaldívar & Hernández, 2001).

The impact of specific ACT components have also been evaluated. Perhaps most importantly is the finding with panic disorder, reviewed earlier, that an ACT acceptance intervention significantly increased patient willingness to undergo exposure following an initial exposure session (using CO_2 inhalation), and reduced the amount of anxiety produced by such exposure (Levitt et al., 2004). Eifert and Heffner (2003) showed that an ACT acceptance intervention (including such ACT metaphors as the finger trap metaphor) had a greater impact on the avoidance, anxiety symptoms, and anxious cognitions of anxious subjects exposed to CO_2 than did a distraction and control comparison condition.

Controlled single case research has demonstrated the effectiveness of ACT with OCD, and two obsessive compulsive spectrum disorders:

Trichotillomania and skin picking (Twohig & Woods, 2004; Twohig, Hayes, & Masuda, in press, 2004). The effectiveness of an eight-session ACT protocol was evaluated as a treatment for OCD in a multiple baseline across participants design (Twohig et al., in press). The intervention decreased compulsions to near zero levels for all participants in the OCD condition, with maintenance of gains at 3-month follow-up. The same protocol decreased four of five adults who skin picked to near zero levels, with moderate maintenance of gains at follow-up, in a pair of multiple baseline designs (Twohig et al., 2004). Finally, ACT plus habit reversal was shown to be effective in decreasing hair pulling to near zero levels for 4 of 6 participants in a pair of multiple baseline designs (Twohig & Woods, 2004). Results were maintained for 3 of the 4 participants at 3-month follow-up.

To date there are two randomized controlled trials of ACT as a treatment for anxiety disorders (Block, 2002; Zettle, 2003). Zettle (2003) compared ACT to systematic desensitization as a treatment for math anxiety. Both treatments were delivered in six, weekly 1-hr sessions. Participants included 37 college students (30 women and 7 men, mean age 31) with math anxiety. Results showed that both groups decreased significantly and equally on math anxiety. Results were maintained at 2-month follow-up for both groups. Experiential avoiders showed a larger change in math anxiety at follow-up within the ACT condition, but not the systematic desensitization condition, suggesting that the two interventions may work through different processes.

Block (2002) compared the effects of ACT to cognitive behavioral group therapy (CBGT), which is an empirically supported treatment for social phobia, and a no-treatment control group in the treatment of social phobia. Participants included 39 college students (13 men, 26 women) who were divided into three groups of 13. All participants reported experiencing at least a moderate degree of social phobia. Treatment consisted of a three-session ACT workshop, a CBGT-based workshop of the same duration, or a no-treatment control group. Results showed that the participants in the ACT group demonstrated an increase in willingness to experience anxiety, a significant decrease in behavioral avoidance during public speaking, and a marginal decrease in anxiety during the exposure exercises as compared with the control group. Participants in the CBGT condition showed a marginal significant increase in willingness, a significant decrease in self-reported avoidance, and a marginal decrease in reported anxiety, relative to the no-treatment control group. There were no significant differences between the two active treatments except on the behavioral measure. ACT participants remained longer in the posttreatment behavioral exposure task than participants in the CBGT group after controlling for pretreatment scores.

There are also several controlled trials that have examined stress or anxiety in populations other than those specifically with anxiety disorders. For example, it has been shown that ACT reduces worksite stress (Bond & Bunce, 2000; Hayes, Bissett, et al., 2004), and anxiety and stress experienced by parents of disabled children (Blackledge, 2004). Thus, although the literature is still very young, the evidence so far is encouraging.

CONCLUSION

ACT began out of work with anxiety disorders, and the underlying model was developed with problems of this kind in mind. Although the data coming in are still preliminary, there are now supportive data both for the ACT model of anxiety and for ACT as a treatment for it. Future research will show how far this model can be pushed as a method of alleviating anxiety disorders.

REFERENCES

Abramowitz, J. S., Tolin, D. F., & Street, G. P. (2001). Paradoxical effects of thought suppression: A meta-analysis of controlled studies. *Clinical Psychology Review, 21*, 683–703.

American Psychiatric Association. (2000). *Diagnostic and statistical manual of mental disorders* (4th ed., Text Revision). Washington, DC: Author.

Bach, P., & Hayes, S. C. (2002). The use of acceptance and commitment therapy to prevent rehospitalization of psychotic patients: A randomized controlled trial. *Journal of Consulting and Clinical Psychology, 70*, 1129–1139.

Batten, S. V., & Hayes, S. C. (2005). Acceptance and commitment therapy in the treatment of co-morbid substance abuse and posttraumatic stress disorder: A case study. *Clinical Case Studies, 4*, 246–262.

Begotka, A. M., Woods, D. W., & Wetterneck, C. T. (2004). The relationship between experiential avoidance and the severity of trichotillomania in a nonreferred sample. *Journal of Behavior Therapy and Experimental Psychiatry, 35*, 17–24.

Blackledge, J. T. (2004). *Using Acceptance and Commitment Therapy in the treatment of parents of autistic children.* Doctoral dissertation, University of Nevada, Reno.

Block, J. A. (2002). Acceptance or change of private experiences: A comparative analysis in college students with public speaking anxiety. *Dissertation Abstracts International: Section B: The Sciences & Engineering, 63*(9-B), 4361.

Bond, F. W., & Bunce, D. (2000). Mediators of change in emotion-focused and problem-focused worksite stress management interventions. *Journal of Occupational Health Psychology, 5*, 156–163.

Bond, F. W., & Bunce, D. (2003). The role of acceptance and job control in mental health, job satisfaction, and work performance. *Journal of Applied Psychology, 88*, 1057–1067.

Carrascoso, L. F. J. (2000). Acceptance and commitment therapy (ACT) in panic disorder with agoraphobia: A case study. *Psychology in Spain, 4*, 120–128.

Dahl, J., Wilson, K. G., & Nilsson, A. (2004). Acceptance and commitment therapy and the treatment of persons at risk for long-term disability resulting from stress and pain symptoms: A preliminary randomized trial. *Behavior Therapy, 35*, 785–802.

Eifert, G. H., & Heffner, M. (2003). The effects of acceptance versus control contexts on avoidance of panic-related symptoms. *Journal of Behavior Therapy and Experimental Psychiatry, 34*, 293–312.

Franklin, M. E., Abramowitz, J. S., Kozak, M. J., Levitt, J. T., & Foa, E. B. (2000). Effectiveness of exposure and ritual prevention for obsessive–compulsive disorder: Randomized compared with nonrandomized samples. *Journal of Consulting and Clinical Psychology, 68*, 594–602.

Gifford, E. V., Kohlenberg, B. S., Hayes, S. C., Antonuccio, D. O., Piasecki, M. M., Rasmussen-Hall, M. L., et al. (2004). Acceptance theory-based treatment for smoking cessation: An initial trial of acceptance and commitment therapy. *Behavior Therapy, 35*, 689–706.

Gutiérrez, O., Luciano, C., Rodríguez, M., & Fink, B. C. (2004). Comparison between an acceptance-based and a cognitive-control-based protocol for coping with pain. *Behavior Therapy, 35*, 767–784.

Hayes, S. C. (1987). A contextual approach to therapeutic change. In N. Jacobson (Ed.), *Psychotherapists in clinical practice: Cognitive and behavioral perspectives* (pp. 327–387). New York: Guilford.

Hayes, S. C. (Ed.). (1989). *Rulegoverned behavior: Cognition, contingencies, and instructional control.* New York: Plenum.

Hayes, S. C. (2004). Acceptance and commitment therapy, relational frame theory, and the third wave of behavioral and cognitive therapies. *Behavior Therapy, 35*, 639–666.

Hayes, S. C., Barnes-Holmes, D., & Roche, B. (Eds.). (2001). *Relational frame theory: A post-Skinnerian account of human language and cognition.* New York: Plenum.

Hayes, S. C., Bissett, R., Korn, Z., Zettle, R. D., Rosenfarb, I., Cooper, L., et al. (1999). The impact of acceptance versus control rationales on pain tolerance. *The Psychological Record, 49*, 33–47.

Hayes, S. C., Bissett, R., Roget, N., Padilla, M., Kohlenberg, B. S., Fisher, et al. (2004). The impact of acceptance and commitment training and multicultural training on the stigmatizing attitudes and professional burnout of substance abuse counselors. *Behavior Therapy, 35*, 821–836.

Hayes, S. C., Hayes, L. J., & Reese, H. W. (1988). Finding the philosophical core: A review of Stephen C. Popper's World Hypotheses. *Journal of Experimental Analysis of Behavior, 50*, 97–111.

Hayes, S. C., Hayes, L. J., Reese, H. W., & Sarbin, T. R. (Eds.). (1993). *Varieties of Scientific Contextualism.* Reno, NV: Context Press.

Hayes, S. C., Masuda, A., Bissett, R., Luoma, J., & Guerrero, L. F. (2004). DBT, FAP, and ACT: How empirically oriented are the new behavior therapy technologies? *Behavior Therapy, 35*, 35–54.

Hayes, S. C., Strosahl, K. D., Bunting, K., Twohig, M. P., & Wilson, K. G. (2004). What is acceptance and commitment therapy? In S. C. Hayes & K. D. Strosahl (Eds.), *A practical guide to acceptance and commitment therapy.* New York: Plenum/Kluwer.

Hayes, S. C. Strosahl, K. D., & Wilson, K. G. (1999). *Acceptance and commitment therapy: An experiential approach to behavior change.* New York: Guilford.

Hayes, S. C., Strosahl, K. D., Wilson, K. G., Bissett, R. T., Pistorello, J., Toarmino, et al. (2004). Measuring experiential avoidance: A preliminary test of a working model. *The Psychological Record, 54,* 553–578.

Hayes, S. C., Wilson, K. G., Gifford, E. V., Follette, V. M., & Strosahl, K. (1996). Emotional avoidance and behavioral disorders: A functional dimensional approach to diagnosis and treatment. *Journal of Consulting and Clinical Psychology, 64,* 1152–1168.

Huerta, F. R., Gomez, S. M., Molina, M. A. M., & Luciano, C. M. (1998). Generalized anxiety disorder: A case study. *Analisis y Modificacion de Conducta, 24,* 751–766.

Ilardi, S. S., & Craighead, W. E. (1994). The role of non-specific factors in cognitive-behavior therapy for depression. *Clinical Psychology: Science and Practice, 1,* 138–156.

Karekla, M., Forsyth, J. P., & Kelly, M. M. (2004). Emotional avoidance and panicogenic responding to a biological challenge procedure. *Behavior Therapy, 35,* 725–746.

Leung, A., & Heimberg, R. (1996). Homework compliance, perceptions of control, and outcome of cognitive–behavioral treatment of social phobia. *Behaviour Research and Therapy, 34,* 423–432.

Levitt, J. T., Brown, T. A., Orsillo, S. M., & Barlow, D. H. (2004). The effects of acceptance versus suppression of emotion on subjective and psychophysiological response to carbon dioxide challenge in patients with panic disorder. *Behavior Therapy, 35,* 747–766.

Marx, B. P., & Sloan, D. M. (2002) The role of emotion in the psychological functioning of adult survivors of childhood sexual abuse. *Behavior Therapy, 33,* 563–577.

Masuda, A., Hayes, S. C., Sackett, C., & Twohig, M. P. (2004). Cognitive defusion and self- relevant negative thoughts: Examining the impact of a ninety year old technique. *Behaviour Research and Therapy, 42,* 477–485.

Miller, J. J., Fletcher, K., Kabat-Zinn, J. (1995). Three-year follow-up and clinical implications of a mindfulness meditation-based stress reduction intervention in the treatment of anxiety disorders. *General Hospital Psychiatry, 17,* 192–200.

Orsillo, S. M., & Batten, S. V. (2005). Acceptance and Commitment Therapy for PTSD. *Behavior Modification, 25,* 95–129.

Purdon, C. (1999). Thought suppression and psychopathology. *Behaviour Research and Therapy, 37,* 1029–1054.

Schmidt, N., & Woolaway-Bickel, K. (2000). The effects of treatment compliance on outcome in cognitive–behavioral therapy for panic disorder: Quality versus quantity. *Journal of Consulting and Clinical Psychology, 68,* 13–18.

Shafran, R. Thordarson, D., & Rachman, S. (1996). Thought action fusion in obses-
    sive compulsive disorder. *Journal of Anxiety Disorders, 5*, 379–391.
Sloan, D. M. (2004) Emotion regulation in action: Emotional reactivity in experien-
    tial avoidance. *Behaviour Research and Therapy, 42*, 1257–1270.
Twohig, M. P., Hayes, S. C., & Masuda, A. (in press). Increasing willingness to
    experience obsessions: Acceptance and commitment therapy as a treatment
    for obsessive compulsive disorder. *Behavior Therapy.*
Twohig, M. P., Hayes, S. C., & Masuda, A. (April, 2004). Acceptance and com-
    mitment therapy as a treatment for OCD and OCD spectrum disorders. In
    M. P. Twohig (Chair), *Acceptance and commitment therapy as a treatment for anxi-
    ety disorders: Recent findings.* Symposium conducted at the Annual Meeting of
    the Association Behavior Analysis, Boston, MA.
Twohig, M. P., & Woods, D. W. (2004). A preliminary investigation of Acceptance
    and Commitment Therapy and habit reversal as a treatment for trichotilloma-
    nia. *Behavior Therapy, 35*, 803–820.
Wilson, K. G., & Hayes, S. C. (1996). Resurgence of derived stimulus relations.
    Journal of the Experimental Analysis of Behavior, 66, 267–281.
Zaldívar, F., & Hernández, M. (2001). Acceptance and commitment therapy (ACT):
    Application to an experiential avoidance with agoraphobic form. *Análisis y
    Modificación de Conducta, 27*(113), 425–454.
Zettle, R. D. (2003). Acceptance and commitment therapy (ACT) vs. systematic
    desensitization in treatment of mathematics anxiety. *Psychological Record, 53*,
    197–215.
Zettle, R. D., & Hayes, S. C. (1986). Dysfunctional control by client verbal behavior:
    The context of reason giving. *The Analysis of Verbal Behavior, 4*, 30–38.

Chapter 5

MINDFULNESS-BASED STRESS REDUCTION

Jeffrey Brantley

INTRODUCTION

Is there a connection between being healthy and being more consciously present? Do meditation practices that emphasize nonjudging awareness promote movement toward greater levels of health, including improvements in anxiety and related disorders? Can one successfully assume a larger degree of responsibility for one's own health by adopting a personal meditation practice? Is it possible to establish an effective and broadly replicable training program in mindfulness meditation that appeals to individuals of diverse social, medical, and spiritual backgrounds who share a common motivation to improve their personal health outcomes? Mindfulness-based stress reduction (MBSR) was born of such questions.

Indeed, MBSR was established in 1979 at the University of Massachusetts Medical Center in Worcester, MA, with two basic intentions (Kabat-Zinn, 2003). First, the program intended to become an effective vehicle for training individuals to practice mindfulness meditation and mindful yoga for reasons of health enhancement and stress reduction. Second, MBSR was developed as a model approach that could be adapted in a variety of health care contexts where stress, pain, illness, and disease were the primary concerns. Since its inception, MBSR programs have had an impact on an enormous number of participants and health care professionals, have generated a growing body of medical research, and have

131

sparked fascinating discussions among researchers and meditators about the nature of the mind–body connection in health and illness.

MINDFULNESS: DEFINITION AND ROOTS

There are a number of definitions of mindfulness that have been discussed in the literature. Here, mindfulness is seen as an awareness that is nonjudging, friendly, and does not seek to add or subtract anything from the experience before it. Mindfulness arises as one pays attention—on purpose—in an allowing, accepting way to inner and outer experience unfolding in the present moment. Mindfulness is not limited to rigid or formulaic methods of meditation, but is available to be experienced in each moment and with every breath. Further, the capacity to be mindful lies in all human beings. Most important to practicing mindfulness, to being "mindful," is "commitment to reside as best one can from moment to moment in awareness with an open heart, a spacious, non-judging, non-reactive mind, and without trying to get anywhere" (Kabat-Zinn, 1994, 2003).

Teachers from diverse faith traditions have pointed to the importance of present moment awareness (Krishnamurti, 1969; Laozi & Mitchell, 1988; Ramana & Venkataramiah, 2000; Tolle, 1999). And, for over 2,500 years, Buddhists have systematically developed meditation methods emphasizing mindfulness. Because of the extensive body of Buddhist meditation experience, familiarity with Buddhist meditation practices by the original developers of MBSR, and because of the simplicity of the meditation instructions, the mindfulness practices taught in MBSR contexts have their origins in traditional Buddhist meditation. Although MBSR borrows from the Buddhist tradition instructions and understanding for teaching and practicing mindfulness, it does not seek to be "Buddhist" or to convert anyone to that tradition. MBSR is firmly rooted in principles of mind–body medicine, and offers itself to anyone who wishes to learn to enhance his or her own health (Kabat-Zinn, 1990).

Historically, the Buddha taught mindfulness to his followers. Among his earliest teachings, he detailed the meditation instructions for mindfulness practice: the Anapanasati Sutra (Rosenberg, 1998) and the Satipatthana Sutra (Smith, 1999). The Anapanasati Sutra details the meditation practice known as *awareness of breathing*, whereas the Satipatthana Sutra describes the *four foundations of mindfulness*, including mindfulness of body, feelings, mind, and dharma.

If mindfulness means bringing an accepting attention to present moment experience, then commentary from several well-known Buddhist teachers may provide further understanding of this process. Rosenberg

(1998) likens mindfulness to a mirror that reflects accurately whatever appears before it. From his perspective, mindfulness is "preconceptual, before thought" (p. 15). The popular meditation teacher, Nhat Hanh (1987), emphasizes the importance of connecting with the present moment, and attitudes of welcome and friendliness in the practice of mindfulness. He says, "... this is the only moment that is real. To be here now, and enjoy the present moment is our most important task" (p. 4). Mindfulness is not about having more thoughts, but includes awareness of thinking as just another aspect of experience. As cited in Smith (1999), the 13th century Zen teacher, Dogen, puts it as follows: "You should therefore cease from practice based on intellectual understanding, pursuing words and following after speech, and learn the backward step that turns your light inwardly to illuminate your self." Feldman (1998), a popular contemporary Buddhist meditation teacher, offers a further perspective on meditation, including mindfulness practices: "There are several core principles which run through all meditative disciplines. Attention, awareness, understanding, and compassion form the basic skeleton of all systems of meditation" (p. 2).

Mindfulness as taught in the MBSR format is especially informed by these elements of accurate reflection, being centered in the present moment, nonconceptual and direct experience, and attitudes of friendliness and compassion toward all experience.

THE MEDICALIZATION OF MINDFULNESS

Drawing from ancient traditions of mindfulness meditation as a vehicle for change and healing in human life, Jon Kabat-Zinn and his colleagues developed the health-focused, stress reduction approach known as mindfulness-based stress reduction (MBSR), and offered the first classes at the University of Massachusetts Medical Center in Worcester, MA, in 1979.

The MBSR approach has always been intended as a complement, not an alternative to therapy. In 1979, the concept of teaching meditation for health was novel, yet in alignment with the emerging field of mind–body medicine. In its early years, the MBSR program required a referral from a physician before accepting a participant. This was a means of firmly establishing the program as a medically appropriate activity. This requirement has changed over the years as the medical use of meditation has become more accepted and widespread.

Over the past 25–30 years there have been four forms of meditation that have received attention from Western medical researchers (Freeman, 2001). As described by Freeman (2001), these forms are transcendental meditation (TM), respiratory one method (ROM), created by Herbert Benson,

M.D.; clinically standardized meditation (CSM), developed by Carrington and others; and mindfulness meditation. Mindfulness meditation differs from the other three forms of meditation significantly in that it emphasizes a "nonconcentrative method" (expanded attention and nonjudgmental observation; Freeman, 2001). Whereas TM, ROM, and CSM approaches to meditation underscore the concentration of attention as a key component of meditation, mindfulness approaches emphasize nonjudging awareness. With their emphasis on nonjudging awareness, mindfulness meditation practices also offer an importantly different meditative approach to health and illness in that they allow the meditator to make changing physical and psychological experience itself the object of attention in meditation (Kabat-Zinn, 1990).

Since the establishment of the MBSR program in 1979, Kabat-Zinn and his colleagues have taught over 15,000 participants to practice mindfulness meditation, not including those trained in over 250 similar programs around the world (Wylie & Simon, 2004). The program has been the subject of a best-selling book, and has been featured in a Bill Moyers television special, "Healing and the Mind." In addition, Kabat-Zinn and his colleagues have developed and delivered a variety of professional training programs in MBSR. About 5,000 medical professionals have now been trained in these programs, about 30–40% being physicians (Wylie & Simon, 2004).

Western psychology and psychotherapists have long been drawn to meditative practices, particularly Buddhist ones. This reference to "Eastern philosophy" includes Freud, and interests in Buddhist practices can be found in the work of Franz Alexander, Carl Jung, Erich Fromm, and Karen Horney, to name a few (Germer, Siegel, & Fulton, 2005). More recently, Linehan (1993) developed an approach to treating borderline personality disorder inspired by the Zen Buddhist tradition and its emphasis on mindfulness. Her program, dialectical behavioral therapy (DBT), integrates Zen principles and practices with cognitive-behavioral therapy.

The interest in applying mindfulness in clinical settings has grown tremendously over the past 25–30 years, with many professionals finding a vehicle in the pioneering work of Kabat-Zinn's MBSR program. A more recent trend is the development of mindfulness-based interventions that are empirically validated and more clinically specific. An example of this is the work of Segal, Williams, and Teasdale (2002) in researching and developing an intervention they call mindfulness-based cognitive therapy for depression.

The MBSR model, with its focus on physical as well as psychological conditions, offers an expanded dimension to the role of meditation practices in clinical settings. Because the MBSR approach explicitly emphasizes "stress" and "stress reduction," it opens the door to meditation practice for individuals interested not only in psychological conditions but also in physical ones, including illness. By openly inviting a heterogeneous population with a diverse set of medical conditions, MBSR has built a foundation for applying mindfulness in a wide variety of physical and psychiatric conditions.

THE MBSR APPROACH: A DESCRIPTION

Stress is the response to the demands placed on the body and mind. The MBSR approach is essentially NOT about developing any particular or special state of mind or body, but IS about being awake and aware of what is happening, of what is present—as fully as possible, in each moment. By paying attention wholeheartedly, attending directly to experience no matter how unpleasant it is, one learns that it is possible to relate differently to stress or pain, or, indeed, any situation (Moyers, Flowers, & Grubin, 1993).

How might individuals be trained to pay attention mindfully to stress and illness in their lives? What follows is a summary of the MBSR model as described by Kabat-Zinn (1990) and Santorelli (1999).

What Is MBSR?

MBSR is not a medical or psychiatric treatment, nor is it intended to be. It is a psychoeducational approach that teaches participants to practice mindfulness meditation in the context of mind–body medicine for the purposes of stress reduction and improved health. Practicing mindfulness, one joins with one's health care provider, and becomes a potent ally in any treatment process he or she is receiving.

One does not have to be a Buddhist (nor even identify as "spiritual") in order to practice mindfulness in this model. The approach emphasizes the universality of mindfulness as a basic human capacity available to anyone who is willing to make the commitment to practice the meditation methods taught in the program.

The Attitudinal Foundation of Mindfulness Practice

A first core principle of MBSR is the belief that "no matter what your condition, here in the MBSR program, we believe that there is more right with you than is wrong with you." This statement summarizes the belief that each person has within him or her an enormous capacity for compassionate and accepting awareness, and that application of this awareness can lead to profound learning, healing, and transformation. It speaks to a paradigm for healing that acknowledges the sacred quality of the healing relationship, and respects each participant as a full human being, rather than as a patient with a problem. A second core principle is one of "being, not doing." Participants learn to recognize and to stop identifying with the habits of busyness and striving that drive so much of experience, and, instead, learn to "be." This means they stop, and simply pay attention without trying to change anything as experience unfolds in each moment—inside and outside the skin. A third core principle offered upon entering an MBSR class is to adopt the "way of not knowing." This simply means to drop all the ideas, judgments, and thoughts about experience, and to be willing to direct attention and to open awareness to direct phenomenal experience as it occurs in the present moment.

In addition to these core principles, there are seven key attitudes that form a foundation for mindfulness practice as taught in the MBSR approach: *nonjudging; patience; beginner's mind; trust; nonstriving; acceptance; and, letting go.* Nonjudging involves learning to recognize the mindstream of labeling and judging experience, and to let it go, as much as possible. When judging does happen, one learns simply to label it as it happens. "Judging, judging, judging." It is not necessary to "judge the judging," or to fight it.

Patience means having the willingness to allow things to unfold in their own time; having the willingness to stay with whatever process is happening in the moment. Beginner's mind involves holding an attitude of freshness toward each experience in the present moment—as if seeing it for the first time. It calls for the recognition that each breath, sensation, or experience is truly unique, happening in this moment, and has unique possibilities. Mindfulness practice fosters the learning to trust oneself and one's basic wisdom and goodness as they are revealed through the practice of mindful attention to mind and body.

Bringing a nonstriving attitude toward mindfulness practice involves letting go of the habit of trying to change things that are noticed during meditation. It means not trying to become anyone or anything else in meditation. For example, boredom, or pain, or sleepiness, or anything else is met by a nonstriving attitude. One need not take any action, but simply pay attention to the sensation or state as closely as possible.

The closely linked concept of acceptance entails means being willing to see things exactly as they are in this moment. It does not mean one has to like what they see, or become passive about everything. It just means starting with attention and the willingness to see things as they are right now.

Finally, the attitude of letting go involves cultivating the attitude of nonattachment. When one starts to pay attention to inner experience in meditation, the mind wants to push away or cling to certain thoughts and feelings. Letting go means letting experience be whatever it is and simply paying attention to it without suppressing it, elevating it or clinging to it.

How Is MBSR Delivered?

The typical structure of an MBSR program is to meet in a classroom setting once a week for 8 weeks. Each class is 2–2.5 hr in length. Activities in the class usually include instruction and practice of a variety of mindfulness methods, plus discussions aimed at strengthening the participants' meditation practice, the application of mindfulness to their specific situation, and linking principles of mind–body health and stress to the practice of mindfulness. Class sizes vary, but may number greater than 30 participants with a single instructor.

In addition to the weekly classes, the MBSR model includes an all-day session called the Day of Mindfulness. This is an intensive, silent meditation retreat experience in which program participants have the opportunity to practice meditation and yoga over several hours with minimal disruption or distraction.

Mindfulness is developed by paying attention on purpose, without trying to change or judge the object of attention. Crucial to the MBSR approach is the principle of making mindfulness a way of living or approaching life, rather than viewing it as a "technique." To this end, participants are taught a variety of practices to support mindfulness. Typically they learn mindfulness of breathing, body scan, mindful walking, mindful yoga, mindful attention to the entire field of sensory experience (open or choiceless awareness), and mindfulness of everyday activities such as eating, doing chores, or dealing with other situations of daily life. In addition, at various times over the 8-week program, meditation practices emphasizing qualities of kindness, compassion, equanimity, or spacious calm may be taught as supports to mindfulness practice itself.

A distinction is made between "formal" meditation and "informal" mindfulness practice. Formal meditation is time each day devoted specifically to practicing one or more of the methods taught in the course. Typically, participants are asked to make a commitment of 45 minutes to 1 hour each day of the 8-week program for formal meditation. Informal practice refers to bringing mindfulness to different situations of daily life. Building on the formal practice experience, the participants are encouraged to stop and pay attention nonjudgmentally and wholeheartedly wherever they find themselves in daily life. For example, this could mean bringing mindful attention to the breath while waiting in traffic, or while undergoing a medical procedure. Or, it could mean paying closer attention to the experience unfolding around a meal, or eating a snack. In any case, the participants are encouraged to engage more fully and consciously with life as it unfolds.

EXPERIENTIAL LEARNING

The word "practice" is used frequently in the MBSR approach. Here, practice does not mean "rehearsal." Nor does it refer to an activity that is somehow different from real life. Practice in the MBSR context does not mean trying to become anything better, or trying to be someone else, or give a better performance. Rather, practice in the MBSR context does mean "... inviting ourselves to interface with this moment in full awareness, with the intention to embody as best we can an orientation of calmness, mindfulness, and equanimity right here and right now" (Kabat-Zinn, 1994).

This experience of approaching life mindfully can only be understood through the direct experience of the individual. No amount of reading or explanation can completely convey the experience of mindfulness through meditation any more than studying a map can completely convey the experience of being in a place. For this reason, to have substantial direct experience being mindful, the MBSR program demands a large commitment from participants to actually meditate daily at home, weekly in class, and over several hours in the day-long intensive. The aim for this commitment to formal and informal mindfulness practices is to cultivate a continuity of awareness in all activities and challenges of daily living (Kabat-Zinn, 2003).

TEACHER QUALIFICATIONS

Instructors in an MBSR program typically meet certain qualifications. Although there is at present no national certification or licensure requirement, MBSR instructors in the UMass program (and some others, including the author's program in the Duke Center for Integrative Medicine) are required to have a variety of educational and meditative skills and a significant base of experience. For example, the qualified instructor typically would have a Master's degree or higher in a health or education field; would have a minimum of 3 years of a daily, personal mindfulness mediation practice, including at least 2-week-long or longer intensive mindfulness meditation retreats; would have significant personal experience with yoga practice; and would have completed a training program for professionals in MBSR.

MBSR AND RESEARCH: AN OVERVIEW

The sheer volume of research aimed at investing the impact of MBSR on the health and well-being of participants, as well as refinements in methodology, has increased markedly in recent years. A review of the current literature suggests that mindfulness interventions may have benefit for participants with a range of medical conditions. The following studies illustrate the broad range of positive impact reported using the MBSR approach. Participants have been found to experience improvements in stress reduction (Astin, 1997); chronic pain (Kabat-Zinn, 1982; Kabat-Zinn, Lipworth, & Burney, 1985; Kabat-Zinn, Lipworth, Burney, & Sellers, 1986); anxiety disorders (Kabat-Zinn et al., 1992; Miller, Fletcher, & Kabat-Zinn, 1995); relapsing depression (Teasdale, Segal, & Williams, 1995; Teasdale et al., 2000); eating disorders (Kristeller & Hallett, 1999); cancer (Speca, Carlson, Goodey, & Angen, 2000); fibromyalgia (Goldenberg et al., 1994; Kaplan, Goldenberg, & Galvin-Nadeau, 1993; Weissbecker et al., 2002); and psoriasis (Kabat-Zinn et al., 1998). Benefits have been found among a mixed group of medical patients (Reibel, Greeson, Brainard, & Rosenzweig, 2001); with a population of inner city residents (Roth & Stanley, 2002); and with premedical and medical students (Rosenzweig, Reibel, Greeson, Brainard, & Hojat, 2003; Shapiro, Schwartz, & Bonner, 1998).

Of additional interest, preliminary work by Davidson, Kabat-Zinn, and others (Davidson et al., 2003) report alterations in brain and immune functions produced by mindfulness meditation. These alterations in brain function are consistent with higher levels of well-being in participants, while immune function is reported to be enhanced in participants who meditate. The possible neuroanatomic basis for subjective feelings of well-being in meditators proposed by Davidson's work is consistent with other mindfulness research in which participants report increased levels of well-being (Brown & Ryan, 2003; Reibel et al., 2001; Rosenzweig et al., 2003).

There is much research still needed. Reviewers of the existing literature (Baer, 2003; Bishop, 2002) have detailed methodological shortcomings in current studies, and pointed out the need for more randomized control studies, and for clarification of mechanisms of action in mindfulness-based approaches. Despite these critiques, however, those same reviewers are in agreement that there already exist enough positive data to warrant further research activity.

MBSR AND ANXIETY

There have been a number of studies that have reported anxiety reductions in individuals who practice mindfulness meditation as taught in the MBSR format. Kabat-Zinn and colleagues (Kabat-Zinn et al., 1992) studied 22 MBSR program participants with diagnosable anxiety disorders. The participants were screened with a structured clinical interview and found to meet *DSM-III-R* criteria for generalized anxiety disorder or panic disorder with or without agoraphobia. Assessments, including self-ratings and therapists' ratings, were obtained weekly before and during participation in the MBSR program, and monthly during a 3-month follow-up period. Significant reductions in scores of anxiety and depression occurred for 20 of the participants. Changes were maintained at follow-up. The number of participants experiencing panic symptoms was also substantially reduced.

Miller and his colleagues (Miller et al., 1995) did a follow-up study of a subgroup of those same participants. In this study, 3-year follow-up data were obtained for 18 of the original 22 study participants. Maintenance of previous gains on a variety of scales, including Hamilton and Beck anxiety scales and the Hamilton panic score, was reported. Ongoing compliance with the meditation practice was also demonstrated, with 10 of the 18 reporting they continued to do a "formal" mindfulness technique 3 years posttraining in MBSR, and 16 of the 18 reporting they continued to practice the "informal" mindfulness technique of awareness of breathing in daily life.

Three studies have examined the impact of MBSR on the anxiety of patients with medical conditions. Speca and colleagues (Speca et al., 2000) taught mindfulness meditation modeled on the MBSR program format to a group of 90 patients heterogeneous in type and stage of cancer. They used a randomized wait-list control design to assess the impact of the intervention on participants. The intervention consisted of a weekly 1.5-hr class and home meditation practice. Patients in the treatment group reported significantly lower levels of anxiety, as well as decreased depression, anger, and confusion.

Reibel and colleagues (Reibel et al., 2001) examined the effects of MBSR on health-related quality of life and physical and psychological symptoms in a population of 136 patients with mixed medical conditions. Participants reported a 38% reduction in general psychological distress, a 44% reduction in anxiety, and a 34% reduction in depression at the end of the program. Thirty percent of the participants responded to a 1-year follow-up survey, and reported maintenance of initial improvements in all three psychological domains.

Tacon and colleagues (Tacon, McComb, Caldera, & Randolph, 2003) reported results of a pilot study of 20 women with anxiety and heart disease, randomized to control and study groups of 10 participants each. Because anxiety correlates significantly with morbidity in heart disease, this study sought to assess the effectiveness of an MBSR approach in reducing anxiety in women with heart disease. Although there were some mixed findings from this study (e.g., no significant differences on a measure of health locus of control), significant reductions were found in the study group comparing pre- to postintervention anxiety scores.

Finally, given the relationship between stress and anxiety, two additional studies that focused on premedical and medical students experiencing stress bear mention. Shapiro and colleagues (Shapiro et al., 1998) used a randomized wait-list control method to measure stress and mood disturbance in a group of premedical and medical students. They reported significant reductions in state and trait anxiety among the participants who participated in MBSR. Similarly, Rosenzweig et al. (2003) reported significant reductions in total mood disturbance, including tension and anxiety, post-MBSR intervention, for 140 2nd-year medical students as compared to 162 control participants.

A PERSONAL MINDFULNESS EXERCISE

Because mindfulness is best understood as a direct experience, this chapter ends with a personal mindfulness meditation exercise. Actual understanding of mindfulness comes only through the repeated practice of mindfulness and the importance of this practice for both participants and instructors is emphasized in MBSR. Intelligent academic discussion and research will also likely benefit when investigators have direct experience of mindfulness meditation through practice. In the spirit of promoting deeper understanding of mindfulness, and greater benefits for all, the following meditation exercise is offered.

(*Note*: As you do this exercise, you may wish to have someone read these meditation instructions to you, or even to record your own voice reading the instructions to support you. It helps if whoever reads the instructions would pause for a breath or two between each sentence. Also, pause a bit longer, perhaps 3–4 breaths, between each paragraph of the instructions.)

OUTER POSTURE

Take a comfortable seat (or lie down if you are physically unable to sit comfortably for any length of time). Adjust your posture and body so that you can relax and remain alert. Let your posture embody ease and the dignity befitting any activity directed at healing and awakening. Let your eyes be at least half closed; fully closed may be even better. Don not let the eyes roam and distract your attention. Do something comfortable with your hands. Perhaps the position the hands take could reflect a sense of ease, relaxation, and safety—of having exactly what you need now, in this moment.

INNER POSTURE

Set your burdens down. Release both the inner and the outer ones. For the period of this meditation, it is not necessary to try to change things, or to become somebody or something else. There is nothing else to accomplish.

Just paying attention—acknowledging in a friendly, sensitive way what is present—is good enough. You are not postponing life when you meditate. Meditation is about being more open and connecting with life. The only time life happens is now—in the present moment.

As you meditate, as best you can, allow yourself to soften and open. Resting in an open, receptive heart. Connecting with your natural inner qualities of awareness and spaciousness. Exploring the sense of inner spaciousness that can contain all experiences. Recognizing the friendliness and compassion present within this spaciousness.

Practicing Meditation: Mindfulness of Breathing

Begin by gathering your attention in the sensations of your body. Feeling the sense of mass and heaviness, and the points of contact of body with the floor or chair. Noticing and allowing the sensations in the feet, the hands, and the face. Noticing sensations in other regions of your body, and allowing those. Now, gently move attention closer to the sensations of your breath. Not controlling the breath in any way, but simply allowing it to flow into and out of the body. Focusing attention at the place in your body where it is easiest to feel the actual sensations of the in-breath, a pause, the out-breath, another pause, and the next in-breath. Perhaps this place is the tip of your nose, or your abdomen, or your chest, rising and falling with each breath.

Paying attention to the direct, bare sensations of breath moving. Noticing long breath, short breath, rapid, slow, rough, smooth breath. Noticing the unique quality of each breath.

No need to control the breath, or to make anything special happen. Simply allowing the breath to flow naturally as you bring a more sensitive and continuous focus to the unfolding sensations and patterns.

There do not have to be any distractions. Whenever your attention wanders, notice that. You have not done anything wrong. Gently return attention to the breath. If you feel especially bothered or distracted, kindly and patiently breathe *with* the distraction. No need to fight the distraction, or to struggle to ignore it. Let it be just as it is as you focus attention on your breath, breathing with the experience. Letting your breath flow in and out, over and under, around and through the distraction as you maintain your primary focus on the changing breath sensations.

Sitting with the breath, *and everything else*. Focused and calm, attending to the breath, and *allowing everything else* for the time of this meditation. Softening, acknowledging, and holding all experience in this moment, in the ever-changing patterns of the breath. Letting the breath and the meditation support you. Continue meditating for as long as you like.

When you are ready to stop this practice, gently open your eyes and begin to move your fingers and toes. Notice how you feel without judgment.

CONCLUSION

Mindfulness is a basic human capacity. In 1979, Jon-Kabat-Zinn and his colleagues at the University of Massachusetts Medical Center in Worcester, MA, began a program for teaching mindfulness meditation and mindful yoga to medical patients referred by physicians. They called this program MBSR. In the 25 years since that time, thousands of people have learned to practice mindfulness meditation in the service of health enhancement and stress reduction through participation in MBSR programs worldwide. Despite this history, the health applications and understanding of mindfulness as a healing practice is still in its infancy. However, after 25 years of MBSR activity, the healing potential of simply being present with compassionate attention is being discovered and appreciated by Western medicine.

REFERENCES

Astin, J. A. (1997). Stress reduction through mindfulness meditation. Effects on psychological symptomatology, sense of control, and spiritual experiences. *Psychotherapy & Psychosomatics, 66*(2), 97–106.

Baer, R. A. (2003). Mindfulness training as a clinical intervention: A conceptual and empirical review. *Clinical Psychology: Science & Practice, 10*(2), 125–143.

Bishop, S. R. (2002). What do we really know about mindfulness-based stress reduction? *Psychosomatic Medicine, 64*(1), 71–83.

Brown, K. W., & Ryan, R. M. (2003). The benefits of being present: Mindfulness and its role in psychological well-being. *Journal of Personality & Social Psychology, 84*(4), 822–848.

Davidson, R. J., Kabat-Zinn, J., Schumacher, J., Rosenkranz, M., Muller, D., Santorelli, S. F., et al. (2003). Alterations in brain and immune function produced by mindfulness meditation. *Psychosomatic Medicine, 65*(4), 564–570.

Feldman, C. (1998). *Thorsons principles of meditation.* London: Thorsons.

Freeman, L. W. (2001). Meditation. In L. W. Freeman & G. F. Lawlis (Eds.), *Mosby's complementary and alternative medicine: A research-based approach* (pp. 166–195). St. Louis, MO: Mosby.

Germer, C. K., Siegel, R. D., & Fulton, P. R. (2005). *Mindfulness and psychotherapy* (1st ed.). New York: Guilford.

Goldenberg, D. L., Kaplan, K. H., Nadeau, M. G., Brodeur, C., Smith, S., & Schmid, C. H. (1994). A controlled study of a stress-reduction, cognitive–behavioral treatment program in fibromyalgia. *Journal of Musculoskeletal Pain, 2*(2), 53–66.

Kabat-Zinn, J. (1982). An outpatient program in behavioral medicine for chronic pain patients based on the practice of mindfulness meditation: Theoretical considerations and preliminary results. *General Hospital Psychiatry, 4*(1), 33–47.

Kabat-Zinn, J. (1990). *Full catastrophe living: Using the wisdom of your body and mind to face stress, pain, and illness.* New York, NY: Delacorte Press.

Kabat-Zinn, J. (1994). *Wherever you go, there you are: Mindfulness meditation in everyday life.* New York: Hyperion.

Kabat-Zinn, J. (2003). Mindfulness-based interventions in context: Past, present, and future. *Clinical Psychology: Science & Practice, 10*(2), 144–156.

Kabat-Zinn, J., Lipworth, L., & Burney, R. (1985). The clinical use of mindfulness meditation for the self-regulation of chronic pain. *Journal of Behavioral Medicine, 8*(2), 163–190.

Kabat-Zinn, J., Lipworth, L., Burney, R., & Sellers, W. (1986). Four year follow-up of a meditation-based program for the self-regulation of chronic pain: Treatment outcomes and compliance. *Clinical Journal of Pain, 2,* 159–173.

Kabat-Zinn, J., Massion, A. O., Kristeller, J., Peterson, L. G., Fletcher, K. E., Pbert, L., et al. (1992). Effectiveness of a meditation-based stress reduction program in the treatment of anxiety disorders. *American Journal of Psychiatry, 149*(7), 936–943.

Kabat-Zinn, J., Wheeler, E., Light, T., Skillings, A., Scharf, M. J., Cropley, T. G., et al. (1998). Influence of a mindfulness meditation-based stress reduction intervention on rates of skin clearing in patients with moderate to severe psoriasis undergoing phototherapy (UVB) and photochemotherapy (PUVA). *Psychosomatic Medicine, 60*(5), 625–632.

Kaplan, K. H., Goldenberg, D. L., & Galvin-Nadeau, M. (1993). The impact of a meditation-based stress reduction program on fibromyalgia. *General Hospital Psychiatry, 15*(5), 284–289.

Krishnamurti, J. (1969). *Freedom from the known.* New York: Harper & Row.

Kristeller, J. L., & Hallett, C. (1999). An exploratory study of a meditation-based intervention for binge eating disorder. *Journal of Health Psychology, 4*(3), 357–363.

Linehan, M. (1993). *Cognitive–behavioral treatment of borderline personality disorder.* New York: Guilford.

Miller, J. J., Fletcher, K., & Kabat-Zinn, J. (1995). Three-year follow-up and clinical implications of a mindfulness meditation-based stress reduction intervention in the treatment of anxiety disorders. *General Hospital Psychiatry, 17*(3), 192–200.

Mitchell, S. (1988). *Tao te ching: A new English version.* New York: Harper & Row.

Moyers, B. D., Flowers, B. S., & Grubin, D. (1993). *Healing and the mind.* New York: Doubleday.

Nhat Hanh, T. (1987). *Being peace.* Berkeley, CA: Parallax Press.

Ramana, M., & Venkataramiah, M. S. (2000). *Talks with Ramana Maharshi: On realizing abiding peace and happiness.* Carlsbad, CA: Inner Directions.

Reibel, D. K., Greeson, J. M., Brainard, G. C., & Rosenzweig, S. (2001). Mindfulness-based stress reduction and health-related quality of life in a heterogeneous patient population. *General Hospital Psychiatry, 23*(4), 183–192.

Rosenberg, L. (1998). *Breath by breath: The liberating practice of insight liberation* (with D. Guy). Boston, MA: Shambhala.

Rosenzweig, S., Reibel, D. K., Greeson, J. M., Brainard, G. C., & Hojat, M. (2003). Mindfulness-based stress reduction lowers psychological distress in medical students. *Teaching & Learning in Medicine, 15*(2), 88–92.

Roth, B., & Stanley, T. W. (2002). Mindfulness-based stress reduction and healthcare utilization in the inner city: Preliminary findings. *Alternative Therapies in Health & Medicine, 8*(1), 60–62.

Santorelli, S. (1999). *Heal thy self: Lessons on mindfulness in medicine.* New York: Harmony/Bell Tower.

Segal, Z. V., Williams, J. M. G., & Teasdale, J. D. (2002). *Mindfulness-based cognitive therapy for depression: A new approach to preventing relapse.* New York: Guilford.

Shapiro, S. L., Schwartz, G. E., & Bonner, G. (1998). Effects of mindfulness-based stress reduction on medical and premedical students. *Journal of Behavioral Medicine, 21*(6), 581–599.

Smith, J. (1999). *Radiant mind: Essential Buddhist teachings and texts* . New York: Riverhead Books.

Speca, M., Carlson, L. E., Goodey, E., & Angen, M. (2000). A randomized, wait-list controlled clinical trial: The effect of a mindfulness meditation-based stress reduction program on mood and symptoms of stress in cancer outpatients. *Psychosomatic Medicine, 62*(5), 613–622.

Tacon, A. M., McComb, J., Caldera, Y., & Randolph, P. (2003). Mindfulness meditation, anxiety reduction, and heart disease: A pilot study. *Family & Community Health, 26*(1), 25–33.

Teasdale, J. D., Segal, Z., & Williams, J. M. (1995). How does cognitive therapy prevent depressive relapse and why should attentional control (mindfulness) training help? *Behaviour Research & Therapy, 33*(1), 25–39.

Teasdale, J. D., Segal, Z. V., Williams, J. M., Ridgeway, V. A., Soulsby, J. M., & Lau, M. A. (2000). Prevention of relapse/recurrence in major depression by mindfulness-based cognitive therapy. *Journal of Consulting & Clinical Psychology, 68*(4), 615–623.

Tolle, E. (1999). *The power of now: A guide to spiritual enlightenment.* Novato, CA: New World Library.

Weissbecker, I., Salmon, P., Studts, J. L., Floyd, A. R., Dedert, E. A., & Sephton, S. E. (2002). Mindfulness-based stress reduction and sense of coherence among women with fibromyalgia. *Journal of Clinical Psychology in Medical Settings, 9*(4), 297–307.

Wylie, M. S., & Simon, R. (2004). The power of paying attention. *Psychotherapy Networker, 28*(6), 59–67.

APPLYING DBT MINDFULNESS SKILLS TO THE TREATMENT OF CLIENTS WITH ANXIETY DISORDERS

Kim L. Gratz, Matthew T. Tull, and Amy W. Wagner

Clinicians and researchers have increasingly begun to acknowledge the potential benefits of incorporating acceptance- and mindfulness-based approaches into cognitive-behavioral treatments for the anxiety disorders (see Orsillo, Roemer, Block, Lejeune, & Herbert, 2004; Orsillo, Roemer, Block-Lerner, & Tull, 2004). As such, the past several years have seen the development of innovative mindfulness- and acceptance-based cognitive-behavioral treatments for several anxiety disorders, including generalized anxiety disorder (Roemer & Orsillo, 2002), panic disorder (PD; Karekla & Forsyth, 2004), posttraumatic stress disorder (PTSD; Orsillo & Batten, 2005), and obsessive–compulsive disorder (OCD; Singh, Wahler, Winton, & Adkins, 2004). Evidence in support of these treatments is provided by both preliminary data on their efficacy (Karekla & Forsyth, 2004; Roemer & Orsillo, 2004) and basic research on the potential benefits of emotional acceptance (relative to suppression) within PD (Levitt, Brown, Orsillo, & Barlow, 2004) and among individuals with heightened anxiety sensitivity (Eifert & Heffner, 2003).

In addition to these new therapies developed specifically for the treatment of anxiety disorders, there are empirically supported mindfulness- and acceptance-based treatments for other clinical disorders that may be usefully adapted for the treatment of anxiety disorders. One such treatment is dialectical behavior therapy (DBT; Linehan, 1993a, 1993b), which offers a pragmatic approach to mindfulness training that may serve as a valuable resource for clinicians who wish to teach mindfulness skills to clients with anxiety disorders. Although DBT was developed to treat parasuicidal women with borderline personality disorder (BPD), research suggests that there are high rates of comorbid anxiety disorders among patients with BPD (see, e.g., Zanarini et al., 1998). Therefore, it is likely that DBT is already being applied to the treatment of anxiety-related symptoms, within the context of BPD. Moreover, certain core characteristics of BPD targeted within DBT, such as experiential avoidance (i.e., attempts to alter the form or frequency of unwanted internal experiences, including emotions, thoughts, memories, and bodily sensations; Hayes, Wilson, Gifford, Follette, & Strosahl, 1996; for the role of experiential avoidance in BPD, see Gratz & Gunderson, in press; Linehan, 1993a), are also common within the anxiety disorders (for a review, see Salters-Pedneault, Tull, & Roemer, 2004), and, as such, may be usefully treated with a similar approach.

In its empirically supported package, DBT includes four treatment components: weekly group skills training, individual psychotherapy, and therapist consultation/supervision meetings, as well as telephone consultation as needed between clients and individual therapists (Linehan, 1993a). Although there is not yet empirical support for the use of only the skills training component of DBT (separate from the other components), it is this component, in particular, that may be usefully adapted for the treatment of anxiety disorders and that will be the focus of this chapter. Specifically, this chapter focuses on the application of one of the four DBT skills training modules, core mindfulness skills, to the treatment of symptoms central to the anxiety disorders.

AN OVERVIEW OF CORE MINDFULNESS SKILLS

Linehan (1993a, 1993b) operationalizes mindfulness practice as a series of discrete behavioral skills that may be taught to clients, and, as such, DBT may be a particularly useful treatment from which to adapt and apply mindfulness training. DBT mindfulness skills promote a present moment focus, nonjudgmental awareness, and attentional flexibility. The overall goal of mindfulness skills training within DBT is to develop a lifestyle of participating with awareness. Underlying this goal is the development of "wise mind," a state of knowing, wisdom, and centeredness, wherein one's emotions ("emotion mind") and reason ("reasonable mind") are integrated to foster a state of mind that is greater than the sum of its parts. To this end, DBT teaches six behavioral skills: three of which focus on *what* to do, and the other three of which focus on *how* to do it. These "what" and "how" skills are designed to be used in conjunction with one another, with the former specifying the behavior to be practiced and the latter specifying the quality or nature of this behavior. These skills will be described briefly below, followed by a discussion of their applicability to specific anxiety-related difficulties. For a thorough description of these skills, as well as step-by-step instructions on how to teach these skills to clients, see Linehan (1993b).

The three DBT "what" skills include *observing*, *describing*, and *participating*, and can be applied only one at a time. Although the overall goal of these skills is to develop a lifestyle of participating with awareness, DBT acknowledges that this is a process, and suggests that observing or describing one's responses may be necessary when a behavior is being learned, a problem is encountered, or a change is required. The first of the "what" skills (i.e., *observing*) involves noticing and attending to internal and external experiences as they occur in the moment. *Observing* involves awareness of each experience as it arises, without labeling it. The second "what" skill (i.e., *describing*) involves labeling what is being observed, and putting words to one's experiences. Clients are encouraged to label their emotions, thoughts, and sensory experiences objectively, and to describe an emotion as just an emotion and a thought as just a thought, etc.—a skill that may be particularly useful for promoting cognitive defusion and deliteralization (i.e., changing the impact of verbal events by changing one's relationship to these events and altering the literal and functional context in which they occur, rather than experiencing verbal events as comparable to the events they represent or responding to thoughts in terms of their literal content (see Hayes, Strosahl, & Wilson, 1999; Masuda, Hayes, Sackett, & Twohig, 2004). The third and final "what" skill is *participating*, and is considered to be the ultimate goal. *Participating* involves entering fully into, and becoming one with, one's experiences. This skill involves throwing oneself completely into an activity (without self-consciousness), and acting intuitively.

The three "how" skills specify the manner in which to *observe*, *describe*, and *participate*, and, unlike the "what" skills, may be applied simultaneously. The first "how" skill is *nonjudgmentally*, which specifies the importance of taking a nonjudgmental and nonevaluative stance. Clients are taught to describe experiences objectively, letting go of evaluations such as "good" or "bad." Similar to other mindfulness-based approaches (for a review, see Baer, 2003; Bishop et al., 2004), a nonjudgmental stance is distinguished from liking something or wanting something, and in no way precludes identifying and describing negative or harmful consequences of behaviors. Moreover, clients are also taught to take a nonjudgmental approach to their own judging (i.e., "not to judge their judging"). The second "how" skill of *one-mindfully* involves focusing attention on one thing in the moment and doing only one activity at a time, with full awareness and undivided attention. Clients are encouraged to let go of distractions and the tendency to do more than one thing at a time and, instead, to focus their attention fully on the activity in which they are engaging. This skill calls for an awareness of being distracted, as well as a gentle "turning of one's mind" back to the activity at hand. Finally, the third "how" skill, *effectively*, involves doing what works and acting skillfully (given the individual's goals and situational demands), as opposed to "cutting off one's nose to spite one's face." This skill involves "playing by the rules" and necessitates awareness of both the environmental contingencies and one's own objectives.

Although empirical support for the efficacy of DBT mindfulness skills in the treatment of anxiety disorders is not yet available, literature on the nature of anxiety and shared characteristics of the anxiety disorders suggests the utility of applying DBT mindfulness skills to the treatment of anxiety-related symptoms. Specifically, common to all anxiety disorders is the tendency to quickly identify, negatively evaluate, and avoid threat (see Barlow, 2002b; Beck & Clark, 1997; McNally, 1995). Although the particular way in which this tendency is expressed and the specific stimuli that are identified as threatening differ across the anxiety disorders, the processes are thought to operate in a similar manner. In the following section, we identify certain characteristics thought to be particularly relevant to the anxiety disorders, and discuss the ways in which DBT mindfulness skills may be usefully applied to the treatment of these anxiety-related processes.

APPLICATION OF DBT MINDFULNESS SKILLS TO PARTICULAR CHARACTERISTICS OF ANXIETY DISORDERS

One of the primary characteristics common across the anxiety disorders is a selective attention to threatening stimuli (Beck & Clark, 1997; McNally, 1995), a bias that may involve either the directing of attentional resources toward potentially threatening stimuli (i.e., a narrowing of attention or "tunnel vision"), or simply a heightened sensitivity to the recognition and detection of these potentially threatening stimuli in one's internal or external environment. For example, individuals with PD have been found to selectively attend to physical threat-related stimuli (Asmundson, Sandler, Wilson, & Walker, 1992) and to exhibit a hypervigilance for certain bodily sensations (i.e., those related to a panic attack; see Schmidt, Lerew, & Trakowski, 1997); individuals with PTSD have been found to demonstrate an attentional bias for stimuli related to their particular trauma (Foa, Feske, Murdock, Kozak, & McCarthy, 1991; Kaspi, McNally, & Amir, 1995); and individuals with social anxiety disorder (SAD) have been found to display both a recognition bias for critical faces (Lundh & Öst, 1996) and increased self-focused attention (Wells et al., 1995).

Because the narrowing of attention may result in the missing of additional, important, non–anxiety-related information in the environment (including information that may counter perceptions of threat), it may be useful to teach clients with anxiety disorders to expand or broaden their awareness to incorporate *all* aspects of their internal and external environment, threatening and not (consistent with other therapies developed specifically for anxiety disorders; see, e.g., Roemer & Orsillo, 2002; Wells, 1990, 1999; Wells, White, & Carter, 1997). Encouraging clients to redirect their attention and broaden their awareness by *observing* phenomena that were previously outside of their awareness may increase the potential for effective and flexible responding (especially during encounters with threat-related stimuli). For example, in order to to counter the tendency within SAD to focus attention on critical faces or one's own internal anxious response, a client with SAD who was giving a speech would be encouraged to expand her or his awareness to observe all aspects of the external environment (e.g., all members of the audience, including those who are responding positively) as well as all aspects of her or his internal emotional response to the situation (e.g., excitement and pride, in addition to fear). Likewise, clients with PTSD may benefit from learning to broaden their awareness to observe all cues in their environment, including those that signal safety (in addition to the more frequently attended to cues that signal threat).

Equally as important as the broadening of awareness, however, is the ability to label one's internal experiences as what they are (e.g., a feeling as just a feeling, a thought as just a thought, etc.). That is, anxiety disorders are characterized not only by a narrowing of attention to certain stimuli (i.e., an attentional bias), but also an interpretation of these stimuli as threatening (i.e., an interpretational bias). For example, PD is associated with the catastrophic misinterpretation of certain bodily sensations that have been paired with the experience of anxiety and panic (e.g., increased heart rate, shortness of breath; Clark et al., 1997), generalized anxiety disorder (GAD) may be associated with the interpretation of worry as being dangerous (e.g., Wells, 1999), and OCD is associated with the interpretation of intrusive thoughts as dangerous (due to the belief that simply having the thought increases the likelihood that the thought will come true and/or is the same as having engaged in some unwanted behavior; referred to as "thought-action fusion," see Shafran, Thordarson, & Rachman, 1996).

Given these interpretational biases, it is important that, in addition to learning to broaden their awareness to include all aspects of an experience, clients with anxiety disorders learn to *describe* their experiences (both those previously attended to and those newly attended to). For example, a client with PD would be encouraged to notice the experience of an increase in his heart rate, describe that experience (e.g., "my heart is beginning to beat faster"), notice any associated thoughts (e.g., "I am having a heart attack"), and then describe those thoughts as just thoughts (e.g., "the thought 'I am having a heart attack' has come into my mind"), rather than buying into the interpretation of an increased heart rate as dangerous and/or responding as if that thought were literally true. Clients with anxiety disorders may be particularly likely to benefit from learning how to describe internal experiences as what they are (e.g., bodily sensations, interpretations, etc.), as it is likely the tendency to "buy into" interpretations of internal experiences as dangerous or threatening that motivates attempts to control or avoid these experiences, paradoxically increasing their severity and frequency. The skill of *describing* these interpretations as just thoughts may eventually function to reduce the extent to which threat is associated with certain internal sensations as clients develop an understanding that these sensations are not inherently harmful.

Similar to this interpretational bias, and another feature common across the anxiety disorders, is a future-oriented focus involving negative, catastrophic expectations. This future focus may take the form of worry regarding the increased likelihood of numerous negative outcomes in GAD (Vasey & Borkovec, 1992), worry regarding the occurrence of future panic attacks in PD (the consequences of which may be as severe as the development of agoraphobia; Craske, Rapee, & Barlow, 1988), and negative expectations regarding future performance and social interactions in SAD (Hofmann & Barlow, 2002). Teaching clients to refocus their attention on the present moment (an aspect underlying all approaches to mindfulness; see Baer, 2003; Bishop et al., 2004; Brown & Ryan, 2003; Kabat-Zinn, 1994; Marlatt & Kristeller, 1999), and to continually bring their attention back to their current experiences and surroundings when they notice that they have become distracted by future-oriented thinking, will help target the negative consequences associated with a rigid future-oriented focus. In particular, having clients practice *one-mindfully observing* or *describing* may assist them in bringing their attention back to the present and provide skills for managing distracting, future-focused thoughts.

Consider, for example, a client with GAD who is continuously worrying about the safety of her son when playing with him. This client would be encouraged to redirect her attention to the present moment by noticing the information coming through her senses in that moment (i.e., *observing*), or describing in detail all aspects of her surroundings and her feelings about these (i.e., *describing*). Moreover, this observing or describing would be done *one-mindfully*, with the client instructed to continually redirect and refocus attention on the process of observing or describing the current moment when distracted by future-focused thoughts. As a result, the client would be less likely to miss out on the positively reinforcing experience of playing with her son and observing his enjoyment.

In addition, teaching clients both to allow thoughts to enter and then leave their mind without attaching to, reacting to, or acting on these thoughts (described by Linehan as having a "Teflon mind"), and to label thoughts as just thoughts may help reduce the tendency to "buy into" future-focused, catastrophic thoughts as literally true. That is, the process of *describing* a thought as just a thought (without trying to change, escape, or avoid it) would be expected to change a client's relationship to her or his thoughts, altering the impact of these thoughts on the client's behavior and decreasing the aversiveness of these thoughts (rather than changing the thoughts themselves). For example, in the case of the client with GAD described above, the practice of having a "Teflon mind" would increase her ability to fully participate in the experience of playing with her son, despite the presence of worrisome thoughts regarding his safety. In addition, not "buying into" these thoughts as truth, and instead labeling them as just thoughts, would likely halt the exacerbation of her worry, increase her contact with the positively reinforcing aspects of playing with her son, and reduce the likelihood that she would avoid playing with her son in the future.

As clearly demonstrated in this example, one way in which negative, future-focused thoughts can adversely affect clients with anxiety disorders is by distracting them from their ongoing experiences and decreasing sensitivity to environmental contingencies. Using the skills of *one-mindfully participating* may target these consequences by teaching clients to bring their full attention and awareness to the one activity in which they are currently engaged. That is, clients would be encouraged to notice their worry and then bring their attention back to the present moment and the activity in which they are presently involved. These skills call for a nonjudgmental awareness of being distracted, as well as a gentle "turning of one's mind" back to the activity at hand. The use of these skills would be expected to increase sensitivity to both environmental contingencies and the positive consequences of participation in valued activities and a life worth living (thereby reinforcing nonavoidance and active participation in life). For example, a client with PD who is engaging in sexual activity may experience worries about the possible negative consequences of an increased heart rate (i.e., an eventual panic attack). These worrisome thoughts would have the potential to distract the client from her experience and its positively reinforcing aspects (e.g., pleasure, intimacy, etc.). This client would likely benefit from learning simply to notice these thoughts and then bring her attention fully back to the present moment, throwing herself completely into the activity in which she is involved.

The avoidance of anxiety and anxiety-related cues is also a central characteristic of the anxiety disorders (Barlow, 2002b; Mowrer, 1960). Clients with anxiety disorders engage in a "seek to avoid" process (Williams, Watts, MacLeod, & Mathews, 1988), detecting threatening stimuli and then attempting to avoid or escape those stimuli. As a result, the complete processing of threat-related stimuli is prevented, maintaining the fear response (Foa & Kozak, 1986). At a basic level, the skill of simply *observing* one's experience may in and of itself target this primary aspect of the anxiety disorders. The act of noticing each and every internal experience as it arises, without trying to push it away or get rid of it, may serve as a form of nonreinforced exposure to anxiety. Similarly, noticing all aspects of one's external experience, including stimuli that may elicit anxiety, is likely to serve as exposure to these cues. As such, simply increasing contact with, and exposure to, previously avoided stimuli (internal and external) is likely to be of benefit.

However, equally as important as *observing* and *describing* previously avoided stimuli is the quality of one's observing and describing; thus, clients must be taught to use the "what" skills of *observing* and *describing* in conjunction with the "how" skill of *nonjudgmentally*. In fact, it is likely this nonevaluative stance (i.e., the description of stimuli as "just is," rather than as "bad" or "good") that underlies many of the potential benefits of the *observing* and *describing* skills, increasing the likelihood that non-reinforced exposure will occur (see Lynch, Chapman, Kuo, Rosenthal, & Linehan, in press). Clients with anxiety disorders may be particularly likely to benefit from learning how to approach their anxiety in a nonjudgmental fashion, as it is likely the evaluation of anxiety as bad or wrong that both motivates attempts to avoid anxiety and leads to the development of secondary emotional responses (e.g., fear or shame; Greenberg & Safran, 1987). A nonjudgmental stance may enable clients to remain present with their anxiety and to view it as a natural part of the human experience.

Moreover, this nonjudgmental approach applies to clients' own judging as well (i.e., clients are taught "not to judge their judging"). That is, while it is important to teach clients to observe and describe their anxiety in a nonjudgmental way, it is equally important to teach them that judgments will not simply disappear (especially early in treatment). For example, the occurrence of anxiety in a male client with PTSD may be followed very quickly by evaluations of this anxiety as bad or a sign of personal weakness. If this client is not taught the importance of taking a nonjudgmental stance with respect to his own judging, he might interpret this overlearned tendency to judge his anxiety as a sign that he is stupid or a failure, and/or that therapy is not working. By learning the importance of not judging one's judging, however, attempts to change one's relationship with anxiety and to approach it in a more accepting way will not be undermined by overlearned evaluations of anxiety. Instead, these evaluations also will be observed as simply another aspect of one's internal environment requiring nonjudgmental observation.

In addition to the avoidance of anxiety and anxiety-related cues, a growing body of evidence suggests that the fear and avoidance of emotional experience *in general* may be central to the anxiety disorders (see Salters-Pedneault et al., 2004). For example, in addition to the fear of fear that may develop among individuals with PD (Chambless & Gracely, 1989), there is evidence that this fear may generalize to other emotions associated with physical sensations perceived as threatening (see Tull, 2005; Williams, Chambless, & Ahrens, 1989), potentially leading to the greater avoidance of emotions in general. Likewise, Mennin, Heimberg, Turk, and Fresco (2002, in press) suggest that individuals with GAD are at greater risk for emotion dysregulation as a result of a predisposition to experience emotions intensely, a poor understanding of emotional experience, reactivity to one's own emotions, and a lack of adaptive emotion regulation strategies, resulting in a tendency to rely on strategies aimed at the avoidance of emotional experience (such as worry). Similar emotion regulation deficits have also been found in SAD (Turk, Heimberg, Luterek, Mennin, & Fresco, 2005). Teaching clients to practice *nonjudgmentally observing* and *describing* all of their emotions may decrease the likelihood of secondary emotional reactions, such as fear or shame (as the primary emotions would not have been evaluated as "bad" or "weak"). Moreover, the use of these skills may help lessen clients' efforts to try to avoid their emotions, thereby intervening in the self-perpetuating cycle of emotional avoidance/control and greater distress that is common across many anxiety disorders (Barlow, Allen, & Choate, 2004; Salters-Pedneault et al., 2004). In addition, the more frequently clients practice the skills of *effectively participating* in their experiences (despite any internal experiences that arise), the more likely they will be to learn that emotions are not threatening (i.e., that they do not have to interfere with a life worth living).

Arguably, the most important characteristics of anxiety disorders that may be targeted by mindfulness skills are behavioral avoidance and inflexible responding. In regard to the former, the development of significant behavioral avoidance is common among clients with anxiety disorders, as they attempt to avoid objects and situations that elicit anxiety. For example, individuals with SAD tend to avoid social situations and/or situations where there is the possibility of social evaluation; individuals with PD may avoid activities that are expected to elicit feared bodily sensations (e.g., exercise, sexual activity, heavy meals, watching exciting movies, etc.); and a rape survivor with PTSD may avoid intimate relationships (out of a fear of sexual activity or men). Overall, evidence suggests that the presence of an anxiety disorder has the potential to put great restrictions on an individual's life (see Barlow, 2002a). Given that the primary goal of DBT mindfulness skills is to develop a lifestyle of participating with awareness, these skills may be particularly useful in targeting this pervasive behavioral avoidance so central to the anxiety disorders. Whereas the skills of *nonjudgmentally observing* and *describing* one's internal and external experiences may assist clients in increasing nonavoidant responses and actively engaging in life, the skill of *participating* specifically targets behavioral avoidance by teaching clients to fully enter into, and become one with, their experiences. Practicing active participation in life would be expected to target the life restriction common among clients with anxiety disorders. For example, a focus on participating may assist the rape survivor with PTSD in pursuing a romantic relationship (despite her valid fears of doing so) if intimate relationships are important to her.

In regard to the characteristic of inflexible responding (usually of an avoidant nature; Beck & Clark, 1997), the DBT skill of *effectively* would be expected to target rigid, inflexible ways of coping with anxiety by emphasizing effective, flexible responding, and doing what works. Moreover, the use of this skill would likely both promote and be promoted by a present moment stance, as effective behavior requires full awareness of the present moment and that which is, so that the most skillful course of action can be determined (given that what is effective in one situation may not be effective in another). For example, although the inflexible use of behavioral avoidance may maintain anxiety in the long run (Mowrer, 1960), there are some situations in which behavioral avoidance may be adaptive. For instance, although a rape survivor might be encouraged to approach certain situations *perceived* as threatening (e.g., the development or maintenance of an interpersonal relationship), other situations might best be avoided (e.g., those associated with heightened risk for harm, such as walking home alone at night). Responding effectively would require full awareness of the present moment and current operating contingencies in order to differentiate *real* threat from *perceived* threat.

CONCLUSIONS

Despite a recent rise in the popularity of mindfulness- and acceptance-based treatments for the anxiety disorders, as well as a growing recognition of the potential benefits of these approaches, these treatments are at relatively early stages of development and are rather few in number. However, well-established treatments for other disorders, such as DBT, have long emphasized the importance and benefits of mindfulness skills training and, as such, hold promise for the treatment of anxiety disorders. As mindfulness-based interventions continue to be incorporated into treatments for a range of clinical disorders, it will be important for researchers and clinicians alike to acknowledge the functional relatedness of problem behaviors across disorders, and the ways in which mindfulness, in general, may effectively target these behaviors (regardless of the disorder with which they are associated). This chapter represents but one example of how this can occur. Specifically, this chapter provided an overview of the mindfulness skills used in DBT and highlighted the applicability of these skills to core characteristics of the anxiety disorders. We would expect these skills to be useful in the treatment of anxiety-related processes either alone or as an adjunct to empirically supported treatments for anxiety disorders (consistent with the growing trend to incorporate acceptance- and mindfulness-based approaches into more traditional, change-focused, cognitive-behavioral approaches for the anxiety disorders; see Karekla & Forsyth, 2004; Roemer & Orsillo, 2002). Of course, future research is needed to determine the effectiveness of these particular mindfulness skills for the treatment of anxiety disorders.

Finally, it is important to recognize that, regardless of the particular treatment from which the interventions are drawn, the use of mindfulness- or acceptance-based approaches may also require a change in perspective on the part of the therapist. That is, from a mindfulness-based perspective, the goal of treatment is not necessarily to reduce anxiety and anxiety-related symptoms, but to change the way in which clients respond to these symptoms (which is expected to indirectly contribute to a reduction of pathological anxiety). Although from session to session certain mindfulness skills may be used to address specific anxiety-related symptoms, the overall goal of these skills is to assist clients in building a life worth living despite the very human experience of anxiety.

REFERENCES

Asmundson, G. J. G., Sandler, L. S., Wilson, K. G., & Walker, J. R. (1992). Selective attention toward physical threat in patients with panic disorder. *Journal of Anxiety Disorders, 6*, 295–303.

Baer, R. A. (2003). Mindfulness training as clinical intervention: A conceptual and empirical review. *Clinical Psychology: Science and Practice, 10*, 125–143.

Barlow, D. H. (2002a). The experience of anxiety: Shadow of intelligence or specter of death? In D. H. Barlow (Ed.), *Anxiety and its disorders* (pp. 1–36). New York: Guilford Press.

Barlow, D. H. (2002b). The nature of anxious apprehension. In D. H. Barlow (Ed.), *Anxiety and its disorders* (pp. 64–104). New York: Guilford Press.

Barlow, D. H., Allen, L. B., & Choate, M. L. (2004). Toward a unified treatment for emotional disorders. *Behavior Therapy, 35*, 205–230.

Beck, A. T., & Clark, D. A. (1997). An information processing model of anxiety: Automatic and strategic processes. *Behaviour Research and Therapy, 35*, 49–58.

Bishop, S. R., Laue, M., Shapiro, S., Carlson, L., Anderson, N. D., Carmody, J., et al. (2004). Mindfulness: A proposed operational definition. *Clinical Psychology: Science & Practice, 11*, 230–241.

Brown, K. W., & Ryan, R. M. (2003). The benefits of being present: Mindfulness and its role in psychological well-being. *Journal of Personality and Social Psychology, 84*, 822–848.

Chambless, D. L., & Gracely, E. J. (1989). Fear of fear and the anxiety disorders. *Cognitive Therapy and Research, 13*, 9–20.

Clark, D. M., Salkovskis, P. M., Öst, L. G., Breitholtz, E., Koehler, K. A., Westling, B. E., et al. (1997). Misinterpretation of body sensations in panic disorder. *Journal of Consulting and Clinical Psychology, 65*, 203–213.

Craske, M. G., Rapee, R. M., & Barlow, D. H. (1988). The significance of panic-expectancy for individual patterns of avoidance. *Behavior Therapy, 19*, 577–592.

Eifert, G. H., & Heffner, M. (2003). The effects of acceptance versus control contexts on avoidance of panic-related symptoms. *Journal of Behavior Therapy and Experimental Psychiatry, 34*, 293–312.

Foa, E. B., Feske, U., Murdock, T. B., Kozak, M. J., & McCarthy, P. R. (1991). Processing of threat-related information in rape victims. *Journal of Abnormal Psychology, 100*, 156–162.

Foa, E. B., & Kozak, M. J. (1986). Emotional processing of fear: Exposure to corrective information. *Psychological Bulletin, 99*, 20–35.

Gratz, K. L., & Gunderson, J. G. (in press). Preliminary data on an acceptance-based emotion regulation group intervention for deliberate self-harm among women with borderline personality disorder. *Behavior Therapy*.

Greenberg, L. S., & Safran, J. D. (1987). *Emotion in psychotherapy: Affect, cognition, and the process of change.* New York: Guilford Press.

Hayes, S. C., Strosahl, K. D., & Wilson, K. G. (1999). *Acceptance and commitment therapy: An experiential approach to behavior change.* New York: Guilford Press.

Hayes, S. C., Wilson, K. G., Gifford, E. V., Follette, V. M., & Strosahl, K. (1996). Experiential avoidance and behavioral disorders: A functional dimensional approach to diagnosis and treatment. *Journal of Consulting and Clinical Psychology, 64*, 1152–1168.

Hofmann, S. G., & Barlow, D. H. (2002). Social phobia (social anxiety disorder). In D. H. Barlow (Ed.), *Anxiety and its disorders* (pp. 454–476). New York: Guilford Press.

Kabat-Zinn, J. (1994). *Wherever you go there you are: Mindfulness meditation in everyday life*. New York: Hyperion.

Karekla, M., & Forsyth, J. P. (2004). A comparison between acceptance enhanced cognitive behavioral and panic control treatment for panic disorder. In S. M. Orsillo (Chair), *Acceptance-based behavioral therapies: New directions in treatment development across the diagnostic spectrum*. Symposium presented at the 38th annual meeting of the Association for Advancement of Behavior Therapy, New Orleans, LA.

Kaspi, S. P., McNally, R. J., & Amir, N. (1995). Cognitive processing of emotional information in posttraumatic stress disorder. *Cognitive Therapy and Research, 19*, 433–444.

Levitt, J. T., Brown, T. A., Orsillo, S. M., & Barlow, D. H. (2004). The effects of acceptance versus suppression of emotion on subjective and psychophysiological response to carbon dioxide challenge in patients with panic disorder. *Behavior Therapy, 35*, 747–766.

Linehan, M. M. (1993a). *cognitive-behavioral treatment of borderline personality disorder*. New York: Guilford Press.

Linehan, M. M. (1993b). *Skills training manual for treating borderline personality disorder*. New York: Guilford Press.

Lundh, L.-G., & Öst, L.-G. (1996). Recognition bias for critical faces in social phobics. *Behaviour Research and Therapy, 34*, 787–794.

Lynch, T. R., Chapman, A. L., Kuo, J. K., Rosenthal, M. Z., & Linehan, M. M. (in press). Mechanisms of change in dialectical behavior therapy: Theoretical and empirical observations. *Journal of Clinical Psychology*.

Marlatt, G. A., & Kristeller, J. L. (1999). Mindfulness and meditation. In W. R. Miller (Ed.), *Integrating spirituality into treatment: Resources for practitioners* (pp. 67–84). Washington, DC: American Psychological Association.

Masuda, A., Hayes, S. C., Sackett, C. F., & Twohig, M. P. (2004). Cognitive defusion and self-relevant negative thoughts: Examining the impact of a ninety year old technique. *Behaviour Research and Therapy, 42*, 477–485.

McNally, R. J. (1995). Automaticity and the anxiety disorders. *Behaviour Research and Therapy, 33*, 747–754.

Mennin, D. S., Heimberg, R. G., Turk, C. L., & Fresco, D. M. (2002). Applying an emotion regulation-framework to integrative approaches to generalized anxiety disorder. *Clinical Psychology: Science and Practice, 9*, 85–90.

Mennin, D. S., Heimberg, R. G., Turk, C. L., & Fresco, D. M. (in press). Preliminary evidence for an emotion dysregulation model of generalized anxiety disorder. *Behaviour Research and Therapy*.

Mowrer, O. H. (1960). *Learning theories and behavior.* New York: Wiley.

Orsillo, S. M., & Batten, S. V. (2005). Acceptance and commitment therapy in the treatment of posttraumatic stress disorder. *Behavior Modification, 29,* 95–129.

Orsillo, S. M., Roemer, L., Block, J., LeJeune, C., & Herbert, J. D. (2004). ACT with anxiety disorders. In S. C. Hayes & K. Strosahl (Eds.), *A practical guide to acceptance and commitment therapy* (pp. 103–132). New York: Springer.

Orsillo, S. M., Roemer, L., Block-Lerner, J., & Tull, M. T. (2004). Acceptance, mindfulness, and cognitive-behavioral therapy: Comparisons, contrasts, and application to anxiety. In S. C. Hayes, M. M. Linehan, & V. M. Follette (Eds.), *Mindfulness, acceptance, and relationships: Expanding the cognitive-behavioral tradition* (pp. 66–95). New York: Guilford Publications, Inc.

Roemer, L., & Orsillo, S. M. (2002). Expanding our conceptualization of and treatment for generalized anxiety disorder: Integrating mindfulness/acceptance-based approaches with existing cognitive-behavioral models. *Clinical Psychology: Science and Practice, 9,* 54–68.

Roemer, L., & Orsillo, S. M. (2004). Acceptance-based behavior therapy for GAD: Preliminary findings from an open trial and a randomized controlled trial. In S. M. Orsillo (Chair), *Acceptance-based behavioral therapies: New directions in treatment development across the diagnostic spectrum.* Symposium presented at the 38th annual meeting of the Association for Advancement of Behavior Therapy, New Orleans, LA.

Salters-Pedneault, K., Tull, M. T., & Roemer, L. (2004). The role of avoidance of emotional material in the anxiety disorders. *Applied and Preventive Psychology, 11,* 95–114.

Schmidt, N. B., Lerew, D. R., & Trakowski, J. H. (1997). Body vigilance in panic disorder: Evaluating attention to bodily perturbations. *Journal of Consulting and Clinical Psychology, 65,* 214–220.

Shafran, R., Thordarson, D. S., & Rachman, S. (1996). Thought–action fusion in obsessive–compulsive disorder. *Journal of Anxiety Disorders, 10,* 379–391.

Singh, N. N., Wahler, R. G., Winton, A. S. W., & Adkins, A. D. (2004). A mindfulness-based treatment of obsessive–compulsive disorder. *Clinical Case Studies, 3,* 275–287.

Tull, M. T. (2005). *A preliminary investigation of emotional avoidance and emotional awareness among a sample of non-treatment seeking panickers.* Unpublished doctoral dissertation, University of Massachusetts, Boston.

Turk, C. L., Heimberg, R. G., Luterek, J. A., Mennin, D. S., & Fresco, D. M. (2005). Emotion dysregulation in generalized anxiety disorder: A comparison with social anxiety disorder. *Cognitive Therapy and Research, 29,* 89–106.

Vasey, M. W., & Borkovec, T. D. (1992). A catastrophizing assessment of worrisome thoughts. *Cognitive Therapy and Research, 16,* 505–520.

Wells, A. (1990). Panic disorder in association with relaxation-induced anxiety: An attentional training approach to treatment. *Behavior Therapy, 21,* 273–280.

Wells, A. (1999). A metacognitive model and therapy for generalized anxiety disorder. *Clinical Psychology and Psychotherapy, 6,* 86–95.

Wells, A., Clark, D. M., Salkovskis, P. M., Ludgate, J., Hackmann, A., & Gelder, M. (1995). Social phobia: The role of in-situation safety behaviors in maintaining anxiety and negative beliefs. *Behavior Therapy, 26,* 153–161.

Wells, A., White, J., & Carter, K. (1997). Attention training: Effects on anxiety and beliefs in panic and social phobia. *Clinical Psychology and Psychotherapy, 4,* 226–232.

Williams, K. E., Chambless, D. L., & Ahrens, A. (1997). Are emotions frightening? An extension of the fear of fear construct. *Behaviour Research and Therapy, 35,* 239–248.

Williams, J., Watts, F. N., MacLeod, C., & Mathews, A. (1988). *Cognitive psychology and emotional disorders.* Chichester, England: Wiley.

Zanarini, M. C., Frankenburg, F. R., Dubo, E. D., Sickel, A. E., Trikha, A., Levin, A., et al. (1998). Axis I comorbidity of borderline personality disorder. *American Journal of Psychiatry, 155,* 1733–1739.

Part III

SPECIFIC POPULATIONS

INTEGRATING ACCEPTANCE AND MINDFULNESS WITH COGNITIVE BEHAVIORAL TREATMENT FOR PANIC DISORDER

Jill T. Levitt and Maria Karekla

It is generally recognized that panic disorder causes functional impairment in those who suffer from it. The diagnosis of panic disorder is related to numerous costs both to the individual and to society at large, such as lost productivity and increased health care utilization (Klerman, Weissman, Oullette, Johnson, & Greenwald, 1991). Fortunately, recent studies illustrate that effective treatment of panic disorder (PD) produces significant medical cost offsets and, most importantly, meaningful improvements in quality of life (Salvador-Carulla, Segui, Fernandez-Cano, & Canet, 1995; Telch, Schmidt, Jaimez, Jacquin, & Harrington, 1995). Thus, effective treatments for PD may not only help patients overcome their anxiety in the short term, but may also help them live more functional lives in the long term. Although traditional cognitive–behavioral treatments (CBT) for PD are moderately effective, dropout rates of 25% and above are common, and, of those offered treatment, only approximately 50% are considered responders at treatment end (e.g., Barlow, Gorman, Shear, & Woods, 2000). Although these numbers are promising, we suggest that the reframing and addition of new techniques drawn from acceptance and mindfulness-based treatments, may decrease dropout rates and enhance the long-term efficacy of traditional CBT for PD. In this chapter we first focus on traditional cognitive–behavioral conceptualizations of PD, and panic control treatment (PCT; Barlow & Craske, 2000), the most widely studied treatment for PD. Next, we describe the limitations of this approach, and we review an alternative conceptualization of PD, the experiential avoidance model. We then describe experimental research supporting the experiential avoidance conceptualization. Following this, we compare and contrast traditional CBT with acceptance-enhanced CBT, a recently developed treatment that integrates acceptance and mindfulness strategies with traditional techniques used in PCT. Finally, we review the implementation of acceptance-enhanced CBT delivered in a group format, and present data from a small randomized trial of acceptance-enhanced CBT as compared with PCT (Karekla, 2004).

DEFINITION AND PREVALENCE

Panic disorder (PD) is an anxiety disorder characterized by recurrent unexpected panic attacks, apprehension about future attacks, or worry about the implications of the attack, and, in the case of PD with agoraphobia, is accompanied by avoidance of situations in which panic attacks are expected to occur (*DSM-IV*; American Psychiatric Association [APA], 1994). A panic attack is a discrete episode of intense fear or discomfort that occurs unexpectedly, and reaches its peak within a period of 10 min. During a panic attack a number of somatic and cognitive symptoms are experienced, which may include racing heart, chest pain, sweating, trembling, shortness of breath, numbing or tingling, fear of dying, and fear of losing control or going crazy. Patients with PD often avoid situations and sensations that have been associated with fear or anxiety. Apprehension or avoidance of situations is termed *agoraphobic avoidance*, whereas avoidance of internal sensations that might trigger panic attacks is often referred to as *interoceptive avoidance* (Barlow, 2002). PD can be diagnosed with and without agoraphobia, although mild agoraphobia is thought to occur in most cases of PD (Brown & Barlow, 2001). Agoraphobia has recently been conceptualized as a coping strategy for dealing with panic attacks, whereby individuals cope with panic attacks by avoiding situations in which they are expected to occur (White & Barlow, 2001). PD with and without agoraphobia typically has a chronic and disabling clinical course (APA, 1994) with low remission and high relapse rates (Keller et al., 1994). Recent epidemiological studies report lifetime prevalence rates of approximately 1.5–3.5% (Eaton, Dryman, & Weissman, 1991; Kessler et al., 1994).

COST OF THE PROBLEM

Panic disorder is associated with significant costs to the individual, including lost productivity, social isolation, decrease in quality of life, and poor health (Klerman et al., 1991; Leon, Portera, & Weissman, 1995; Markowitz, Weissman, Ouellette, Lish, & Klerman, 1989). Individuals with PD have been found to overuse both emergency department and general medical services, as they present with high rates of unexplained cardiac symptoms and dizziness (Beitman, Thomas, & Kushner, 1992; Katon, 1994). In fact, those suffering from PD show the highest rates of emergency medical service utilization for problems with an emotional basis (Rees, Richards, & Smith, 1998). Direct (e.g., hospitalization) and indirect (e.g., work productivity) costs to the health care system are significant (Salvador-Carulla et al., 1995). Individuals suffering from PD also appear more likely to experience adverse workplace outcomes such as work loss due to absenteeism than do nonanxious individuals (DuPont et al., 1996). Patients who have been diagnosed with PD are therefore impaired emotionally, physically, and economically, and this impairment affects not only the individual, but society at large.

CONDITIONING ACCOUNT OF THE ETIOLOGY AND MAINTENANCE OF PD

The most widely researched treatment for PD is PCT (Barlow & Craske, 2000), which is based on Barlow's conditioning theory of the etiology of PD (Barlow, 2002). We will first describe Barlow's conditioning account, and next review the treatment stemming from this model. The conditioning theory of PD originated from the observation that the experience of unexpected panic attacks seems to be relatively common in the general population, and that these attacks rarely progress to PD. Individuals experiencing "nonclinical" panic attacks show little concern over the possibility of experiencing additional attacks. Rather, they typically dismiss the attacks, believing that the panic attack was associated with some trivial and potentially controllable event (Bouton, Mineka, & Barlow, 2001). In contrast, individuals with PD develop anxiety focused on the next potential attack. According to this model, the tendency to fear the next panic attack may occur because of biological factors, fearful cognitions about physical sensations, or the presence of life stress (see Barlow, 2002; Bouton et al., 2001, for reviews). Individuals who develop PD begin to anticipate the next attack with apprehension, and become extremely vigilant for somatic symptoms that might signal the beginning of the next attack. Barlow (2002) noted that during an early panic attack, panic symptoms could be conditioned to internal physiological stimuli reflecting the process of interoceptive conditioning. According to this view, an individual will learn to associate internal bodily sensations that accompany the early onset of a panic attack with the rest of the attack. There is a positive feedback loop that begins with the experience of somatic sensations, and then selective focus of attention to these sensations, followed by conditioned anxiety (as a result of repeated associations between somatic cues and states of panic), which serves to intensify the feared somatic cues (Bouton et al., 2001). Thus, as a result of interoceptive conditioning, modest changes in heart rate or the onset of shallow breathing might become signals that can later trigger a full-blown attack (Barlow, 2002).

EFFICACY OF PSYCHOSOCIAL INTERVENTIONS FOR PD

Since the 1980s, evolving conceptualizations of PD have led to the development of CBT directed specifically at unexpected panic attacks, and the cognitive interpretation of the meaning and consequences of the physical symptoms of panic. PCT is a CBT based on Barlow's conditioning model of the etiology and maintenance of PD. This treatment has been widely studied and has received more research and clinical support than any other therapy for PD. PCT consists of four main components: (1) psychoeducation regarding the nature of anxiety and panic attacks, (2) cognitive restructuring (challenging panic-related anxious thoughts and the misinterpretation of panic-related symptoms), (3) interoceptive exposure (repeated exposure to frightening internal sensations), and (4) situational or in vivo exposure (exposure to feared or avoided situations). Interoceptive and situational exposure both stem directly from Barlow's conditioning model of panic disorder, whereby interoceptive exposure aims to weaken associations between specific bodily cues and panic reactions, and situational exposure aims to weaken relations between panic attacks and avoided situations that occasion such attacks. In contrast, psychoeducation and cognitive restructuring are intended to directly challenge incorrect beliefs about the consequences of panic (see Craske & Barlow, 1994, for a detailed presentation of each component part).

PCT is a 12-session CBT that is classified as an empirically supported treatment for PD by the American Psychological Association Division 12 Task Force on the Promotion and Dissemination of Psychological Procedures (Chambless et al., 1998). Several clinical trials have demonstrated that PCT is efficacious (Barlow, Craske, Cerny, & Klosko, 1989; Barlow et al., 2000; Craske, Brown, & Barlow, 1991; Craske, DeCola, Sachs, Pontillo, 2003; for a review, see Levitt, Hoffman, Grisham, & Barlow, 2001).

The first controlled study of PCT (Barlow et al., 1989) included three treatment conditions (PCT alone, progressive muscle relaxation [PMR] alone, and PCT combined with relaxation) compared to a waitlist control condition. After 12 weekly sessions, 85% of the PCT group and 87% of the combined treatment group were panic-free, compared to 36% of the waitlist group and 60% of the PMR group. The PCT and combined treatment groups evidenced significantly more improvement than the waitlist, whereas the PMR group did not. Subsequent studies have supported the findings presented by Barlow and colleagues, providing additional evidence for the efficacy of individual PCT (e.g., Craske et al., 1991; Klosko, Barlow, Tassinari, & Cerny, 1990).

PCT has also been delivered and tested in group settings. Craske and collegues (2003) examined the efficacy of group PCT delivered in 16 weekly, 90-min sessions. This study compared the efficacy of PCT with and without the addition of in vivo exposure, and found that both conditions were efficacious in the reduction of frequency and severity of panic attacks and related agoraphobic avoidance. At posttreatment, 79% of the sample reported no panic attacks. The majority of this sample was categorized as having moderate to severe agoraphobia at pretreatment (82%), compared to 29% in the moderate to severe range at posttreatment. Telch and colleagues (1993) also found favorable results after eight sessions of group PCT. The results illustrated that 85% of patients in the PCT group and 30% in the waitlist control condition were panic-free at posttreatment. Clinical trials have also examined the efficacy of PCT compared to pharmacological treatments. Klosko and colleagues (1990) reported greater improvement immediately following treatment in patients receiving PCT than in those receiving alprazolam.

The most recent data on the efficacy of PCT are the product of a multicenter clinical trial comparing PCT, imipramine (the pharmacological treatment of choice at the time the study was conducted), and their combination (Barlow et al., 2000). This study entailed a randomized, double-blind placebo design, with a total of 312 patients with PD with and without mild agoraphobia receiving either imipramine, PCT, a pill placebo, or a combination of PCT and medication or PCT and placebo. The main objective of this study was to evaluate whether PCT and drug therapy were each better than placebo, whether either was more effective than the other, and whether the combination of PCT and drug therapy was superior to either treatment administered individually. For all groups, the acute treatment phase consisted of 11 sessions conducted within a 12-week period, which was followed by a maintenance phase comprised six monthly sessions. All treatment was discontinued after the maintenance phase, and patients underwent a follow-up assessment 6 months later. The results of this study indicate that both imipramine and PCT were significantly superior to placebo for the acute treatment phase, and that they were not significantly different from each other after acute treatment or 6 months of maintenance. In addition, the combination of PCT and medication was not superior to either treatment alone at posttreatment. Six months after discontinuation of all treatment, response rates were significantly higher for the PCT plus placebo group and the PCT alone group, than for either the imipramine alone group, or the combination of both active treatments. This was due to a deterioration in treatment gains in those who received imipramine and the combination of imipramine and PCT. The results of this study indicate that PCT is an efficacious treatment for PD, and that it is at least as effective as imipramine in the short term, and seemingly more durable in the long term.

LIMITATIONS OF CURRENT RESEARCH ON COGNITIVE–BEHAVIORAL THERAPY FOR PD

Though much research indicates that PCT is an efficacious treatment for PD, a careful look at the literature suggests that many patients do not respond to PCT (e.g., Barlow et al., 2000), and that relapse after treatment is common (Beck & Zebb, 1994). Using an intent-to-treat analysis, which includes all participants who entered treatment, most studies have found only modest responder rates, ranging from 30 to 50%. For example, Craske et al. (2003) found clinically significant improvement at posttreatment in 32–42% of those who began PCT, whereas Barlow et al. (2000) found intent-to-treat responder rates of 49% for those who began PCT. Twenty-seven percent of those who began the PCT alone condition in the Barlow et al. (2000) study dropped out before completion of the acute phase of treatment. This indicates that over half of those who began PCT either dropped out, or did not respond to treatment.

Additional caveats associated with PCT have been described in the literature. For example, studies investigating the efficacy of PCT have not been consistent with regard to the methodology and outcome measures used. Experimenters utilize different inclusion criteria in treatment outcome studies (e.g., varying degree of panic severity and extent of agoraphobic avoidance) and different criteria for defining treatment success (ranging from decreases in help-seeking behaviors to decreases in panic frequency to decreases in levels of distress). With regard to inclusion criteria, most studies to date enroll individuals with only mild levels of agoraphobia, thus limiting the generalizability of treatment results (see Hofmann &

Spiegel, 1999, for a review). It seems likely that the efficacy of PCT for individuals diagnosed with moderate to severe agoraphobia is lower than that for less avoidant patients.

Studies that utilize stringent criteria for treatment success (e.g., individuals treated no longer experience any panic symptomatology) find lower response rates than those with less stringent criteria. For example, Brown and Barlow (1995) found that when stringent criteria were applied (i.e., recurrence of a panic attack) to 68% of panic-free patients at treatment end, only 40% were classified as being panic-free at 3-month posttreatment. At 24-month follow-up one third of patients classified as "panic-free" had experienced a panic attack in the preceding year, and almost one third had obtained further treatment for PD. These results suggest that relapse after treatment is common and that PCT does not work for all patients, leading some individuals to require additional treatment after undergoing PCT.

Finally, nearly all studies of PCT have involved cross-sectional designs (Hofmann & Spiegel, 1999) and evidence as to the long-term efficacy of treatment (beyond the 2-year period) is lacking. In some studies the number of patients showing clinical improvement decreases from posttreatment to follow-up (White & Barlow, 2001). At present, it is unclear whether treatment gains from PCT will be maintained over longer follow-up periods. More longitudinal research is needed to investigate rates and reasons for relapse, and to better understand whether individual difference factors may contribute to panic remission.

In an attempt to understand relapse rates, some have speculated that forgetfulness might contribute to relapse and thus the inclusion of booster sessions following treatment has been suggested (Tsao & Craske, 2000; Wilson, 1992). In addition, researchers have proposed a variety of modifications to PCT, in part to improve the long-term durability of the treatment. Such modifications include combining PCT with situational exposure, including significant others in treatment, or adding a relapse prevention component to the treatment (see Hofmann & Spiegel, 1999, for a review). Though such modifications may prove to be beneficial, we hypothesize that the integration of acceptance and mindfulness techniques may serve to decrease dropout rates (for reasons that will be explained later in this chapter), and improve short- and long-term efficacy. In addition, because the primary focus of acceptance-based treatments is increasing awareness of all sensations, promoting action despite painful thoughts and feelings, and improving quality of life, we also suggest that studies of acceptance-based treatments include outcome measures that assess such changes, rather than including only measures of panic symptoms as is common in studies of PCT.

EXPERIENTIAL AVOIDANCE AND PD

Before discussing the use of acceptance and mindfulness in the treatment of PD, we first review literature that supports the experiential avoidance conceptualization of the etiology and maintenance of PD. Experiential avoidance is said to occur when a person "is unwilling to remain in contact with particular private experiences (e.g., bodily sensations, emotions, thoughts, memories, behavioral predispositions) and takes steps to alter the form or frequency of these events and the contexts that occasion them" (Hayes, Strosahl, & Wilson, 1999, p. 58). Interoceptive avoidance, or the avoidance of internal sensations that might trigger panic attacks, is one form of experiential avoidance. Experiential avoidance also includes suppression of emotions or thoughts. Experiential avoidance has been suggested to be a fundamental emotion regulation process relevant to panic and other anxiety disorders (Hayes et al., 1999).

At the core of the experiential avoidance conceptualization of anxiety disorders is the view that attempts to directly alter the frequency or intensity of aversive internal experiences can in fact exacerbate such experiences and thereby lead one to feel helpless and out of control (Hayes et al., 1999). According to this conceptualization, individuals who are high in experiential avoidance would be more likely to develop fear and avoidance after having an unexpected panic attack than those who are more accepting of their internal experiences. Experiential avoidance is then maintained and may even escalate to the more severe condition of agoraphobia, because situational avoidance reduces the frequency and intensity of panic attacks in the short term. Panic attacks, and any forms of anxiety, fear, or worry become unwanted internal experiences that further prompt attempts at avoidance, leading to a negative spiral of increased severity of symptoms. In this way, experiential avoidance may contribute to both the etiology and maintenance of PD. In support of this model, there is evidence that individuals with PD with agoraphobia not only avoid public places but also avoid experiencing private events such as thoughts and emotions that are associated with panic (Friman, Hayes, & Wilson, 1998). Similarly, it is evident that patients with PD often avoid engaging in activities that might heighten awareness of internal physical sensations, such as physical exertion (Barlow, 2002).

Research on emotion and thought suppression supports the idea that attempts to reduce the intensity of aversive experience can have a paradoxical effect, and instead increase symptoms. This research has primarily involved nonclinical populations, although it seems likely that repeated attempts to avoid negative thoughts and emotions through the use of suppression could exacerbate psychological symptoms in clinical samples as well. Research in nonclinical samples suggests that efforts to suppress thoughts under mental load can create increased accessibility of the suppressed thought (Wegner & Erber, 1992), intended mood control under mental load can lead to greater accessibility of thoughts relevant to the unwanted mood (Wegner, Erber, & Zanakos, 1993), and intended relaxation under load can promote arousal (Wegner, Broome, & Blumberg, 1997). In addition, the paradoxical effects of thought and emotional suppression have been implicated in cognitive–behavioral models of several psychological disorders (Abramowitz, Tolin, & Street, 2001). Specifically, suppression is believed to contribute to the development or maintenance of depression (Wegner, 1994), generalized anxiety disorder (Becker, Rink, Roth, & Margraf, 1998), obsessive compulsive disorder (Purdon, 2004), specific phobias (Thorpe & Salkovskis, 1997), and posttraumatic stress disorder (Ehlers & Steil, 1995). In addition, related research on coping skills indicates that greater use of avoidant coping (including various experiential avoidance strategies) is related to greater symptoms of depression (DeGenova, Patton, Jurich, & MacDermid, 1994), and increased symptoms related to childhood sexual abuse (Leitenberg, Greenwald, & Cado, 1992). However, it is important to note that methodological differences in thought suppression paradigms and varying measures of coping have led to inconsistent results in the literature.

A number of recent studies have examined the impact of experiential avoidance on response to a carbon dioxide (CO_2) challenge in nonclinical samples. The CO_2 challenge is a laboratory paradigm that induces panic symptoms in patients with PD, and provides an experimental paradigm in which hypotheses regarding the relationship between experiential avoidance and panic responses can be tested. In one study, individuals high in experiential avoidance endorsed more panic symptoms, more severe cognitive symptoms, and more fear and uncontrollability than their less avoidant counterparts (Karekla, Forsyth, & Kelly, in press). A second study found that participants classified as high in emotional avoidance reported significantly lower efficacy in terms of their perceived ability to regulate their emotional responses during a CO_2 challenge (Feldner, Zvolensky, Eifert, & Spira, 2003). The experiential avoidance group also reported significantly greater levels of anxiety in response to the challenge, and significantly greater levels of displeasure relative to the low emotional avoidance group. Finally, the high emotional avoidance group reported greater emotional dyscontrol than low emotional avoidance participants during the CO_2 challenge (Feldner et al., 2003). These studies indicate that individuals who have a general tendency to avoid internal experiences are more distressed and feel more out of control during a CO_2 challenge than those who have a tendency to be more accepting of their internal experience.

ACCEPTANCE AND PD

Building on the experiential avoidance conceptualization of the etiology and maintenance of psychopathology, Hayes et al. (1999) have designed a treatment entitled "acceptance and commitment therapy" (ACT), which is based on the idea that acceptance of internal experiences is an effective alternative approach to coping with thoughts and feelings. ACT and other acceptance and mindfulness-based approaches challenge the idea that internal experiences need to be regulated in order for clinical improvement to occur, and, in contrast, suggest that attempts at internal control may be the problem, rather than the solution. Mindfulness, or the "art of conscious living," is a form of acceptance that is used to facilitate awareness, rather than avoidance (Kabat-Zinn, 1994). In ACT and other acceptance and mindfulness-based approaches, patients are taught to feel emotions and bodily sensations fully and without avoidance, and to focus on behavior change in valued directions, rather than the modification of thoughts and feelings. The explicit goal of acceptance-based treatments is to reduce attempts at internal control and experiential avoidance, while increasing behavioral control and willingness to experience a range of emotions. Although symptom reduction is expected to occur over the long term, a significant improvement in quality of life is the explicit goal of this treatment. This is in contrast to many CBTs in which the explicit goal is to directly reduce the frequency and intensity of panic attacks.

Recent experimental research provides support for the potential utility of acceptance as an alternative to suppression or emotional avoidance. Eifert and Heffner (2003) compared a brief acceptance intervention to breathing retraining in a sample of undergraduates with high anxiety sensitivity in the context of a CO_2 challenge. Individuals in the acceptance group exhibited less avoidance behavior, and reported less intense fear and fewer catastrophic thoughts than those in the breathing retraining and no-instruction conditions in response to the CO_2 challenge. The results indicate that a brief acceptance intervention may attenuate anxious responding in a nonclinical population, and may facilitate willingness to engage in future unpleasant interoceptive tasks. Only one experimental study has been conducted in a clinical sample of patients with panic disorder (Levitt, Brown, Orsillo, & Barlow, 2004). Sixty patients with PD were randomly assigned to one of three conditions: a 10-min audiotape describing one of two potential responses to panic-related symptoms (acceptance or suppression) or a neutral narrative (control group) prior to undergoing a 15-min 5.5% CO_2 challenge. The acceptance group was significantly less anxious and less avoidant than the suppression or control groups in terms of subjective anxiety during the task and willingness to participate in a second challenge. In addition, greater use of suppression was related to more subjective anxiety during the challenge, whereas greater use of acceptance was related to more willingness to participate in a second challenge. The results of both of these studies suggest that acceptance may be a useful intervention for reducing subjective anxiety and avoidance in patients with PD.

As a way of improving treatment effectiveness for PD, it may be beneficial to explore treatments that focus on reducing the key dysfunctional elements of the disorder, namely experiential avoidance and excessive attempts to control thoughts and feelings. Additionally, verbal-linguistic functions may underlie experiential avoidance in PD. One common example of this is getting caught up in verbal rules such as "I cannot go to the mall unless my anxiety disappears," although there is nothing inherent in feeling anxious that prevents anyone from entering a mall (this has been described in the acceptance literature as cognitive fusion and disjunction with environmental contingencies; Hayes et al., 1999). In turn, these processes appear to be closely related to difficulties associated with rule-governed behavior (i.e., behavior controlled by verbal antecedents; see Hayes et al., 1999), again suggesting that ACT and other acceptance and mindfulness-based treatments may be beneficial in the treatment of PD. Further, the future-oriented nature of anxiety and the common fear of impending danger that characterizes PD both suggest that training in present-focused mindful awareness may provide a useful alternative way of responding. This alternative response may lead to acceptance of internal sensations for what they are, and a realization of the unworkability of the control agenda. Finally, a focus on valued living and desired action in accordance with stated goals is likely to increase functional behaviors and quality of life. The experiential avoidance conceptualization of PD, and the preliminary evidence suggesting that acceptance may be a useful alternative, has led us to attempt to integrate some of the effective elements of PCT with elements of mindfulness and acceptance-based treatments (specifically ACT), in the treatment of PD with and without agoraphobia.

ACCEPTANCE-BASED APPROACHES VERSUS TRADITIONAL CBT

As indicated above, traditional CBT and acceptance-based interventions are based on different conceptualizations of psychopathology. Although both types of treatments recognize the important role that cognitions and private experiences play in the development and maintenance of psychopathology, one of the main differences is the mechanism used to achieve change. PCT focuses on directly altering the content of private experiences (e.g., challenging anxious thoughts), whereas ACT and other acceptance-based treatments seek to alter the broader context in which thoughts and feelings are experienced (e.g., reduce experiential avoidance/increase willingness to experience emotions). Unlike PCT, acceptance-based approaches are not set within a mastery and control framework, but rather an acceptance and mastery of experiencing framework. Furthermore, the experiential avoidance conceptualization posits that psychopathology results from avoidance and unsuccessful control strategies over unwanted thoughts and emotions. From this perspective, PCT may be less efficacious in the long term, as it plays into the very system that creates and maintains symptoms (i.e., "I need to be better at controlling my thoughts and feelings and the therapist is going to teach me better ways to do just that"). Thus, acceptance-based interventions regard PCT's focus on symptom reduction as counterproductive. Instead, acceptance-based treatments offer an alterative whereby patients are taught to become better at experiencing the full range of thoughts and emotions, while also teaching clients to make commitments to valued life activities.

PCT, in accordance with the cognitive model of panic, holds that faulty cognitions are an important maintaining factor of this disorder, and thus PCT targets such cognitions during treatment (Barlow & Craske, 2000). In contrast, acceptance-based treatments assume that excessive attempts to control negative internal events are a risk factor leading to disorders such as PD. Emphasis is therefore placed on accepting the inevitability of life events, distinguishing between feelings and actions, and living life according to one's values despite unwanted thoughts and emotions. Additionally, ACT is based on the idea that emotional avoidance may be a product of confusing thoughts with real events and thus taking too literally beliefs about the self and/or the world. Thus, in ACT, attempts are made to teach skills such as mindfulness, so as to increase willingness to experience negative emotions and build greater awareness of the self, while also helping the client to distinguish between evaluative thoughts, thoughts that tend to distort direct experience, and descriptive thoughts of direct experiences. Finally, in acceptance-based treatments, willingness to experience uncomfortable thoughts and feelings is encouraged in order to facilitate living life according to one's values.

The use of an acceptance and mindfulness approach in the treatment of PD, and other anxiety disorders, makes conceptual sense. Though traditional CBT and acceptance-based approaches may view the development of psychopathology from different perspectives, they both seek to initiate behavior change in clients. Furthermore, both types of treatments aim to alter the way a suffering individual views the world and their own problems and both employ elements of exposure in achieving the goal of teaching a person not to misinterpret their physical and emotional sensations as something other than what they are. Therefore, the two treatments do not present entirely conflicting approaches, but instead have numerous common components. For example, CBT and acceptance-based approaches may ultimately operate via similar mechanisms such as interoceptive and situational exposure.

PRACTICAL SUGGESTIONS FOR INTEGRATING ACCEPTANCE AND MINDFULNESS INTO THE TREATMENT OF PD

The acceptance-enhanced CBT approach that we propose here retains the following active treatment elements from the original PCT: psychoeducation, relaxation, and exposure, all presented within an acceptance-based context and not a mastery and control-focused context as in PCT. The psychoeducation component introduces a model of anxiety and panic, including the purpose and function of anxiety and panic, the different components of anxious responding, the costs of anxiety, the maintaining effects of avoidance, the utility of early cue detection, and difficulties of emotional control. Relaxation, presented as an alternative to anxious responding, includes multiple forms of relaxation such as progressive muscle relaxation and diaphragmatic breathing but also incorporates mindfulness exercises assumed to aid in loosening patterns of habitual responding and increasing present-moment focus. Perhaps the most effective component of PCT is exposure to interoceptive and exteroceptive cues using traditional techniques such as symptom induction exercises. In fact, exposure has repeatedly been found to be one of the key elements of successful treatment for all anxiety disorders (Barlow, 2002; Fava, Zielezny, Savron, & Grandi, 1995; Jansson, Jerremalm, & Ost, 1986; Jansson & Ost, 1982; O'Brien & Barlow, 1984). Gould, Otto, and Pollack (1995) in a large meta-analysis of treatment outcome studies for PD reported an average effect size of 0.53 for exposure; the largest effect size yielded for any treatment component, including pharmacotherapy. Rather than presenting exposure with a habituation rationale, in the acceptance-enhanced treatment model, exposure is conducted for the purpose of living life in accordance with one's own values despite feelings of anxiety, and taking specific behavioral actions consistent with such values.

Additional elements borrowed from ACT and other mindfulness-based treatments are incorporated throughout the proposed acceptance-enhanced model, such as mindfulness techniques to heighten awareness of patterns of anxious responding. A number of specific ACT elements and techniques are integrated into this approach and we will mention these techniques by name (the interested reader is referred to Hayes et al., 1999, for a full description of the ACT terminology and techniques). The acceptance-enhanced treatment we have developed includes elements from ACT such as the presentation of willingness as an alternative to control, and cognitive defusion and deliteralization of language via presentation of how to disrupt troublesome language practices.

To illustrate this acceptance-enhanced CBT approach to PD we now present a session-by-session outline of components presented. We have chosen to retain elements of PCT that focus on reducing experiential avoidance (e.g., interoceptive and situational exposure), but have eliminated elements that are not consistent with an acceptance-based approach such as cognitive restructuring. Given that this integrated CBT and acceptance approach was originally designed to be compared to group PCT, we have attempted to sustain a parallel structure (equal session frequency and length) between the two treatments. The approach presented here is just one possible way of integrating acceptance with current CBT practices and it is likely that many other effective variations can be developed. The acceptance-enhanced CBT we propose was developed for use in a group format and consists of ten 90-min weekly group sessions. However, we are currently developing a similar treatment for use in individual format that will consist of twelve 60-min weekly individual sessions. In this chapter we describe the 10-session 90-min group acceptance-enhanced CBT.

Session 1 of acceptance-enhanced CBT begins similarly to PCT with an overview of treatment, where the model, purpose, and the different components of anxiety and panic are discussed. The functions and costs of anxiety are also emphasized. Next, clients are asked to present prior coping attempts used to control or decrease their anxiety, both successful and unsuccessful. The focus is on "creative hopelessness," or the therapist's creative use of the hopeless state induced in clients when they start to see that they have tried everything that was logical to attempt to get rid of their problems, but the problems remain. The therapist uses this state to encourage the client to abandon the "get rid of symptoms" agenda, and to try a new approach to coping with unwanted internal experience. Next, the importance of self-monitoring of panic and anxiety are discussed and clients are provided with self-monitoring forms and are taught how to complete these forms.

Session 2 presents more on psychoeducation regarding the nature of anxiety and panic in a manner similar to that presented in PCT, and specifically discusses the connection between panic-related cognitions, behaviors, and physiological reactions. Next, clients are presented with a breathing/mindfulness exercise, as a way of centering themselves and becoming aware of their internal and external surroundings. Therefore, breathing in acceptance-enhanced CBT is used as a mindfulness technique and an exposure exercise (rather than an attempt to reduce anxiety), because through breathing clients are asked to focus on and explore their internal sensations, a process that individuals suffering from PD tend to avoid at all costs.

The next session reviews diaphragmatic breathing and then discusses the function of emotions. Following this, the therapist introduces the rationale for PMR, again with a focus on using this technique in order to increase awareness of internal sensations and as a way of accepting any and all sensations. Clients are encouraged to use the exercise to aid in becoming more aware of the ways they struggle with their "internal world" and what this struggle means for them. The eight-muscle group PMR is completed in the session and following the exercise the clients' reactions are reviewed and any problems or difficulties are addressed. Next, clients are asked to describe examples of failed attempts to control emotions such as anxiety (e.g., distraction, avoidance, drinking alcohol). An emphasis is placed on recognizing how previous efforts to reduce symptoms have really been efforts aimed at controlling private events. In addition, the futility of attempts to control internal experience is reviewed. Metaphors, such as the "Polygraph Metaphor," which illustrate that the harder one tries to "not feel anxious" the more anxious one feels, are used. Metaphors are provided as aids in understanding concepts that are hard to describe in ordinary language (Lieb & Kanofsky, 2003). Clients are provided with a recording of the PMR exercise to use for practice during the upcoming week.

After reviewing the PMR homework and concepts presented in the previous session, Session 4 introduces the four-muscle group PMR and this is practiced in session, again with an emphasis placed on experiencing emotions and as a way to refocus and become aware of one's surroundings. In addition, acceptance of unwanted experience and willingness to engage in situations despite anxiety are presented as an alternative to control. Cognitive defusion (separating oneself from one's thoughts), deliteralization of language (learning to not take one's thoughts so literally), and willingness to enter previously avoided situations and feel previously avoided feelings as the goal of deliteralization are presented (see Hayes et al., 1999). In this session, patients learn strategies to disrupt troublesome language, so that they are less likely to take their own thoughts as fact. Again, patients are provided with monitoring forms and are asked to practice mindful relaxation during the upcoming week.

The emphasis of Session 5 is on valued directions, and each person is encouraged to explore his or her own values. The discussion includes teaching clients how values create a sense of life meaning and direction. Also, individuals are encouraged to clarify their values and distinguish between choice and judgment. Furthermore, clients are asked to define how their values suggest specific life goals, and to list the actions needed to accomplish these goals. The valued directions are used to present the rationale for exposure and the importance of facing one's fears. For instance, a patient might be encouraged to face her fear of going to the mall not for the purpose of habituation, but rather because she wants to spend more time with her children, and avoiding the mall interferes with these relationships (i.e., her stated value is to be a better parent). Symptom induction exercises are presented as a form of interoceptive exposure, and patients are encouraged to experience feared sensations in order to move in the direction of their stated values. Like PMR, interoceptive exposure is also an experiential exercise, designed to increase contact with, and acceptance of, uncomfortable sensations.

In Session 6, interoceptive exposure exercises are carried out, and the concepts of acceptance, willingness, and valued directions are strongly emphasized to facilitate exposure. Clients rank different exercises (e.g., breathing through a straw to induce the symptom of lightheadedness) on the basis of the amount of fear experienced and formulate their fear hierarchy to be used for exposure. Again, exposure is encouraged in order to increase contact with physical sensations so that patients can engage in meaningful life activities. The therapist also addresses any problems or difficulties the clients experience during the exercises. The homework for this session involves practicing these exercises at home.

After reviewing the valued directions clients identified in previous sessions, Session 7 encourages clients to take specific actions consistent with these values and problem solve any difficulties, with an emphasis on understanding the "hooks" that pull the client out of a valued process of living. Next, techniques and strategies consistent with each person's valued directions are presented, and clients are encouraged to face their fears. Dealing with frightening memories of panic attacks is also discussed and a mindfulness and deliteralization exercise (such as "The Observer Exercise") is used to aid each client in coming into contact with and facing these frightening memories. Specifically, "The Observer Exercise" aims to have a client become an objective observer of his or her thoughts and feelings, as he or she is guided through an exercise of visualizing certain experiences in his or her life, like his or her first panic attack. Practicing exposure outside of the therapy sessions constitutes the homework for Session 7.

During Session 8, the importance of facing additional fears such as a being alone and away from home (i.e., agoraphobic avoidance) is discussed within a framework consistent with each individual's stated values. Session 8 also includes a review of concepts learned during the treatment to date.

Session 9 comprises a discussion about different types of anxiety medications, how they work, and proper ways to stop them if a person chooses to do so. Finally, in this session the issue of treatment termination is explored (see also Barlow & Craske, 2000).

In the final session the clients are encouraged to recognize their accomplishments and evaluate their progress. Clients are asked to plan for the future by deciding on their next steps, making a commitment to continuing to face their fears and move toward their valued directions, and discussing how to maintain progress, and deal with high-risk situations in the future.

Overall, combining notions of acceptance and mindfulness with current cognitive–behavioral practices for treating PD appears to make conceptual sense for this disorder. On the basis of research supporting the efficacy of PCT, this acceptance-enhanced approach retains several of the active and effective treatment components of PCT and builds on this to de-emphasize notions of experiential control and at the same time emphasize committed action directed by the person's values. The approach presented here is one possible way of integrating the two approaches and it is likely that there are other variations. It is not clear yet whether this approach will offer benefits beyond those found with the traditional approach; however, some evidence appears to support the efficacy of the proposed treatment for PD.

EVIDENCE FOR THE POTENTIAL EFFICACY OF ACCEPTANCE-ENHANCED CBT

As mentioned earlier, most evidence for the possible efficacy of an acceptance-based approach to treating PD is derived from analog studies, which provide preliminary support for the conceptual basis of integrating notions of acceptance and mindfulness into the treatment of PD (e.g., Eifert & Heffner, 2003; Feldner et al., 2003; Karekla et al., in press; Levitt et al., 2004). Some outcome studies and small scale randomized clinical trials for a variety of anxiety conditions have also been promising (e.g., Block, 2002; Orsillo, Roemer, & Barlow, 2003).

To date, the aforementioned acceptance-enhanced CBT approach to PD has been tested in only one modest randomized controlled clinical trial

(Karekla, 2004). This study aimed to examine the efficacy of the acceptance-enhanced CBT as compared to PCT alone for the treatment of individuals suffering from PD. Twenty-two individuals (17 women; ages 18–65) with a primary diagnosis of PD were enrolled in the study. Of them 10 were randomly assigned to the PCT group and 12 were assigned to the acceptance-enhanced CBT group. Treatment was carried out in a group format of approximately 5–6 individuals in each group and followed the treatment outline presented above. Fourteen individuals completed the full 10 weeks of the treatment (6 in PCT and 8 in acceptance-enhanced CBT). Preliminary results support the efficacy of this approach.

This study utilized both traditional symptom reduction measures (so as to enable comparisons between the results of this study and previous findings from the literature on panic treatment) and acceptance process measures, and a measure of quality of life. Participants in both conditions evidenced significant decreases in self-reported general distress, trait anxiety, avoidance, and depression, as assessed by the State Trait Anxiety Inventory (STAI-T; Spielberger, Gorsuch, Lushene, Vagg, & Jacobs, 1983), Acceptance and Action Questionnaire (AAQ; Hayes et al., 2004), Automatic Thoughts Questionnaire (ATQ; Hollon & Kendall, 1980), and Beck Depression Inventory (BDI; Beck, Rush, Shaw, & Emery, 1979) from pretreatment to posttreatment. Similarly, participants in both groups reported significantly lower levels of anxiety sensitivity, agoraphobic cognitions, panic rates, and panic severity as assessed by the Anxiety Sensitivity Inventory (ASI; Reiss, Peterson, Gursky, & McNally, 1986; Peterson & Reiss, 1992), Agoraphobic Cognitions Questionnaire (ACQ; Chambless, Caputo, Bright, & Gallagher, 1984), Panic and Agoraphobia Scale (Bandelow, 1999), and Panic Disorder Severity Scale (PDSS; Shear et al., 1992) from pretreatment to posttreatment. Additionally, some parameters of participants' reported quality of life (SF-36 Health Survey; Stewart, Hays, & Ware, 1988) and specifically mental health and social functioning significantly increased across assessment time points for both conditions. Further, weekly ratings of anxiety of each individual's five worst fears was found to decrease across the 10 weeks, whereas weekly ratings of willingness to enter each of the five most feared and avoided situations increased across the duration of treatment. However, no differences in the aforementioned measures were found between the two groups, suggesting that both treatments resulted in similar clinical benefits at posttreatment. A 6-month follow-up is currently under way. Given that this treatment did not specifically target decreases in rates and severity of anxiety and panic but instead increases in a person's life and activity repertoire in accordance with their stated values, it was hypothesized that clinical benefits from the acceptance-enhanced condition would become more evident at the follow-up points. In addition, the small sample size in the current study is related to decreased power to detect significant differences between the two treatment groups.

One area where differences between groups were detected was in the pattern, but not the rate, of treatment attrition (4 participants dropped out of each group). The majority of individuals in the PCT condition dropped out of treatment at Session 6 following the introduction of the exposure component of treatment. Such a pattern was not evident in the acceptance-enhanced condition where no individuals dropped out at Session 6 and the pattern of dropout was dispersed evenly across treatment sessions. Consistent with an acceptance-based conceptualization, it may be the case that presenting an acceptance and values-laden rationale better prepares individuals for engaging in exposure. On a cautionary note, the results presented here are preliminary and resulted from a modest clinical trial suffering from limited power and should therefore be interpreted with caution. Further research utilizing this approach is warranted prior to making any conclusive statements as to the efficacy of this approach. These results, however, are overall promising and present preliminary support for the efficacy of acceptance-enhanced CBT in the treatment of PD.

In summary, although there is substantial evidence to support the efficacy of CBT for PD, there is also much room for improvement. Acceptance-based theories and therapies are extremely relevant to the diagnosis of PD, and they hold promise in their ability to enhance the efficacy of traditional CBT. Although research on the application of acceptance-enhanced CBT for PD is only beginning, preliminary research suggests that this treatment has the potential to bring about clinically meaningful changes in quality of life. We hypothesize that acceptance-based interventions may improve participant engagement in interoceptive and situational exposure, and in this way acceptance-based interventions may also serve to decrease dropout rates, and improve traditional measures of treatment outcome (e.g., agoraphobic avoidance). Additional randomized controlled trials are needed in order to further examine whether acceptance and mindfulness interventions do in fact enhance CBT, and laboratory studies focused on mechanisms of action are also needed in order to better articulate acceptance and mindfulness processes and their relation to other behavioral processes such as habituation and extinction. Although this area of research is only in its infancy, the integration of acceptance and mindfulness techniques with traditional CBT holds potential for further improving the lives of those who suffer from PD.

REFERENCES

Abromowitz, J. S., Tolin, D. F., & Street, G. P. (2001). Paradoxical effects of thought suppression: A meta-analysis of controlled studies. *Clinical Psychology Review, 21*, 683–703.

American Psychiatric Association. (1994). *Diagnostic and statistical manual of mental disorders* (4th ed.). Washington, DC: Author.

Bandelow, B. (1999). *Panic and Agoraphobia Scale (PAS)*. Seattle, WA: Hogrefe & Huber Publishers.

Barlow, D. H. (2002). *Anxiety and its disorders: The nature and treatment of anxiety and panic* (2nd ed.). New York: Guilford.

Barlow, D. H., & Craske, M. G. (2000). *Mastery of your anxiety and panic: Client workbook for anxiety and panic*. San Antonio, TX: Graywind Psychological Corporation.

Barlow, D. H., Craske, M. G., Cerny, J. A., & Klosko, J. S. (1989). Behavioral treatment of panic disorder. *Behavior Therapy, 20*, 261–282.

Barlow, D. H., Gorman, J. M., Shear, M. K., & Woods, S. W. (2000). Cognitive–behavioral therapy, imipramine, or their combination for panic disorder: A randomized controlled trial. *Journal of the American Medical Association, 283*, 2529–2536.

Beck, A. T., Rush, A. J., Shaw, B. F., & Emery, G. (1979). *Cognitive therapy of depression*. New York: Guilford.

Beck, J. G., & Zebb, B. J. (1994). Behavioural assessment and treatment of panic disorder: Current status, future directions. *Behavior Therapy, 25*, 581–611.

Becker, E. S., Rink, M., Roth, W. T., & Margraf, J. (1998). Don't worry and beware of white bears: Thought suppression in anxiety patients. *Journal of Anxiety Disorders, 12*, 39–55.

Beitman, B. D., Thomas, A. M., & Kushner, M. G. (1992). Panic disorder in the families of patients with normal coronary arteries and non-fear panic disorder. *Behaviour Research and Therapy, 30*, 403–406.

Block, J. A. (2002). *Acceptance or change of private experiences: A comparative analysis in college students with a fear of public speaking*. Doctoral dissertation. University at Albany, State University of New York.

Bouton, M. E., Mineka, S., & Barlow, D. H. (2001). A modern learning theory perspective on the etiology of panic disorder. *Psychological Review, 108*, 4–32.

Brown, T. A., & Barlow, D. H. (1995). Long-term outcome in cognitive–behavioral treatment of panic disorder: Clinical predictors and alternative strategies for assessment. *Journal of Consulting and Clinical Psychology, 63*, 754–765.

Brown, T. A., & Barlow, D. H. (2001). Classification of anxiety and mood disorders. In D. H. Barlow (Ed.), *Anxiety and its disorders: The nature and treatment of anxiety and panic*. New York: Guilford.

Chambless, D. L., Baker, M. J., Baucom, D. H., Beutler, L., Calhoun, K. S., Crits-Cristoph, P., et al. (1998). Update on empirically validated therapies, II. *The Clinical Psychologist, 51*, 3–16.

Chambless, D. L., Caputo, G. C., Bright, P., & Gallagher, R. (1984). Assessment of 'fear of fear' in agoraphobics: The Body Sensations Questionnaire and the Agoraphobic Cognitions Questionnaire. *Journal of Consulting and Clinical Psychology, 52,* 1090–1097.

Craske, M. G., & Barlow, D. H. (1994). Panic disorder and agoraphobia. In D. H. Barlow (Ed.), *Clinical Handbook of Psychological Disorders.* New York: Guilford.

Craske, M. G., Brown, T. A., & Barlow, D. H. (1991). Behavioral treatment of panic disorder: A two-year follow-up. *Behavior Therapy, 22,* 289–304.

Craske, M. G., DeCola, J. P., Sachs, A. D., & Pontillo, D. C. (2003). Panic control treatment for agoraphobia. *Journal of Anxiety Disorders, 17,* 321–333.

DeGenova, M. K., Patton, D. M., Jurich, J. A., & MacDermid, S. M. (1994). Ways of coping among HIV-infected individuals. *Journal of Social Psychology, 134,* 655–663.

DuPont, R. L., Rice, D. P., Miller, L. S., Shiraki, S. S., Rowland, C. R., & Harwood, H. J. (1996). Economic costs of anxiety disorders. *Anxiety, 2,* 167–172.

Eaton, W. W., Dryman, A., & Weissman, M. M. (1991). Panic and phobia. In L. N. Robins & D. A. Regier (Eds.), *Psychiatric disorders in America: The epidemiological catchment area study.* New York: Free Press.

Ehlers, A., & Steil, R. (1995). Maintenance of intrusive thoughts in posttraumatic stress disorder: A cognitive approach. *Behavioural and Cognitive Psychotherapy, 23,* 217–249.

Eifert, G. H., & Heffner, M. (2003). The effects of acceptance versus control contexts on avoidance of panic-relates symptoms. *Journal of Behavior Therapy and Experimental Psychiatry, 34,* 293–312.

Fava, G. A., Zielezny, M., Savron, G., & Grandi, S. (1995). Long-term effects of behavioral treatment for panic disorder and agoraphobia. *British Journal of Psychiatry, 166,* 87–92.

Feldner, M.T., Zvolensky, M.J., Eifert, G.H., & Spira, A.P. (2003). Emotional avoidance: An experimental test of individual differences and response suppression using biological challenge. *Behaviour Research and Therapy, 41,* 403–411.

Friman, P. C., Hayes, S. C., & Wilson, K. G. (1998). Why behavior analysts should study emotion: The example of anxiety. *Journal of Applied Behavior Analysis, 31,* 137–156.

Gould, R. A., Otto, M. W., & Pollack, M. H. (1995). A meta-analysis of treatment outcome for panic disorder. *Clinical Psychology Review, 15,* 819–844.

Hayes, S. C., Strosahl, K. D., & Wilson, K. G. (1999). *Acceptance and commitment therapy: An experiential approach to behavior change.* New York: Guilford.

Hayes, S. C., Strosahl, K. D., Wilson, K. G., Bissett, R. T., Pistorello, J., Toarmino, D., et al. (2004). Measuring experiential avoidance: A preliminary test of a working model. *The Psychological Record, 54,* 553–578.

Hofmann, S. G., & Spiegel, D. A. (1999). Panic control treatment and its applications. *Journal of Psychotherapy Practice and Research, 8,* 3–11.

Hollon, S. D., & Kendall, P. C. (1980). Cognitive self-statements in depression: Development of an automatic thoughts questionnaire. *Cognitive Therapy and Research, 4,* 383–395.

Jansson, L., Jerremalm, A., & Ost, L. G. (1985). Applied relaxation in the treatment of agoraphobia: Two experimental case studies. *Scandinavian Journal of Behaviour Therapy, 14*(4), 169–176.

Jansson, L., & Ost, L. G. (1982). Behavioral treatments of agoraphobia: An evaluative review. *Clinical Psychology Review, 2*, 311–336.

Kabat-Zinn, J. (1994). *Wherever you go there you are.* New York: Hyperion.

Karekla, M. (2004). *A comparison between acceptance enhanced cognitive behavioral and panic control treatment for panic disorder.* Doctoral dissertation. University at Albany, State University of New York.

Karekla, M., Forsyth, J. P., & Kelly, M. (2004). Emotional avoidance and panicogenic responding to a biological challenge procedure. *Behavior Therapy, 35*(4), 725–746.

Katon, W. (1994). Primary care-psychiatry panic disorder management module. In: B. E. Wolfe & J. D. Maser (Eds.), *Treatment of panic disorder: A consensus development conference* (pp. 4–56). Washington, DC: American Psychiatry Press.

Keller, M. B., Yonkers, K. A., Warshaw, M. G., Pratt, L. A., Golan, J., Mathews, A. O., et al. (1994). Remission and relapse in subjects with panic disorder and agoraphobia: A prospective short interval naturalistic follow-up. *Journal of Nervous and Mental Disorders, 182*, 290–296.

Kessler, R. C., McGonagle, K. A., Zhao, S., Nelson C. B., Hughes, M., Eshleman, S., et al. (1994). Lifetime and 12-month prevalence of DSM-III-R psychiatric disorders in the United States: Results from the National Comorbidity Survey. *Archives of General Psychiatry, 51*, 8–19.

Klerman, G. L., Weissman, M., Ouellette, R., Johnson, J., & Greenwald, S. (1991). Panic attacks in the community: Social morbidity and health care utilization. *Journal of the American Medical Association, 265*, 742–746.

Klosko, J. S., Barlow, D. H., Tassinari, R., & Cerny, J. A. (1990). A comparison of alprazolam and behavior therapy in treatment of panic disorder. *Journal of Consulting and Clinical Psychology, 58*, 77–84.

Leitenberg, H., Greenwald, E., & Cado, S. (1992). A retrospective study of long-term methods of coping with having been sexually abused during childhood. *Child Abuse and Neglect, 16*, 399–407.

Leon, A. C., Portera, L., & Weissman, M. M. (1995). The social costs of anxiety disorders. *British Journal of Psychiatry, 166*(Suppl. 27), 19–22.

Levitt, J. T., Brown, T. A., Orsillo, S. M., & Barlow, D. H. (2004). The effects of acceptance versus suppression of emotion on subjective and psychophysiological response to carbon dioxide challenge in patients with panic disorder. *Behavior Therapy, 35*, 747–766.

Levitt, J. T., Hoffman, E. C., Grisham, J. R., & Barlow, D. H. (2001). Empirically supported treatments for panic disorder. *Psychiatric Annals, 31*, 478–487.

Lieb, R. J., & Kanofsky, S. (2003). Towards a constructionist control mastery theory: An integratioln with narrative therapy. *Psychotherapy Theory, Research, Practice, and Training, 40*(3), 187–202.

Markowitz, J. S., Weissman, M. M., Ouellette, R., Lish, J. D., & Klerman, G. L. (1989). Quality of life in panic disorder. *Archives of General Psychiatry, 46*, 984–992.

O'Brien, G. T., & Barlow, D. H. (1984). Agoraphobia. In S. M. Turner (Ed.), *Behavioral treatment of anxiety disorders*. New York: Plenum.

Orsillo, S. M., Roemer, L., & Barlow, D. H. (2003). Integrating acceptance and mindfulness into existing cognitive–behavioral treatment for GAD: A case study. *Cognitive and Behavioral Practice, 10*, 223–230.

Peterson, R. A., & Reiss, S. (1992). *Anxiety sensitivity index manual* (2nd ed.). Worthington, OH: International Diagnostic Systems.

Purdon, C. (2004). Empirical investigations of thought suppression in OCD. *Journal of Behavior Therapy and Experimental Psychiatry, 35*, 121–136.

Rees, C. S., Richards, J. C., & Smith, L. M. (1998). Medical utilization and costs in panic disorder: A comparison with social phobia. *Journal of Anxiety Disorders, 12*, 421–435.

Reiss, S., Peterson, R. A., Gursky, D. M., & McNally, R. J. (1986). Anxiety sensitivity, anxiety frequency and the predictions of fearfulness. *Behaviour Research and Therapy, 24*, 1–8.

Salvador-Carulla, L., Segui, J., Fernandez-Cano, P., & Canet, J. (1995). Costs and offset effects in panic disorders. *British Journal of Psychiatry, 166*(Suppl. 27), 23–28.

Shear, M. K., Brown, T. A., Sholomskas, D. E., Barlow, D. H., Gorman, J. M., Woods, S. W., et al. (1992). *Panic Disorder Severity Scale (PDSS)*. Pittsburgh, PA: Department of Psychiatry, University of Pittsburg School of Medicine.

Spielberger, C. D., Gorsuch, R. L., Lushene, R. E., Vagg, P. R., & Jacobs, G. A. (1983). *Manual for the State-Trait Anxiety Inventory (Form Y)*. Palo Alto, CA: Consulting Psychologists Press.

Stewart, A. L., Hays, R. D., & Ware, J. E. (1988). The MOS short-form general health survey: Reliability and validity in a patient population. *Medical Care, 26*, 724–735.

Telch, M. J., Lucas, J. A., Schmidt, N. B., Hanna, H. H., Jaimez, T. S., Lucas, R. A. (1993). Group cognitive–behavioral treatment of panic disorder, *Behaviour Research and Therapy, 31*, 279–287.

Telch, M. J., Schmidt, N. B., Jaimez, T. L., Jacquin, K. M., & Harrington, P. J. (1995). Impact of cognitive behavioral treatment on quality of life in panic disorder patients. *Journal of Consulting and Clinical Psychology, 63*, 823–830.

Thorpe, S. J., & Salkovskis, P. M. (1997). Animal phobias. In: G. C. L. Davey (Ed.), *Phobias: A handbook of theory, research and treatment* (pp. 81–105). New York: Wiley.

Tsao, J. C. I., & Craske, M. G. (2000). Panic disorder. In M. Hersen & M. Biaggio (Eds.), *Effective brief therapies: A clinician's guide* (pp. 63–78). San Diego, CA: Academic Press.

Wegner, D. M. (1994). Ironic processes of mental control. *Psychological Review, 101*, 34–52.

Wegner, D. M., Broome, A., & Blumberg, S. J. (1997). Ironic effects of trying to relax under stress. *Behaviour Research and Therapy, 35*, 11–21.

Wegner, D. M., & Erber, R. (1992). The hyperaccessibility of suppressed thoughts. *Journal of Personality and Social Psychology, 63*, 903–912.

Wegner, D. M., Erber, R., & Zanakos, S. (1993). Ironic processes in the mental control of mood and mood-related thought. *Journal of Personality and Social Psychology*, *65*, 1093–1104.

White K. S., & Barlow, D. H. (2001). Panic disorder and agoraphobia. In D. H. Barlow (Ed.), *Anxiety and its disorders: The nature and treatment of anxiety and panic*. New York: Guilford.

Wilson, P. H. (1992). Relapse prevention: Conceptual and methodological issues. In P. H. Wilson (Ed.), *Principles and practice of relapse prevention* (pp. 1–22). New York: Guilford.

AN ACCEPTANCE AND MINDFULNESS-BASED PERSPECTIVE ON SOCIAL ANXIETY DISORDER

James D. Herbert and LeeAnn Cardaciotto

Social anxiety disorder (SAD), also known as social phobia, is a common and often debilitating anxiety disorder. The cardinal features of SAD are anxiety in and avoidance of situations involving interpersonal behavior, social performance, or both. Pathological social anxiety is characterized by extreme concerns over humiliation, embarrassment, or similar emotional consequences resulting from fear of negative evaluation by others. The disorder is associated with serious impairment in multiple areas of functioning, including romantic and nonromantic relationships, academic functioning, and occupational functioning (e.g., Davidson, Hughes, George, & Blazer, 1993; Schneier, Johnson, Hornig, Liebowitz, & Weissman, 1992). SAD is also associated with increased risk of comorbid psychopathology, especially depression other anxiety disorders and substance abuse (e.g., Magee, Eaton, Wittchen, McGonagle, & Kessler, 1996; Schneier et al., 1992).

Although research on pathological social anxiety and avoidance extends back several decades, the condition was only recognized as a distinct disorder upon publication of the third edition of the *Diagnostic and Statistical Manual of Mental Disorders* (*DSM-III*) in 1980 (American Psychiatric Association, 1980). The *DSM-III* originally conceptualized SAD as fear and avoidance of one or more discrete social situations such as public speaking, eating in front of others, or using public toilets. Research quickly demonstrated, however, that many individuals with the condition fear and avoid multiple social situations, and the revision of the *DSM-III* published in 1987 distinguished a "generalized" subtype, in which anxiety extends to most social situations. The distinction between discrete and generalized subtypes of SAD continues to be made in the most recent edition of the *DSM* (American Psychiatric Association, 2000).

Research on SAD has increased dramatically over the past two decades. The National Comorbidity Survey found that SAD is the third most common mental disorder in the United States, with lifetime prevalence estimates of 13.3% (Kessler et al., 1994). Although many individuals with the disorder, especially those with the generalized subtype, report having been shy and socially anxious for as long as they can remember, the onset of SAD as a clinical disorder appears to follow a bimodal pattern, with one peak in early childhood and another in mid-adolescence (Dalrymple, Herbert, & Gaudiano, 2005; Juster & Heimberg, 1995; Stein, Chavira, & Jang, 2001). Despite its high prevalence, the disorder often goes unrecognized by professionals, and therefore untreated (Herbert, Crittenden, & Dalrymple, 2004; Wittchen, Stein, & Kessler, 1999). Without intervention, SAD tends to follow a chronic, unremitting course. The high prevalence of SAD, along with the high levels of distress and impairment associated with it, makes the disorder a major public health concern (Kashdan & Herbert, 2001; Lang & Stein, 2001).

The etiology of SAD remains unknown, although data suggest a role for both genetic and environmental factors. Family studies have revealed robust familial linkages for the disorder (e.g., Fyer, Mannuzza, Chapman, Liebowitz, & Klein, 1993; Mannuzza, Schneier, Chapman, Liebowitz, & Klein, 1995; Reich & Yates, 1988; Stein et al., 1998). The temperamental style of behavioral inhibition in early childhood, characterized by shyness and restraint, avoidance, and distress in the face of novel situations, has been found to be associated with the subsequent development of SAD in adolescence (Schwartz, Snidman, & Kagan, 1999). Retrospective reports indicate that individuals with SAD perceive their parents to have been socially isolated and to have encouraged excessive concerns about evaluation by others as well as social isolation. Approximately half of individuals with SAD recall a traumatic event that they believe caused or contributed to their condition (Stemberger, Turner, Beidel, & Calhoun, 1995). Further, cognitive models propose that SAD results from dysfunctional cognitive content as well as biased information processing. Although it is generally accepted that SAD results from the interplay of both genetic and environmental factors, the specific nature of these interactions has not been established.

PSYCHOTHERAPY FOR SAD

BEHAVIOR THERAPY

There is little evidence to support traditional models of psychotherapy (e.g., psychodynamic or supportive psychotherapy) for SAD, although relatively little research has examined such approaches. Most contemporary psychotherapies for SAD are behaviorally oriented, and share the component of systematic exposure to anxiety-provoking stimuli. Exposure therapy can be conducted in vivo, through behavioral stimulations, and in imagery. In each case, the therapist and client together develop a hierarchy of phobic situations, and then systematically expose the client to increasingly anxiety-provoking stimuli. For example, an initial exposure for a client who fears and avoids conversations might be to introduce herself to a stranger. She might subsequently initiate a conversation and maintain it for 1 min. Later exposures might entail initiating a conversation with a group of individuals at a dinner party and maintaining it for at least 5 min. The difficulty of the exposure exercises is gradually increased over a number of treatment sessions. Several meta-analyses have found exposure to be effective in the treatment of SAD (Fedoroff & Taylor, 2001; Feske & Chambless, 1995; Taylor, 1996).

A unique feature of exposure therapy for SAD is the emphasis placed on simulated exposure, often referred to as role-play exercises. A simulation of many social situations, including both interpersonal situations such as conversations or dating as well as performance situations such as public speaking, can be readily created in the clinic. Initially the therapist can play the role of various other people in such simulations, and eventually other staff, including both professional staff (e.g., other therapists) and lay staff (e.g., administrative support persons), can be incorporated. There are several advantages of simulated exposure, including the ability to target a wide range of situations and the high level of control they afford the clinician to titrate the level of difficulty. Moreover, clients are often surprised at how realistic such stimulations appear once they are underway. Simulated exposures conducted in the therapist's office can be followed up with therapist-guided in vivo exposures in the community, as well as homework assignments involving further in vivo exposure.

Another commonly used behavioral treatment strategy is social skills training (SST). Research demonstrates that SAD is associated with problems with social performance, although the degree to which such impairments reflect actual skills deficits or the pernicious effects of anxiety remains unknown (Heimberg & Becker, 2002; Herbert, 1995; Norton & Hope, 2001). In any case, like exposure, SST has been shown to be an effective treatment for SAD (Fedoroff & Taylor, 2001; Taylor, 1996). After an individualized assessment to highlight specific areas of problematic social behavior, the therapist targets each area by modeling, conducting role-played practice, and providing veridical feedback. Role plays conducted for the purpose of SST are typically brief initially, lasting anywhere from a few seconds to a minute, and may be repeated several times. This permits the clinician to focus on one or two specific skills at a time. As increasingly complex skills are targeted, the duration of role plays may be extended to several minutes, affording the opportunity for simulated exposure as well. Although SST has been shown to be an effective treatment for SAD, it is not clear if the beneficial effects of SST on social anxiety and behavioral performance are due to skill acquisition per se or to the effects of exposure provided by the role plays.

A multicomponent treatment that includes SST is social effectiveness therapy (SET; Turner, Beidel, Cooley, Woody, & Messer, 1994). In addition to targeting social skills, SET includes psychoeducation, in vivo and/or imaginal exposure exercises, and programmed practice through homework. Although there has been limited research on SET, initial results are promising (Turner et al., 1994; Turner, Beidel, & Cooley-Quille, 1995).

COGNITIVE BEHAVIOR THERAPY

The most popular contemporary treatments for SAD are variations of cognitive–behavioral therapy (CBT), which are based on cognitive models of the disorder, discussed further below. In addition to incorporating systematic exposure, CBT targets exaggerated negative thoughts and beliefs about the degree of threat associated with social situations, the adequacy of one's social performance, and the actual consequences of social *faux pas* and other negative outcomes. Therapy aims to modify these cognitions using a variety of techniques. For example, cognitive restructuring involves identifying "automatic thoughts" evoked by feared social situations, identifying the characteristic errors and biases in such thoughts, and then systematically correcting these errors.

The most popular and widely researched form of CBT for SAD is cognitive–behavioral group therapy (CBGT) developed by Heimberg and colleagues (Heimberg & Becker, 2002; Heimberg et al., 1990). A unique feature of CBGT is that cognitive restructuring is conducted within the context of simulated exposure exercises, such that the two components are fully integrated. The primary goal of simulated exposure exercises is not habituation to anxiety-provoking situations but rather to present experiential evidence to counter-specific negatively biased cognitions. For example, a client who believes that his mind will "go blank" and will therefore be unable to engage in conversation might be asked to have a conversation in the context of a role-play exercise. The therapist then counts the number of verbalizations he makes during the exercise, and presents these data to him following the conversation to illustrate the inaccuracy of his prediction about his performance. Regular homework in the form of self-monitoring and correcting biased cognitions, as well as practicing previously avoided behaviors, is assigned following each session.

A substantial literature has supported the effectiveness of CBGT (e.g., Gelernter et al., 1991; Heimberg, Salzman, Holt, & Blendell, 1993; Hope, Herbert, & White, 1995; Otto et al., 2000). Moreover, several variations of the program have recently been evaluated. Several studies have found that individual treatment is as effective as the group format (e.g., Gould, Buckminster, Pollack, Otto, & Yap, 1997; Herbert, Rheingold, Gaudiano, & Myers, 2004; Scholing & Emmelkamp, 1993), and one study found that individual treatment may be even more effective (Stangier, Heidenreich, Peitz, Lauterbach, & Clark, 2003). Brief (e.g., 6-week) versions of individual CBT based on the CBGT model have been shown to be effective (Herbert, Rheingold, & Goldstein, 2002). A recent study found that the effects of CBGT were augmented by the inclusion of SST (Herbert et al., 2005; see also Franklin, Feeny, Abramowitz, Zoellner, & Bux, 2001). Despite the overall effectiveness for CBGT and its variations, the specific mechanisms responsible for these effects remain unclear.

A similar CBT program for SAD has been developed by Clark (2001). Clark argues that exposing patients to social situations, even in the context of cognitive restructuring, may have limited impact on anxiety reduction and meaningful cognitive change without explicit efforts to shift the focus of attention outward and to eliminate the use of safety behaviors (e.g., not speaking much or scripting speech; wearing a turtleneck sweater to hide sweating; avoiding eye contact in conversations). Like standard CBT treatments, exposure exercises and cognitive restructuring techniques are conducted to help clients test negative predictions and beliefs. However, a unique feature of the Clark program is that feared situations are role played under two conditions, once while engaging in self-focused attention and employing safety behaviors and then again while focusing attention outward and without using safety behaviors. Therapy encourages clients to shift to an external focus of attention and to drop safety behaviors during social interactions, including simulated interactions in session as well as in vivo interactions through homework assignments. In addition, videotaped feedback is used to provide realistic information about how the client actually appears to others.

LIMITS TO EFFICACY OF CURRENT TREATMENT APPROACHES

Although traditional behavioral and cognitive–behavioral programs are reasonably effective for SAD, there remains much room for improvement. A substantial number of patients fail to respond to these therapies. Moreover, the majority of those who do respond continue to experience residual symptoms and associated impairment. For example, Turner, Beidel, and Wolff (1994) found that only 33% of those with the generalized subtype SAD achieved at least moderate end-state functioning following a course of behavior therapy. Similarly, Hope et al. (1995) found that only 18% of patients with generalized SAD were rated by independent evaluators as fully remitted following a course of CBT. Brown, Heimberg, and Juster (1995) likewise found that only 44% of patients with generalized SAD were classified as treatment responders following CBT.

Augmentation with antidepressant medication has not been found to result in meaningful increases in overall response rates, especially in the long term (Heimberg, 2002; Huppert, Roth, Keefe, Davidson, & Foa, 2002). In fact, Haug et al. (2003) found that patients with SAD who received combined treatment (sertraline plus exposure therapy) demonstrated poorer long-term outcome than those who received exposure therapy alone. Thus, there is a need for treatment innovations to target nonresponders to standard therapy and to enhance the magnitude of therapeutic effects among treatment responders.

A promising variation to standard CBT are programs that highlight mindfulness and acceptance strategies. Such programs have recently attracted considerable attention in the treatment of a wide range of conditions, including various mood and anxiety disorders, psychotic disorders, and personality disorders, among others. Following a discussion of theoretical conceptualizations of SAD, we will return to the question of mindfulness and acceptance-based interventions for the disorder.

COGNITIVE MODELS OF SAD

Given the centrality of negative cognitions in SAD, it is not surprising that popular models of the disorder focus primarily on cognitive–verbal processes. There is broad consensus that such processes are critical to the development and maintenance of SAD, although the specific mechanisms are not yet clear. Cognitive theories emphasize the role of negative cognitions and hold that information-processing biases play a central role in the etiology and maintenance of SAD. Current cognitive theories are based on the general model of clinical anxiety developed by Beck, Emery, and Greenberg (1985), which proposes that dysfunctional cognitions that operate largely beyond conscious awareness influence information processing by biasing attention toward stimuli congruent with the cognitions. These dysfunctional cognitions result in vulnerability to anxiety. Individuals with SAD perceive themselves as vulnerable to social threat, leading to information-processing biases that reinforce beliefs about the threat.

Clark and Wells (1995) and Rapee and Heimberg (1997) have developed cognitive models of SAD derived largely from the Beck et al. (1985) model. Both Clark and Wells and Rapee and Heimberg highlight attentional biases that occur before, during, and after a social situation, the influence of past memories of social events, the role of focus on the self, and the tendency to perceive threat in the world. However, there are key differences with regard to why anxiety is generated. Clark and Wells suggest that individuals with SAD develop dysfunctional assumptions about themselves and social situations, which lead them to appraise social situations as dangerous. The appraisal then generates anxiety, leading individuals with SAD to become self-focused (i.e., attention is shifted away from the actual situation and inward on negative thoughts and feelings). Faulty inferences made about how one appears to others and processing of external cues biased in favor of negatively interpreting others' responses both contribute to the vicious cycle that generates and maintains anxiety. According to Rapee and Heimberg, however, anxiety is induced and maintained by the continued comparison and discrepancy between the expectation of how one should be performing with the ongoing mental representation of one's performance. Rappe and Heimberg argue that individuals with SAD form mental representations of their external appearance and behavior, and make faulty predictions based on past experiences and perceived internal and external cues about how others will perceive them. Anxiety is influenced by the perception of success or failure, which depends upon the degree of match between the two mental representations.

In support of cognitive models of SAD, a growing body of research has demonstrated various information processing biases associated with the disorder, including biases involving attention, interpretation of ambiguous information, and possibly memory. With regard to attention, individuals diagnosed with SAD have shown to score higher on measures of public self-consciousness (i.e., attention to aspects of the self that can be observed by others; Bruch & Heimberg, 1994; Saboonchi, Lundh, & Ost 1999). Individuals high in social anxiety report higher levels of self-focused attention during social situations (Mellings & Alden, 2000), and exhibit enhanced ability to detect negative external social cues, such as negative audience behaviors (e.g., yawning, looking at watch) rather than positive behaviors (e.g., smiling, nodding; Veljaca & Rapee, 1998). There is some evidence to suggest that socially anxious individuals exhibit preferential memory for threat-related information, including poorer memory for details from a recent social interaction (Daly, Vangelisti, & Lawrence, 1989; Kimble & Zehr, 1982; Mellings & Alden, 2000) and selective retrieval of negative public self-referent words when anticipating public speaking (Mansell & Clark, 1999). However, for nonclinical socially anxious individuals the bias only occurs if a socially anxious state is evoked at the time of retrieval (Heinrichs & Hofmann, 2001). Individuals with SAD also form excessively negative appraisals of social situations. Those with SAD have a tendency to interpret ambiguous social events negatively; this negative interpretation is specific to the performance of the socially anxious individual himself or herself, and occurs only during social situations (Amir, Foa, & Coles, 1998; Stopa & Clark, 2000). Highly socially anxious individuals also use internal information (e.g., physiological arousal) to make markedly negative inferences about how they appear to others (e.g., Mellings & Alden, 2000; Wells & Papageorgiou, 2001). In comparison to independent raters, socially anxious individuals underestimate how well they come across to others (Stopa & Clark, 1993).

Although the research reviewed above is generally consistent with cognitive models of SAD, it is important to note that the causal role of cognitive variables in the etiology or maintenance of the disorder has not been established. It is possible that biased information processing is a concomitant or result of social anxiety, rather than a cause. In addition, the implication of extant cognitive models of SAD is that effective intervention requires correcting distorted cognitive content and processes. We now turn to an alternative perspective that may provide new insights in understanding and treating SAD.

MINDFULNESS

Modern descriptions of mindfulness in clinical psychology are derived from traditional Buddhist conceptualizations. Mindfulness in the Buddhist tradition has been referred to as "bare attention," or a nondiscursive registering of events without reaction or mental evaluation. The emphasis is on the *process* of sustained attention rather than the *content* to what is attended (Thera, 1972). Among the descriptions in Western psychology, the most frequently cited definition of mindfulness is provided by Kabat-Zinn (1994) as "paying attention in a particular way: on purpose, in the present moment, and nonjudgmentally" (p. 4). Reflected in Kabat-Zinn's definition and consistent with most other descriptions of mindfulness are two central components: present-moment awareness and nonjudgmental acceptance. Awareness in this context refers to the continuous monitoring of both one's inner experience and external perceptions (Deikman, 1996). This awareness focuses on the ongoing stream of experience in the present, rather than attention to past or future events (Roemer & Orsillo, 2003). The second component of mindfulness concerns the psychological stance in which present-moment awareness is conducted: nonjudgmentally, with an attitude of acceptance and openness to one's experience. Acceptance has been defined as "experiencing events fully and without defense, as they are" (Hayes, 1994, p. 30), during which one is fully open to the experience of the present moment without evaluating the truth or value of that experience (Roemer & Orsillo, 2003). Acceptance implies refraining from attempts to change, avoid, or escape from one's experience, regardless of its specific content.

Bishop et al. (2004) recently proposed a similar operational definition of mindfulness that focuses on two components: sustained attention to present experience and an attitude of openness, curiosity, and acceptance. Although a useful advance over earlier attempts to define the construct, one problem with their definition is that any self-regulation of attention is inconsistent with an attitude of thoroughgoing acceptance (Brown & Ryan, 2004). That is, one cannot be fully open and accepting of the full range of psychological experience if one is simultaneously attempting to direct attention in any particular way (e.g., away from external stimuli, as in certain forms of concentrative meditation).

Although most descriptions of mindfulness reflect the components of awareness and nonjudgmental acceptance, the distinction between the two is generally not emphasized. In fact, Brown and Ryan (2003, 2004) argue on both theoretical and empirical grounds that the acceptance component of mindfulness is redundant with the awareness component. It is often assumed that increased present-focused awareness will necessarily occur with an attitude of enhanced acceptance, and conversely that enhancing one's stance of nonjudgmental acceptance will necessarily lead to increased awareness. However, the degree to which changes in either component tend to affect changes in the other is an open question, and it should not be assumed that the two components are inextricably linked. For example, high levels of awareness need not be accompanied by high levels of acceptance. Research demonstrates that panic disorder is associated with increased awareness of internal physiological cues (e.g., Ehlers & Breuer, 1992, 1996), but this awareness is certainly not accepted nonjudgmentally by the panicker; quite the contrary in fact. Conversely, one can adopt a highly accepting perspective without necessarily being highly aware of ongoing experience. For example, an athlete focusing on performing an event might learn to decrease attention to both internal sensations such as pain and external distractions such as the audience's cheering, yet adopt an accepting attitude to distractions when they do arise in awareness. Csikszentmihalyi (1990) describes a psychological state he terms "flow," in which attention is so highly focused on a particular task that one's experience of both the internal and external environment is temporarily attenuated. It is possible that such a state is associated with relatively low levels of present-moment awareness of the internal and external environments, yet relatively high levels of acceptance of whatever experience does enter consciousness. We therefore propose that the concept of mindfulness be conceptualized as consisting of two factors: (a) enhanced awareness of the full range of present experience and (b) an attitude of nonjudgmental acceptance of that experience. As will become clear below, the distinction between these components becomes important in conceptualizing SAD and its treatment from a mindfulness perspective.

A large literature supports the beneficial effects of mindfulness. For example, Kabat-Zinn and colleagues (1992) found a mindfulness meditation-based stress reduction program to be effective for medical outpatients with generalized anxiety disorder (GAD) or panic disorder; Miller, Fletcher, and Kabat-Zinn (1995) found these results to be maintained at a 3-year follow-up. Orsillo, Roemer, and Barlow (2003) report pilot data suggesting the value of incorporating mindfulness techniques into an existing group CBT program for GAD. Davidson and colleagues (2003) report that mindfulness meditation produces brain activation in a region typically associated with positive affect, and beneficial effects of immune functioning. In addition, Carlson, Speca, Patel, and Goodey (2003) found significant improvements in quality of life, symptoms of stress, and sleep quality in breast and prostate cancer patients after participation in a mindfulness-based stress reduction program.

Despite these encouraging results, the research to date has generally not clearly distinguished the two constituents of the mindfulness concept. It is therefore unclear if the beneficial effects of increased mindfulness are due to increased awareness, increased acceptance, or both. Moreover, confounding the two components of mindfulness may obscure their individual effects in theoretical models of psychopathology. We now turn to a model of SAD in which awareness and acceptance each play a unique role.

AN ACCEPTANCE-BASED MODEL OF SAD

As discussed above, standard cognitive models of SAD focus on distorted or dysfunctional cognitive content (e.g., negative thoughts about one's social performance) and biased information processing (e.g., attentional, memory, and judgmental biases). Consideration of the construct of

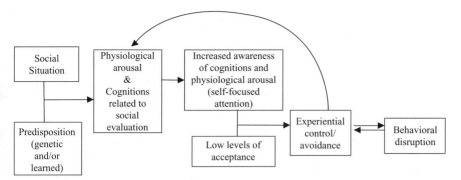

FIGURE 1. An Acceptance-Based Model of Social Anxiety Disorder

mindfulness and its constituent components yields variations to these models that suggest additional theoretical mechanisms and alternative intervention strategies.

Our model of SAD is illustrated in Figure 1. First, phobic social situations, in the context of a predisposition toward social anxiety, produce both physiological arousal and negative thoughts related to social evaluation. There are several noteworthy points to this first step. First, both a phobic stimulus and a predisposition toward social anxiety are required to produce anxiety-related thoughts and feelings. Without the predisposition toward social anxiety, a social situation will produce minimal arousal, and in the absence of a specific phobic situation the predisposition is not operative. Second, we use the term "social situation" broadly to include any stimulus, internal or external, that functions to trigger anxiety. For example, thoughts of an upcoming social situation might serve to trigger anxiety in a vulnerable individual. Third, both the predisposition to anxiety and the specific phobic stimuli are conceptualized as continuous variables rather than as discrete categories. That is, both constructs are assumed to vary quantitatively across individuals. Hence, the level of cognitive and physiological arousal experienced by a given individual will depend on his or her quantitative levels of each of these factors. Fourth, the distal cause of the predisposition may be genetically based, learned, or (most likely) a combination of both. As discussed above, there are data consistent with genetic influences on the development of social anxiety (e.g., family studies, temperament), as well as environmental factors (e.g., retrospective reports of parenting style). In either case, we are far from being able to prevent the development of the disorder through modification of either process. As it is not clear how (or even if) one can change one's predisposition to social anxiety, and given the ubiquity of social situations, the first step in the model does not provide for direct targets for intervention.

As anxiety-related thoughts and feelings are elicited, they in turn trigger an increase in internal awareness, and a corresponding decrease in awareness of external cues. Although triggered automatically by increased arousal, this self-focused attention is nevertheless theoretically distinct. The nonjudgmental acceptance component is critical at this stage, because the effects of increased awareness of internal arousal will depend upon the individual's level of acceptance. It is worth noting that acceptance in this context is hypothesized to represent a quasi-stable trait, yet one that can nevertheless be modified, as discussed below. In the context of a high level of nonjudgmental acceptance, one will simply notice the cognitive and physiological arousal without attempting to control, escape from, or avoid it. The impact on behavioral performance will therefore be minimal. On the other hand, in the context of low acceptance, one will reflexively engage in a variety of experiential control strategies designed to alter the form and/or frequency of the thoughts and feelings. For example, one might attempt to "talk back" to or rationalize one's thoughts, or try to suppress or distract oneself from unpleasant feelings.

Although such experiential control strategies may sometimes work at least temporarily, they often fail. For example, thought suppression has been found to be associated with heightened pain experience (Sullivan, Rouse, Bishop, & Johnston, 1997), increased anxiety (Koster, Rassin, Crombez, Naring, 2003), poorer ratings of quality of sleep and longer estimates of sleep-onset latency when thoughts are suppressed during the presleep period (Harvey, 2003), and increases in the reinforcing effect of alcohol when urges to drink were suppressed by heavy drinkers (Palfai, Monti, Colby, & Rohsenow, 1997). In addition, although Belloch, Morillo, and Gimenez (2004) found that suppression of intrusive or neutral thoughts had no effect on their frequency, their results suggested that suppression efforts may nevertheless interfere with habituation to the thought, whereas a lack of control leads to a marked decrease in thought frequency. Fehm and Margraf (2002) report data suggesting that thought suppression may be particularly relevant to SAD. Relative to agoraphobics and nonanxious controls, persons with SAD demonstrated impaired ability to suppress not only socially relevant thoughts, but thoughts related to other topics as well. Other research suggests that attempts to control feelings may be equally problematic. For example, Strahan (2003) found that high levels of emotional control at baseline predicted poorer academic performance over a year later.

Furthermore, the greater the perceived cost of failing to control one's internal experiences, the less successful such efforts are likely to be. An experiential exercise known as the polygraph metaphor nicely illustrates this point (Hayes, Strosahl, & Wilson, 1999). Imagine being connected to the world's best polygraph machine, which provides an ongoing index in real time of your level of physiological arousal. Your task is to stay very relaxed, and your ongoing level of relaxation will be recorded by the machine. In order to provide extra incentive to stay relaxed, imagine that a shotgun is mounted on a table next to you and aimed at your head. When the machine is activated, nothing will happen as long as you remain perfectly calm. But any increase in arousal will trigger the gun to go off, killing you instantly. Most clients, and especially those with anxiety disorders, readily grasp the paradoxical implications of this metaphor: The greater the cost associated with controlling one's internal experience the harder it becomes to do so, and in fact the greater the likelihood that the experience will become even more salient and disruptive.

Returning to Figure 1, experiential control efforts therefore tend to backfire, leading to even further increases in anxiety-related arousal. This establishes a vicious cycle of increased arousal, increased awareness, and further efforts at experiential control, including escape behaviors. Behavioral disruption occurs as one becomes preoccupied with controlling unpleasant thoughts and feelings. This disruption can take many forms, including avoidance of anxiety-provoking situations, impaired performance in social or performance situations, and a constriction of one's behavioral repertoire. This behavioral disruption in turn leads to further efforts at experiential control. For example, an individual who struggles to control feelings of nervousness in a conversation with an attractive potential dating partner may have difficulty focusing on the conversation, and may stumble over his words. In an effort to make the conversation flow more smoothly, he works even harder to control his nervousness, thereby setting up a vicious cycle.

IMPLICATIONS FOR INTERVENTION

There are several implications of this model for intervention. First, in principle one could arrest the vicious cycle by targeting either of the two components of mindfulness: awareness or acceptance. According to the model, a *decrease* in internal awareness would theoretically result in decreased experiential control, especially since self-focused attention has been shown to lead to increases in social anxiety rather than task-focused attention (Boegels & Lamers, 2002). In fact, traditional CBT, especially as practiced by Clark and colleagues, may owe its effectiveness in part to this mechanism. Strategies designed to decrease self-focused attention and to increase externally focused attention may serve to decrease efforts to control anxiety-related arousal, thereby resulting in less behavioral disruption (e.g., Wells & Papageorgiou, 1998). The difficulty with this strategy is that direct efforts to decrease attention toward internal experiences run the risk of paradoxically increasing attention to those very experiences in some individuals.

A potentially more powerful strategy would be to focus on increasing levels of nonjudgmental acceptance of one's experience. If one is able to embrace fully one's experience without defense, there is no need to engage in control efforts, and *all* of one's efforts can therefore be directed to the task at hand, rather than struggling to control thoughts and feelings. By adopting a stance of nonjudgmental acceptance, the content of one's experience becomes irrelevant; one is willing to experience whatever occurs. From a mindfulness perspective, an advantage of focusing on changing levels of nonjudgmental acceptance, rather than awareness, is that clients can more directly learn to increase levels of acceptance. In contrast, even if it were possible to control fully the target or content of one's awareness, efforts to do so would run the risk of amplifying the very experiences the client wishes to avoid.

Although the proposed mechanisms of traditional cognitive-based treatment approaches are theoretically different from mindfulness-based approaches, both may share some common mechanisms. In the case of depression, for example, there is evidence that the effects of both traditional CBT and mindfulness-based CBT are mediated by increases in "metacognitive awareness," or holding one's thoughts and feelings as distinct from the self (Teasdale et al., 2001, 2002). It should be noted, however, that the actual degree of acceptance in measures of metacognitive awareness is not clear. As used by Teasdale et al., metacognitive awareness refers to the process of "decentering" and "disidentification" with one's thoughts so that they are distinguished from the self. Although this distance from one's internal experience may foster an attitude of nonjudgmental acceptance, the degree of acceptance per se is not explicitly measured and is therefore unknown.

Although traditional CBT may indeed result in increases in metacognitive awareness when it is effective, it remains the case that the basic therapeutic stance is fundamentally at odds with an acceptance orientation. Regardless of the differences between the specific interventions, all standard cognitive therapy programs for SAD propose that therapeutic change is mediated by modification of biased or dysfunctional cognitions. That is, standard CBT holds that changes in the content and/or frequency of thoughts is what produces changes in affect, physiological arousal, and behavior. Thus, performance is only enhanced after anxiety reduction. In contrast, from an acceptance perspective, the specific content or frequency of thoughts is essentially irrelevant. Instead, how one relates to one's private events is more important, and adopting a stance of nonjudgmental acceptance allows one to be willing to experience whatever occurs regardless of its emotional valence. One can have physiological arousal, negative social–evaluative thoughts, or both, and nevertheless continue to perform effectively. Given that experiential control strategies often appear to backfire, this suggests that directly targeting acceptance may prove to be an especially powerful intervention strategy.

ACCEPTANCE AND COMMITMENT THERAPY

One therapeutic perspective that highlights the importance of experiential acceptance and that has recently attracted considerable attention is acceptance and commitment therapy (ACT), developed by Steven Hayes and colleagues (Hayes et al., 1999). ACT is based on a behavioral theory of language known as relational frame theory (RFT; Hayes, Barnes-Holmes, & Roche, 2001), and is situated within the philosophical perspective known as functional contextualism. RFT proposes that much psychological distress is a byproduct of natural language processes, which encourage futile efforts to control private experiences. ACT utilizes a variety of experiential exercises and metaphors, integrated with standard behavioral interventions, to foster nonjudgmental acceptance of one's psychological experience. This experiential acceptance is not considered an end in and of itself, but rather is viewed as a tool explicitly linked to promoting action toward personally relevant goals. These goals are in turn explicated through the process of examining one's personal values across major life domains. In fact, ACT is more explicit than most other mindfulness and acceptance-oriented psychotherapies in linking experiential acceptance directly to behavioral progress toward chosen goals and values.

The ACT model has been applied to a variety of forms of psychopathology, including the anxiety disorders (Orsillo, Roemer, Block-Lerner, LeJeune, & Herbert, 2004). To date, no controlled studies have evaluated the efficacy of ACT with generalized SAD. One small study evaluated brief public speaking workshops based on ACT versus CBT, relative to a no-treatment comparison group, for college students with fear of public speaking (Block, 2003). Both treatments resulted in significant improvement on measures of anxiety and avoidance relative to the control condition. There were few differences between treatments, although the ACT condition showed greater decreases in behavioral avoidance during public speaking.

Herbert and Dalrymple (2004) developed a detailed treatment manual of ACT for generalized SAD, and a pilot study based on this program is currently underway. This program builds on earlier treatment protocols that utilize cognitive therapy integrated with simulated exposure (e.g.,

Heimberg & Becker, 2002), although cognitive therapy techniques, particularly cognitive restructuring, are not conducted. Following thorough assessment and construction of a hierarchy of feared social situations, the initial stage of treatment focuses on exploring the various strategies the client has attempted to utilize to control her anxiety. Strategies such as deep breathing, relaxation, attempting to "talk through" negative thoughts, and drinking alcohol prior to or during social events are commonly reported; in fact, clients typically list anxiety reduction as their primary goal of treatment. Inevitably such strategies have not been successful, or the client would not be presenting for treatment. This exploration leads to a discussion of the paradoxical nature of experiential control efforts. Various exercises and metaphors are used to demonstrate the futility of efforts to control one's anxiety, such as the polygraph metaphor described above.

The next step involves the introduction of the idea of willingness to experience whatever thoughts and feelings arise as an alternative to experiential control. The goal of increased willingness is discussed, using the two-scale metaphor (Hayes et al., 1999). In this metaphor, anxiety on the one hand and willingness to experience private events (including feelings of anxiety) on the other are conceptualized as two distinct scales. The client has focused her efforts exclusively on the anxiety scale, monitoring it closely and attempting to keep anxiety low. Yet her experience has demonstrated that such efforts are futile, at least in the long term. By shifting the focus to the willingness scale, which she actually can influence, the anxiety scale becomes increasingly irrelevant. At this stage, and continuing throughout the remainder of the program, stimulated and in vivo exposure to phobic social situations is conducted. The goal of the exposure exercises, however, is explicitly *not* to reduce anxiety, but rather to foster acceptance and willingness while simultaneously practicing social behaviors that are consistent with one's goals (e.g., initiating and maintaining conversations, asking someone out on a date, being assertive, public speaking). During role-play exercises, the therapist periodically "checks in" with the client, reminding her simply to notice what internal experiences are occurring without attempting to change them, and asking her to provide ratings of her willingness. Although anxiety reduction may occur and in fact frequently does, the client is repeatedly warned against making anxiety reduction the goal or becoming too attached to the experience of low anxiety, as doing so is tantamount to abandoning willingness in favor of experiential control. One cannot be fully accepting of one's psychological experience while simultaneously engaged in experiential control efforts, no matter how indirect or subtle, to modify that very experience. This emphasis reflects another unique feature of ACT: its radical perspective on acceptance. Many current applications of mindfulness in psychotherapy claim to promote nonjudgmental acceptance of psychological experience on the one hand while suggesting that such acceptance will lead to the goal of reducing or eliminating distressing thoughts and feelings on the other. Upon reflection, the contradiction is obvious. One cannot be fully accepting of one's psychological experience while simultaneously engaged in experiential control efforts, no matter how indirect or subtle, to modify that very experience. Consistent with our model of SAD (Figure 1), the danger with any attempt to control, avoid, or escape from internal experience is that such efforts can lead to behavioral disruption as well as further increases in anxiety.

Various exercises are utilized to enhance experiential willingness during both simulated exposure exercises and in vivo exposures conducted in the clinic and as homework assignments. The difficulty of the exposures is gradually increased throughout the course of therapy as the client progresses up his fear hierarchy, and homework assignments are linked to exposure exercises conducted in the session. A final stage of therapy concerns values clarification and goal-setting. ACT conceptualizes values as general life directions, analogous to points on a compass, whereas goals are specific, attainable mileposts along the way toward a valued direction. Both values and goals are choices made by the client, as the ACT therapist is careful to avoid coercing or even advocating for any specific value, and this work serves two useful purposes. First, it encourages the client to take full ownership of his values and goals. Second, it highlights goals that might not otherwise be obvious, and that may not in fact relate directly to social anxiety (e.g., increasing religious or spiritual practices, increasing physical fitness).

Although data collection is currently underway, our initial experience with this program has been quite encouraging. Our experience suggests that this program appears to be especially useful with difficult, entrenched, or treatment refractory cases, although controlled research is needed to evaluate these observations.

CONCLUSIONS AND FUTURE DIRECTIONS

Labeled "the neglected anxiety disorder" less than 20 years ago (Liebowitz, Gorman, Fyer, & Klein, 1985), the past two decades have witnessed a dramatic increase in research on the etiology, phenomenology, and treatment of SAD. This research has caused a shift in the conceptualization of the disorder from a relatively minor phobia of a specific social situation to a chronic, unremitting, and often debilitating disorder that typically affects multiple domains of functioning. The most popular current models of the disorder emphasize biases in information processing. Research has been largely consistent with hypotheses derived from these models, finding that individuals with SAD exhibit specific biases in attention, memory, and judgment. Nevertheless, the causal status of these biases with respect to SAD has not been demonstrated. In addition, current treatment approaches based on these models, although generally effective, leave considerable room for improvement.

We suggest that the concept of mindfulness, properly deconstructed, holds considerable promise in both the understanding and treatment of SAD. The nonjudgmental acceptance component of mindfulness may be especially important in understanding the maintenance of the disorder, and in treatments designed to increase experiential acceptance as a tool for promoting action toward chosen goals, and life values have been developed and are currently being evaluated. The importance of methodologically sound research in this area cannot be overstated. Although we clearly believe that the concept of mindfulness has considerable utility, the rapid increase in interest in the concept runs the risk of transforming it into yet another psychotherapy fad, only to be subsequently dismissed as the next innovation comes along. To prevent this fate, in addition to ongoing clinical development, the concept of mindfulness should be subjected to critical analysis, and strong tests of resulting hypotheses should be conducted. Our hope is that this chapter may serve as an impetus to such research.

REFERENCES

American Psychiatric Association. (1980). *Diagnostic and statistical manual of mental disorders* (3rd ed.). Washington, DC: Author.

American Psychiatric Association. (2000). *Diagnostic and statistical manual of mental disorders* (4th ed., text revision). Washington, DC: Author.

Amir, N., Foa, E. B., & Coles, M. E. (1998). Negative interpretation bias in social phobia. *Behavior Research & Therapy, 36,* 945–957.

Beck, A. T., Emery, G., & Greenberg, R. L. (1985). *Anxiety disorders and phobias: A cognitive perspective.* New York: Basic Books.

Belloch, A., Morillo, C., & Gimenez, A. (2004). Effects of suppressing neutral and obsession-like thoughts in normal subjects: beyond frequency. *Behavior Research and Therapy, 42,* 841–857.

Bishop, S. R., Lau, M., Shapiro, S., Carlson, L., Anderson, N. D., Carmody, J., et al. (2004). Mindfulness: A proposed operational definition. *Clinical Psychology: Science and Practice, 11,* 230–241.

Block, J. A. (2003). Acceptance or change of private experiences: A comparative analysis in college students with public speaking anxiety. *Dissertation Abstracts International: Section B: The Sciences and Engineering, 63*(9-B), 4361.

Boegels, S. M., & Lamers, C. T. J. (2002). The causal role of self-awareness in blushing-anxious, socially-anxious, and social phobics individuals. *Behaviour Research & Therapy, 40,* 1367–1384.

Brown, E. J., Heimberg, R. G., & Juster, H. R. (1995). Social Phobia subtype and avoidant personality disorder: Effect on severity of social phobia, impairment, and outcome of cognitive behavioral treatment. *Behavior Therapy, 26,* 467–486.

Brown, K. W., & Ryan, R. M. (2003). The benefits of being present: Mindfulness and its role in psychological well-being. *Journal of Personality and Social Psychology, 84,* 822–848.

Brown, K. W., & Ryan, R. M. (2004). Perils and promise in defining and measuring mindfulness: Observations from experience. *Clinical Psychology: Science and Practice, 11,* 242–248.

Bruch, M. A., & Heimberg, R. G. (1994). Differences in perceptions of parental and personal characteristics between generalised and nongeneralised social phobics. *Journal of Anxiety Disorders, 8,* 155–168.

Carlson, L. E., Speca, M., Patel, K. D., & Goodey, E. (2003). Mindfulness-based stress reduction in relation to quality of life, mood, symptoms of stress, and immune parameters in breast and prostate cancer outpatients. *Psychosomatic Medicine, 65,* 571–581.

Clark, D. M. (2001). A cognitive perspective on social phobia. In W. R. Crozier & L. E. Alden (Eds.), *International handbook of social anxiety: Concepts, research, and interventions relating to the self and shyness* (pp. 405–430). New York: Wiley.

Clark, D. M., & Wells, A. (1995). A cognitive model of social phobia. In R. Heimberg, M. Liebowitz, D. A. Hope, & F. R. Schneier (Eds.), *Social phobia: Diagnosis, assessment and treatment* (pp. 69–93). New York: Guilford.

Csikszentmihalyi, M. (1990). *Flow: The psychology of optimal experience.* New York: Harper & Row.

Dalrymple, K. L., Herbert, J. D., & Gaudiano, B. A. (2005). *Onset of illness and developmental factors in social anxiety disorder: Findings from a retrospective interview.* Manuscript under editorial review.

Daly, J. A., Vangelisti, A. L., & Lawrence, S. G. (1989). Self-focused attention and public speaking anxiety. *Personality & Individual Differences, 10,* 903–913.

Davidson, J. R. T., Hughes, D. L., George, L. K., & Blazer, D. G. (1993). The epidemiology of social phobia: Findings from the Duke Epidemiological Catchment Areas Study. *Psychological Medicine, 23,* 709–718.

Davidson, R. J., Kabat-Zinn, J., Schumacher, J., Rosenkranz, M., Muller, D., Santorelli, S. F., et al. (2003). Alterations in brain and immune function produced by mindfulness meditiation. *Psychosomatic Medicine, 65,* 564–570.

Deikman, A. J. (1996). "I" _ awareness. *Journal of Consciousness Studies, 3,* 350–356.

Ehlers, A., & Breuer, P. (1992). Increased cardiac awareness in panic disorder. *Journal of Abnormal Psychology, 101,* 371–382.

Ehlers, A., & Breuer, P. (1996). How good are patients with panic disorder at perceiving their heartbeats? *Biological Psychology, 42,* 165–182.

Fedoroff, I. C., & Taylor, S. (2001). Psychological and pharmacological treatments of social phobia: A meta-analysis. *Journal of Clinical Psychopharmacology, 21,* 311–324.

Fehm, L., & Margraf, J. (2001). Thought suppression: Specificity in agoraphobia versus broad impairment in social phobia? *Behaviour Research and Therapy, 40*, 57–66.

Feske, U., & Chambless, D. L. (1995). Cognitive behavioral versus exposure only treatment for social phobia: A meta-analysis. *Behavior Therapy, 26*, 695–720.

Franklin, M. E., Feeny, N. C., Abramowitz, J. S., Zoellner, L. A., & Bux, D. A. (2001). Comprehensive cognitive behavior therapy: A multi-component treatment for generalized social phobia. *Psicoterapia Cognitiva e Comportamentale, 7*, 211–221.

Fyer, A. J., Mannuzza, S., Chapman, T. F., Liebowitz, M. R., & Klein, D. F. (1993). A direct interview family study of social phobia. *Archives of General Psychiatry, 50*, 286–293.

Gelernter, C. S., Uhde, T. W., Cimolic, P., Arnkoff, D. B., Vittone, B. J., Tancer, M. E., et al. (1991). Cognitive–behavioral and pharmacological treatments for social phobia: A controlled study. *Archives of General Psychiatry, 48*, 938–945.

Gould, R. A., Buckminster, S., Pollack, H. M., Otto, M. W., & Yap, L. (1997). Cognitive behavioral and pharmacological treatment for social phobia: A meta-analysis. *Clinical Psychology: Science and Practice, 4*, 291–306.

Harvey, A. G. (2003). The attempted suppression of presleep cognitive activity in insomnia. *Cognitive Therapy & Research, 27*, 593–602.

Haug, T. T., Blomhoff, S., Hellstrom, K., Holme, I., Humble, M., Madsbu, H. P., et al. (2003). Exposure therapy and sertraline in social phobia: 1-year follow-up of a randomised controlled trial. *British Journal of Psychiatry, 182*, 312–318.

Hayes, S. C. (1994). Content, context, and the types of psychological acceptance. In S. C. Hayes, N. S. Jacobsen, V. M. Follette, & M. J. Dougher (Eds.), *Acceptance & change: Content and context in psychotherapy* (pp. 13–32). Reno, NV: Context Press.

Hayes, S. C., Barnes-Holmes, D., & Roche, B. (Eds.). (2001). *Relational frame theory: A post-Skinnerian account of human language and cognition*. New York: Plenum.

Hayes, S. C. Strosahl, K., & Wilson, K. G. (1999). *Acceptance and commitment therapy*. New York: Guilford.

Heimberg, R. G. (2002, November). *The understanding and treatment of social anxiety: What a long strange trip it's been (and will be)*. Paper presented at the Association for Advancement of Behavior Therapy, Reno, NV.

Heimberg, R. G., & Becker, R. E. (2002). *Cognitive–behavioral group therapy for social phobia: Basic mechanisms and clinical strategies*. New York: Guilford.

Heimberg, R. G., Dodge, C. S., Hope, D. A., Kennedy, C. R., Zollo, L., & Becker, R. E. (1990). Cognitive behavioral group treatment of social phobia: Comparison to a credible placebo control. *Cognitive Therapy and Research, 14*, 1–23.

Heimberg, R. G., Salzman, D., Holt, C. S., & Blendell, K. (1993). Cognitive behavioral group treatment of social phobia: Effectiveness at 5-year follow-up. *Cognitive Therapy and Research, 17*, 325–339.

Heinrichs, N., & Hofmann, S. G. (2001). Information processing in social phobia: A critical review. *Clinical Psychology Review, 21*, 751–770.

Herbert, J. D. (1995). An overview of the current status of social phobia. *Applied and preventive Psychology, 4*, 39–51.

Herbert, J. D., Crittenden, K., & Dalrymple, K. L. (2004). Knowledge of social anxiety disorder relative to attention deficit hyperactivity disorder among educational professionals. *Journal of Clinical Child & Adolescent Psychology, 33*, 366–372.

Herbert, J. D., & Dalrymple, K. L. (2004). *Acceptance and commitment therapy for social anxiety disorder: A treatment manual.* Unpublished manuscript, Drexel University, Philadelphia, PA.

Herbert, J. D., Gaudiano, B. A., Rheingold, A., Harwell, V., Dalrymple, K., & Nolan, E. M. (2005). Social skills training augments the effectiveness of cognitive behavior group therapy for social anxiety disorder. *Behavior Therapy, 36*, 125–138.

Herbert, J. D., Rheingold, A. A., Gaudiano, B. A., & Myers, V. H. (2004). Standard versus extended cognitive behavior therapy for social anxiety disorder: A randomized controlled trial. *Behavioural and Cognitive Psychotherapy, 32*, 1–17.

Herbert, J. D., Rheingold, A. A., & Goldstein, S. G. (2002). Brief cognitive behavioral group therapy for social anxiety disorder. *Cognitive and Behavioral Practice, 9*, 1–8.

Hope, D. A., Herbert, J. D., & White, C. (1995). Social phobia subtype, avoidant personality disorder, and psychotherapy outcome. *Cognitive Therapy and Research, 19*, 339–417.

Huppert, J. D., Roth, D. A., Keefe, F. J., Davidson, J. R. T., & Foa, E. B. (2002, November). *Comprehensive CBT, Fluoxetine, and their combination: A randomized, placebo-controlled trial.* Paper presented at the Association for Advancement of Behavior Therapy, Reno, NV.

Juster, H. R., & Heimberg, R. G. (1995). Social phobia: Longitudinal course and long-term outcome of cognitive–behavioral treatment. *The Psychiatric Clinics of North America, 18*, 821–842.

Kabat-Zinn, J. (1994). *Wherever you go, there you are: Mindfulness meditation in everyday life.* New York: Hyperion.

Kabat-Zinn, J., Massion, A. O., Kristeller, J., Peterson, L. G., Fletcher, K. E., Pbert, L., et al. (1992). Effectiveness of a meditation-based stress reduction program in the treatment of anxiety disordes. *American Journal of Psychiatry, 149*, 936–943.

Kashdan, T. B., & Herbert, J. D. (2001). Social anxiety disorder in childhood and adolescence: Current status and future directions. *Clinical Child and Family Psychology Review, 4*, 37–61.

Kessler, R. C., McGonagle, K. A., Zhao, S., Nelson, C. B., Hughes, M., Eschleman, S., et al. (1994). Lifetime and 12 month prevalence of DSM-III-R psychiatric disorders in the United States: Results from the National Comorbidity Survey. *Archives of General Psychiatry, 51*, 8–19.

Kimble, C. E., & Zehr, H. D. (1982). Self-consciousness, information load, self-presentation, and memory in a social situation. *Journal of Social Psychology, 118*, 39–46.

Koster, E. H. W., Rassin, E., Crombez, G., & Naring, G. W. B. (2003). The paradoxical effects of suppressing anxious thoughts during imminent threat. *Behaviour Research & Therapy, 41,* 1113–1120.

Lang, A. J., & Stein, M. B. (2001). Social phobia: Prevalence and diagnostic threshold. *Journal of Clinical Psychiatry, 62,* 5–10.

Liebowitz, M. R., Gorman, J. M., Fyer A. J., & Klein, D. F. (1985). Social phobia: Review of a neglected anxiety disorder. *Archives of General Psychiatry, 42,* 729–736.

Magee, W. J., Eaton, W. W., Wittchen, H.-U., McGonagle, K. A., & Kessler, R. C. (1996). Agoraphobia, simple phobia, and social phobia, in the National Comorbidity Survey. *Archives of General Psychiatry, 53,* 159–168.

Mannuzza, S., Schneier, F. R., & Chapman, T. F., Liebowitz, M. R., & Klein, D. F. (1995). Generalized social phobia. *Archives of General Psychiatry, 52,* 230–237.

Mansell, W., & Clark, D. M. (1999). How do I appear to others? Social anxiety and processing of the observable self. *Behaviour Research & Therapy, 37,* 419–434.

Mellings, T. M. B., & Alden, L. E. (2000). Cognitive processes in social anxiety: The effects of self-focus, rumination and anticipatory processing. *Behaviour Research & Therapy, 38,* 243–257.

Miller, J., Fletcher, K., & Kabat-Zinn, J. (1995). Three-year follow-up and clinical implications of a mindfulness meditation-based stress reduction intervention in the treatment of anxiety disorders. *General Hospital Psychiatry, 17,* 192–200.

Norton, P. J., & Hope, D. A. (2001). Analogue observational methods in the assessment of social functioning in adults. *Psychological Assessment, 13,* 59–72.

Orsillo, S., Roemer, L., & Barlow, D. H. (2003). Integrating acceptance and mindfulness into existing cognitive–behavioral treatment for GAD: A case study. *Cognitive and Behavioral Practice, 10,* 222–230.

Orsillo, S. M., Roemer, L., Block-Lerner, J., LeJeune, C., & Herbert, J. D. (2004). ACT with anxiety disorders. In S. C. Hayes & K. Strosahl (Eds.) *A clinician's guide to acceptance and commitment therapy* (pp. 103–132). New York: Springer.

Otto, M. W., Pollack, M. H., Gould, R. A., Worthington, J. J., McArdle, E. T., Rosenbaum, J. F., et al. (2000). A comparison of the efficacy of clonazepam and cognitive–behavioral group therapy for the treatment of social phobia. *Journal of Anxiety Disorders, 14,* 345–358.

Palfai, T. P., Monti, P. M., Colby, S. M., & Rohsenow, D. J. (1997). Effects of suppressing the urge to drink on the accessibility of alcohol outcome expectancies. *Behaviour Research & Therapy, 35,* 59–65.

Rapee, R. M., & Heimberg, R. (1997). A cognitive–behavioral model of anxiety in social phobia. *Behavior Research & Therapy, 35,* 741–756.

Reich, J., & Yates, W. (1988). Family history of psychiatric disorders in social phobia. *Comprehensive Psychiatry, 29,* 72–75.

Roemer, L., & Orsillo, S. M. (2003). Mindfulness: A promising intervention strategy in need of further study. *Clinical Psychology: Science & Practice, 10,* 172–178.

Saboonchi, F., Lundh, L. G., & Ost, L. G. (1999). Perfectionism and self-consciousness in social phobia and panic disorder with agoraphobia. *Behaviour Research & Therapy, 37,* 799–808.

Schneier, F. R., Johnson, J., Hornig, C. D., Liebowitz, M. R., & Weissman, M. M. (1992). Social phobia: Comorbidity and morbidity in an epidemiologic sample. *Archives of General Psychiatry, 49,* 282–288.

Schwartz, C. E., Snidman, N., & Kagan, J. (1999). Adolescent social anxiety as an outcome of inhibited temperament in childhood. *Journal of the American Academy of Child & Adolescent Psychiatry, 38,* 1008–1015.

Stangier, U., Heidenreich, T., Peitz, M., Lauterbach, W., & Clark, D. M. (2003). Cognitive therapy for social phobia: Individual versus group treatment. *Behaviour Research & Therapy, 41,* 991–1007.

Stein, M. B., Chavira, D. A., & Jang, K. L. (2001). Bringing up bashful baby: Developmental pathways to social phobia. *Psychiatric Clinics of North America, 24,* 661–676.

Stemberger, R. T., Turner, S. M., Beidel, D. C., & Calhoun, K. S. (1995). Social phobia: An analysis of possible developmental factors. *Journal of Abnormal Psychology. 104,* 526–531.

Stopa, L., & Clark, D. M. (1993). Cognitive processes in social phobia. *Behaviour Research & Therapy, 31,* 255–267.

Stopa, L., & Clark, D. M. (2000). Social phobia and interpretation of social events. *Behavior Research & Therapy, 38,* 273–283.

Strahan, E. Y. (2003). The effects of social anxiety and social skills on academic performance. *Personality and Individual Differences, 34,* 347–366.

Sullivan, M. J. L., Rouse, D., Bishop, S., & Johnston, S. (1997). Thought suppression, catastrophizing, and pain. *Cognitive Therapy & Research, 21,* 555–568.

Taylor, S. (1996). Meta-analysis of cognitive–behavioral treatments for social phobia. *Journal of Behavior Therapy and Experimental Psychiatry, 27,* 1–9.

Teasdale, J. D., Moore, R. G., Hayhurst, H., Pope, M., Williams, S., & Segal, Z. V. (2002). Metacognitive awareness and prevention of relapse in depression: Empirical evidence. *Journal of Consulting & Clinical Psychology, 70,* 275–287.

Teasdale, J. D., Scott, J., Moore, R. G., Hayhurst, H., Pope, M., & Paykel, E. S. (2001). How does cognitive therapy prevent relapse in residual depression? Evidence from a controlled trial. *Journal of Consulting and Clinical Psychology, 69,* 347–357.

Thera, N. (1972). *The power of mindfulness.* San Francisco, CA: Unity Press.

Turner, S. M., Beidel, D. C., Cooley, M. R., Woody, S. R., & Messer, S. C. (1994). A multicomponent behavioral treatment of social phobia: Social effectiveness therapy. *Behaviour Research & Therapy, 32,* 381–390.

Turner, S. M., Beidel, D. C., & Cooley-Quille, M. R. (1995). Two year follow-up of social phoics treated with social effectiveness therapy. *Behaviour Research & Therapy, 33,* 553–556.

Turner, S. M., Beidel, D. C., & Wolff, P. L. (1994). A composite measure to determine improvement following treatment for social phobia: The Index of Social Phobia Improvement. *Behaviour Research and Therapy, 4,* 471–476.

Veljaca, K., & Rapee, R. M. (1998). Detection of negative and positive audience behaviours by socially anxious subjects. *Behaviour Research & Therapy, 36,* 311–321.

Wells, A., & Papageorgiou, C. (1998). Social phobia: Effects of external attention on anxiety, negative beliefs, and perspective taking. *Behavior Therapy, 29*, 357–370.

Wells, A., & Papageorgiou, C. (2001). Social phobic interoception: Effects of bodily information on anxiety, beliefs and selfprocessing. *Behaviour Research & Therapy, 39*, 1–11.

Wittchen, H.-U., Stein, M. B., & Kessler, R. C. (1999). Social fears and social phobia in a community sample of adolescents and young adults: Prevalence, risk factors, and co-morbidity. *Psychological Medicine, 29*, 309–323.

CHAPTER 9

AN ACCEPTANCE-BASED BEHAVIOR THERAPY FOR GENERALIZED ANXIETY DISORDER

LIZABETH ROEMER AND SUSAN M. ORSILLO

Generalized anxiety disorder (GAD) is a disorder characterized by chronic, pervasive, uncontrollable worry (as well as associated somatic complaints; American Psychiatric Association, 1994) for which we have yet to develop sufficiently successful interventions. The National Comorbidity Study yielded a lifetime prevalence estimate of 5.1% for GAD, and revealed, contrary to the common assumption that it is a mild disorder, that GAD is associated with significant psychosocial impairment (Wittchen, Zhao, Kessler, & Eaton, 1994). GAD is unlikely to remit on its own (Yonkers, Warshaw, Massion, & Keller, 1996) and remains more chronic than panic disorder after pharmacotherapy (Woodman, Noyes, Black, Schlosser, & Yagia, 1999). In addition, GAD is associated with high rates of comorbidity (most commonly other anxiety or mood disorders), and this comorbidity is associated with increased functional impairment (Wittchen et al., 1994) and health care utilization/cost (Souetre et al., 1994). Further, GAD has been associated with impaired well-being and life satisfaction beyond its association with major depression in a community study of 15–64 year olds (Stein & Heimberg, 2004), as well as with impaired quality of life, beyond that accounted for by comorbid diagnoses, among older

213

adults (Wetherall et al., 2004). Recent studies in primary care settings have consistently found that "pure" (noncomorbid) GAD is associated with impairment in multiple domains (see Kessler, Walters, & Wittchen, 2004, for a review).

GAD differs from other anxiety disorders in that it is not characterized by a focal target of fear, anxiety, and worry or by behavioral avoidance. Studies attempting to uncover a specific focus of worry among individuals diagnosed with GAD have shown that GAD worry is not characterized by any particular fears, but instead by more frequent worries about a range of topics, as well as idiosyncratic and minor worries (Brown, Barlow, & Liebowitz, 1994; Roemer, Molina, & Borkovec, 1997). These worries take the form of catastrophic predictions of low-probability negative events in the future (Borkovec, Shadick, & Hopkins, 1991; Dugas et al., 1998), which are readily accessible due to information-processing biases toward threatening information (Matthews, 1990) and a tendency to overestimate risk (Butler & Matthews, 1987). The pervasive nature of worry is also evident in the consistent clinical observation that individuals with GAD seem to move from one worry domain to another, rather than worrying exclusively on one topic for an extended period of time (Borkovec & Roemer, 1994; Butler, 1994). Studies have also revealed that GAD worry is characterized by worry about worry or meta-worry (Wells & Carter, 1999). These findings have been incorporated in the *DSM-IV* definition of GAD, in which worry is characterized as pervasive and uncontrollable, but no specific content of worry is defined.

Just as GAD is not characterized by reactions to circumscribed phobic stimuli, it is also not generally considered to be associated with specific phobic behavioral avoidance (Borkovec, Hazlett-Stevens, & Diaz, 1999; Butler, Gelder, Hibbert, Cullington, & Klimes, 1987). However, the majority of individuals with GAD do report some form of behavioral avoidance (Butler et al., 1987), suggesting that the absence of focal avoidance behaviors should not be seen as evidence for the irrelevance of behavioral avoidance to this disorder (as discussed more fully below).

EFFICACY OF EXISTING TREATMENTS FOR GAD

Several cognitive-behavioral treatments have been developed for GAD. These cognitive-behavioral treatments typically include psychoeducation, self-monitoring, and either applied relaxation, cognitive therapy, coping imagery, or some combination of these elements. Borkovec and Ruscio (2001) review 13 controlled GAD treatment outcome studies and conclude that cognitive-behavioral approaches yield significant changes (with large effect sizes) that are maintained or improved at follow-up. This review concludes that cognitive-behavioral treatments have been found more effective than waitlist control conditions (e.g., Barlow, Rapee, & Brown, 1992), and have most often been found more effective than nonspecific treatment conditions (e.g., Borkovec & Costello, 1993). Whereas some studies that have compared components of cognitive-behavioral treatment (CBT) to a full package of CBT have found the full package to yield larger effects (e.g., Butler, Fennell, Robson, & Gelder, 1991), others have found the dismantled and full packages comparable (e.g., Barlow et al., 1992). Outcome studies published more recently provide further support for the conclusions drawn from this review. A CBT that directly targets intolerance of uncertainty, a construct proposed to be central to GAD, has been found to be more efficacious than waitlist control when delivered in both individual (Ladouceur et al., 2000) and group (Dugas et al., 2003) format. Two studies have found that applied relaxation (Öst, 1987) and cognitive therapy (based on Beck & Emery, 1985) both result in significant, comparable, symptom reduction (Arntz, 2003; Öst & Brietholtz, 2000). Borkovec, Newman, Lytle, and Pincus (2002) found comparable, efficacious results for a combined applied relaxation and coping desensitization treatment, cognitive therapy, and a treatment package that combined all three elements.

Although efficacious interventions have been developed for GAD, it remains the least successfully treated of the anxiety disorders (Brown et al., 1994; Roemer, Orsillo, & Barlow, 2002). Despite the apparent efficacy of cognitive-behavioral approaches, none have yielded high end-state functioning (defined by most outcomes within normative range) for a large proportion of the treated sample. Ladouceur et al. (2000) and Borkovec and Costello (1993) found that 58% of those clients receiving CBT demonstrated high end-state functioning at 12-month follow-up, whereas Borkovec and colleagues (2002) yielded somewhat lower proportions of clients meeting criteria for high end-state functioning (29–48% across conditions at 12-month follow-up and 38–52% across conditions at 24-month follow-up), despite providing a longer duration of treatment. In addition, little is known about the sustained efficacy of these treatments (Westen & Morrison, 2001). Only Borkovec et al. (2002) included a 24-month follow-up period, and only 38% of clients in their combined CBT condition met criteria for high end-state functioning at this assessment. (Clients in the other two conditions—cognitive therapy and self-control desensitization—fared better, but still only about half met these criteria.) None of the extant studies have examined the impact of treatments on quality of life and functioning. Thus, more efficacious treatments are needed, as are more extensive investigations (with longer follow-up periods and broader assessments of outcomes) of these treatments.

One explanation for the relatively weaker success treating GAD with cognitive-behavioral approaches may be the absence of focal fears and avoidance behaviors among these individuals. Successful interventions for other anxiety disorders involve exposure to feared stimuli, which are more easily identified in disorders characterized by focal fears (e.g., inte-roceptive cues in panic disorder, social situations in social phobia, feared thoughts and images in obsessive–compulsive disorder). Researchers have begun to turn their attention to other characteristics of worry and GAD, hoping to develop interventions that will more effectively treat this chronic disorder. These efforts have included targeting the interpersonal and expe-riential aspects of GAD (e.g., Newman, Castonguay, Borkovec, & Molnar, 2004), emotion regulation difficulties in GAD (e.g., Mennin, 2004), in-tolerance of uncertainty (e.g., Dugas, Buhr, & Ladouceur, 2004), and meta-worry (or worry and other negative responses to one's worry; Wells, 2004). Of these approaches, only Dugas et al. (2004) have published data supporting the efficacy of their treatment (in comparison to a waitlist con-trol condition; Ladouceur et al., 2000). Our own work has focused on developing a treatment for GAD that specifically targets the experien-tial and behavioral avoidance that characterize this disorder, in order to improve quality of life in addition to targeting symptoms of GAD. This approach arose from the convergence of accumulated knowledge from basic research and theories of GAD and worry with new developments in behavioral interventions for other disorders, which suggested the po-tential efficacy of integrating mindfulness/acceptance elements and tradi-tional cognitive-behavioral techniques. In the next section, we review the empirically based conceptualization of GAD on which our treatment is based.

AN ACCEPTANCE-BASED CONCEPTUALIZATION OF GAD

Research and theory in the area of worry and GAD, as well as advances in the understanding and treatment of other disorders, converge to sup-port a proposal that individuals with GAD have negative reactions to their own internal experiences, and are motivated to try to avoid these experi-ences, which they do both behaviorally and cognitively (through repeated engagement in the worry process). This conceptualization suggests that treatments that promote experiential acceptance, which would counteract this reactivity and experiential avoidance, may be particularly beneficial. Broader acceptance-based models for psychopathology are reviewed else-where in this volume (e.g., Orsillo, Roemer, & Holowka, 2005; Twohig, Masuda, Varra, & Hayes, 2005) Here we focus specifically on GAD-specific theory and research that supports this model and connects to related work in the field.

The Experientially Avoidant Function of Worry

Borkovec (e.g., Borkovec, Alcaine, & Behar, 2004) has proposed an avoidance model of worry in which worry is negatively reinforced by the reduction in internal distress that accompanies it (as well as the superstitious perceived avoidance of low-frequency catastrophic events that individuals with GAD predict). The association between worry and *reductions* in internal distress seems counterintuitive, yet it is supported by research and provides a compelling model for understanding the persistence of worry as well as a potential target for intervention.

Although individuals with GAD report subjective distress associated with their worry, and certainly find worry to be an unpleasant experience, experimental evidence demonstrates that worry is associated with initial *reductions* in reactivity. Speech phobic participants who worried prior to imagining giving a speech did not experience an increase in heart rate during the imaginal exposure, in contrast to those who engaged in relaxation prior to the exposure (Borkovec & Hu, 1990). Similarly, participants who worried after exposure to a gruesome film reported less immediate anxiety than those who engaged in imaginal rehearsal (Wells & Papageorgio, 1995). In contrast to other anxious states, neither chronic nor state worry is associated with increased sympathetic activation; instead they are associated with reduced autonomic flexibility (Connor & Davidson, 1998; Hoehn-Saric & McLeod, 1988). Although this reduced variability (associated with decreased vagal tone; Lyonfields, Borkovec, & Thayer, 1995) has detrimental long-term consequences, the short-term effect of diminished activation is likely to be negatively reinforcing, increasing the frequency of worrisome responding. Individuals with GAD seem to be somewhat aware of the association between worry and reduced distress: self-report of the use of worry to distract from more distressing topics was the only reason for worrying that reliably distinguished participants with GAD from subclinical cases (Borkovec & Roemer, 1995; Freeston, Rheaume, Letarte, Dugas, & Ladouceur, 1994). These data taken together suggest that the most striking form of avoidance in GAD may be experiential; that is, individuals with GAD may be actively and/or automatically avoiding unpleasant internal experiences by focusing on multiple future events.

Borkovec (2002) notes that this emphasis on the future keeps individuals with GAD from living in the present moment. The success of worry in reducing distress may in part be due to the fact that it removes individuals from painful experiences that they are having in the present moment: current fears, sad feelings, angry thoughts, and so on are avoided by a focus on a more distal future. However, this removal from the present moment has detrimental long-term consequences. Individuals distracted from the present moment by their worry are unable to respond to current environmental contingencies and learn adaptively. If they are avoiding their emotional experience, they are also unable to use their emotions adaptively to provide information about their current environment (e.g., noting that they are dissatisfied with a relationship or work situation, recognizing that someone has mistreated them) and respond effectively. Also, because increased anxiety is a necessary component of functional exposure (Foa & Kozak, 1986), worry may interfere with successful emotional processing and maintain threatening associations over the long-term (Borkovec et al., 2004). In the study described above, although worrying before phobic imagery reduced heart rate response to an imagined speech, it also interfered with habituation to repeated presentations of the image, whereas those who engaged in relaxing thinking prior to exposure evidenced reductions in heart rate over time (Borkovec & Hu, 1990). Similarly, worrying after exposure to a gruesome film reduced anxiety initially, but led to increased intrusions over the next few days, compared to imaginal rehearsal (Wells & Papageorgio, 1995).

This model of worry (that it is associated with short-term reductions in internal distress but long-term maintenance of this distress along with difficulties responding adaptively to the environment) corresponds closely to Hayes and colleagues' model of experiential avoidance as an important functional dimension in psychopathology (Hayes, Strosahl, & Wilson, 1999; Hayes, Wilson, Gifford, Follette, & Strosahl, 1996). These researchers have noted that several clinically problematic behaviors seem to be aimed at instrumental control of internal experiences (thoughts, feelings, and bodily sensations). They argue that these efforts to experientially avoid distress are inherently flawed because our internal experience is not subject to the same instrumental control as our behavior. Further, these efforts often have paradoxical effects (e.g., Gross & Levenson, 1993, 1997; Wegner, 1994; but see Purdon, 1999, for a full review of this literature). According to Hayes and colleagues, targeting internal experience with these efforts at control leads individuals to fail to exercise instrumental control where it would be more beneficial: in choosing their actions. Hayes and colleagues have developed a treatment called acceptance and commitment therapy (ACT), which targets these difficulties, and from which we draw substantially for our treatment of GAD. Research supports the proposed connection between experiential avoidance and GAD: levels of experiential avoidance have been found to be associated with both severity of GAD and level of worry (Roemer, Salters, Raffa, & Orsillo, 2005).

Associating Threat with Internal Experiences

In Hayes et al.'s (1999) model, experiential avoidance stems from a learned association of threat with internal experiences. Similarly, Borkovec and Sharpless (2004) suggest that individuals with GAD have difficulty with their "reactions to their reactions"; in other words, they respond with distress or worry to their initial cognitive and emotional reactions, prompting more distress or worry. Wells (2004) has also noted that individuals with GAD may come to experience their own worry (another internal experience) as threatening, which may exacerbate anxiety and perpetuate the cycle of worry. A central problem among individuals with GAD (along with individuals with other clinical disorders) may be their association of threat with their internal experiences, leading to reactivity to these experiences and subsequent efforts to avoid or escape these experiences.

Reactivity to one's emotions (an internal experience that may be particularly important in the treatment of GAD) is one of the central elements of Mennin and colleagues' (in press) emotion regulation model of GAD, along with intensity of emotion, difficulty understanding emotion, and engagement in maladaptive management of emotions. Individuals with GAD have been found to report higher levels of reactivity to their own emotions than controls, in terms of both anxiety sensitivity (Taylor, Koch, & McNally, 1992) and a broader fear of emotions (Mennin, Heimberg, Turk, & Fresco, in press; Roemer et al., 2005). The importance of reactivity to one's emotions in GAD is further supported by findings that it remains associated with GAD, even when controlling for worry (Mennin et al., in press; Roemer et al., 2005), as does experiential avoidance (Roemer et al., 2005). Taken together, these findings suggest that a tendency to find one's emotions threatening and therefore attempt to avoid them may be an important factor in GAD, both because of the relationship of these phenomena with worry, and also because of a broader association with GAD symptomatology. These findings suggest that specifically targeting these phenomena may be beneficial in the treatment of GAD.

Other Correlates of GAD with Clinical Relevance

Several clinically observed and empirically demonstrated characteristics of GAD may be related to these reactive and avoidant processes. In particular, narrowed awareness (focused on threat and the future), amplification of distressing internal experiences, and restrictions in behavior stemming from avoidance seem to be important processes in the phenomenology of GAD and its associated functional impairment. A better understanding of these phenomena, along with directly targeting them in treatment, may result in more efficacious treatments for this chronic disorder.

Narrowed Awareness and Focus on the Future

As is common across the anxiety disorders, individuals with GAD demonstrate a preattentive bias toward threatening material and a tendency to interpret ambiguous situations in a threatening manner (MacLeod & Rutherford, 2004). Thus, attentional processes in GAD are narrowed toward potential threat. Attention is further narrowed by its emphasis on future possibilities as opposed to current realities. As a result, individuals with GAD are likely not attending to current environmental contingencies that might facilitate adaptive responding. This narrowing of attention seems to occur internally as well. Our clients report that they attend to their internal experiences; however, although they easily register the presence of anxiety or general distress, they seem less able to detect or differentiate the broader, more complex, or more subtle range of emotions that accompany these responses (such as sadness or anger that may accompany or underlie anxiety). In fact, individuals with GAD do report poor understanding and clarity of their emotional responses (Mennin et al., in press; Salters-Pedneault, Roemer, Tull, Rucker, & Mennin, in press). Expanded internal and external awareness (for instance, through mindfulness practice, described more fully below) might allow these individuals to better perceive and more effectively use the information these internal and external cues can offer, and simultaneously reduce the exaggerated perception of threat that accompanies these attentional biases.

Amplification of Internal Experiences

The narrowing of attention toward threatening or undesirable internal experiences, coupled with reactivity toward and efforts to avoid these experiences, may paradoxically lead to amplification of internal responses. This may explain the consistent association between emotional intensity and GAD (Mennin et al., in press; Turk, Heimberg, Luterek, Mennin, & Fresco, 2005), although it may also be that individuals with GAD have more intense initial emotional responses and that attempts to suppress or avoid these intense emotions simply further intensify responding (Mennin et al., in press). Judgments of one's emotional responses or thoughts can increase distress associated with this internal content, and, as noted above, efforts to control these experiences can lead them to be more pronounced (e.g., Gross & Levenson, 1993, 1997; Wegner, 1994). These processes may also further contribute to the lack of clarity individuals with GAD have regarding their internal experiences. Negative reactions to, judgments of, and efforts to avoid internal experiences lead to increased distress and additional emotional responses and thoughts that "muddy" or reduce the clarity of one's response, similar to Hayes and colleagues' (1999) concept of "dirty" emotions. This amplification also provides the individual with experiential evidence that his or her emotions are extreme and unpleasant, likely prompting more judgments, reactions, and efforts to avoid. Although an experiential accepting stance will not necessarily alter initial or primary emotional responses (Greenberg & Safran, 1987), and engaging in acceptance for the purpose of reducing distress would constitute another avoidance strategy (Hayes et al., 1999), an accepting stance may reduce amplification of these responses by reducing judgment, reactivity, and avoidance strategies (e.g., secondary emotional responses, Greenberg & Safran, 1987), thus leading to clearer emotional responses that the individual can use more effectively and that are less likely to interfere with behavior.

Rigid, Habitual, and Ineffective Behavior Driven by Avoidance

As noted above, although individuals with GAD do not typically present with marked focal behavioral avoidance, they do endorse avoidance behaviors (Butler et al., 1987). Their habitual anxious responding results in rigidity in behavioral responding as well (Borkovec et al., 2004), and their lack of attention to current environmental contingencies likely interferes with adaptive responses to those contingencies. In addition, behavioral repertoires can become restricted and ineffective as individuals relinquish opportunities to engage in personally relevant and meaningful activities and interactions (such as attending a party, asserting one's needs, or pursuing a desired position at work) in an effort to avoid unwanted internal experiences (Hayes et al., 1999). In these cases, individuals may not even be aware that they are avoiding these actions; their avoidance may be so habitual that it appears inevitable to them, rather than a conscious choice. Thus, it may be particularly important to target these subtle, automatic avoidance behaviors, most notably to improve quality of life among individuals who may be retreating from important areas of their lives in order to avoid the internal experiences that inevitably arise when one engages fully in one's life.

We have also found that often the avoidance our clients engage in is even more subtle than automatically failing to engage in a given behavior. Many of our clients report that they are engaging in behaviors in all the domains that they value. However, when we have them monitor these behaviors, it becomes clear that they are not fully attending to what they are doing; they are on "automatic pilot." Clients sometimes report feeling like a spectator in their own lives; they are so focused on future potential threats that they are disengaged from what is actually happening in the present moment. This distraction may serve an experientially avoidant function; worry about what one is going to do at work tomorrow might be less distressing than experiencing the sadness associated with feeling poorly understood by one's partner or emotionally distant from one's child. However, this experiential avoidance precludes recognition of these important circumstances, which could lead to corrective actions aimed at ameliorating these problems. Although present-moment awareness during one's actions may feel more painful initially, it is likely to contribute to a more satisfying life over time.

Drawing from the emphasis in ACT on promoting action in valued domains (Hayes et al., 1999; Wilson & Murrell, 2004), we directly target these avoidance behaviors in our treatment by exploring what matters to clients in their lives, increasing their awareness of their actions in these domains, and assisting them in taking actions, regardless of the cognitive and emotional responses that occur. We describe this approach more fully below.

OVERVIEW OF AN ACCEPTANCE-BASED BEHAVIOR THERAPY FOR GAD

The preceding conceptual understanding of GAD, coupled with treatment development advances over the past decade in behaviorally or cognitively oriented acceptance-based interventions, led us to develop an acceptance-based behavior therapy for GAD that combines traditional cognitive-behavioral approaches (drawing from Borkovec's efficacious treatment for GAD; Borkovec et al., 2002) with elements of these acceptance-based interventions (most notably ACT; Hayes et al., 1999; but also MBCT; Segal, Williams, & Teasdale, 2002; MBSR; Kabat-Zinn, 1990; and DBT; Linehan, 1993a, 1993b). We consider this treatment an acceptance-based behavioral approach because it combines an emphasis on acceptance (which includes mindfulness training as a way to promote experiential acceptance) with an emphasis on behavioral change. This is similar to the dual emphasis in ACT and the dialectical approach in DBT. Clearly, nonbehavioral treatments also emphasize acceptance (e.g., Greenberg, 2002; Rogers, 1961) and distally influence our treatment; here we particularly emphasize the more proximal influences from within the cognitive-behavioral tradition. An earlier, less developed version of this treatment is presented in Orsillo, Roemer, and Barlow (2003).

In our current outcome study, we provide this treatment in individual format. The course of treatment is 16 sessions. The first 4 sessions aimed at orienting our clients to our treatment model last 90 min and the remaining 12 sessions are an hour in length. To encourage consolidation and generalization of treatment gains, we taper sessions at the end of treatment; specifically, the final two sessions occur biweekly. Each session begins with a formal mindfulness exercise designed to foster this skill in our clients and to prepare both the client and the therapist for the work of the session. The first seven sessions introduce important concepts from the treatment through psychoeducation, experiential exercises, metaphors, and between session self-monitoring assignments. Regular outside-of-session mindfulness practice is also emphasized during these sessions, and clients concurrently explore what is important to them in various areas of their lives. The latter sessions are primarily focused on guiding behavioral action in areas that matter to the client, as well as continuing to strengthen and broaden mindfulness practice, particularly to challenging contexts. Below we review the major components of our treatment.

PRESENTATION OF OUR MODEL

Similar to all cognitive-behavioral approaches, we begin treatment by introducing clients to our model of anxiety, worry, and GAD as well as the rationale for our treatment. Through handouts, self-monitoring assignments, experiential exercises, and discussion, we develop a shared conceptualization of the client's difficulties that is connected to our treatment plan. We emphasize the habitual nature of anxiety, illustrating how anxious responses (such as attentional bias toward threat) elicit more distress and anxiety in an escalating spiral. We explore the reasons that people may engage in worry (e.g., superstitious, preparation, motivation; Borkovec et al., 1999) and review the model of worry and GAD presented earlier in this chapter. We suggest that worry may function at least in part as a way of avoiding greater distress and illustrate how anxiety and worry can interfere with engaging in one's life, particularly through a narrowed focus on threat and the future rather than an expanded experience of the present. Thus, clients are introduced early on to the idea that they may be attempting to avoid their own distress and subtly avoiding engagement in their lives. Although clients differ in the degree to which they are aware of these forms of avoidance, they are commonly able to see them after in-session and out-of-session exercises highlight these processes. When clients are skeptical about the model, we encourage them to attend to their own experience, be open to the possibility that some of these concepts may apply to them, and try them on for a few weeks and then check back in to see if they fit or alter them appropriately.

In order to prepare clients for the utility of experiential acceptance, and because research suggests that individuals with GAD may have difficulty using their emotions adaptively (Mennin et al., in press), we spend an early session discussing the function of emotions (e.g., Linehan, 1993b), which has not been a typical component of CBT for GAD. We note that emotions prepare us for action, communicate important information to ourselves and others, and enhance our experience. Through in-session exercises and between-session monitoring, clients observe the ways that even unpleasant emotions can be beneficial (for instance, providing information that our needs are not being met). However, we also note that these emotional responses are sometimes less useful because they are "muddy" rather than "clear," due to carryover emotional responses from our past, present, or anticipated future, or due to other factors such as lack of sleep or dysregulated eating. Another session is devoted to exploring the ways that our efforts to control our emotions and thoughts tend to be unsuccessful (drawing heavily from ACT exercises), commonly intensifying our internal experiences and making them even less clear and useful. We validate clients' experience that these thoughts and feelings can be painful and it is natural (and is often a learned and instructed behavior) to want to avoid them. However, we encourage them to notice the long-term detrimental consequences of these efforts and to entertain the possibility that it may not be helpful in the long run to engage in these efforts. Between these sessions, clients monitor their emotional responses, their responses to their responses, and the degree to which their emotions are clear and muddy.

Finally, we suggest that these efforts to control internal experience often result in restrictions in the ways individuals are living their lives and invite clients to observe if this is true for them through writing assignments, discussions with the therapist, and monitoring between sessions. For instance, clients monitor the degree to which they are engaging in actions that they value, whether they are mindful in those contexts, and what is getting in the way of action if they choose not to do something they value. We suggest that rather than exerting efforts to change internal experiences, clients can turn their efforts toward living in ways that matter to them ("valued action"; Hayes et al., 1999; Wilson & Murrell, 2004).

Acceptance and Mindfulness-Based Strategies

As early sessions begin to establish the ways that clients have been (1) narrowing attention toward future threat, (2) reacting negatively (both emotionally and cognitively) to their own natural and often functional internal experiences, (3) engaging in potentially futile and often paradoxical efforts to reduce these distressing thoughts and feelings, and (4) avoiding aspects of life that might be painful, we introduce the possibility of an alternative stance. That is, in order to alter these life-interfering responses to internal experiences, we encourage clients to cultivate a a nonjudgmental, compassionate, expansive stance in which they accept internal and external stimuli as being what they are, and are willing to engage in actions that matter to them, regardless of the emotional responses that might accompany these actions.

Often, although clients may begin to see the futility and cost of control efforts, they will be hesitant to engage in willingness or acceptance as they fear it suggests resignation or defeat. We correct any misconceptions clients have at this point in therapy about the nature of acceptance. Acceptance involves "having what you already have got" (Hayes et al., 1999), seeing what is actually present in a given moment, feeling a feeling when it arises. In other words, an acceptance stance means acknowledging you are having sad feelings, when sad feelings emerge. Even if it is unfair that you just got fired, if you did, you must accept that reality to be able to move through and beyond the moment. Further, an acceptance standpoint suggests that if you take a risk, you will likely feel vulnerable. However, acceptance does not mean resigning yourself to your current situation (e.g., "I will have an anxiety disorder forever and so I will never be able to apply for a new job"). As is obvious from the larger description of our treatment, acceptance involves making room for the full myriad of thoughts, feelings, and bodily sensations that will inevitably arise as you engage in actions that are personally relevant and meaningful.

Cultivating an acceptance perspective involves skill building and practice. Here again, we draw from traditional cognitive-behavioral interventions by using extensive self-monitoring in order to increase clients' awareness of their external context and their internal processes. We also use relaxation techniques, such as progressive muscle relaxation (PMR; Bernstein, Borkovec, & Hazlett-Stevens, 2000) and diaphragmatic breathing, to promote present-moment awareness. However, we add to this an explicit emphasis on the type of awareness clients are practicing (nonjudgmental, compassionate, expansive) and draw heavily from mindfulness and other acceptance-based strategies in order to facilitate this alternative way of responding to one's experience. In particular, we are careful to emphasize that, although some of these strategies may lead to reduced distress at times, such a reduction is not the goal. Instead clients are encouraged to notice whatever arises for them internally, recognize that these are just thoughts, feelings, or sensations, bring compassion to these experiences, and choose to act in valued ways regardless.

We have found that mindfulness-based practices (both formally within and between session and informally throughout the clients' day) are particularly helpful ways of promoting an open, accepting stance to counteract our clients' habitual ways of responding. We introduce the concept of mindfulness ("paying attention in a particular way: on purpose, in the present moment and nonjudgmentally"; Kabat-Zinn, 1994, p. 4) during the second session. Clients engage in several exercises so that they can experience, rather than try to intellectually understand, what it means to notice internal and external stimuli with an open, curious attitude. We emphasize the importance (and difficulty) of bringing compassion to one's experience, rather than judgment, and describe how the process may unfold by noticing and not judging one's own judgments, which inevitably arise (as opposed to judging one's judgments, which only perpetuates the cycle). Clients are encouraged to begin to view their thoughts and feelings as separate from themselves (from a "decentered" perspective, Segal et al., 2002). We emphasize the process of mindfulness (using the common mindfulness instruction to gently bring one's attention back 101 times, when it wanders 100 times) and note that it is not a state we achieve, but a practice we continually engage in.

We have clients engage in formal mindfulness practices that progress throughout the course of therapy from a focus on their breath and other internal sensations (using diaphragmatic breathing and PMR as awareness exercises), to slowly and carefully identifying and tuning into sensations such as sight, taste, and sound (e.g., The Raisin Exercise, Mindfulness of Sounds; Segal et al., 2002), to the challenge of emotions and thoughts (e.g., *The Guest House*, Segal et al., 2002; Clouds exercise, Linehan, 1993b; Leaves on a Stream, Hayes et al., 1999), to developing self-compassion (e.g., "The Wild Geese" by Mary Oliver, as cited in Segal et al., 2002), to the development of a transcendent sense of self (e.g., the mountain meditation, Kabat-Zinn, 1994). Clients also engage in informal practices throughout their day, bringing awareness to tasks such as eating, washing dishes, having conversations, and driving to work (e.g., Nhat Hanh, 1992). Over time they are encouraged to bring mindfulness to more challenging daily contexts, such as disagreements with a loved one, new social situations, or stressful tasks at work. We emphasize the importance of fully participating in life (Linehan, 1993b), with formal practices designed to help develop the skills that allow one to bring mindfulness to these life activities.

Similar to Borkovec's approach to treating GAD, we try to increase our clients' flexibility in responding by introducing them to numerous types of mindfulness practices and encouraging them to try all of them, and commit to regular practice of those they find most beneficial. Although we embrace this flexible approach, we are also careful to encourage clients to try practices they find particularly challenging, and that they may want to avoid, as these may encourage the mindfulness skills they most need to work on. For example, we have had clients who dislike longer, more formal mindfulness exercises because they fear they are wasting time sitting quietly or because they find prolonged periods of quiet time difficult to tolerate. Consistent with the rest of our treatment, we encourage clients here to pay attention to the urge to avoid and see if there is something important to be learned. We emphasize that clients should feel free to choose mindfulness exercises, rather than compelled toward or away from them. So if they feel particularly pulled toward or away from one form of practice, some further attention to and exploration of the area may be warranted. We do not require our clients to have a traditional sitting practice, although we do ask them to engage in some type of formal practice for at least 15 min a day. This flexibility in our protocol means that one client may engage in extensive formal sitting practice, another might practice PMR and diaphragmatic breathing as his or her mindfulness practice, and a third might practice mindful breathing during his or her subway commute. Although common principles are emphasized across all clients, variability is allowed in the practices they regularly commit to.

Our clinical experience suggests that compassion is a particularly important, and challenging, aspect of mindfulness practice for our GAD clients (and preliminary data from an undergraduate sample suggest that self-compassion is uniquely related to both GAD symptom severity and excessive worry, beyond shared associations with depression and anxiety symptoms, as well as mindful awareness; Roemer, Salters-Pedneault, & Mennin, 2005). When our clients begin to practice mindfulness, they often report a lot of critical thoughts and judgments about their internal experience (e.g., "I shouldn't worry about that," "I don't know why I can't get this out of my head," "I'm so overreactive to things") and their external actions ("I should be doing more," "Other people are more productive than I am"). Clients sometimes report concerns that a more compassionate response to their internal experience or their external behaviors would result in complacency and prevent change. One client reported that this would involve "letting [herself] off the hook." These clients are asked to observe whether these judgments are in fact promoting more change in their lives. They are also asked to test out a more compassionate response and see what its effects are, tolerating the anxiety that may arise from letting oneself "off the hook." Therapists may also share their own experiences of noticing how their self-judgments often get in the way of adaptive responding, while bringing compassion to their experience opens up options for more flexible behavioral responding in a given situation, even though it might feel like the effects would be reversed. Clients are encouraged to practice responding to their own experiences as they might respond if a close friend or family member were sharing his or her thoughts and feelings. Therapists also convey compassion toward their clients' reported experiences, validating the human nature of their responses. This validation commonly increases clients' compassion toward themselves (Rogers, 1961).

Drawing from ACT, we explicitly promote experiential acceptance as something we engage in to help us lead a meaningful life, rather than in order to alter our internal experience. However, we acknowledge that individuals may choose to make some efforts to alter their internal experience (such as breathing deeply in an effort to relax themselves). We review clients' own experience that such efforts do not always have the desired effect, particularly during the times they most want them to be effective. We therefore encourage clients not to attach to an emotion-altering outcome for these strategies, and to continue to engage in their lives fully, regardless of whether these desired internal changes take place.

One way we convey this concept is through an adaptation of the swamp metaphor from ACT. We note that if we want to go to a beautiful mountain and there is a swamp between us and the mountain, we may have to go through the swamp to get there. On the other hand, if the swamp is on the side of our path, there is no reason to walk over and roll around in it. Also, we can try to place a board across the swamp, or put on big boots in an effort to get less muddy while we are crossing the swamp. There is nothing particularly noble about wallowing in the muck of the swamp. However, we also recognize that we might trip and fall on our way through, no matter how big our boots or how wide our board. And if this happens, and we want to get to the mountain or travel on this path, we will have to pick ourselves up and keep moving. So acceptance is a stance that helps us move through whatever needs to be moved through, or carry with us whatever arises, while we are doing what matters to us.

In addition to mindfulness practices (drawn from MBCT, MBSR, DBT, and ACT) and modeling acceptance within the therapeutic relationship, we use several strategies from ACT that help clients experience their thoughts and reactions as separate from themselves and their direct experience, thus facilitating acceptance and nonavoidance of these internal experiences. We encourage clients to use the practice of labeling thoughts and feelings as thoughts and feelings, in order to bring awareness to the distinction between these reactions and judgments (e.g., "I'm having the thought that I am a failure," "I am having an anxious reaction") and reality (as suggested by "I am a failure" or "I am anxious"). We also encourage clients to replace the word *but* with the word *and* in sentences like "I wanted to ask her out, but I was anxious" because this change in language opens up the possibility that one could be experiencing anxiety and still engage in a valued action. This stance runs counter to a typical stance of taking internal experiences as a reason not to engage in actions, due to our ingrained patterns of experiential avoidance. These language practices help increase flexibility and awareness that our actions are a choice, regardless of our internal experience.

BEHAVIORAL CHANGE

As part of the informed consent process, we communicate to our clients that from our perspective, GAD is problematic in the way that it erodes quality of life, and thus our treatment involves attending to the way they are living their lives and making changes in this arena. This conceptualization of their problem often runs counter to clients' initial reasons for entering treatment (to reduce their anxiety); however, in our experience, at some deep level clients can often connect with the idea that anxiety has distanced them from the people and activities they personally value and agree that this is a worthwhile focus of treatment.

Drawing from ACT, we distinguish between goals and values, emphasizing the process of behaving in ways that are consistent with what matters, rather than the goal of achieving certain outcomes. For example, often our clients will present as very dissatisfied with their current jobs and they will have the goal of obtaining a new job. Although having such a goal can be useful in that it can help a client to organize his or her behavior to achieve the goal, focusing solely on this goal can be disruptive. For instance, by its very definition a goal is future-oriented and it implies that wherever the client is in this moment is not good enough. Additionally, once a goal is met (the client gets a new job), a new goal must be set to organize purposeful behavior in this domain of living. On the other hand, values in the work domain might include ongoing attributes or "ways of being," such as communicating openly and effectively with co-workers, taking on challenging tasks, working collaboratively with team members, and so on. These values can be pursued in the client's current position while he or she searches for a new job and they can be continuously pursued if a new position is attained. Further, in our experience, clients sometimes set goals as an avoidance behavior. A client may be dissatisfied in his or her current position because he or she is avoiding connecting with co-workers or taking on challenges and rather than accepting those feelings and taking action, he or she daydreams about a future job that would solve all the current stressors and problems (goal). We have found that often when a client identifies values he or she can pursue in a current job, relationship, and so forth, the need to move becomes less pressing.

We begin our efforts at behavioral change by increasing clients' awareness of what matters to them and the ways that they are not acting consistently with these values. Before treatment, we assess the importance of certain areas of life (e.g., family relationships, intimate relationships, work, recreation, health) and the consistency with which clients are living as they would like to be in each of these valued domains (Wilson & Groom, 2002). Clients then engage in a series of between-session writing assignments that ask them to deeply explore their thoughts and feelings, focusing first on the obstacles they experience in living consistent with their values in three central domains of life (we organize and collapse the areas of life into interpersonal, occupational/educational, and personal interests/care) and then on how they would like to be in each of these domains (e.g., how open they want to be in their relationships, what sort of attributes are important to them as they pursue a particular career). Subsequent assignments help clients identify one or two central core values within each domain that will guide behavioral assignments over the course of therapy. Values are explicitly individualized and therapists work with clients toward whatever matters most to them, and allow this process of identifying values to unfold throughout the course of therapy.

Drawing from the concept of pliance discussed by Hayes and colleagues (1999), we emphasize the importance of clients determining what actually matters to them, not what they think "should" matter, or what we think matters. Although this is a simple concept, it can be quite difficult in practice as social sanctioning of values is so strong. Further, it can be difficult to determine if a particular action is values driven or avoidance driven. For instance, we treated a client who was unclear on whether she valued her current, low stress work environment as it allowed her more time to engage in other valued activities or whether she was simply avoiding taking risks with her career. We steer clients away from using logical, rational analysis to sort out these dilemmas, instead underscoring the freedom of making choices without having to justify or rationalize the reasons (e.g., like choosing vanilla over chocolate ice cream). In our experience, often once the pressure of making the right decision is removed, the client will use his or her own wisdom to make valued choices.

Once a client has deeply explored, and emotionally processed through a series of writing assignments, the ways in which anxiety and avoidance may be affecting his or her life, and identified certain core values, a period of careful self-monitoring begins during which the client observes his or her own valued behavior and missed opportunities. For instance, a client who identified a value of open communication with his partner would then monitor communication with his partner throughout the week, noting when he openly communicated and when he did not, as well as what got in the way of his open communication. Once internal (thoughts and feelings) and external (limited time with partner because of work schedules) barriers to valued action are identified, clients then begin the process of committing to certain actions within each domain throughout the course of the week, monitoring how these actions unfold, and adjusting subsequent planned actions accordingly. Particular attention is paid to the obstacles that clients encounter, with mindfulness and acceptance being practiced when the obstacle is internal, and problem-solving being engaged when the obstacle is external. Again, valued directions may also unfold and change as a result of experiences while engaging in these actions, and this is also discussed in therapy.

The process of identifying one's values and noticing the ways that one is not living a valued life can be a painful process. Often clients express sadness at their feelings of detachment from others in their lives, dissatisfaction with their jobs, or a sense of emptiness or loneliness that underlies their generally anxious state. We encourage clients to practice mindfulness and experiential acceptance as these feelings arise, and we validate the pain inherent in recognizing the ways that their lives have become limited and restricted.

Often clients who have had no difficulty with the idea of acceptance early in treatment begin to exhibit increased experiential avoidance when they begin trying out valued action. We predict that engaging in these actions will often increase distress at least initially, given that experiential avoidance is one reason these actions have been avoided in the past. As these patterns of nonaccepting responding reemerge, we revisit the model of treatment along with experiential exercises that promote acceptance, and also review with clients their desire to engage in these chosen actions. We encourage clients to try engaging in their chosen behaviors and to "take their anxiety with them" as they do. Once they repeatedly engage in these behaviors, they often experience a renewed commitment to making these behavioral changes and an increased willingness to experience the distress associated with fully engaging in their lives.

Toward the end of treatment, time is devoted to relapse prevention efforts. Therapists and clients review the progress made, noting strategies, exercises, and metaphors each client found particularly helpful and making a list of these for future reminders. Clients are reminded that anxiety is a natural human response and that they are likely to experience increases in anxiety as their lives unfold. They are cautioned not to interpret increases in anxiety as evidence that their progress was illusory, but rather to see it as part of the natural ebb and flow of life and as a reminder to bring attention back to the elements of treatment that were particularly helpful. Clients are given a notebook of all the handouts from treatment, as well as a list of mindfulness resources (many of which have been recommended by former clients). Clients are also encouraged to continue some form of regular mindfulness practice (some clients do regular sitting meditation, others do yoga, some practice mindfulness in particular contexts, such as while riding on the subway or sitting in a church) and to develop reminders to place around their environments that will help them bring their attention back to the present moment. Clients also develop a list of their values and are encouraged to check in with themselves from time to time to see if they are making choices that are consistent with these values.

PRELIMINARY DATA

The treatment described above was developed as part of a treatment development grant. During the first half of the grant, we implemented and revised the treatment, while assessing outcome on those clients treated, providing us with open trial data on its effectiveness. For the second half of the grant (which is still underway), clients were randomly assigned to a treatment or waitlist condition in order to obtain an initial indication of its efficacy.

Sixteen clients completed the treatment in the open trial. Five of these clients were treated by the developers of the treatment (L.R. and S.O.) and the other 11 were treated by graduate and postdoctoral level clinicians supervised by these developers. The sample of completers was 56.3% female, whereas 87.5% identified as White, with one client identifying as Latina and one as White/Southeast Asian. They had an average age of 36.44 years ($SD = 12.34$). All clients were assessed before and after treatment by an independent clinical assessor who administered the Anxiety Disorder Interview Schedule—IV (ADIS-IV; DiNardo, Brown, & Barlow, 1994). Clients' average clinical severity rating for GAD was 5.93 (on a scale of 0 to 8, with 4 as a clinical cutoff; $SD = 0.93$). Two clients presented with comorbid principal diagnoses of depression (a population that is typically omitted from GAD clinical trials), and the overall sample presented with an average of 1.31 additional diagnoses (ranging from 0 to 3). Social anxiety disorder, specific phobia, panic disorder, and major depressive disorder were the most common additional diagnoses. Six of these clients were taking psychiatric medications (anxiolytics, antidepressants, or both) and were asked to stay at constant dosages throughout treatment, although two chose to discontinue their medications during the course of therapy.

These 16 clients demonstrated significant reductions in clinician ratings of severity of GAD and in self-report measures of anxiety, worry, and depressive symptoms from pre- to posttreatment. Clients also demonstrated a significant reduction in frequency of additional diagnoses, suggesting that the treatment also targeted non-GAD symptomatology. Further, clients demonstrated significant increases in self-reported quality of life, an outcome that has not been investigated in previous investigations of GAD. Clients also demonstrated significant decreases in measures of proposed mechanisms of change (experiential avoidance and fear of emotional responses), suggesting the treatment may be effectively targeting intended psychological processes. All of these were large effects; large effects were also revealed on measures at 3-month follow-up.

To date, 17 clients have completed the randomized controlled trial (10 randomly assigned to treatment). These clients presented with an average GAD severity of 5.66 ($SD = 0.61$) and an average of 0.88 ($SD = 0.86$) additional diagnoses. Two clients presented with comorbid principal diagnoses of MDD and one client presented with a comorbid principal diagnosis of dysthymia (other comorbid conditions included social phobia, specific phobia, and obsessive–compulsive disorder). Five clients were taking psychiatric medications (anxiolytics, antidepressants, or both) and were asked to keep at a constant level throughout treatment, although one discontinued medication use during treatment. Clients were an average of 31.81 ($SD = 9.06$) years old. The majority of clients identified as White, with one Latino and one Asian American client. There were 9 women in the sample. The treatment and waitlist group did not differ significantly in demographic variables or pretreatment levels of any of the outcome and process variables.

In analyses controlling for pretreatment levels of each variable, the treatment group demonstrated significantly better outcomes in GAD clinician severity rating, number of additional diagnoses, anxiety, worry, and depressive symptoms, and quality of life. Significantly lower levels of experiential avoidance, fear of emotions, and emotion dysregulation were also revealed for the treatment group. Again, effect sizes were all large. Among those clients who have currently completed a posttreatment assessment, 62% meet criteria for high end-state functioning using criteria similar to those used in other trials (Borkovec & Costello, 1993; Ladouceur et al., 2000), suggesting comparable or slightly improved outcomes to previous trials, although such comparisons should be considered extremely preliminary at this point. As data collection is still underway, long-term follow-up data are not yet available. It remains to be seen whether this intervention is more efficacious than an alternative credible treatment; we are planning a study to examine this next. Thus, although current findings are promising, more research is needed to determine whether the novel elements of this intervention increase efficacy in treating GAD.

DIRECTIONS FOR FUTURE RESEARCH

Clearly, a great deal of further research is needed exploring the utility of using an acceptance-based behavior therapy to treat GAD. First, it will be important to compare the efficacy of this approach to a credible alternative treatment in order to determine whether the observed effects are due to specific ingredients in this treatment as opposed to more nonspecific factors. It will also be important to determine whether this treatment is efficacious through the proposed mechanisms (e.g., experiential acceptance, emotional openness, expanded awareness, mindfulness). In order to do this, we need to continue to develop more sensitive and valid self-report (Block-Lerner, Salters-Pedneault, & Tull, 2005) and laboratory-based (Zvolensky, Feldner, Leen-Feldner, & Yartz, 2005) measures of these constructs so that we can determine whether this treatment and others like it lead to changes in these phenomena and whether those changes account for the symptom and quality of life changes that are observed. Relatedly, it will be interesting to explore whether similar mechanisms account for the efficacy of treatments that do not explicitly target these phenomena (similar to Teasdale and colleagues', 2002, finding that both cognitive therapy and mindfulness-based cognitive therapy led to increased metacognitive awareness, as well as reductions in depressive relapse).

It will also be important to investigate pretherapy predictors of outcome, so that one might determine which clients are most likely to benefit from this approach. In our preliminary data, medication status, comorbidity, level of pretreatment depression, and level of pretreatment experiential avoidance all failed to significantly predict outcome. However, studies with larger sample sizes are needed with more extensive pretreatment assessments of potentially relevant variables. Further, we need to investigate long-term outcome and stability of change in order to determine whether the changes we are observing are persistent or transitory. Also, we need to include more comprehensive assessments of quality of life (e.g., relational and occupational functioning, physical health status) in order to determine the broader impact of this (and other) treatments.

Our current data demonstrate that this treatment can be efficacious in a research-based clinic, with the treatment developers overseeing its implementation. It will be important to explore the portability of the treatment and to determine optimal modes of training that are cost-effective and yet sufficiently in-depth so that clinicians are able to flexibly and effectively use the treatment manual. It will also be important to explore the effectiveness of the treatment with people from different ethnic, racial, and socioeconomic backgrounds, given that our sample so far has been predominantly White and middle-class. Our very limited experience with the few ethnic minority and working class clients we have treated has been encouraging.

We believe that the emphasis on client-defined valued areas and the flexibility we give clients in trying multiple forms of mindfulness and acceptance-based practice, but committing to those practices that suit them best, enhances the acceptability and applicability of the treatment. However, considerable research is needed to determine the extent to which this is accurate as well as any culturally specific adaptations that should be made.

Finally, in order to determine the causal relationship between acceptance-based processes and various outcomes, it will be important to conduct basic research aimed at isolating components of these processes and determining their unique effects. Although dismantling designs in treatment outcome research are also an important way to determine active ingredients (and allow for tests of causal effects within the therapeutic context, which is important), outcome studies are extremely labor and time intensive. Coupling them with basic experimental research that strives to develop externally valid analogues for clinically relevant interventions and outcomes is an ideal way to increase our knowledge regarding the mechanisms of these treatment methodologies (see Eifert & Heffner, 2003; Levitt, Brown, Orsillo, & Barlow, 2004, for examples of this methodology). It is particularly challenging to devise ways to reproduce experiential acceptance or a mindful stance in a laboratory setting, and limits in the external validity of these interventions need to be noted; nonetheless this is an important area for future methodological developments that will advance the field.

Treatment approaches that incorporate acceptance and mindfulness-based strategies with behavior change techniques seem to hold promise in the treatment of many clinical disorders. Given the apparent centrality of experiential avoidance and reactivity to emotions in GAD, it may be that those approaches similarly hold promise in the treatment of this chronic anxiety disorder for which we have yet to develop sufficiently efficacious treatments. Further research will help us determine whether our approach or others like it can be beneficial in treating both the symptoms and the functional impairment associated with GAD.

ACKNOWLEDGMENTS: Preparation of this chapter was supported in part by National Institute of Mental Health Grant MH63208 to the first and last authors. The authors thank Dave Barlow for his support of this research. We also thank the therapists and clients involved in the grant whose wisdom and shared experience greatly enhance this treatment.

REFERENCES

American Psychiatric Association. (1994). *Diagnostic and statistical manual of mental disorders* (4th ed.). Washington, DC: Author.

Arntz, A. (2003). Cognitive therapy versus applied relaxation as treatment of generalized anxiety disorder. *Behaviour Research and Therapy, 41*, 633–646.

Barlow, D. H., Rapee, R. M., & Brown, T. A. (1992). Behavioral treatment of generalized anxiety disorder. *Behavior Therapy, 23*, 551–570.

Beck, A. T., & Emery, G. (1985). *Anxiety disorders and phobias: A cognitive perspective.* New York: Basic Books.

Bernstein, D. A., Borkovec, T. D., & Hazlett-Stevens, H. (2000). *New directions in progressive relaxation training: A guidebook for helping professionals.* Westport, CT: Praeger Publishers.

Block-Lerner, J., Salters-Pedneault, K., & Tull, M.T. (2005). Assessing mindfulness and experiential acceptance: Attempts to capture inherently elusive phenomena. In S. M. Orsillo & L. Roemer (Eds.), *Acceptance and mindfulness-based approaches to anxiety: Conceptualization and treatment* (pp. 71–99). New York: Springer.

Borkovec, T. D. (2002). Life in the future versus life in the present. *Clinical Psychology: Science and Practice, 9*, 76–80.

Borkovec, T. D., Alcaine, O. M., & Behar, E. (2004). Avoidance theory of worry and generalized anxiety disorder. In R. G. Heimberg, C. L. Turk, & D. S. Mennin (Eds.), *Generalized anxiety disorders: Advances in research and practice* (pp. 77–108). New York: Guilford.

Borkovec, T. D., & Costello, E. (1993). Efficacy of applied relaxation and cognitive-behavioral therapy in the treatment of generalized anxiety disorder. *Journal of Consulting and Clinical Psychology, 61*, 611–619.

Borkovec, T. D., Hazlett-Stevens, H., & Diaz, M. L. (1999). The role of positive beliefs about worry in generalized anxiety disorder and its treatment. *Clinical Psychology and Psychotherapy, 6*, 126–138.

Borkovec, T. D., & Hu, S. (1990). The effect of worry on cardiovascular response to phobic imagery. *Behaviour Research and Therapy, 28*, 69–73.

Borkovec, T. D., Newman, M. G., Lytle, R., & Pincus, A. (2002). A component analysis of cognitive behavioral therapy for generalized anxiety disorder and the role of interpersonal problems. *Journal of Consulting and Clinical Psychology, 70*, 288–298.

Borkovec, T. D., & Roemer, L. (1994). Generalized anxiety disorder. In R. T. Ammerman & M. Hersen (Eds.), *Handbook of prescriptive treatments for adults* (pp. 261–281). New York: Plenum.

Borkovec, T. D., & Roemer, L. (1995). Perceived functions of worry among generalized anxiety disorder subjects: Distraction from more emotionally distressing topics? *Journal of Behavior Therapy and Experimental Psychiatry, 26*, 25–30.

Borkovec, T. D., & Ruscio, A. M. (2001). Psychotherapy for generalized anxiety disorder. *Journal of Clinical Psychiatry, 62*, 37–45.

Borkovec, T. D., Shadick, R., & Hopkins, M. (1991). The nature of normal and pathological worry. In R. Rapee & D. H. Barlow (Eds.), *Chronic anxiety: Generalized anxiety disorder and mixed anxiety-depression* (pp. 29–51). New York: Guilford.

Borkovec, T. D., & Sharpless, B. (2004). Generalized anxiety disorder: Bringing cognitive-behavioral therapy into the valued present. In S. C. Hayes, V. M.

Follette, & M. M. Linehan (Eds.), *Mindfulness and acceptance: Expanding the cognitive-behavioral tradition* (pp. 209–242). New York: Guilford.

Brown, T. A., Barlow, D. H., & Liebowitz, M. R. (1994). The empirical basis of generalized anxiety disorder. *American Journal of Psychiatry, 151,* 1272–1280.

Butler, G. (1994). Treatment of worry in generalized anxiety disorder. In G. C. L. Davey & F. Tallis (Eds.), *Worrying: Perspectives on theory, assessment and treatment* (pp. 35–59). New York: Wiley.

Butler, G., Fennell, M., Robson, P., & Gelder, M. (1991). Comparison of behavior therapy and cognitive behavior therapy in the treatment of generalized anxiety disorder. *Journal of Consulting and Clinical Psychology, 59,* 167–175.

Butler, G., Gelder, M., Hibbert, G., Cullington, A., & Klimes, I. (1987). Anxiety management: Developing effective strategies. *Behaviour Research and Therapy, 25,* 517–522.

Butler, G., & Matthews, A. (1987). Anticipatory anxiety and risk perception. *Cognitive Therapy and Research, 11,* 551–565.

Connor, K. M., & Davidson, J. R. T. (1998). Generalized anxiety disorder: Neurobiological and pharmacotherapeutic perspectives. *Biological Psychiatry, 44,* 1286–1294.

DiNardo, P. A., Brown, T. A., & Barlow, D. H. (1994). *Anxiety Disorders Interview Schedule for DSM-IV.* Albany, NY: Graywind Publications.

Dugas, M. J., Buhr, K., & Ladouceur, R. (2004). The role of intolerance and uncertainty in etiology and maintenance. In R. G. Heimberg, C. L. Turk, & D. S. Mennin (Eds.), *Generalized anxiety disorders: Advances in research and practice* (pp. 164–186). New York: Guilford.

Dugas, M. J., Freeston, J. H., Ladouceur, R., Rheaume, J., Provencher, M., & Boisvert, M. M. (1998). Worry themes in primary GAD, secondary GAD and other anxiety disorders. *Journal of Anxiety Disorders, 12,* 253–261.

Dugas, M. J., Ladouceur, R., Leger, E., Freeston, M. H., Langlois, Provencher, M. D., et al. (2003). Group cognitive-behavioral therapy for generalized anxiety disorder: Treatment outcome and long-term follow-up. *Journal of Consulting and Clinical Psychology, 71,* 821–825.

Eifert, G. H., & Heffner, M. (2003). The effects of acceptance versus control contexts on avoidance of panic-related symptoms. *Journal of Behavior Therapy and Experimental Psychiatry, 34,* 293–312.

Foa, E. B., & Kozak, M. J. (1986). Emotional processing of fear: Exposure to corrective information. *Psychological Bulletin, 99,* 20–35.

Freeston, M. H., Rheaume, J., Letarte, H., Dugas, M. J., & Ladouceur, R. (1994). Why do people worry? *Personality and Individual Differences, 17,* 791–802.

Greenberg, L. S. (2002). *Emotion-focused therapy: Coaching clients to work through their feelings.* Washington, DC: American Psychological Association.

Greenberg, L. S., & Safran, J. D. (1987). *Emotions in psychotherapy.* New York: Guilford.

Gross, J. J., & Levenson, R. W. (1993). Emotional suppression: Physiology, self-report, and expressive behavior. *Journal of Personality and Social Psychology, 64,* 970–986.

Gross, J. J., & Levenson, R. W. (1997). Hiding feelings: The acute effects of inhibiting negative and positive emotion. *Journal of Abnormal Psychology, 106,* 95–103.

Hayes, S. C., Strosahl, K. D., & Wilson, K. G. (1999). *Acceptance and commitment therapy: An experiential approach to behavior change.* New York: Guilford.

Hayes, S. C., Wilson, K. G., Gifford, E. V, Follette, V. M., & Strosahl, K. (1996). Experiential avoidance and behavioral disorders: A functional dimensional approach to diagnosis and treatment. *Journal of Consulting and Clinical Psychology, 64,* 1152–1168.

Hoehn-Saric, R., & McLeod, D. R. (1988). The peripheral sympathetic nervous system: Its role in normal and pathological anxiety. *Psychiatric Clinics of North America, 11,* 375–386.

Kabat-Zinn, J. (1990). *Full catastrophe living: Using the wisdom of your body and mind to face stress, pain and illness.* New York: Delacorte.

Kabat-Zinn, J. (1994). *Wherever you go there you are.* New York: Hyperion.

Kessler, R. C., Walters, E. E., & Wittchen, H.-U. (2004). Epidemiology. In R. G. Heimberg, C. L. Turk, & D. S. Mennin (Eds.), *Generalized anxiety disorder: Advances in research and practice* (pp. 29–50). New York: Guilford.

Ladouceur, R., Dugas, M. J., Freeston, M. H., Leger, E., Gagnon, F., & Thibodeau, N. (2000). Efficacy of a new cognitive-behavioral treatment for generalized anxiety disorder: Evaluation in a controlled clinical trial. *Journal of Consulting and Clinical Psychology, 68,* 957–964.

Levitt, J. T., Brown, T. A., Orsillo, S. M., & Barlow, D. H. (2004). The effects of acceptance versus suppression of emotion on subjective and psychophysiological response to carbon dioxide challenge in patients with panic disorder. *Behavior Therapy, 35,* 747–766.

Linehan, M. M. (1993a). *cognitive-behavioral treatment of borderline personality disorder.* New York: Guilford.

Linehan, M. (1993b). *Skills training manual for cognitive behavioral treatment of borderline personality disorder.* New York: Guilford.

Lyonfields, J. D., Borkovec, T. D., & Thayer, J. F. (1995). Vagal tone in generalized anxiety disorder and the effects of aversive imagery and worrisome thinking. *Behavior Therapy, 26,* 457–466.

MacLeod, C., & Rutherford, E. (2004). Information-processing approaches: Assessing the selective functioning of attention, interpretation, and retrieval. In R. G. Heimberg, C. L. Turk, & D. S. Mennin (Eds.), *Generalized anxiety disorders: Advances in research and practice* (pp. 109–142). New York: Guilford.

Matthews, A. (1990). Why worry? The cognitive function of anxiety. *Behaviour Research and Therapy, 28,* 455–468.

Mennin, D. S. (2004). Emotion regulation therapy for generalized anxiety disorder. *Clinical Psychology and Psychotherapy, 11,* 17–29.

Mennin, D. S., Heimberg, R. G., Turk, C. L., & Fresco, D. M. (in press). Preliminary evidence for an emotion dysregulation model of generalized anxiety disorder. *Behaviour Research and Therapy.*

Newman, M. G., Castonguay, L. G., Borkovec, T. D., & Molnar, C. (2004). Integrative psychotherapy. In R. G. Heimberg, C. L. Turk, & D. S. Mennin (Eds.), *Generalized* anxiety disorder: Advances in Research and Practice (pp. 320–350). New York: Guilford.

Nhat Hanh, T. (1992). Peace is every step: The path of mindfulness in everyday life. New York: Bantam Books.

Orsillo, S. M., Roemer, L., & Barlow, D. H. (2003). Integrating acceptance and mindfulness into existing cognitive-behavioral treatment for GAD: A case study. Cognitive and Behavioral Practice, 10, 223–230.

Orsillo, S. M., Roemer, L., & Holowka, D. W. (2005). Acceptance-based behavioral therapies for anxiety: Using acceptance and mindfulness to enhance traditional cognitive-behavioral approaches. In S. M. Orsillo & L. Roemer (Eds.), Acceptance and mindfulness-based approaches to anxiety: Conceptualization and treatment (pp. 3–35). New York: Springer.

Öst, L. (1987). Applied relaxation: Description of a coping technique and review of controlled studies. Behaviour Research and Therapy, 25, 397–409.

Öst, L. G., & Breitholtz, E. (2000). Applied relaxation vs. cognitive therapy in the treatment of generalized anxiety disorder. Behaviour Research and Therapy, 38, 777–790.

Purdon, C. (1999). Thought suppression and psychopathology. Behaviour Research and Therapy, 37, 1029–1054.

Roemer, L., Molina S., & Borkovec, T. D. (1997). An investigation of worry content among generally anxious individuals. Journal of Nervous and Mental Disease, 185, 314–319.

Roemer, L., Orsillo, S. M., & Barlow, D. H. (2002). Generalized anxiety disorder. In D. H. Barlow (Ed.), Anxiety and its disorders: The nature and treatment of anxiety and panic (2nd ed.). New York: Guilford.

Roemer, L., Salters, K., Raffa, S., & Orsillo, S. M. (2005). Fear and avoidance of internal experiences in GAD: Preliminary tests of a conceptual model. Cognitive Therapy and Research, 29, 79–88.

Roemer, L., Salters-Pedneault, K., & Mennin, D. S. (2005). The role of mindfulness and self-compassion in generalized anxiety disorder. Unpublished dataset.

Rogers, C. R. (1961). On becoming a person: A therapist's view of psychotherapy. Boston: Houghton Mifflin Company.

Salters-Pedneault, K., Roemer, L., Tull, M. T., Rucker, L., & Mennin, D. S. (in press). Evidence of broad deficits in emotion regulation associated with chronic worry and generalized anxiety disorder. Cognitive Therapy Research.

Segal, Z. V., Williams, J. M. G., & Teasdale, J. D. (2002). Mindfulness-based cognitive therapy for depression: A new approach to preventing relapse. New York: Guilford.

Souetre, E., Lozet, H., Cimarosti, I., Martin, P., Chignon, J. M., Ades, J., et al. (1994). Cost of anxiety disorders: Impact of comorbidity. Journal of Psychosomatic Research, 38, 151–160.

Stein, M. B., & Heimberg, R.G. (2004). Well-being and life satisfaction in generalized anxiety disorder: Comparison to major depressive disorder in a community sample. Journal of Affective Disorders, 79, 161–166.

Taylor, S., Koch, W. J., & McNally, R. J. (1992). How does anxiety sensitivity vary across the anxiety disorders? Journal of Anxiety Disorders, 6, 249–259.

Teasdale, J. D., Moore, R. G., Hayhurst, H., Pope, M., Williams, S., & Segal, Z. V. (2002). Metacognitive awareness and prevention of relapse in depression: Empirical evidence. *Journal of Consulting and Clinical Psychology, 70,* 275–287.

Turk, C. L., Heimberg, R. G., Luterek, J. A., Mennin, D. S., & Fresco, D. M. (2005). Delineating emotion regulation deficits in generalized anxiety disorder: A comparison with social anxiety disorder. *Cognitive Therapy and Research, 29,* 89–106.

Twohig, M. P., Masuda, A., Varra, A. A., & Hayes, S. C. (2005). Acceptance and Commitment Therapy as a treatment for anxiety disorders. In S. M. Orsillo & L. Roemer (Eds.), *Acceptance and mindfulness-based approaches to anxiety: Conceptualization and treatment* (pp. 101–129). New York: Springer.

Wegner, D. M. (1994). Ironic processes of mental control. *Psychological Review, 101,* 34–52.

Wells, A. (2004). A cognitive model of GAD: Meta-cognition and worry. In R. G. Heimberg, C. L. Turk, & D. S. Mennin (Eds.), *Generalized anxiety disorders: Advances in research and practice* (pp. 164–186). New York: Guilford.

Wells, A., & Carter, K. (1999). Preliminary tests of a cognitive model of generalized anxiety disorder. *Behaviour Research and Therapy, 37,* 585–594.

Wells, A., & Papageorgio, C. (1995). Worry and the incubation of intrusive images following stress. *Behaviour Research and Therapy, 33,* 579–583.

Westen, D., & Morrison, K. (2001). A multi-dimensional meta-analysis of treatments for panic, depression and generalized anxiety disorder: An empirical examination of the status of empirically supported treatments. *Journal of Consulting and Clinical Psychology, 69,* 875–899.

Wetherell, J. L., Thorp, S. R., Patterson, T. L., Golshan, S., Jeste, D., & Gatz, M. (2004). Quality of life in geriatric generalized anxiety disorder: A preliminary investigation. *Psychiatric Research, 38,* 305–312.

Wilson, K. G., & Groom, J. (2002). *The Valued Living Questionnaire.* (Available from the first author at Department of Psychology, University of Mississippi, Oxford.)

Wilson, K. G.., & Murrell, A. R. (2004). Values work in acceptance and commitment therapy: setting a course for behavioral treatment. In S. C. Hayes, V. M. Follette, & M. M. Linehan (Eds.), *Mindfulness and acceptance: Expanding the cognitive-behavioral tradition* (pp. 120–151). New York: Guilford.

Wittchen, H.-U., Zhao, S., Kessler, R. C., & Eaton, W. W. (1994) DSM-III-R generalized anxiety disorder in the National Comorbidity Survey. *Archives of General Psychiatry, 51,* 355–364.

Woodman, C. L., Noyes, R., Black, D. W., Schlosser, S., & Yagia, S. J. (1999). A five year follow-up study of generalized anxiety disorder and panic disorder. *Journal of Nervous and Mental Disease, 187,* 3–9.

Yonkers, K. A., Warshaw, M. G., Massion, A. O., & Keller, M. B. (1996). Phenomenology and course of generalized anxiety disorder. *British Journal of Psychiatry, 168,* 308–313.

Zvolensky, M. J., Feldner, M. T., Leen-Feldner, E. W., & Yartz, A. R. (2005). Exploring basic processes underlying acceptance and mindfulness. In S. M. Orsillo & L. Roemer (Eds.), *Acceptance and mindfulness-based approaches to anxiety: Conceptualization and treatment* (pp. 325–357). New York: Springer.

ACCEPTANCE AND MINDFULNESS-BASED APPROACHES TO THE TREATMENT OF POSTTRAUMATIC STRESS DISORDER

Sonja V. Batten, Susan M. Orsillo,
and Robyn D. Walser

Posttraumatic stress disorder (PTSD) is the only anxiety disorder for which a specific event is seen as responsible for the etiology of the symptoms. More specifically, PTSD is diagnosed when a person has been exposed to a potentially traumatic event (e.g., sexual assault, combat, motor vehicle accident), during which the person experienced intense fear, helplessness, or horror (American Psychiatric Association, 1994), followed by a particular constellation of resulting symptoms. There are three main classes of symptoms in PTSD: reexperiencing, avoidance, and arousal. Reexperiencing symptoms may include distressing memories, nightmares, flashbacks, and intense distress or physiological reactivity upon exposure to internal or external cues related to the event. Avoidance symptoms may include avoidance of thoughts, feelings, situations, or people associated with the event, problems with memory for the event, anhedonia, and restricted range of affect. Finally, symptoms of increased arousal may consist of trouble sleeping or concentrating, irritability or anger, hypervigilance, and exaggerated startle response.

The National Comorbidity Survey estimated an overall lifetime prevalence rate of PTSD of 7.8%, with the rate for women (10.4%) more than twice that for men (5.0%; Kessler, Sonnega, Bromet, Hughes, & Nelson, 1995). There is considerable variation in the proportion of individuals exposed to a traumatic event who develop PTSD (8 to 60%) with variables such as trauma type, gender, and preexisting psychopathology influencing risk (Kessler et al., 1995). A diagnosis of PTSD is often associated with significant lifetime comorbidity (approximately 80% of individuals diagnosed with PTSD meet criteria for at least one additional lifetime disorder) and a notably chronic course, with more than one third of individuals diagnosed with PTSD still meeting criteria for the disorder 5 years later (Kessler et al., 1995).

Because of its diagnostic categorization within the anxiety disorders, most of the treatments developed for PTSD have been based upon an understanding of posttraumatic symptoms as they relate to problems with fear and anxiety responses. Although this original conceptualization of PTSD as an anxiety disorder has led to several effective treatments (most notably exposure therapy), it has recently been argued that PTSD can be more thoroughly understood as a disorder of experiential avoidance (Orsillo & Batten, 2005). That is, the symptoms experienced by individuals who meet criteria for PTSD can largely be explained within a model that proposes that chronic, pervasive efforts to avoid thoughts, feelings, and memories related to the traumatic event produce long-term exacerbation of these private events and ensuing functional impairment. We believe that acceptance-based behavioral therapies that follow from this model of experiential avoidance have the potential to add significantly to the effectiveness and comprehensiveness of the current PTSD treatment armamentarium.

TRADITIONAL TREATMENT APPROACHES FOR PTSD

The past three decades have witnessed significant advances in the psychotherapeutic treatment of PTSD. In fact, a recent meta-analysis indicates that the most widely used psychotherapies for PTSD lead to large improvements in symptoms from baseline (Bradley, Greene, Russ, Dutra, & Westen, 2005). The treatment approaches for PTSD with the most empirical support are exposure therapy, cognitive–behavioral therapies that focus on building skills for managing anxiety and/or challenging dysfunctional ways of thinking following a traumatic event, and eye movement desensitization and reprocessing. Basic descriptions of the differences between these treatments will be briefly reviewed here, followed by an analysis of the limitations of these treatments and description of the ways in which acceptance-based treatments can add to the existing tools available for the treatment of PTSD.

Exposure Therapy

One of the most consistently empirically supported treatments for PTSD is exposure therapy, a behavioral intervention in which the client is repeatedly presented with imaginal or in vivo cues associated with the traumatic event. The objective of exposure therapy is to engage fear and anxiety that arise upon remembering the trauma and to maintain contact with those emotions without avoidance, until habituation of emotional responding occurs. Exposure therapy has demonstrated efficacy with clients who have experienced a variety of traumatic events (Bryant, Moulds, Guthrie, Dang, & Nixon, 2003; Marks, Lovell, Noshirvani, Livanou, & Thrasher, 1998; Tarrier et al., 1999), including motor vehicle accidents (Fecteau & Nicki, 1999), sexual and physical assault (Foa et al., 1999; Foa, Rothbaum, Riggs, & Murdock, 1991), and combat (Glynn et al., 1999; Keane, Fairbank, Caddell, Zimering, & Bender, 1989).

Anxiety Management Training

Another treatment approach shown to be efficacious for PTSD is anxiety management training (AMT). In AMT, clients are taught a collection of cognitive and behavioral skills to help them manage the emotional responses that are common to PTSD. One of the primary components in AMT is relaxation training, whether through diaphragmatic breathing, progressive muscle relaxation, or relaxing guided imagery. Other components of AMT are psychoeducation about trauma, communication skills training, and anger management training (Chemtob, Novaco, Hamada, & Gross, 1997; Keane et al., 1989). Although not as widely researched as exposure therapy, AMT has been shown to be efficacious (Foa et al., 1991, 1999), and is more appealing to some clients and therapists because it does not specifically require that the client discuss and process the traumatic event.

Combined Treatment Approaches

On the basis of the established efficacy of both exposure therapy and more skills-based approaches, such as AMT, several combined treatment packages have been developed. Keane, Fisher, Krinsley, and Niles (1994) proposed an example of such an approach and recommended a treatment sequence consisting of six phases: (i) behavioral stabilization, (ii) trauma education, (iii) anxiety management skills, (iv) trauma focus work, (v) relapse prevention skills, and (vi) aftercare availability. Preliminary support has been found for such an approach, incorporating cognitive therapy techniques, for combat-related PTSD (Frueh, Turner, Beidel, Mirabella, & Jones, 1996). However, the most well-developed and fully researched combination therapy is Resick and Schnicke's (1992) cognitive processing therapy (CPT) for rape-related PTSD, which combines elements of cognitive therapy, exposure therapy, and AMT. CPT has demonstrated efficacy in several studies that have investigated its utility with sexual assault survivors (Nishith, Resick, & Griffin, 2002; Resick, Nishith, Weaver, Astin, & Feuer, 2002).

Eye Movement Desensitization and Reprocessing

One of the more controversial treatment developments in the field of PTSD is eye movement desensitization and reprocessing (EMDR, 1989, 1995). In EMDR, the client is asked to focus on an image of the traumatic event or negative cognitions associated with the trauma while engaging in repeated sets of lateral eye movements. Although a recent meta-analysis demonstrated that the application of EMDR results in clinical improvement, there is no evidence that EMDR is superior to exposure therapy and no support for the unique contribution of eye movements on outcome (Davidson & Parker, 2001), leading many to criticize the conceptual foundation of this approach (e.g., Lohr, Tolin, & Lilienfeld, 1998).

Limitations of Existing Treatments

The field of PTSD treatment development has made impressive progress in the creation and refinement of interventions available for the amelioration of posttraumatic symptoms. Meta-analysis of psychotherapy for PTSD has demonstrated that, on average, 67% of patients who complete one of the treatments described above no longer meet criteria for PTSD posttreatment, with a recovery rate of 56% if all participants are included in an intent-to-treat analysis (Bradley, et al., 2005). These results are encouraging, especially given the chronic and pernicious course that PTSD can take when left untreated. However, despite the accumulating positive findings from randomized controlled trials (RCTs), there are a number of methodological issues that potentially limit the generalizability of these findings to clinical practice.

On the basis of their review of the literature, Bradley and colleagues (2005) identified several important issues in the treatment of PTSD that deserve recognition. First, stringent exclusion criteria for participation in clinical trials for PTSD may be sacrificing external validity for internal validity. Although the overall exclusion rate across studies was only 30%, many of the most commonly cited exclusion criteria such as general comorbidity, comorbid substance dependence, and suicidality are common characteristics found among individuals diagnosed with PTSD. For instance, Tarrier and Gregg (2004) found a majority of individuals diagnosed with PTSD reported issues related to suicidality, with 38% reporting suicidal ideation, 8.5% admitting to a plan, and an additional 9.6% disclosing at least one previous attempt. Further, high rates of comorbidity with PTSD have been reported consistently across clinical and community samples. In the National Comorbidity Survey, a lifetime history of at least one additional psychiatric disorder was documented among 88.3% of men and 79% of women diagnosed with PTSD (Kessler et al., 1995). In that same sample, a lifetime history of a substance use disorder was present in 25% of the women and half of the men diagnosed with PTSD. Excluding potential participants from randomized-controlled trials assessing the efficacy of PTSD treatments based on these common characteristics may severely limit the generalizability of the findings to typical clinical practice.

Additionally, although a majority of participants in RCTs no longer meet criteria for PTSD at posttreatment, the use of this indicator as a criterion of successful outcome may be less than ideal. Bradley and colleagues (2005) accurately point out that individuals can fall below diagnostic thresholds by improving with regard to only one or two symptoms while remaining highly symptomatic. Broader evidence of the clinical significance of the changes associated with existing PTSD treatment is needed to ensure the sufficiency of these approaches. Further, the long-term maintenance of gains from existing PTSD treatments has not been sufficiently demonstrated (Bradley et al., 2005).

Bradley et al. (2005) also found the lowest effect sizes for treatment that was delivered to individuals with combat-related PTSD and hypothesized that factors such as multiple traumatization, more severe psychopathology, limited disclosure of traumatic events, and delayed opportunities for exposure and social support in this group, could all be potentially important factors that might complicate treatment. It is exactly these sorts of clients, who have struggled with untreated PTSD for long periods of time, who come to us with the most difficult and treatment-resistant presentations. In our experience, these individuals have incorporated their avoidant styles and resulting behavioral problems into most domains of their lives, and thus experience problems not just with reexperiencing and hyperarousal, but also with interpersonal relationships, vocational functioning, and general quality of life (Medlowicz & Stein, 2000). For these clients, traditional exposure therapy or cognitive–behavioral therapy may be effective in reducing PTSD symptoms, but may be less systematically focused on addressing the broader dysfunction in other psychosocial domains that leads to these individuals' distress and unsatisfying day-to-day functioning.

Thus, despite the significant progress that has been made with regard to PTSD treatment, continued development, refinement, and innovation are still needed to address the wide-ranging problems associated with this chronic disorder. Given the high levels of psychiatric comorbidity with PTSD (Kessler et al., 1995), treatments are needed that can cut across diagnostic categories and begin to treat presenting problems based on functional dimensions (Hayes, Wilson, Gifford, Follette, & Strosahl, 1996). In addition to symptom reduction, treatment must address interpersonal and occupational functioning, along with overall quality of life. Recently, several innovative treatments have been introduced and preliminarily tested for their efficacy in reducing PTSD symptomatology and addressing a number of the potential shortcomings discussed above (e.g., Cloitre, Koenen, Cohen, & Han, 2002; Turner, Beidel, & Frueh, 2005). We have suggested that acceptance-based behavioral approaches to treating PTSD, such as acceptance and commitment therapy (ACT; Hayes, Strosahl, & Wilson, 1999), that draw from the extant empirical literature linking avoidance with the development and maintenance of PTSD may be particularly beneficial in informing future treatment development (Orsillo & Batten, 2005). Before further describing this approach to treatment, we will briefly examine the role of avoidance in the development, maintenance, and treatment resistance of PTSD.

A BROAD AVOIDANCE-BASED CONCEPTUALIZATION OF PTSD

A core diagnostic feature of PTSD is engagement in efforts aimed at avoiding trauma-related thoughts and feelings (American Psychiatric Association, 1994), behaviors that are consistent with the concept of experiential avoidance. Experiential avoidance has been defined as a process by which individuals engage in strategies designed to alter the frequency or experience of private events, such as thoughts, feelings, memories, or bodily sensations (Hayes et al., 1996), and the resulting model holds avoidance as key in the development and maintenance of a variety of psychological disorders. For instance, experiential avoidance has been offered as a unifying conceptualization of the disparate problems (e.g., substance use, behavioral avoidance, thought suppression, self-harm) that often develop following exposure to a traumatic experience (Polusny & Follette, 1995). From this perspective, these problems and clinical disorders all reflect regulatory processes that function to minimize the experience and expression of painful trauma-related thoughts and emotions (Polusny & Follette, 1995). Although such regulatory processes may be negatively reinforced in the short term because they result in reduced immediate distress, they are likely to cause increased symptoms and behavioral problems over time. Thus, experiential avoidance can be seen as a contributory factor in the development and maintenance of PTSD, as well as the broad diversity of disorders that commonly present as comorbid conditions (Orsillo & Batten, 2005).

Research from a variety of domains related to emotional functioning in trauma survivors confirms the prominence of experiential avoidance in PTSD. This exacerbation of unwanted, trauma-related private events is predicted by both the general literature on the effects of thought and emotion suppression (Gross & Levenson, 1993, 1997; Purdon, 1999; Wegner, 1994), as well as by studies on suppression in clinical samples (see Purdon, 1999, for a review). Although the results are not totally consistent, research on the effects of suppression shows that control efforts are often ineffective and can actually result in a paradoxical increase in the thoughts and feelings that the individual was attempting to avoid. Extending this area of research to a traumatized population, Shipherd and Beck (1999) found that this suppression effect was particularly strong for women with rape-related PTSD. Suppression can thus be proposed as a key variable influencing the cyclical relationship between the avoidance and reexperiencing symptom clusters in PTSD.

The coping literature also provides ample support for a model that would predict that effortful attempts at coping through avoidance are often not only ineffective, but quite problematic as well. Although correlational, a wide range of studies have consistently found that the use of avoidant coping methods, such as emotional suppression, denial, detachment, and wishful thinking, are associated with negative outcomes and posttraumatic symptoms for traumatized individuals. This effect has been found in adult survivors of child sexual abuse (Batten, Follette, & Aban, 2001), rape survivors (Boeschen, Koss, Figueredo, & Coan, 2001; Valentiner, Foa, Riggs, & Gershuny, 1996), motor vehicle accident survivors (Nightingale & Williams, 2000), Gulf War veterans (Benotsch et al., 2000), and African American youth exposed to inner-city violence (Dempsey, 2002; Dempsey, Overstreet, & Moely, 2000). It has also been suggested that avoidant coping by suppression is more distinctive to PTSD than to other anxiety disorders (Amir et al., 1997).

Recently, investigators have begun to test more directly and rigorously the role of experiential avoidance in posttraumatic functioning.

Experiential avoidance has been shown to predict the severity of posttraumatic psychological functioning over and above the effects of trauma severity (Plumb, Orsillo, & Luterek, 2004). Experiential avoidance has also been shown to fully mediate the relationship between childhood sexual abuse and global psychological distress (Marx & Sloan, 2002) and trauma-related psychological distress (Rosenthal, Rasmussen, Hall, Palm, Batten, & Follette, 2005) in adulthood. Similarly, avoidance has been shown to partially mediate the relationship between adolescent sexual victimization and negative outcomes in adulthood (Polusny, Rosenthal, Aban, & Follette, 2004). Additionally, emotional avoidance and inhibition have been found to mediate the relationship between adult psychological distress and several factors that commonly exist in trauma survivors, history of childhood emotional invalidation (Krause, Mendelson, & Lynch, 2003) and affect intensity (Lynch, Robins, Morse, & Krause, 2001). Furthermore, evidence for inhibition of the expression of emotion in trauma survivors has also been found when comparing levels of facial expressivity to emotionally evocative stimuli versus self-reported levels of emotional activation (Litz, Orsillo, Kaloupek, & Weathers, 2000; Orsillo, Batten, Plumb, Luterek, & Roessner, 2004; Wagner, Roemer, Orsillo, & Litz, 2003).

Many traditional approaches to cognitive–behavioral therapy for PTSD acknowledge the key role of avoidance in PTSD. For instance, one mechanism of change in exposure therapy is proposed to be the reduction of fear and avoidance that occurs during habituation. However, we argue that the experiential avoidance in PTSD involves a wider range of complex emotional responses and that another potential shortcoming that has affected treatment development for PTSD is the narrow focus on fear- and anxiety-based conceptualizations of PTSD. PTSD is associated with a heterogeneous set of emotional responses including guilt (Kubany, Abueg, & Ownes, 1995), anger (Riggs, Dancu, & Gershuny, 1992), and sadness/depression (Kessler et al., 1995). Further, negative attitudes toward emotional experience (Joseph et al., 1997), difficulties in emotion regulation (Roth, Newman, Pelcovitz, van der Kolk, & Mandel (1997), and dissociation, which has been behaviorally conceptualized as an emotional control process (Wagner & Linehan, 1998), have all been shown to be positively correlated with PTSD severity.

An accumulation of data underscores the significance of these complex emotional responses and regulation strategies in the course and treatment of PTSD. Prospective studies following individuals exposed to traumatic events suggest that dissociation (Cardena & Spiegel, 1993; Koopman, Classen & Spiegel, 1994) and delayed peak emotional reactions to a traumatic event (Gilboa-Schechtman & Foa, 2001) are associated with the later development of more severe posttraumatic symptomatology. In addition, certain emotions and emotional styles, such as an inability or unwillingness to experience and express trauma-related emotions, seem to interfere with traditional cognitive–behavioral therapy. Specifically, individuals reporting higher pretreatment levels of both anger (Foa, Riggs, Massie, & Yarczower, 1995) and guilt (Pitman et al., 1991) have been shown to benefit less from exposure therapy. Further, clients who display more intense facial fear expressions (Foa et al., 1995) and those who report higher subjective anxiety ratings (reflecting higher emotional engagement; Jaycox, Foa & Morral, 1998) in the first session of exposure therapy achieve better results from such treatment.

ACCEPTANCE-BASED BEHAVIORAL TREATMENT FOR POSTTRAUMATIC PROBLEMS IN LIVING

Given the proposed prominence of experiential avoidance in the development and maintenance of PTSD and the efficacy of exposure in the treatment of PTSD, we argue that treatment development in this area must be aimed at the reduction of experiential and behavioral avoidance and the enhancement of a willingness and acceptance to experience the full range of internal events that characterize individuals with PTSD. We believe that acceptance-based behavioral interventions focused on the balance of acceptance and change hold significant promise in the next wave of treatments for PTSD. In our treatment development for PTSD, we have focused on combining traditional exposure therapy practices with mindfulness training (e.g., Segal, Williams, & Teasdale, 2002), dialectical behavior therapy (DBT) skills (Linehan 1993a, 1993b), and ACT (Hayes et al., 1999).

Collectively, these approaches, along with others, have been referred to as representing a third generation of behavior therapy (Hayes, 2005). They share common ground in that they emphasize the importance of facilitating the development of broad, flexible repertoires of responding to problems in daily living among clients, over the goal of narrowly defined symptom reduction (Hayes, 2005). Further, they aim to understand and address the context and function of psychological phenomena (e.g., experiential avoidance), rather than simply focusing on their form (e.g., specific symptom expression). We will describe our use of each of these sets of interventions below, along with special considerations for acceptance-based treatment with specific populations or circumstances.

MINDFULNESS PRACTICES

Mindfulness can be described as a psychological state in which one focuses awareness on the present moment, with acknowledgment of both internal and external stimuli, but without trying to change or evaluate any part of the experience (Kabat-Zinn, 1994; Segal et al., 2002). We have found that both of the major components of mindfulness, an increased awareness of one's internal and external environment and a change in the relationship one has with his or her internal experiences, to be especially useful for the trauma survivors with whom we work. In our experience with clients diagnosed with PTSD, their habitual focus on potential threat cues and the time and energy that is invested in attempting to avoid and control unwanted private events severely limits their awareness of subtle and complex cues and responses. This pattern of limited awareness has been clinically described, in part, as alexythymia, a state that is characterized by difficulties identifying and distinguishing between feelings and bodily sensations, difficulties describing emotional experience, and externally oriented thinking (Taylor, Bagby, & Parker, 1997). In addition, our clients with PTSD are frequently unable to distinguish between thoughts, feelings, memories, and behavioral urges, and this lack of distinction can cause them to engage in undesirable behaviors (such as using substances or self-harming) that feel as if they are outside of their personal control.

Mindfulness is aimed at developing an observer perspective from which an individual can notice and allow for internal experiences such as thoughts, feelings, and memories, while still retaining control of overt personal behavior. This sense of self is similar to the behavioral understanding of self described by Kohlenberg and Tsai (1991) as the ability to label the types of experiences that are evoked by private stimuli, such as "I feel, want, like, etc." Often, clients with traumatic histories, particularly those who experienced abuse or severe emotional invalidation in childhood, lack the skills and experience necessary to label these events solely on the basis of private stimuli and are more likely to identify what they think/feel/prefer based on public stimuli or the behavior of others.

A first step toward increasing awareness and ability to label the full range of internal and external events in any given moment involves a willingness to turn toward, rather than away from, potentially painful experiences. Our clients with PTSD typically have a long personal and shared history of labeling and judging painful experiences as bad, dangerous, and to be avoided. Mindfulness practice involves constantly working toward noticing and acknowledging the habitual tendency to label and avoid internal experiences while practicing a willingness to allow whatever experiences might be present in any given moment.

Mindfulness-based therapy has been described in more detail earlier in this volume, so we will not review all of the possible methods of facilitating mindfulness here. However, we should note that we have found a progressive approach to mindfulness to be most beneficial in working with clients with PTSD. Early in therapy, clients (and therapists!) practice mindfulness of one sensory modality (e.g., sound, taste, smell) at a time to gently and progressively develop some basic skills of awareness and attending. For example, listening to a piece of music together or eating a segment of orange can provide the opportunity to notice, in a new, open, and curious way, the variety of thoughts, feelings, and sensations that can arise in a given moment. Once some basic mindfulness skills have been established, the focus of mindfulness can shift to more personal, and potentially painful experiences such as thoughts, feelings, images, memories, and physiological sensations that arise across many daily life situations. Mindfulness exercises such as watching thoughts and feelings go by on an imaginary conveyer belt, or on clouds that float across the sky can be used to help clients begin to practice observing and labeling their subtle and complex thoughts and feelings as they are, while also noticing the urge to label, avoid, and control them. For those clients who have a hard time even recognizing what it is that they are feeling, additional shaping by the therapist may be necessary, and the supplemental use of a list of feeling words can be very helpful. We find that it is often useful to conduct mindfulness exercises at the beginning of each group or individual therapy session as repeated practice and refinement of these skills is necessary, and engagement in mindfulness exercises can be a powerful way for the therapist and client to increase their awareness and presence in session.

When practiced over time, mindful meditation offers an alternative to experiential avoidance and inattention and allows clients to relate to internal experience from a broadened perspective—as psychological events, rather than accurate reflections of reality. Mindfulness is also seen as an important skill for improving quality of life. Clients with PTSD are typically consumed with thoughts and memories of traumatic events, and much of their internal efforts and external behaviors are aimed at attempting to avoid or control these experiences. Thus, clients often feel detached from important people and activities in their lives. Mindfulness is a skill that can potentially help clients live more in the present, be more available to and involved with people and activities, engage more fully in the moment, be less consumed with trauma-related, past events. Through the act of mindfulness practice, clients diagnosed with PTSD may begin to view associated thoughts and feelings from a new perspective. This may also create a new context from which the trauma survivor can view the world and the self, facilitating efforts to take healthy action and make life-enhancing behavioral changes, while still mindfully acknowledging emotion and thought.

DIALECTICAL BEHAVIOR THERAPY SKILLS

Recent developments in the treatment of PTSD, especially for those with childhood sexual abuse histories, have focused on a model in which grounding methods and skills training are provided to clients before moving into the work of exposure therapy (Becker & Zayfert, 2001; Cloitre et al., 2002; Follette, Palm, & Hall, 2004). We likewise agree that those individuals with complicated trauma histories and pervasive problems with emotion regulation may benefit from a skills training approach before beginning more intensive exposure-based treatment, although empirical support for the efficacy of a combined approach as compared to exposure alone has yet to be established (Cahill, Zoellner, Feeny, & Riggs, 2004). In addition to the skills provided in AMT approaches, we have found DBT skills training (Linehan, 1993a, 1993b) to be extremely helpful in this area. DBT is one of the most widely known psychological treatments based on the tension between acceptance and change. Although it was originally developed for the treatment of individuals with borderline personality disorder (BPD), we have found the skills taught in DBT to be applicable to individuals with PTSD who have notable difficulties with emotion regulation, even when they do not meet criteria for BPD. However, it should be noted that the empirical support for DBT is based primarily on the traditional application of this therapy in its multimodal form, including individual therapy, group skills training, skills-coaching phone calls, and a consultation team for therapists (e.g., Linehan, Armstrong, Suarez, Allmon, & Heard, 1991; Linehan et al., 1999). The addition of DBT skills training without implementation of a full DBT model has had mixed empirical results thus far (e.g., Linehan, Heard, & Armstrong, 1993; Telch, Agras, & Linehan, 2000), and further evaluation of such an approach is necessary.

DBT skills training covers four basic domains: core mindfulness skills, interpersonal effectiveness skills, emotional regulation skills, and distress tolerance skills. Although all four components have utility with this population, the two modules that we find to be most important in preparing individuals for further work on their trauma histories are the core mindfulness and distress tolerance skills. As described in the previous section, the core mindfulness skills are key to improvement for those with chronic problems with experiential avoidance. In addition to the basic mindfulness skills taught in this module, we have also found the introduction of the "wise mind" perspective to be very important to developing a sense of self (a la Kohlenberg and Tsai, 1991) as well as to providing a perspective of self-as-context for experiencing private events (described more fully in the ACT section below). The wise mind is described as a perspective that allows integration of both emotional and rational sources of information, and over time, work in this area may help the client learn to trust his or her own private experiences as valid.

We have also found the distress tolerance module of DBT skills training to be especially important and useful in the beginning stages of treatment. The skills explicated in this unit provide the client with several strategies that can be used to get through a crisis without acting impulsively or self-destructively. Examples of these skills include mindful breathing exercises, techniques for self-soothing using the five senses, and a variety of modes of distraction. When viewed carefully, the distraction techniques are actually actively teaching clients how to practice avoidance. At its core, this is antithetical to an acceptance-based model, and we have had to work to reconcile the pragmatic utility of these skills that we see in practice with our overall conceptualization that argues that avoidance-based modes of coping are not helpful and can even be harmful in the long term.

We now teach these skills regularly to our clients with PTSD, but with a caveat included in the rationale for their use. We will often say something like,

> As we've discussed, the long-term goal for our therapy is for you to be able to experience your thoughts, feelings, and memories without having to avoid or distract yourself from them. However, I don't think it's fair to ask you to give up the avoidance strategies you've been using for years without giving you something to put in their place at first. The distress tolerance skills I'm going to teach you are likely not going to fix the problems that you have, and in fact, our goal is going to be to continue to work toward willingness and acceptance without distraction. Until we get there, though, the clients with PTSD that I've worked with generally find that these skills are really useful in getting through a difficult moment without doing something that will hurt you or that you'll regret later.

As the work of therapy progresses, we help the client gradually reduce use of distress tolerance skills and focus more on willingness to experience private events in the present moment.

ACCEPTANCE AND COMMITMENT THERAPY

Once beginning mindfulness skills have been developed and the client has been taught some functional emotional regulation skills, we have found that ACT (Hayes et al., 1999) provides one of the most effective ways of targeting willingness and openness to experience in individuals with PTSD. ACT has also been described in more detail earlier in this volume, so we will not review the basic components of that treatment approach. Rather, we will provide specific examples of how we tailor an ACT approach to traumatized populations, based on the special considerations that arise with our clients with PTSD.

In our work with clients who have been struggling with PTSD for long periods of time, the first stage of ACT, creative hopelessness, seems to have a powerful impact. We have used a number of strategies to demonstrate creative hopelessness, which can be conducted in either individual or group therapy. One of the more effective has been to first list on a white board, the many emotions and thoughts that the clients struggle with, followed by a list of all of the ways that they have tried to change the thoughts and feelings listed. Response to the written material ranges from anger to deep sadness. A number of clients have commented that when they have seen the struggle and efforts laid out before them in written form it seems to poignantly highlight the problem of being stuck. Despite these feelings, the clients have generally tended to feel validated, because they have recognized for years that their efforts have gone unrewarded.

At this moment of realization, understandably, clients will often ask the therapist for the answer or the "magic" solution to the problem. Although in some ways there is a deceptively simple answer to the problem, rather than avoiding experiences the client may need to work toward acceptance, it is generally our experience that this understanding needs to be reached experientially, over time, and cannot be didactically taught. A potential trap at this stage of therapy is for acceptance to be provided to a client as the answer to his or her problem and for the client to use "acceptance" as a potential way to control internal experiences. At this stage in therapy, it is important for both the client and therapist to notice the urge to provide quick answers or "fixes," to acknowledge the difficulty and frustration associated with the futility of past attempts at control, and to accept that true change may be a slow and progressive process.

We have generally found that creative hopelessness not only has a powerful impact on clients who have tried for many years to control their emotions and thoughts, but it can also have an impact on individuals who have less experience in the paradoxical effects of efforts at avoidance. Having older clients in group therapy with younger clients, for instance, can help the younger clients to understand vicariously the futility of such avoidance efforts. We have had a number of younger clients say, "I don't want to end up there, what can I do now to help myself?"

On the other hand, given the pervasive message in our culture that changing internal states is possible (and desirable), the success that clients have had with some control efforts (e.g., I can drink to get rid of my feelings), and the misperceptions some clients with limited awareness have about the true efficacy of their control efforts and/or the costs associated with control (e.g., the way I survive is by shutting down all my feelings), these same clients may still hold out significant hope for the change agenda. It is not uncommon to have clients who adamantly report that thought/emotion control works and that it has been successful for them. From our perspective, it is not useful, and in fact it can be harmful to the therapeutic relationship, to try and convince clients that these change efforts have not been successful. At this point, we have found two approaches to be useful. First, mindfulness practice aimed at increasing a client's awareness of his or her actions and consequences can gradually provide new evidence that may challenge the rule that control always works or that control works without any significant cost. Second, we ask clients if they are willing to simply consider that there might be some costs associated with control, and some possible alternative ways of living, as therapy progresses to the control as the problem stage of therapy.

When working with chronic PTSD, issues of control are intense and long-standing. Not only are many of the symptoms of PTSD about gaining control of private experience, but so are many of the associated disorders, such as substance abuse, eating disorders, and other anxiety disorders. Trauma often occurs under conditions of no personal control and individuals who have experienced traumatic events may subsequently attempt to overcompensate by being in control of as many aspects of their life and experience as possible. Thus, it is understandable that when clients come to therapy, a large part of their agenda may be to gain "control," and they would like the therapist to teach them how to control their internal experience "even better." A number of strong reactions and misunderstandings can emerge during this stage of therapy.

Clients will often voice a number of concerns during this stage, such as, "So do you mean we just need to give up control and let our lives fall apart?" or "It is control that is keeping me just enough together to be here," or some form of, "If I give up control, I will destroy myself and those around me." Here we focus more heavily on the areas where control works. We will explore the workability of controlling internal experience versus the workability of controlling one's life. Clients will sometimes misunderstand the concept of "workability" and believe that we are trying to suggest to them that attempting to control is "wrong" or "bad," whereas be willing to accept is "good." When this issue arises, it is important to refocus treatment toward what works and does not work for this particular client as he or she tries to live a valued and vital life. Another common reaction to this stage of treatment is a belief that the therapist is suggesting that the client resign him or herself to living with significant distress, intense emotional anguish, and PTSD. Here it is important to distinguish continually between painful emotions that are an inevitable part of human existence and the chronic and intense distress that is likely the consequence of habitual nonacceptance, negative evaluation, and failed attempts to control primary emotional responses. Finally, clients can sometimes overgeneralize the potential futility of control efforts and ask if they need to resign themselves to giving up control over all aspects of life despite the explicit focus on behavioral action in ACT. The therapist's role in this situation is to facilitate the client's ability to connect with all the potential behavioral options available to the client, particularly when the struggle with internal control is dropped.

In our clinical experience, clients who have experienced sexual trauma and those who struggle with intense anger and rage as a part of their profile seem to have particular difficulty with accepting the limits to experiential control. The sexually traumatized client will often equate "letting go" of some control efforts as giving in, giving up, or allowing oneself to be submissive or weak, a position that can be reminiscent of the original traumatic experience. Clients who regularly experience extreme anger and rage may view "letting go" as permission to behave poorly when angry. It is the therapist's task to carefully delineate the difference between the importance of control over one's behavior versus the futility of control over one's internal experience. In these situations, the therapist can validate the desire for control and acknowledge the containment it appears to give, while at the same time working with the client to address the costs of control, pointing to such things as loss of relationships, fear of connection, shutting down, and so forth. Again, the use of mindfulness and self-monitoring to increase the client's awareness of what actually happens when he or she engages in a control strategy can greatly enhance this work.

A noteworthy piece in this work related to feelings of anger may need some direct attention. The feeling of anger and the actions associated with anger are closely linked; for instance, clients with PTSD who experience angry outbursts frequently report that the emotion and reaction are simultaneous and therefore cannot be helped. This issue can be addressed in therapy in a few ways. First, the therapist can draw attention to emotions that may be underlying anger and help the client notice how connecting with and holding on to angry feelings can often serve as a tool for avoidance of some other emotion (e.g., it is often easier or more comfortable to feel anger than to feel sadness or disappointment). In many instances, we suggest that if the client could "peel" the anger off and see what is underneath, there is often a feeling of hurt or "being wronged" in some way. Drawing from mindfulness skills aimed at allowing those feelings to be present and paying attention to their origin, the therapist can validate the client's experience and help the client act in accordance with his or her values, even in the presence of those painful feelings.

Additionally, anger is often related to conceptions of right and wrong. With many clients who have PTSD, there is a fundamental conceptual link between being right-versus-wrong and being safe-versus-threatened. In this case, to give up taking the "right" action means to put one's own or others' lives at risk. Deliteralization techniques can be useful when addressing this issue. One exercise that can be used is the "Right and Wrong Card Game." In this exercise, the therapist uses a set of 3×5 index cards that say "RIGHT" on half of the cards and "WRONG" on the other half. Using experiences that are linked with problematic anger either that emerge in session or that can be elicited from the client's history, with the client's permission, the therapist engages in a demonstration of the ultimate consequences of being right or wrong. While the client generates thoughts about an anger-provoking experience, the therapist listens for connections with being "RIGHT" or "WRONG." When the therapist detects an "I'm right about this" kind of thought or response, then he hands a "RIGHT" card to the client and the therapist takes a "WRONG" card. If the client makes him or herself "WRONG," then the therapist takes a "RIGHT" card and hands the client a "WRONG" card. The goal is to get a stack of "RIGHT" and "WRONG" cards for both players.

Once a good-sized stack of each has developed, the therapist can suggest to the client the result of the game is that sometimes the client was right and other times wrong, yet the problem remains unsolved. By "deliteralizing" right and wrong, the therapist makes some room for the possibility that aiming all of one's actions toward always being right may not bring one the happiness or sense of safety he or she is seeking. The therapist can then introduce the possibility of an alternative—to let go of the importance of having to be right in exchange for focusing efforts on actions and behaviors that will bring the client a fuller and more vital and effective life. Some therapists are hesitant to do this exercise with clients for fear that it may invalidate the client's experience or elicit anger in session. Once a strong therapeutic relationship is established that involves a radical respect on the part of the therapist for the client and a compassionate understanding of the struggle we all engage in with our internal experiences, an irreverent approach to dealing with difficult issues such as acted-out anger and the struggle to be acknowledged as "right" can be a powerful tool for increasing deliteralization and making room for radical changes in how clients relate to their own internal experiences.

As described above in our application of mindfulness to PTSD, working on self-as-context is an important aspect of therapy with individuals diagnosed with PTSD. For instance, women who were chronically sexually abused and neglected as children, and often repeatedly revictimized thereafter, can have a difficult time locating the transcendent, constant observer self that experiences emotions and thoughts. An inherent aspect of being sexually victimized is the invalidation of one's internal experiences. For instance, the perpetrator may force the client to engage in activities against her will, sometimes making false declarations about her thoughts and feelings (e.g., "you really wanted to have sex, you are enjoying this"). In the chaotic family environments that often accompany sexual assault, children are often told what they should think and feel, and little opportunity exists for the development and nurturing of self-observational skills. Repeated exposure to people and situations that consistently invalidate a person's internal experience may lead him or her to rely on external sources to ascertain thoughts, feelings, and values.

One goal of therapy, therefore, is to work with the client to reestablish his or her ability to observe personal behavior, including thoughts and feelings. In and outside of session, clients are asked to notice what they are experiencing and to notice the constant observer who can engage in this task. A number of exercises can be used to strengthen a client's awareness of the observer self, including an imagery task that involves having the client localize past memories and events and connect with the constant observer who was present across different contexts and situations. The establishment of a sense of self as context is critical in that this stance allows clients to experience difficult memories or emotional pain as content that may come and go, while a stable sense of self remains constant and unthreatened. We have found the Mountain Meditation (Kabat-Zinn, 1990) also to be a useful exercise that facilitates the client's connection with the core mountain that remains stable despite the changing seasons and sometimes turbulent conditions.

Another obstacle to the establishment of an observer self that is sometimes encountered in work with clients with PTSD is an overidentification with the "conceptualized self" or the content by which we identify ourselves and explain our behavior. It is a universal human experience to describe and define ourselves using particular content (e.g., I am a mother, I have an anxious personality). However, an overidentification with particular content can limit our willingness to experience content that is incompatible with our conceptualized self and restrict our behavior to actions consistent with this sense of self. For instance, many Vietnam veterans who have chronic PTSD strongly identify themselves as "Vietnam Veterans" along with all of the cultural characteristics that accompany that identity. On the surface, this identification with content can seem positive in that it can allow veterans to feel connected with others who share similar experiences and struggles. However, an overidentification with any particular content can severely limit an individual's freedom to experience the full range of emotions, thoughts, and actions available. Someone who defines himself as a Vietnam Veteran who is "messed up and angry" be-cause of his history may find himself stuck and unable to move forward with different life choices. Once again, mindfulness and deliteralization exercises can be used strengthen the sense of self as context or the observer of content and to loosen the ties a conceptualized sense of self may have on the clients' behavior.

As discussed above, clients with chronic PTSD often expend signifi-cant energy and resources in an attempt to manage their internal distress as-sociated with trauma memories and reminders. The impact of this chronic burden on clients' lives can be remarkable. Many of the clients with whom we work have become so removed from personal choice and valued living (e.g., intimate connections, meaningful and industrious vocational activ-ity, and recreational activities) that in many senses their lives have become "unlivable." Although working with clients with chronic PTSD to increase their acute awareness of the consequences of their behavioral restriction and to develop and define their personal values can be an arduous task for both the therapist and client, it is in many ways the core feature of ACT. The explicit goal of the therapy is to improve the quality of the client's life in a clinically significant and meaningful way. The pain associated with creative hopelessness, letting go of control, enhancing acceptance, and de-veloping a sense of self as context is all in the service of valued living. Often, clients with PTSD initially struggle with the notion that they can hold personal values without having to justify or explain them. They may not trust their own choices and seek external direction and validation of their behavior. However, it is our experience that, in a safe and support-ive therapeutic relationship, many clients can eventually describe what is important to them and begin to accomplish actions that are aligned with these individual values.

ADAPTATIONS TO EXPOSURE EXERCISES

As described above, the empirical evidence for the treatment of PTSD in-dicates that one of the most effective components of treatment for this anx-iety disorder is exposure, whether in vivo or imaginal. The use of exposure therapy is in many ways consistent with an acceptance-based approach to treatment, and we will frequently use exposure exercises when work-ing with traumatized clients. Many of the methods of exposure used in acceptance-based approaches are conducted exactly as they are in other cognitive–behavioral treatment packages, such as imaginal exposure exer-cises in which the client is asked to write about a memory of a specific trau-matic event, repeating the description of this memory over and over, and even listening repeatedly to recordings of verbal accounts of the traumatic event(s). However, the rationale used to describe exposure exercises from an acceptance standpoint differs significantly from the traditional rationale. Most importantly, we do not suggest that recounting the trauma multiple times will result in habituation or diminution of difficult private events, as this rationale highlights exposure as another method aimed at experiential control. Rather, we discuss the possibility that approaching, instead of avoiding, these traumatic memories and the associated thoughts and affect, will change the context in which these private events are experienced and the nature of the relationship that the client has with these experiences. Consequently, this change in context then allows for more behavioral flexibility and increased ability to make steps forward in valued directions. Additionally, in-vivo exposure is also conducted regularly as an integral part of acceptance-based therapy for PTSD, although the form of the exposure, and the rationale, may differ. For instance, a client may be encouraged to attend a party (a previously avoided activity), not with the purpose of habituating to anxiety in that situation, but with the explicit goal of engaging in a behavior that is consistent with the client's value of developing and maintaining relationships.

UNIQUE BENEFITS OF AN ACCEPTANCE-BASED APPROACH TO TREATING PTSD

We believe that mindfulness, DBT skills, and the core approaches in ACT allow therapists to deal with many of the limitations in traditional PTSD treatments. An acceptance-based treatment for posttraumatic reactions is not confined to addressing only those symptoms associated with PTSD or to a primarily fear-based response. Working on increasing willingness and experiential acceptance is broad-based and applicable to the full spectrum of emotional responses, including anger, guilt, and sadness, as well as fear. Furthermore, another limitation of traditional exposure is that it is difficult to employ when a clear memory of a specific event is not accessible. In addition, there is no clear algorithm in exposure therapy for dealing with multiple events that may have occurred at different times and in various contexts, or for what to do when a person has experienced too many different events to deal with each individually (as can be the case in child sexual abuse or combat). In contrast, mindfulness and willingness can be implemented successfully, even in such cases.

An additional benefit is that treatment based on the functional dimension of avoidance can be used for clients who have a variety of the comorbid conditions that frequently accompany PTSD. ACT already has demonstrated utility for depression (Zettle & Raines, 1989), substance use disorders (Hayes, Wilson et al., 2004), and psychotic disorders (Bach &

Hayes, 2002)—all of which have been found either to complicate PTSD treatment or lead to exclusion from existing PTSD treatments. Especially in the case of substance use disorders, comorbidity with PTSD is extremely prevalent (Chilcoat & Menard, 2003; Ouimette, Brown & Najavits, 1998), and it has been argued (Batten & Hayes, 2005) that it is more efficient and effective to target functional domains that PTSD and substance use have in common than to attempt to treat them in an artificially sequential manner.

ROLE OF THE THERAPEUTIC RELATIONSHIP

ACT and DBT have always placed great emphasis on the value of the therapeutic relationship (Hayes et al., 1999; Linehan, 1993a). However, this aspect of treatment may be even more crucial in the treatment of individuals who have experienced interpersonal traumas. Most trauma survivors have been profoundly disappointed by the people in their lives and are extremely sensitive to any sign of untrustworthiness or rejection. It is important for the trauma therapist using an acceptance-based approach to maintain a transparent and straightforward manner, as it is our clinical experience that trauma survivors have a notably heightened awareness of other people's feelings and behaviors. In these types of treatments, therapeutic boundaries are functional, not arbitrary, and the therapist is quick to acknowledge that the problems that are dealt with in session are common to the human condition. At all times, the therapist must work based on the assumption that the client is not pathological or broken, and that he or she already has the capacity to live a vital and meaningful life. The therapist has faith in the client's ability to experience difficult private events—clients do not need to be rescued from their own feelings and memories. Similarly, therapists need to be willing to experience their own difficult thoughts and feelings that will be elicited throughout the course of therapy.

The therapist should take seriously the impact of PTSD on a client's life. At times, if not done carefully, the irreverent therapeutic style in DBT and some of the deliteralization methods of ACT can have the appearance of undermining the seriousness of an individual's experience of PTSD and its associated problems. When working with these techniques it is very important to be present compassionately with the client, acknowledging the difficulty of the struggle. We have had individuals in group therapy comment that a particular session or therapeutic technique seems to negate the "true" experience of trauma. As noted by Hayes and colleagues (1999), it is important to keep the playing field level and watch out for one-upsmanship. The ACT therapist is instructed to notice the inevitable pull to try and convince the client of something—these are likely times that the therapist is working to support a particular agenda, rather than mindfully connecting with the client in his or her current state. For instance, in a recent session on living a valued life, a woman who had PTSD related to rape shared her experience that the therapists just did not understand how hard it is to live with the symptoms. She reported thinking that in asking her to take a valued action, we were asking her to not be affected by her rape and the accompanying symptoms. In response to this disclosure, we slowed the session down and connected with the client's painful experience of the trauma and her long-standing feeling of "stuckness." We allowed the client to see that our request that she take valued action came with a genuine understanding of her pain, radical respect for all the choices available to her, and a hopeful perspective that she might be able to have both the thoughts and feelings she was experiencing and still choose to take valued action.

The therapeutic relationship in an acceptance-based treatment provides a model for the way in which clients are being encouraged to relate to their own thoughts and feelings. It is accepting and compassionate, basing its direction on long-term values, not short-term comfort. Therapists working from an acceptance-based perspective are aware of their personal susceptibility to avoidance, judgment, and lack of mindfulness of their own thoughts, and seek consultation to help ensure that they maintain a willing, accepting and open stance while conducting therapy. The supervisory relationship, likewise, is strong and accepting, modeling the essential interpersonal characteristics of the effective therapeutic relationship (Follette & Batten, 2000).

EVIDENCE FOR EFFICACY OF ACCEPTANCE-BASED APPROACHES TO PTSD

The existing empirical evidence for the efficacy of the approaches to the treatment of PTSD described in this chapter is limited, although the preliminary data that are available are supportive of the utility of acceptance- and mindfulness-based approaches in this population. Walser and colleagues have investigated the feasibility and acceptability of ACT with male and female clients in inpatient PTSD treatment programs (Walser, Loew, Westrup, Gregg, & Rogers, 2002; Walser, Westrup, Rogers, Gregg, & Loew, 2003). The investigators also assessed issues specifically targeted and expected to change from an ACT standpoint, before and after therapy, as well as at 3-month follow-up. Both male and female clients reported positive response to ACT both in terms of helpfulness and in terms of valued choice. Pre- to postmeasures of the frequency of occurrence of automatic thoughts did not differ significantly; however, measures of believability of those same thoughts decreased significantly from before to after treatment, and ability to take action in the face of difficult emotion, as measured by the Acceptance and Action Questionnaire (Hayes, Strosahl et al., 2004), also improved.

Batten and Hayes (2005) have also demonstrated preliminary efficacy in a case study using ACT to treat comorbid PTSD and substance abuse. At 1-year follow-up, the client described in this case study maintained significant reductions in depression, general psychological distress, and experiential avoidance and was making notable behavioral changes in her life to move her closer to those things in life that she valued.

SUMMARY

Cognitive–behavioral approaches to PTSD treatment are rooted in experimental learning theory, and they seem to offer significant promise in the amelioration of PTSD. However, innovative treatment refinement and reformulation may be useful in enhancing the outcomes associated with these approaches and increasing the accessibility and acceptability of treatment to a wide variety of clients with PTSD and associated features. PTSD theory and research underscore the importance of experiential avoidance in the development, maintenance, and treatment of PTSD. Thus, the integration of acceptance-based approaches with traditional behavioral methods may be an important next step in the treatment of PTSD. Although preliminary findings are encouraging, more systematic evaluation of the potential efficacy and effectiveness of these approaches is clearly needed.

REFERENCES

American Psychiatric Association. (1994). *The diagnostic and statistical manual of mental disorders* (4th ed.). Washington, DC: Author.

Amir, M., Kaplan, Z., Efroni, R., Levine, Y., Benjamin, J., & Kotler, M. (1997). Coping styles in posttraumatic stress disorder (PTSD) patients. *Personality and Individual Differences, 23,* 399–405.

Bach, P., & Hayes, S. C. (2002). The use of acceptance and commitment therapy to prevent the rehospitalization of psychotic patients: A randomized controlled trial. *Journal of Consulting and Clinical Psychology, 70,* 1129–1139.

Batten, S. V., Follette, V. M., & Aban, I. B. (2001). Experiential avoidance and high risk sexual behavior in survivors of child sexual abuse. *Journal of Child Sexual Abuse, 10,* 101–120.

Batten, S. V., & Hayes, S. C. (2005). Acceptance and commitment therapy in the treatment of comorbid substance abuse and posttraumatic stress disorder: A case study. *Clinical Case Studies, 4,* 246–262.

Becker, C. B., & Zayfert, C. (2001). Integrating DBT-based techniques and concepts to facilitate exposure treatment for PTSD. *Cognitive and Behavioral Practice, 8,* 107–122.

Benotsch, E. G., Brailey, K., Vasterling, J. J., Uddo, M., Constans, J. L, & Sutker, P. B. (2000). War zone stress, personal and environment resources, and PTSD symptoms in Gulf War veterans: A longitudinal perspective. *Journal of Abnormal Psychology, 109,* 205–213.

Boeschen, L. E., Koss, M. P., Figueredo, A. J., & Coan, J. A. (2001). Experiential avoidance and post-traumatic stress disorder: A cognitive mediational model of rape recovery. *Journal of Aggression, Maltreatment and Trauma, 4,* 211–245.

Bradley, R., Greene, J., Russ, E., Dutra, L., & Westen, D. (2005). A multidimensional meta-analysis of psychotherapy for PTSD. *American Journal of Psychiatry, 162,* 214–227.

Bryant, R. A., Moulds, M. L., Guthrie, R. M., Dang, S. T., & Nixon, R. D. V. (2003). Imaginal exposure alone and imaginal exposure with cognitive restructuring in treatment of posttraumatic stress disorder. *Journal of Consulting and Clinical Psychology, 71,* 706–712.

Cahill, S. P., Zoellner, L. A., Feeny, N. C., & Riggs, D. S. (2004). Sequential treatment for child-abuse related posttraumatic stress disorder: Methodological comment on Cloitre, Koenen, Cohen, and Han (2002). *Journal of Consulting and Clinical Psychology, 72,* 543–548.

Cardena, E., & Spiegel, D. (1993). Dissociative reactions to the San Francisco Bay Area Earthquake of 1989. *American Journal of Psychiatry, 150,* 474–478.

Chemtob, C. M., Novaco, R. W., Hamada, R. S., & Gross, D. M. (1997). Cognitive behavioral treatment of severe anger in posttraumatic stress disorder. *Journal of Consulting and Clinical Psychology, 65,* 184–189.

Chilcoat, H. D., & Menard, C. (2003). Epidemiological investigations: Comorbidity of posttraumatic stress disorder and substance use disorder. In P. Ouimette & P. J. Brown (Eds.), *Trauma and substance abuse: Causes, consequences, and treatment of comorbid disorders* (pp. 9–28) Washington DC: American Psychological Association.

Cloitre, M., Koenen, K. C., Cohen, L. R., & Han, H. (2002). Skills training in affective interpersonal regulation followed by exposure: A phase-based treatment for PTSD related to childhood abuse. *Journal of Consulting and Clinical Psychology, 70,* 1067–1074.

Davidson, P. R., & Parker, K. C. (2001). Eye movement desensitization and reprocessing (EMDR): A meta-analysis. *Journal of Consulting and Clinical Psychology, 69,* 305–316.

Dempsey, M. (2002). Negative coping as a mediator in the relation between violence and outcomes in inner-city African American youth. *Journal of Orthopsychiatry, 72,* 102–109.

Dempsey, M., Overstreet, S., & Moely, B. (2000). "Approach" and "avoidance" coping and PTSD symptoms in inner-city youth. *Current Psychology: Developmental, Learning, Personality, Social, 19,* 28–45.

Fecteau, G., & Nicki, R. (1999). Cognitive behavioural treatment of posttraumatic stress disorder after motor vehicle accident. *Behavioural and Cognitive Psychotherapy, 27,* 201–214.

Foa, E. B., Dancu, C. V., Hembree, E. A., Jaycox, L. H., Meadows, E. A., & Street, G. P. (1999). A comparison of exposure therapy, stress inoculation training, and their combination for reducing posttraumatic stress disorder in female assault victims. *Journal of Consulting and Clinical Psychology, 67,* 194–200.

Foa, E. B., Riggs, D. S., Massie, E. D., & Yarczower, M. (1995). The impact of fear activation and anger on the efficacy of exposure treatment for posttraumatic stress disorder. *Behavior Therapy, 26,* 487–499.

Foa, E. B., Rothbaum, B. O., Riggs, D. S., & Murdock, T. B. (1991). Treatment of posttraumatic stress disorder in rape victims: A comparison between cognitive–behavioral procedures and counseling. *Journal of Consulting and Clinical Psychology, 59,* 715–723.

Follette, V. M., & Batten, S. V. (2000). The role of emotion in psychotherapy supervision: A contextual behavioral analysis. *Cognitive and Behavioral Practice, 7,* 306–312.

Follette, V. M., Palm, K. M., & Hall, M. L. R. (2004). Acceptance, mindfulness, and trauma. In S. C. Hayes, V. M. Follette, & M. M. Linehan (Eds.), *Mindfulness and acceptance: Expanding the cognitive–behavioral tradition* (pp. 192–208). New York: Guilford.

Frueh, B. C., Turner, S. M., Beidel, D. C., Mirabella, R. F., & Jones, W. J. (1996). Trauma management therapy: A preliminary evaluation of a multicomponent behavioral treatment for chronic combat-related PTSD. *Behavior Research and Therapy, 34,* 533–543.

Gilboa-Schechtman, E., & Foa, E. B. (2001). Patterns of recovery from trauma: The use of intraindividual analysis. *Journal of Abnormal Psychology, 110,* 392–400.

Glynn, S. M., Eth, S. Randolph, E. T., Foy, D. W., Urbaitis, M., Boxer, L., et al. (1999). A test of behavior family therapy to augment exposure for combat-related posttraumatic stress disorder. *Journal of Consulting and Clinical Psychology, 67,* 243–251.

Gross, J. J., & Levenson, R. W. (1993). Emotional suppression: Physiology, self-report, and expressive behavior. *Journal of Personality and Social Psychology, 64,* 970–986.

Gross, J. J., & Levenson, R. W. (1997). Hiding feelings: The acute effects of inhibiting negative and positive emotion. *Journal of Abnormal Psychology, 106,* 95–103.

Hayes, S. C. (2005). Acceptance and commitment therapy, relational frame theory, and the third wave of behavioral and cognitive therapies. *Behavior Therapy, 35,* 639–665.

Hayes, S. C., Strosahl, K. D., & Wilson, K. G. (1999). *Acceptance and commitment therapy: An experiential approach to behavior change.* New York: Guilford.

Hayes, S. C., Strosahl, K. D., Wilson, K. G., Bissett, R. T., Pistorello, J., Toarmino, D., et al. (2004). Measuring experiential avoidance: A preliminary test of a working model. *The Psychological Record, 54,* 553–578.

Hayes, S. C., Wilson, K. G., Gifford, E. V., Bissett, R. T., Piasecki, M., Batten, S. V., et al. (2004). A preliminary trial of twelve-step facilitation and acceptance and commitment therapy with polysubstance-abusing methadone-maintained opiate addicts. *Behavior Therapy, 35,* 667–688.

Hayes, S. C., Wilson, K. G., Gifford, E. V., Follette, V. M., & Strosahl, K. G. (1996). Experiential avoidance and behavioral disorders: A functional dimensional approach to diagnosis and treatment. *Journal of Consulting and Clinical Psychology, 64,* 1152–1168.

Jaycox, L. H., Foa, E.B., & Morral, A. R. (1998). Influence of emotional engagement and habituation on exposure therapy for PTSD. *Journal of Consulting and Clinical Psychology, 66,* 185–192.

Joseph, S., Dalgleish, T., Williams, R., Yule, W., Thrasher, S., & Hodgkinson, P. (1997). Attitudes towards emotional expression and post-traumatic stress in survivors of the Herald of Free Enterprise disaster. *British Journal of Clinical Psychology, 36,* 133–138.

Kabat-Zinn, J. (1990). *Full Catastrophe Living: Using the wisdom of you body and mind to face stress, pain, and illness.* New York: Dell.

Kabat-Zinn, J. (1994). *Wherever you go there you are.* New York: Hyperion.

Keane, T. M., Fairbank, J. A., Caddell, J. M., Zimering, R. T., & Bender, M. E. (1989). Implosive (flooding) therapy reduces symptoms of PTSD in Vietnam combat veterans. *Behavior Therapy, 20,* 245–260.

Keane, T. M., Fisher, L. M., Krinsley, K. E., & Niles, B. L. (1994). Posttraumatic stress disorder. In M. Hersen & R. T. Ammerman (Eds.), *Handbook of prescriptive treatments for adults* (pp. 237–260). New York: Plenum.

Kessler, R. C., Sonnega, A., Bromet, E., Hughes, M., & Nelson, C. (1995). Posttraumatic stress disorder in the National Comorbidity Survey. *Archives of General Psychiatry, 52,* 1048–1060.

Kohlenberg, R. J., & Tsai, M. (1991). *Functional analytic psychotherapy.* New York: Plenum.

Koopman, C., Classen, C., & Spiegel, D. A. (1994). Predictors of posttraumatic stress symptoms among survivors of the Oakland/Berkeley, California firestorm. *American Journal of Psychiatry, 151,* 888–894.

Krause, E. D., Mendelson, T., & Lynch, T. R. (2003). Childhood emotional invalidation and adult psychological distress: The mediating role of emotional inhibition. *Child Abuse & Neglect, 27,* 199–213.

Kubany, E. S., Abueg, F. R., & Ownes, J. A. (1995). Initial examination of a multidimensional model of trauma-related guilt: Applications to combat veterans and battered women. *Journal of Psychopathology and Behavioral Assessment, 17,* 353–376.

Linehan, M. M. (1993a). *Cognitive behavioral treatment for borderline personality disorder.* New York: Guilford

Linehan, M. M. (1993b). *Skills training manual for treating borderline personality disorder.* New York: Guilford.

Linehan, M. M., Armstrong, H. E., Suarez, A., Allmon, D., & Heard, H. L. (1991). Cognitive–behavioral treatment of chronically parasuicidal borderline patients. *Archives of General Psychiatry, 48,* 1060–1064.

Linehan, M. M., Heard, H. L., & Armstrong, H. E. (1993). Naturalistic follow up of a behavioral treatment for chronically parasuicidal borderline patients. *Archives of General Psychiatry, 50*, 971.

Linehan, M. M., Schmidt, H., Dimeff, L. A., Craft, J. C., Kanter, J., & Comtois, K. A. (1999). Dialectical behavior therapy for patients with borderline personality disorder and drug-dependence. *American Journal on Addiction, 8*, 279–292.

Litz, B. T., Orsillo, S. M., Kaloupek, D., & Weathers, F. (2000). Emotional processing in posttraumatic stress disorder. *Journal of Abnormal Psychology, 109*, 26–39.

Lohr, J. M., Tolin, D. F., & Lilienfeld, S. O. (1998). Efficacy of eye movement desensitization and reprocessing: Implications for behavior therapy. *Behavior Therapy, 29*, 123–156.

Lynch, T. R., Robins, C. J., Morse, J. Q., & Krause, E. D. (2001). A mediational model relating affect intensity, emotion inhibition, and psychological distress. *Behavior Therapy, 32*, 519–536.

Marks, I., Lovell, K., Noshirvani, H., Livanou, M., & Thrasher, S. (1998). Treatment of posttraumatic stress disorder by exposure and/or cognitive restructuring. *Archives of General Psychiatry, 55*, 317–324.

Marx, B. P., & Sloan, D. M. (2002). The role of emotion in the psychological functioning of adult survivors of childhood sexual abuse. *Behavior Therapy, 33*, 563–577.

Mendlowicz, M. V., & Stein, M. B. (2000). Quality of life in individuals with anxiety disorders. *American Journal of Psychiatry, 157*, 669–682.

Nightingale, J., & Williams, R. M. (2000). Attitudes to emotional expression and personality in predicting post-traumatic stress disorder. *British Journal of Clinical Psychology, 39*, 243–254.

Nishith, P., Resick, P. A., & Griffin, M. G. (2002). Pattern of change in prolonged exposure and cognitive-processing therapy for female rape victims with posttraumatic stress disorder. *Journal of Consulting and Clinical Psychology, 70*, 880–886.

Orsillo, S. M., & Batten, S. V. (2005). Acceptance and commitment therapy in the treatment of posttraumatic stress disorder. *Behavior Modification, 29*, 95–129.

Orsillo, S. M., Batten, S. V., Plumb, J. C., Luterek, J. A., & Roessner, B. M. (2004). An experimental study of emotional responding in women with posttraumatic stress disorder related to interpersonal violence. *Journal of Traumatic Stress, 17*, 241–248.

Ouimette, P. C., Brown, P. J., & Najavits, L. M. (1998). Course and treatment of patients with both substance use and posttraumatic stress disorders. *Addictive Behaviors, 23*, 785–795.

Pitman, R. K., Altman, B., Greenwald, E., Longpre, R. E., Macklin, M. L., Poire, R. E., et al. (1991). Psychiatric complications during flooding therapy for posttraumatic stress disorder. *Journal of Clinical Psychiatry, 52*, 17–20.

Plumb, J. C., Orsillo, S. M., & Luterek, J. A. (2004). A preliminary test of the role of experiential avoidance in post-event functioning. *Journal of Behavior Therapy and Experimental Psychiatry, 35*, 245–257.

Polusny, M. A., & Follette, V. M. (1995). Long-term correlates of child sexual abuse: Theory and review of the empirical literature. *Applied and Preventive Psychology, 4,* 143–166.

Polusny, M. A., Rosenthal, M. Z., Aban, I., & Follette, V. M. (2004). Experiential avoidance as a mediator of the effects of adolescent sexual victimization on negative adult outcomes. *Violence and Victims, 19,* 109–120.

Purdon, C. (1999). Thought suppression and psychopathology. *Behaviour Research and Therapy, 37,* 1029–1054.

Resick, P. A., Nishith, P., Weaver, T. L., Astin, M. C., & Feuer, C. A. (2002). A comparison of cognitive-processing therapy with prolonged exposure and a waiting condition for the treatment of chronic posttraumatic stress disorder in female rape victims. *Journal of Consulting and Clinical Psychology, 70,* 867–879.

Resick, P. A., & Schnicke, M. K. (1992). Cognitive processing therapy for sexual assault victims. *Journal of Consulting and Clinical Psychology, 60,* 748–756.

Riggs, D. S., Dancu, C. V., & Gershuny, B. S. (1992). Anger and post-traumatic stress disorder in female crime victims. *Journal of Traumatic Stress, 5,* 613–625.

Roemer, L., & Borkovec, T. D. (1994). Effects of suppressing thoughts about emotional material. *Journal of Abnormal Psychology, 103,* 467–474.

Rosenthal, M. Z ., Rasmussen Hall, M. L., Palm, K., Batten, S. V., & Follette, V. M. (2005). Chronic avoidance helps explain the relationship between severity of childhood sexual abuse and psychological distress in adulthood. *Journal of Child Sexual Abuse, 14,* 25–41.

Roth, S., Newman, E., Pelcovitz, D., van der Kolk, B., & Mandel, F. (1997). Complex PTSD in victims exposed to sexual and physical abuse: Results from the DSM-IV field trial for posttraumatic stress disorder. *Journal of Traumatic Stress, 10,* 539–555.

Segal, Z. V., Williams, J. M., & Teasdale, J. D. (2002). *Mindfulness-based cognitive therapy for depression: A new approach to preventing relapse.* New York: Guilford.

Shapiro, F. (1989). Eye movement desensitization: A new treatment for posttraumatic stress disorder. *Journal of Behavior Therapy and Experimental Psychiatry, 20,* 211–217.

Shapiro, F. (1995). *Eye movement desensitization and reprocessing: Basic principles, protocols, and procedures.* New York: Guilford.

Shipherd, J. C., & Beck, J. G. (1999). The effects of suppressing trauma-related thoughts on women with rape-related posttraumatic stress disorder. *Behaviour Research and Therapy, 37,* 99–112.

Tarrier, N., & Gregg, L. (2004). Suicide risk in civilian PTSD patients: Predictors of suicidal ideation, planning and attempts. *Social Psychiatry & Psychiatric Epidemiology, 39,* 655–661.

Tarrier, N., Pilgrim, H., Sommerfield, C., Faragher, B., Reynolds, M., Graham, E., et al. (1999). A randomized trial of cognitive therapy and imaginal exposure in the treatment of chronic posttraumatic stress disorder. *Journal of Consulting and Clinical Psychology, 67,* 13–18.

Taylor, G. J., Bagby, R. M., & Parker, J. D. A. (1997). *Disorders of affect regulation: Alexithymia in medical and psychiatric illness.* Cambridge, England: Cambridge University Press.

Telch, C. F., Agras, W. S., & Linehan, M. M. (2000). Group dialectical behavior therapy for binge eating disorder: A preliminary uncontrolled trial. *Behavior Therapy, 31*, 569–582.

Turner, S. M., Beidel, D. C., & Frueh, B. C. (2005). Multicomponent behavioral treatment for chronic combat-related posttraumatic stress disorder: Trauma management therapy. *Behavior Modification, 29*, 39–69.

Valentiner, D. P., Foa, E. B., Riggs, D. S., & Gershuny, B. S. (1996). Coping strategies and posttraumatic stress disorder in female victims of sexual and nonsexual assault. *Journal of Abnormal Psychology, 105*, 455–458.

Wagner, A. W., & Linehan, M. M. (1998). Dissociative behavior. In V. M. Follette, J. L. Ruzek, & F. R. Abueg (Eds.), *Cognitive–behavioral therapies for trauma* (pp. 191–225). New York: Guilford.

Wagner, A. W., Roemer, L., Orsillo, S. M., & Litz, B. T. (2003) Emotional experiencing in women with posttraumatic stress disorder: Congruence between facial expressivity and self-report. *Journal of Traumatic Stress, 16*, 67–75.

Walser, R. D., Loew, D., Westrup, D., Gregg, J., & Rogers, D. (2002, November). *Acceptance and commitment therapy: Theory and treatment of complex PTSD.* International Society of Traumatic Stress Studies, Baltimore, MD.

Walser, R. D., Westrup, D., Rogers, D., Gregg, J., & Loew, D. (2003, November). *Acceptance and commitment therapy for PTSD.* International Society of Traumatic Stress Studies, Chicago, IL.

Wegner, D. M. (1994). Ironic processes of mental control. *Psychological Review, 101*, 34–52.

Zettle, R. D., & Raines, J. C. (1989). Group cognitive and contextual therapies in treatment of depression. *Journal of Clinical Psychology, 45*, 438–445.

Chapter 11

MINDFULNESS- AND ACCEPTANCE-BASED BEHAVIOR THERAPY FOR OBSESSIVE–COMPULSIVE DISORDER

Scott E. Hannan and David F. Tolin

Obsessive–compulsive disorder (OCD) is a chronic anxiety disorder, marked by recurrent, intrusive, and distressing thoughts (obsessions) and/or repetitive behaviors (compulsions) (American Psychiatric Association, 2004). Epidemiological data suggest a 6-month prevalence of 1–2% (Myers et al., 1984) and a lifetime prevalence of 2–3% (Robins et al., 1984). OCD symptoms often severely disrupt social and vocational functioning (Leon, Portera, & Weissman, 1995), and OCD is associated with a 40% unemployment rate (Steketee, Grayson, & Foa, 1987). A survey of individuals with OCD indicated that 20% spent 5–8 hr per day engaged in rituals, with 13% spending more than 17 hr per day during the most severe period of the disorder (Gallup Organization Inc., 1990).

BEHAVIORAL TREATMENT OF OCD

Behavioral interventions for OCD have taken many forms over the past three decades. For the purpose of this chapter, we categorize these treatments into two broad categories: those that emphasize controlling one's unwanted or unpleasant thoughts or feelings (private events), and those that de-emphasize control of private events. The latter treatments direct patients toward an acceptance of thoughts and feelings and instead emphasize control over voluntary, maladaptive behaviors.

One of the oldest (and still most widely used) behavioral interventions for OCD is *thought stopping* (Bain, 1928; Wolpe, 1990). In this intervention, patients are initially taught to respond to obsessive thoughts by saying "Stop!" out loud. Next, they are instructed to whisper the word to themselves, and finally to merely think the word "Stop!" Augmentations to vocal or subvocal thought stopping have included strategies such as electric shock or snapping the wrist with a rubber band (Reed, 1985; Wolpe, 1990). Despite its wide use, however, empirical results for the use of thought stopping have generally shown this technique to be ineffective for OCD (Emmelkamp & Kwee, 1977; Salkovskis & Westbrook, 1989).

Relaxation training has a long-standing history as a treatment intervention in medicine and mental health (E. Jacobson, 1929). The use of progressive muscle relaxation (PMR) has been particularly prolific in the treatment of anxiety disorders, as entire treatments have been based around variants of muscle relaxation (Haugen, Dixon, & Dickel, 1963). Some authors have suggested that PMR is a useful component of OCD treatment, particularly with children (March & Mulle, 1998). PMR has been shown to decrease symptoms of anxiety disorders such as agoraphobia (Michelson, Mavissakalian, & Marchione, 1985), and generalized anxiety disorder (Borkovec & Costello, 1993). Although PMR has demonstrated benefits in treating anxiety, other forms of cognitive–behavioral therapy have been found to be superior to relaxation training alone (Borkovec & Costello, 1993; Clark et al., 1994; Greist et al., 2002). When treating some disorders (e.g., panic disorder), the use of relaxation along with other treatment components may even detract from treatment efficacy (Murphy, Michelson, Marchione, Marchione, & Testa, 1998; Schmidt et al., 2000). PMR strategies such as relaxation have not been shown to be an effective component of treatment for OCD (Marks, 1987).

The aim of *cognitive therapy* (CT) for OCD is to teach patients to identify and correct dysfunctional beliefs about feared situations (e.g., Freeston et al., 1997). Two of the most widely utilized variants of CT are rational–emotive therapy (RET), now called rational-emotive behavior therapy, in which irrational beliefs are identified and targeted via rational debate; or CT along the lines of Beck, Emery, and Greenberg (1985), in which Socratic questioning and behavioral experiments are used to challenge the validity of distorted thoughts and biased thought processes. Both of these forms of

CT require patients to elaborate on their "automatic" appraisals of feared situations, to identify the logical inconsistencies in those thoughts, and to practice more adaptive ways of thinking. The specific efficacy of CT for OCD is not clear. In comparison studies, both RET (Emmelkamp, Visser, & Hoekstra, 1988) and CT (Cottraux et al., 2001; van Balkom et al., 1998; van Oppen et al., 1995) did not differ in efficacy from exposure and response prevention (ERP), a more behaviorally oriented treatment described below. In a group setting, however, CT yielded moderate results that were not as strong as those obtained using group ERP (McLean et al., 2001). In each of these CT comparison studies, we note that ERP sessions were briefer and more widely spaced than were those used in other ERP studies (Foa et al., 2005), and did not emphasize prolonged, therapist-assisted exposures, likely attenuating the efficacy of the ERP treatment (Tolin & Hannan, in press). In an augmentation trial, treatment with ERP was not enhanced by the addition of RET (Emmelkamp & Beens, 1991). Similarly, CT did not add to the effects of ERP to a greater extent than did a placebo condition (relaxation training; Vogel, Stiles, & Götestam, 2004). However, in an open trial utilizing a novel and intense variant of CT, five adult patients who had failed to respond to pharmacotherapy and ERP experienced a decrease in self-reported OCD symptoms (Krochmalik, Jones, & Menzies, 2001).

In summary, treatments that emphasize control over private events such as thoughts, feelings, and physiological sensations have shown mixed efficacy for OCD. In particular, the (arguably) most "control-based" treatments, thought stopping and PMR, have been found generally ineffective for the treatment of OCD. CT may be effective, although we note that many features of this treatment overlap substantially with the more behavioral treatments described below. For example, patients are often encouraged to conduct "behavioral experiments" that closely resemble the procedures used in exposure and ritual prevention. Therefore, the efficacy of CT may stem less from the client establishing control over their thoughts as from the client behaving in a manner that increases exposure to feared stimuli and control over voluntary behaviors. This appears to be the case for CT of depression, in which the more "behavioral" aspects of the treatment appear to explain much of the treatment outcome (N. S. Jacobson et al., 1996). Although meta-analytic findings (Abramowitz, 1997) show roughly equivalent effect sizes between cognitive and behavioral treatments, further inquiry suggests that the effects of CT for the treatment of OCD are driven largely not by establishing cognitive control, but rather by the "behavioral experiments" (exposures) used to challenge maladaptive beliefs (Abramowitz, Franklin, & Foa, 2002). Furthermore, cognitive change does not appear to require the strategies of cognitive therapy: patients receiving exposure-based therapy, for example, show changes in dysfunctional beliefs that are as pronounced and durable as are those seen in patients receiving CT (McLean et al., 2001). As Rachman (1997, p. 19) noted, "It appears that negative cognitions can decline after a direct attack or after an indirect attack." Segal, Williams, and Teasdale (2002) have suggested that CT may lead to change not through the alteration of thought content, but rather through "decentering," in which the individual learns to switch from a perspective that thoughts represent reality to one in which their thoughts are viewed as only an internal event.

In contrast to the control-based strategies described above, other interventions for OCD tend to de-emphasize direct attempts to control thoughts and feelings, and instead focus on altering voluntary behaviors. The clearest example of such a treatment is ERP. ERP consists of graded, prolonged exposure to fear eliciting stimuli or situations, combined with instructions for strict abstinence from compulsive behaviors. For example, a patient with an obsessive fear of being contaminated might be asked to touch objects of increasing "dirtiness," such as a doorknob, the floor, and bathroom fixtures, while simultaneously refraining from washing or cleaning behaviors. A patient with an obsessive fear of hitting pedestrians with a car may be encouraged to drive down a busy city street without checking to see if anyone was harmed. Rather than emphasizing to the patient that they should try to feel less anxious, or not to think about the possible catastrophic results of the exposure, in ERP the emphasis is often on encouraging the patient to experience his or her fearful thoughts and emotions fully, without attempting to change them. ERP's rationale is based on the habituation response, in which repeated exposures paired with the blocking of escape and avoidance behaviors such as compulsions result in reduced emotional and physiological responding to the feared stimuli, although, as Rachman noted above, "indirect" cognitive change may also be a mechanism of action.

Unlike the various "control-oriented" treatments described above, numerous controlled studies attest to the efficacy of ERP for patients with OCD (Cottraux, Mollard, Bouvard, & Marks, 1993; Fals-Stewart, Marks, & Schafer, 1993; Foa et al., 2005; Lindsay, Crino, & Andrews, 1997; van Balkom et al., 1998). In addition, open trials suggest that ERP is also effective when used in general clinical practice as opposed to a research context (Franklin, Abramowitz, Kozak, Levitt, & Foa, 2000; Warren & Thomas, 2001), and is at least moderately effective for patients who have not responded adequately to multiple medications for OCD (Tolin, Maltby, Diefenbach, Hannan, & Worhunsky, 2004).

Thus, unlike many control-based treatments, ERP appears to be an efficacious and effective intervention for OCD. Curiously, however, this treatment has yet to achieve the widespread acceptance that the more control-based therapies enjoy. In a survey of patients treated at specialty anxiety disorder clinics, strategies aimed at controlling private events were much more widely used than was ERP. Percentages of patients receiving various treatments were as follows: thought stopping (48%), distraction (44%), relaxation (40%), and cognitive therapy, broadly defined (52%). By comparison, only 28% of patients had received either in vivo or imaginal exposure (Goisman et al., 1993). In a survey of psychologists who treat OCD, 67% of respondents indicated that they frequently used CT, and 40% indicated that they frequently used relaxation training. By comparison, 37% of respondents indicated that they frequently used ERP (Freiheit, Vye, Swan, & Cady, 2004). In short, although ERP is the most clearly supported psychological treatment of OCD, clinicians are more likely to use strategies aimed at increasing control over thoughts and feelings, despite the relative lack of empirical support for such interventions.

THE ROLE OF ACCEPTANCE IN ERP

Recently, there has been increased interest in behavioral and cognitive–behavioral approaches that emphasize the importance of accepting, rather than attempting to change, internal experiences such as thoughts, feelings, images, and bodily sensations. This interest seems to be driven by approaches that incorporate mindfulness practice and/or acceptance into traditional cognitive–behavioral therapy. *Mindfulness* has been defined as the process by which one attends to their thoughts and feelings in the present moment without making any judgments as to their meaning or value (Baer, 2003; Brantley, 2003; Linehan, Armstrong, Suarez, Allmon, & Heard, 1993; Segal et al., 2002). A related concept is acceptance, a process by which one moves away from viewing thoughts and feelings as reality or things that need to be changed, and toward embracing them simply as internal events that do not need to be altered (Hayes, Strosahl, & Wilson, 1999; Roemer & Orsillo, 2003). The overarching goal of acceptance-based behavior therapy approaches is to reorient patients away from mal-adaptive attempts to alter their thoughts and feelings, and toward making positive, sustained behavioral change that is consistent with one's values and goals—essentially, to *live* better, rather than to *think and feel* better.

We do not view acceptance- and mindfulness-based approaches as being distinctly different from ERP. Rather, we view ERP as a treatment that is entirely compatible with these approaches. We thus conceptual-ize acceptance-based approaches as a vehicle for effective delivery of ERP and an alternative method of communicating its basic principles. In its

current form (Kozak & Foa, 1997), ERP is presented to patients largely at
the level of technique and strategy, with explanations based on the principle of habituation and change in beliefs. Patients are instructed that by
coming into contact with stimuli they believe to be dangerous or extremely
uncomfortable, without the use of rituals, they will experience a reduction
in anxiety. For many patients, this explanation is satisfactory. However,
the 25% refusal rate for ERP (Franklin & Foa, 2002) suggests that for at
least some patients, this rationale is not sufficiently compelling. In our
clinical experience, even among patients who initially accept the current
rationale for ERP, some appear to struggle with understanding the approach during the early stages of treatment. We often find that additional
explanation, providing patients with a "bigger picture" view of ERP, can
help less-motivated patients decide to engage in treatment (Tolin, Maltby,
Diefenbach, & Worhunsky, 2004). In addition, although a large number of
patients benefit from ERP, one study showed that at post-treatment follow-
up, nearly 40% of ERP patients intent-to-treat were considered treatment
nonresponders (Foa et al., 2005). Thus, ERP may benefit from additional
attention to the rationale and model provided to patients, as well as an
emphasis on coping with anxiety in a manner that does not add to the
problem.

The various acceptance-based approaches (e.g., acceptance and commitment therapy [ACT], dialectical behavior therapy [DBT], and mindfulness based cognitive therapy [MBCT]) can offer a basic philosophical
framework for the specific strategies used in treatment, which may help
some patients understand the rationale and spirit of ERP more clearly. In
addition, techniques such as mindfulness meditation and the metaphors
used in ACT may help those patients who are resistant to the idea of exposure. We may be accused of putting "old wine into new bottles"; however,
we suggest that, for some patients at least, this particular bottle may make
the wine more palatable.

AN EXPERIENTIAL AVOIDANCE-BASED
CONCEPTUALIZATION OF OCD

Experiential avoidance, a process by which individuals engage in strategies designed to alter the frequency or experience of private events, such
as thoughts, feelings, memories, or bodily sensations, has been described
as a functional dimension that may be key in the development and maintenance of many psychological disorders (Hayes, Wilson, Gifford, Follette, &
Strosahl, 1996). An experiential avoidance model of psychopathology
matches well with current views of OCD. From this perspective, OCD

is related to metacognitive beliefs about, and behavioral attempts to control, internal experiences such as thoughts and emotions. OCD patients evaluate and engage their thought processes in a manner that intensifies the struggle and thus the anxiety and discomfort they experience. Subsequently, they engage in behaviors that, although they may appear to provide short-term anxiety relief, actually increase long-term anxiety.

Dysfunctional beliefs have been hypothesized to play a factor in OCD (Frost & Steketee, 2002; Obsessive Compulsive Cognitions Working Group, 1997). Specific beliefs thought to characterize OCD include threat overestimation, beliefs that one's thoughts are important and are equivalent to action, beliefs that one needs to keep control of one's thoughts, intolerance of uncertainty, inflated responsibility, and perfectionism. Beliefs that one's thoughts are important (e.g., the same as performing an action) and must be controlled appear prominent in OCD (Shafran & Rachman, 2004), suggesting a central role of such beliefs in the maintenance of OCD symptoms (Tolin, Woods, & Abramowitz, 2003; Tolin, Worhunsky, & Maltby, 2004). These associations suggest that a key problem in OCD is the belief that obsessive thoughts are in some way important or "bad" and must be controlled. In many ways this concept is similar to the metacognitive model of generalized anxiety disorder proposed by Wells (1999), which shows some overlap with OCD symptoms (Wells & Papageorgiou, 1998). The relationship between these thought processes and OCD symptoms coincides with the experiential avoidance model that negative evaluation of one's thoughts and emotions keeps patients in a struggle to avoid the possibility of negative emotions (Hayes et al., 1999).

The concept that thoughts are equivalent to action and must be controlled is most easily observed in the phenomenon termed "thought action fusion," the explicit or implicit belief that one's thoughts will make an event more likely to occur (likelihood thought action fusion), or that having a "bad" thought is the moral equivalent of performing a "bad" act (moral thought action fusion; Shafran & Rachman, 2004; Shafran, Thordarson, & Rachman, 1996). An example of thought action fusion in OCD is a patient seen in our clinic who presented with intrusive, obsessive thoughts that she would harm her infant daughter. These thoughts, quite understandably, elicited intense feelings of anxiety. Upon questioning, she indicated two distinct reactions to the thoughts, both of which illustrate the concept of thought action fusion: First, she believed that if she "allowed" herself to experience these intrusive thoughts, the probability that she would actually harm her child would increase. That is, she believed that her thoughts would influence her actual behavior. Second, she believed that, regardless of whether she actually harmed her child, the presence of these thoughts meant she was dangerous, immoral, crazy, and a bad mother. Her evaluations of her own self worth, therefore, were based primarily on her private events, rather than on her overt behaviors.

Even among patients who do not present with clear examples of thought action fusion, as the woman described above, a more subtle form of fusion with one's cognitive appraisals may still be present. For example, one of our patients presented with the persistent belief that the university from which he had graduated many years before was "contaminated." He was unable to articulate specifically how or why it was contaminated, other than the fact that the thought had occurred in his mind. In fact, this was one of the reasons he gave for accepting the idea so uncritically: "If I think it this strongly and this often, there must be something to it." He had accepted the label of "contaminated" as reality, and acted accordingly by going to great lengths to avoid reminders of his university. It is perhaps noteworthy, from an associative learning perspective, that he denied any history of adverse experiences at the university—in fact, he reported being quite happy there. In this case, the unconditioned stimulus was not an actual experience, but rather a verbal label that, from his perspective, was accepted as real.

In addition to evaluating obsessive thoughts, OCD patients make attempts to reduce or eliminate aversive thoughts and emotions. These behavioral attempts at anxiety reduction typically take two forms of avoidance, with most patients exhibiting both kinds: Passive avoidance, in which patients avoid stimuli or situations that elicit obsessions or anxiety; and active avoidance, which is the repetitive, ritualistic behavior enacted to prevent or reduce feelings of anxiety or discomfort. For example, the man who thought his university was contaminated engaged in passive avoidance by refusing to travel to the state in which the school was located, ceasing contact with his friends from college, and staying away from his gym where he believed an alumnus of that university now worked; all of these behaviors served to reduce his perceived sense of risk that the "contamination" would somehow infect him. His active avoidance (the overt compulsions) took the form of repeated handwashing, showering, and cleaning, whenever he encountered *or even thought of* anything remotely related to his university. Like the capacity for thoughts to become unconditioned stimuli, this man's avoidance behavior in response to his own thoughts highlights the importance that OCD patients attribute to private events.

Many authors have suggested that OCD patients are characterized by the excessive use of thought suppression (Freeston & Ladouceur, 1997), and research suggests that these patients use thought suppression to a greater degree than do nonanxious controls (Abramowitz, Whiteside, Kalsy, &

Tolin, 2003; Amir, Cashman, & Foa, 1997). Although attempts to suppress thoughts may be effective for limited periods of time, evidence suggests that with time, these thoughts will paradoxically increase (Abramowitz, Tolin, & Street, 2001; Wegner, Schneider, Carter, & White, 1987). This paradoxical effect appears to be even greater among OCD patients than among nonanxious and anxious controls (Tolin, Abramowitz, Przeworski, & Foa, 2002). Furthermore, when thought suppression attempts eventually fail, OCD patients appear to attribute such failure not to the inherent unworkability of thought suppression, but rather to internal factors such as mental weakness or the "badness" of the thought itself (Tolin, Abramowitz, Hamlin, Foa, & Synodi, 2002). Such attributions in turn may further enhance the perceived need to try harder to suppress. In our research using the Obsessive Beliefs Questionnaire (Obsessive Compulsive Cognitions Working Group, 2001), we have found that beliefs that one's thoughts are important and need to be controlled differentiate OCD patients from those with other anxiety disorders (Tolin, Worhunsky, & Maltby, 2004), and that such beliefs are associated with self-reported use of maladaptive thought control strategies (Tolin, Worhunsky et al., 2003).

In summary, OCD can be conceptualized from an experiential avoidance-based perspective as a disorder of evaluation and control. The process by which one experiences his or her thoughts and emotions as a reality, rather than as internal events, is associated with an increase in obsessions and compulsions. It may be difficult for patients to stop viewing thoughts as reality due to the emotional arousal connected to their obsessions. In addition, some may believe that their thoughts are equivalent to actually performing the feared behavior or that it will make them more likely to engage in the feared behavior. Responding to their negative evaluation of their cognitive and emotional state, patients will attempt to eliminate what they believe to be the root of the problem (i.e., the presence of obsessions, or the negative outcomes that their obsessions predict). However, acceptance-based therapies (and to a lesser extent, ERP) involve teaching the patient that the main source of their suffering is neither obsessions (e.g., thoughts about being contaminated) nor the predicted consequences (e.g., contracting a fatal disease), but rather the patient's understandable but ultimately unhelpful attempts to avoid or control these private events. Such attempts typically involve passive and active avoidance, resulting in short-term relief, but a long-term increase in anxiety. Furthermore, as noted at the beginning of this chapter, these strategies often interfere substantially with quality of life. Studies using quality-of-life measures have found OCD to be associated with poorer self-reported quality of life than are disorders such as diabetes or schizophrenia (Bystritsky et al., 2001; Koran, Thienemann, & Davenport, 1996).

IMPLEMENTATION OF ACCEPTANCE BASED STRATEGIES FOR OCD PATIENTS

As discussed above, we do not view acceptance-based strategies as alternatives to ERP; rather, in our practice we use the perspectives of acceptance and mindfulness to convey the principles of ERP. The core aim of each intervention is to undermine patients' chronic and maladaptive experiential avoidance strategies, to teach distancing from private events such as intrusive thoughts, and to shape more adaptive behavior patterns. Below, we discuss some of the core acceptance and mindfulness strategies (e.g., Hayes et al., 1999) and discuss how they are used to complement ERP. In our work, we draw most heavily from ACT (Hayes et al., 1999).

One aim of early treatment, often in the first session, is to help the patient recognize that compulsions, avoidant behavior, and thought suppression have not been successful in solving their problems in the long term. Although these rituals and avoidance behaviors appear to make sense, they have not been helpful, except with short-term anxiety relief. At times, even the use of medication and psychological therapy may be illustrative of this pattern, to the extent that the sole aim of such treatment was short-term anxiety reduction rather than durable behavior change. The message to be conveyed is that the pursuit of anxiety relief may keep patients anxious in the long term, rather than helping them improve.

The acceptance-based rationale for this step differs subtly but perhaps importantly from the usual rationale for ERP. Rather than merely presenting the argument that "ritualizing will make you feel worse, and not ritualizing will make you feel better," the emphasis from an acceptance perspective is to help the patient examine the ways in which compulsions and avoidance have been not only unhelpful, but have also had an impact on his or her ability to live according to his or her personal values and goals. For example, a patient who values his or her role as a parent might be engaged in a discussion of how their coping strategies have led them to spend more time with their OCD than with their children. Thus, the initial emphasis is not on immediate anxiety reduction, but rather on quality-of-life issues.

Jane's primary obsessions involve a fear that she will be contaminated by anthrax, a fear that developed abruptly after the 2001 anthrax mailings on the East Coast. In this session, the therapist attempts to increase her willingness to consider alternatives to her usual control strategies. For the purpose of this chapter, the transcripts are abbreviated; however, this exploration can take time as patient and therapist work together to undermine the patient's control strategies.

T: Can you tell me about some of the ways that you've tried to solve this problem in the past?

C: Well, mostly I just avoid the mail. I have my husband open it, or sometimes my kids will do it. Sometimes I have to have them open the mail outside or in the garage, to make sure the house doesn't get contaminated.

T: Okay, so avoiding things that might be contaminated is one way that you've tried to control things. How has that worked for you?

C: Well, I definitely don't get as anxious when someone else opens the mail as I would if I had to do it myself.

T: How about in the long term? That is, how successful has avoidance been in making this problem actually get better?

C: I guess it hasn't been very successful. The problem has pretty much gotten worse over the last couple of years.

T: You told me that you're a wife and mother. How important is that to you?

C: That means everything to me! It's who I am; it's who I want to be. It's the one thing I can really take pride in. I may screw up a lot of things in my life but I really want to be the best wife and mom I can be.

T: How does OCD affect that?

C: It's totally messed up my life. It's not just that I can't touch the mail; I can't even touch things that touched the mail. Like after my kids or my husband open the mail, they have to shower and change their clothes before I can even go near them.

T: Wow, so for example, you wouldn't hug your husband or your kids when they come home?

C: Not unless they've showered and changed clothes. And it goes beyond that, too. I used to make lunches for my kids before they went to school, but now that the kitchen is contaminated I can't even go in there and touch stuff, so my husband has to make the lunches and do all the cooking.

T: So you don't hug your family when they come home, don't make lunches for the kids. How does that fit with your desire to be the best wife and mom you can be?

C: (pause) It doesn't. Not at all. Instead of being a good wife and mom, I've become a problem. A burden. (becomes tearful)

T: I can see that even thinking about this is really affecting you. I can see how important that is for you, and I can imagine how frustrating it must be to not be living the kind of life you want to live. You used to have all this energy and time to put into doing wife and mom stuff, and now you put that energy and time . . .

C: Into my OCD.

T: So it's like OCD has robbed you of the things that are most important to you. I have a question for you: what aspect of OCD has done the most damage?

C: I'm not sure I get what you mean.

T: Well, I mean that your OCD is made up of a lot of different things, like intrusive thoughts about contamination, anxious feelings, compulsive washing, and avoiding dirty things. So some of the ingredients of OCD are things that happen inside you, like thoughts and feelings, and other ingredients are things you do, like washing and avoiding. What ingredients are the ones that actually take you away from being the kind of wife and mom you want to be?

C: (pause) I guess it's the avoiding. If I didn't avoid so much, I might be able to do more. And maybe the washing, too, because it takes up so much of my time that I used to spend hanging out with my family.

T: I think maybe there's something very important about that. It's not the thoughts and feelings that have done the damage? It's the actions?

C: Yeah, but the actions come from the thoughts and feelings.

T: Perhaps we could reword that and say that when you feel anxious and think about anthrax, you try to manage those thoughts and feelings by avoiding and washing.

C: Yeah, I guess that sounds right.

T: And it's the avoiding and washing that have done the biggest damage to your life?

C: Hmmm . . . maybe.

The therapist continued this line of questioning in regard to Jane's compulsive handwashing, showering, and cleaning. In each case, Jane was able to recognize that her control strategies had backfired. A metaphor from ACT underscores this point.

T: One way we could think about this problem is that you've fallen into a hole that we call OCD. We're not entirely sure about how you fell in, but there you are nevertheless. So you reach into your toolbox and pull out the best tool you can see, which happens to be a shovel. And so you start trying to dig your way out. When you wash your hands, that's like taking one scoop of dirt with the shovel. And when you ask your husband to open the mail, there's another scoop. You dig and dig; you're going through the motions of solving the problem, but every time you look up from digging you realize you're still in the hole, maybe even a bit deeper in the hole. So you do what seems logical; you dig harder! But all the digging in the world won't get you out of that hole. You are stuck.

C: So are you saying that it's hopeless? That there's no way out of the hole?

T: Not at all. I think there is a way out of the hole. What I am saying is that digging is definitely not it. And it's not that you're not digging hard enough—it's not that you haven't washed enough, or that you haven't found just the right avoidance strategy. It's that washing, avoidance, and so on cannot make your OCD get better. Part of the problem is that as long as you keep digging, it's hard for you to see any other solutions. So even if someone threw a ladder down the hole, presented a really different way for you to solve the problem, as long as you keep digging—as long as you keep washing and avoiding—you won't be able to take advantage of it. First, you have to have the courage to put the shovel down, scary as that prospect might be. It will take courage for you to give up washing and avoiding.

Once the patient has developed an understanding that his or her current efforts to control OCD has not been working, the therapist can begin to help undermine their maladaptive control strategies by illustrating the paradoxical nature of thought suppression and by presenting the alternative concept of willingness. As discussed above, OCD patients appear to overutilize thought suppression, often with paradoxical effects. The thought suppression paradox is suggested in standard ERP (Abramowitz, Franklin, & Cahill, 2003) and can be a useful tool in acceptance-based therapies (Hayes et al., 1999).

Robert presented for OCD treatment with a persistent fear that he would impulsively harm a family member, friend, or stranger. He reported extensive efforts to distract himself from these thoughts or otherwise force them from his mind. The therapist used a thought suppression exercise to help Robert recognize the paradoxical effects of these strategies.

T: You've mentioned that you do whatever you can to stop thinking about hurting people. You might try to distract yourself to prevent these thoughts from entering your mind, or if you notice that thought occurring, you'll immediately try to think of something else in order to get it out of your mind.

C: Right. The thought is really scary to me; it seems so real. So I just can't stand having it. I want to get rid of it as fast as I can to make sure I don't lose control of myself.

T: You've also mentioned, though, that this strategy hasn't been very successful in really solving this problem. The thought just keeps coming back again and again. I want to talk a bit about that strategy, and maybe show you what it's really doing to you. Let's try an exercise together. Close your eyes for a moment and I'm going to ask you to try something (Robert and the therapist close their eyes). In a second, I'm going to ask you not to think about something and I really want you to try not to think about it. Try very hard not to let it into your mind at all. Ready? The thing I want you not to think about is a white bear. Don't think about what it looks like, or sounds like, and do not even think the words "white bear." I'll give you some time to not think about it (waits 30 seconds). Okay, that's fine; you can open your eyes when you're ready. Tell me what you experienced.

C: Well, I knew I wasn't supposed to think about a white bear, so I started going over my shopping list for later today as a way to distract myself.

T: So you tried to distract yourself from the thought. What happened to the white bear while you were doing that?

C: I'd be thinking about my shopping list, but the picture of a white bear kept popping up in my mind.

T: So we kind of made a mini-obsession there, didn't we? A thought that you couldn't get rid of, even though you tried. Do you think maybe it's because you didn't try hard enough? What if you'd tried harder? Like if I told you I'd give you a million dollars if you didn't think of a white bear?

C: I think I still wouldn't be able to stop myself from thinking about it.

T: You wouldn't, would you? Neither would I. The fact is, no one can do that very well. At best, we can distract ourselves for a short while, but our brains aren't very good at not thinking about things.

Because the rule you tell yourself, "Don't think about a white bear," contains the very words "white bear!" It's like every time you remind yourself of what you're supposed to be doing, you bring up the forbidden thought. Now, this was just for 30 seconds or so. What do you think would happen if I told you not to think about a white bear for the rest of the day?

C: I'd be seeing white bears all over the place!

T: Exactly. You'd have white bear OCD. Just out of curiosity, do white bears have any special meaning for you? Are they important in some way to you?

C: No. I saw polar bears at the zoo once, but that was when I was a kid. I never gave them much thought.

T: Okay, so white bears are pretty meaningless to you. Now, here's the million-dollar question: What do you think would happen if the thought were meaning*ful* to you? Maybe even scary? For example, what if, instead of a white bear, I asked you not to think about murdering someone?

C: (Pause) I guess it would be worse.

T: Exactly. The stakes would be higher, and so you'd try harder to control it. And the harder you tried . . .

C: The more the thought would bother me.

T: And there's a lesson there, that is critical to understanding OCD: Everything works backward. If you try not to think about something, what happens?

C: I think about it more.

T: Exactly. In other words, if you're unwilling to experience the thought, you'll see more of it. And so, if you really want to overcome a problem thought . . .

C: (Pause) I should think about it more? So does that mean that if I think about murdering people more, it will make me stop thinking about it?

T: Not necessarily. Actually, since the thought probably occurs to a lot of people from time to time, it would be kind of strange if you *never ever* thought about it again. But maybe the thought wouldn't hold so much meaning for you. Maybe, just maybe, you wouldn't care too much whether the thought came into your mind or not.

Using this thought suppression exercise, the therapist has helped the patient recognize that his attempts to control his private events, although they make intuitive sense to the patient, have actually become part of the problem. Note also that the therapist used this discussion to begin to lead the patient toward the concept of therapeutic exposure to his distressing thoughts. The patient has begun to express some recognition that confronting unpleasant thoughts and feelings may be a more workable alternative to avoiding or suppressing them. Note as well that the therapist steered Robert away from the notion that exposure is a way to rid himself of unwanted thoughts. When exposure is conducted in this manner, the patient may experience the same paradoxical effects seen in thought suppression (Wegner et al., 1987): after conducting the exposure, the patient would continue to monitor his thoughts for signs of the "forbidden" thought, thus increasing the likelihood of their occurrence and detection. Detection of the unwanted thought could then be interpreted by the patient as a sign of failure or a need to "try harder," thus perpetuating the cycle of attempts to control internal events. Instead, the therapist emphasized the "distancing" aspects of exposure, in which exposure would help him react less strongly to the thoughts and learn to treat them as mere internal events. Thus, the actual occurrence of intrusive thoughts is de-emphasized and given less importance.

Continuing with Robert, the therapist demonstrates how repeated exposure to unwanted thoughts can strip them of their assigned meaning.

T: So if suppressing thoughts makes them seem worse, then maybe addressing them can make them seem like less of a problem. Let's try something else. When you think the words, "white bear," what comes to mind?

C: A big white teddy bear, like a polar bear.

T: And how real does that bear seem to you right now? That is, how vividly can you imagine it, see it, feel it, and so on?

C: It seems pretty real. I can just imagine it sitting on a shelf in my kid's room.

T: Okay, now try something. Pick it up.

C: You mean imagine picking it up?

T: No, I mean really pick it up and hold it in your hands.

C: (Pause) Well, I can't do that for real.

T: Why not?

C: Because there isn't actually any bear here.

T: But just a second ago you said it was really vivid; you could see it, feel it, it was on your kid's shelf, and so on. So what's the problem?

C: It's not real.

T: So no matter how real it seems in your mind, that doesn't make it real?

C: Right.

T: Thoughts are not the same as real things?

C: No.

T: I agree. But maybe it's different if the thought is about something important. If we were to sit here and think about murdering someone, do you think we could get arrested for murder?

C: (Laughs) No, because we didn't actually kill someone; we just thought about it.

T: But what if we thought about it really, really vividly, so it seemed very real in our minds?

C: It still wouldn't be real.

T: You are exactly right. Thoughts are not real. They're just thoughts, whether they're good or bad, happy or unhappy, comfortable or scary. Now, a minute ago you had a really radical idea that just might work. You said that if you really want to overcome a thought, one way to do that might be to think about it more, not less. Let's try an exercise. For the next two minutes, we'll both say "white bear" over and over again. Ready? Go! (Robert and the therapist say "white bear" repeatedly and rapidly for 2 minutes, with the therapist periodically encouraging Robert to keep going, go faster, etc.). Okay, let's stop now. Tell me what you experienced.

C: Well, it was kind of boring, just saying the words over and over.

T: Yeah. At the beginning, you said that white bear seemed very real to you, very vivid. What happened with that?

C: After a while, it just became words, like I wasn't thinking about a white bear any more; just the words. And then even the words didn't really make sense; they were just sounds. It was kind of like a tongue-twister when we started going really fast.

T: I see. So by saying it over and over again, it stopped having that special meaning? The words "white bear" stopped giving you the realistic experience of an actual bear?

C: Right. The bear that I saw in my mind just kind of went away and I was just making noise.

T: And that's all it really was in the first place. Just noise. But because the noise was in our heads, we tend to feel like it's real. But by repeating it over and over again, we started to see it as noise again. Now let's try something a little closer to home. This might be a little uncomfortable at first. Could we try the same exercise, but using a different word? This time, let's try the word "kill."

C: The idea of doing that is pretty scary, but I guess we can try.

T: How vivid and scary is that word right now, say, on a scale from 0–10?

C: About an 8. It seems pretty real.

T: Okay, so let's try saying "kill" over and over again, just like last time. Ready? Go! (Robert and the therapist say "kill" for 2 minutes in the same fashion). Okay, let's stop now. Now how vivid and scary is that word for you?

C: About a 2. It's just sound, just like the white bear.

T: Absolutely right. Just noise.

One important aspect of approaching exposure from an acceptance-based perspective is that reduction in the frequency of obsessive thoughts, or reduction in anxious feelings, is de-emphasized compared to traditional ERP. For example, in traditional ERP, the success of an exposure is identified using the Subjective Units of Discomfort (SUD) Scale, in which patients rate their anxiety on a numeric scale. This conflicts somewhat with the spirit of an acceptance-based therapy: it is difficult to persuade patients to increase their willingness to experience anxiety, while simultaneously asking them every 5 minutes whether they still feel anxious. Once the patient demonstrates a clear understanding of the fact that control of obsessions is an indirect, rather than direct, process, this is less of an issue. However, in the early stages of treatment, as shown above, it may be preferable to focus on other aspects of the thought, such as the degree to which it is perceived as "real."

The alternative to perceiving a thought as "real" is to observe that thought from a detached perspective, a notion central to mindfulness. In MBCT (Segal et al., 2002), patients learn to attend to internal processes without evaluation, to move away from a focus on trying to alter the internal processes, and to increase willingness to allow all thoughts and feelings to be present. Mindfulness meditation exercises as suggested by Segal et al. (2002) can be performed utilizing neutral stimuli, such as the body scan. As patients learn a nonevaluative observation of internal events, they can be guided toward a willingness to face anxiety-provoking stimuli. A focus on private events is an important component of ERP.

Research suggests that for maximum efficacy, exposure exercises must be paired with response prevention (Foa, Steketee, & Milby, 1980). Thus, the patient is asked to do two things simultaneously: decrease attempts to control private events (e.g., obsessions) and increase attempts to control voluntary behaviors and mental neutralization (e.g., compulsions). We often utilize a "bully" metaphor to explain this concept.

T: OCD can often behave like a schoolyard bully. He approaches other kids looking to get a reaction. One day he approaches two different kids. He does the same thing to both; he calls the names and tells them how he can beat them up. One student yells back in protest and argues with the bully. The other student acknowledges the bully without protest, "O.K. whatever you say" and goes about his recess. What do you think will happen to these two kids?

C: Well, he's a bully. He'll keep picking on them.

T: You're probably right. Let's imagine that you are the bully. You go up to the first student and he argues with you. As a bully what would you do?

C: I'll probably laugh at him, maybe push him down to the ground.

T: What if he gets backs up and tries to push you back?

C: Well maybe I'll punch him.

T: O.K. What about the second kid on the playground, who doesn't argue back with you?

C: As a bully I'll probably keep after him for a while, but I'll probably go looking for the first kid. I can really push his buttons.

T: It may be helpful to think of OCD as that bully. For a while now you've been fighting back with him and he keeps pushing you around. Now that you are starting exposure and response prevention you are like that second kid on the playground. The bully is going to keep testing you out. It's very hard not to fight back with him. All your instincts keep telling you to fight him, argue with him, and so on. Maybe we cannot control his behavior, just as we have found we cannot control obsessions. In fact, the first child was trying hard to control the bully and ended up having to deal with the bully for much longer. If, however, we are willing to let the bully say what he wants we can go on with our recess.

C: So, I should just be a pushover and let the bully control me?

T: Not at all. It's no fun being a pushover and I know I wouldn't want my life to be like that. Let's think about it some more. With this bully scenario, what is beyond your control?

C: What the bully says to me.

T: Right. You can't shut him up, and the more you try, the louder and more obnoxious he gets. So what *can* you control?

C: What I do?

T: Exactly. So, let's say, the bully says that you're a big dummy and your mother dresses you funny. How much control do you have here?

C: Basically none. He's going to say what he's going to say. But I guess I have control over whether I argue with him or not.

T: That's right. The only thing you can control is you. Okay, what if the bully says, "Give me your lunch money or I'll beat you up?" Now how much control do you have?

C: Well . . . I guess I have control over whether or not I give him the money.

T: You don't have control over him demanding the money from you?

C: No. I can't stop him from demanding it, but I can control how I respond to him.

T: I think you have it. What do you suppose will happen when you refuse to give him the money?

C: He'll beat me up?

T: Maybe. Or perhaps he's all talk. If our bully is OCD, remember that OCD is just a bunch of thoughts and feelings and brain signals. Can those things beat you up?

C: No, they're just inside me.

T: Like the white bear! You can see it in front of you, but you can't actually pick it up because it's not a real thing. So this is the kind of bully that's all talk.

C: Yeah, but I bet when I refuse to give him the money he'll get a lot more threatening, maybe threaten to beat up my friends and family, too.

T: Yeah, that seems pretty likely. That's what bullies do. And then?

C: And then, when he sees I'm not going to back down, maybe he'll go bother some other kid.

T: So the goal here, the way to beat this bully, is...

C: Not to get into arguments with him and not to do what he says.

As has been discussed previously, one subtle aspect of acceptance-based strategies is that interventions not be used as substitute attempts to change internal events. Thus, at this point the therapist may assess whether or not the patient is using this as a way to escape their feelings.

T: So, by ignoring the bully, what do you hope will happen?

C: Hopefully he'll go away.

T: Here's the difficulty with this bully. He's in the schoolyard. You're in the schoolyard. And there's a big fence around the whole thing. In the case of OCD, he's inside your brain and we can't just open up your head and make him leave. So he's probably not going anywhere.

C: Well, maybe I need to just go about my life and do what I normally do, even though he's there.

T: Perhaps that's a better solution. Maybe he can do his thing, and you do yours? And I bet, since he's a bully, he'll still occasionally give you a dirty look, or call you a name. What then?

C: Maybe I should just say to myself, "There he goes again, doing his thing."

T: So it's kind of like learning to co-exist with him?

C: Right.

T: And what would be the point of doing that, if you know he's not going to go away? What would be the reason for learning to co-exist?

C: Well, then I could get on with doing the things I want to do instead of always worrying about him and what he's going to do.

T: Right. You could do your work, play your sports, or whatever else it is you want to do in the schoolyard, rather than devoting all of your time, effort, and attention to him.

As patients learn to be more aware and accepting of their thoughts, it is often helpful to direct them to *seek out* their unwanted thoughts, rather than passively waiting for them to occur. This strategy increases patients' sense of control and mastery over the process and ensures ample opportunity to practice adaptive coping strategies. Susan presented for treatment with fears that she was responsible for preventing harm to others.

If she saw objects on the sidewalk such as a stick or a banana peel, she would go back to pick it up out of fear that someone would trip and get hurt. One exposure exercise involved dropping pieces of banana peels on a city sidewalk. The therapist acted as her mind as she performed this exercise.

> **T:** Susan, in this exercise I'm going to be your OCD and you will be you. Your job is to do today's exposure exercise, walking around and dropping these pieces of banana peel on the sidewalk. My job is to try to scare you out of it, to get you to stop doing it—because that's what your OCD does normally. But I bet, from our previous discussions, that you have a pretty good sense of how to deal with me.
>
> **C:** Yup. I should not argue with you or engage with you, but I also shouldn't try to run away from you or get you to shut up.
>
> **T:** Right. And when I tell you to do something?
>
> **C:** I shouldn't obey you.
>
> **T:** Absolutely right. Okay, let's start.
>
> **C:** (Dropping peels)
>
> **T:** Are you sure you want to drop that there? Someone could get really hurt.
>
> **C:** Should I pick it up?
>
> **T:** Don't listen to OCD! Just keep doing what you're doing.
>
> **C:** (Looking hesitant). Okay. But how do I know if it's safe to drop it here?
>
> **T:** Remember what we discussed. I'm your OCD. I am not a good judge of what is going to happen in reality. In fact, the more you ask me how dangerous something is, the more I'll come up with more dangerous situations. Your job is to do whatever you want with this banana peel, now matter how dangerous I tell you it is.
>
> **C:** (Begins to throw peels again).
>
> **T:** Are you sure you want to do that? This is a busy street. Someone could slip into the road and get hit by a car.
>
> **C:** (Continues to throw peels).
>
> **T:** What if an old person walks by? They could get really hurt.

This exercise continued as Susan continued to throw peels around the sidewalks. She noticed her anxiety decreasing, and felt the banter from the therapist (her OCD) less compelling and "real." The therapist then asked Susan to join in and say some of these scary thoughts herself.

> T: You're doing great. Now let's try something extra. Can you play the part of your OCD as well? That is, all of these scary things I'm saying, can you try saying them too? That way, you'll know you can handle them even when they are coming from inside you. So we'll invite OCD to come over and let him say whatever he has to say.

> C: I can try. (Continues to drop peels)

> T: You'd better go pick those up. I see a couple of kids coming by, and there is a big bus on the road. You know kids never look where they are going.

> C: Yeah, those kids could slip on the peels and fall right into the path of the bus and get run over. We may even see the big accident on the evening news! (laughs)

As the patient was more willing to "hear" her obsessive thoughts, she found that those thoughts no longer elicited intense feelings of anxiety or an urge to ritualize. Not only was she willing to experience those thoughts, she was willing to bring them on (i.e., exposure to distressing thoughts).

SUMMARY AND CONCLUSIONS

We have suggested that cognitive–behavioral interventions for OCD can be divided into those that emphasize control over private events versus those that emphasize acceptance of private events and control of voluntary behavior. In general, control-based strategies such as relaxation training and thought stopping have not been found effective for OCD (Emmelkamp & Kwee, 1977; Marks, 1987; Salkovskis & Westbrook, 1989). Cognitive therapy, another control-based treatment, may be efficacious; however, the mechanism of change is not clear and it appears that patients may improve not because of increased control over their thoughts, but because of therapist-directed behavioral changes (Abramowitz et al., 2002). By comparison, ERP has a robust track record of clinical efficacy, with both exposure and response prevention appearing necessary for durable change.

The spirit of ERP appears quite consistent with that of acceptance-based strategies. As such, in this chapter we have presented acceptance and mindfulness not as distinct interventions, but rather as a means of delivering the principles of ERP in a "user-friendly" and theoretically coherent manner. In both ERP and acceptance-based therapies, a presumed core mechanism of change is undermining patients' maladaptive control attempts such as thought suppression, experiential avoidance, and ritualistic behavior. Once weakened, these strategies are replaced with deliberate confrontation of frightening thoughts and the situations that elicit such thoughts, and increased emphasis on controlling voluntary behavior. As patients learn to shift their control attempts away from their thoughts and toward their behavior, their obsessions begin to seem less real and are perceived as the "brain noise" that they are.

The role of acceptance and mindfulness in OCD treatment, of course, will ultimately need to be determined at an empirical level. It would be helpful to compare the efficacy of acceptance-based treatments with that of existing treatments such as ERP and cognitive therapy. Furthermore, it would be important to determine whether the mechanisms of change are the same in each of these forms of treatment. Alternatively, in keeping with the spirit of this chapter in which we define *acceptance* and *mindfulness* as helpful adjuncts to ERP, it would be informative to study whether the efficacy (as well as factors such as ease of use, tolerability, attrition rate, etc.) of ERP is augmented by acceptance-based strategies.

REFERENCES

Abramowitz, J. S. (1997). Effectiveness of psychological and pharmacological treatments for obsessive–compulsive disorder: a quantitative review. *Journal of Consulting and Clinical Psychology, 65*, 44–52.

Abramowitz, J. S., Franklin, M., & Cahill, S. P. (2003). Approaches to common obstacles in the exposure-based treatment of obsessive–compulsive disorder. *Cognitive and Behavioral Practice, 10*, 14–22.

Abramowitz, J. S., Franklin, M. E., & Foa, E. B. (2002). Empirical status of cognitive–behavioral therapy for obsessive–compulsive disorder: A meta-analytic review. *Romanian Journal of Cognitive and Behavioral Psychotherapies, 2*, 89–104.

Abramowitz, J. S., Tolin, D. F., & Street, G. P. (2001). Paradoxical effects of thought suppression: a meta-analysis of controlled studies. *Clinical Psychology Review, 21*, 683–703.

Abramowitz, J. S., Whiteside, S., Kalsy, S. A., & Tolin, D. F. (2003). Thought control strategies in obsessive–compulsive disorder: A replication and extension. *Behaviour Research and Therapy, 41*, 529–540.

American Psychiatric Association. (2004). *Diagnostic and Statistical Manual of Mental Disorders* (4th ed. Text Rev.). Washington, DC: Author.

Amir, N., Cashman, L. A., & Foa, E. (1997). Strategies of thought control in obsessive–compulsive disorder. *Behaviour Research and Therapy, 35*, 775–777.

Baer, R. A. (2003). Mindfulness training as a clinical intervention: A conceptual and empirical review. *Clinical Psychology: Science & Practice, 10*, 125–143.

Bain, J. A. (1928). *Thought control in everyday life*. New York: Funk & Wagnalls.

Beck, A. T., Emery, G., & Greenberg, R. L. (1985). *Anxiety disorders and phobias: A cognitive perspective*. New York: Basic Books.

Borkovec, T. D., & Costello, E. (1993). Efficacy of applied relaxation and cognitive–behavioral therapy in the treatment of generalized anxiety disorder. *Journal of Consulting and Clinical Psychology, 61*, 611–619.

Brantley, J. (2003). *Calming your anxious mind: How mindfulness and compassion can free you from anxiety, fear, and panic*. Oakland, CA: New Harbinger.

Bystritsky, A., Liberman, R. P., Hwang, S., Wallace, C. J., Vapnik, T., Maindment, K., et al. (2001). Social functioning and quality of life comparisons between obsessive–compulsive and schizophrenic disorders. *Depression and Anxiety, 14*, 214–218.

Clark, D. M., Salkovskis, P. M., Hackmann, A., Middleton, H., Anastasiades, P., & Gelder, M. (1994). A comparison of cognitive therapy, applied relaxation and imipramine in the treatment of panic disorder. *British Journal of Psychiatry, 164*, 759–769.

Cottraux, J., Mollard, E., Bouvard, M., & Marks, I. (1993). Exposure therapy, fluvoxamine, or combination treatment in obsessive–compulsive disorder: One-year followup. *Psychiatry Research, 49*, 63–75.

Cottraux, J., Note, I., Yao, S. N., Lafont, S., Note, B., Mollard, E., et al. (2001). A randomized controlled trial of cognitive therapy versus intensive behavior therapy in obsessive compulsive disorder. *Psychotherapy and Psychosomatics, 70*, 288–297.

Emmelkamp, P. M., & Beens, H. (1991). Cognitive therapy with obsessive–compulsive disorder: A comparative evaluation. *Behaviour Research and Therapy, 29*, 293–300.

Emmelkamp, P. M., & Kwee, K. G. (1977). Obsessional ruminations: A comparison between thought-stopping and prolonged exposure in imagination. *Behaviour Research and Therapy, 15*, 441–444.

Emmelkamp, P. M., Visser, S., & Hoekstra, R. J. (1988). Cognitive therapy vs exposure in vivo in the treatment of obsessive–compulsives. *Cognitive Therapy and Research, 12*, 103–144.

Fals-Stewart, W., Marks, A. P., & Schafer, J. (1993). A comparison of behavioral group therapy and individual behavior therapy in treating obsessive–compulsive disorder. *Journal of Nervous and Mental Disease, 181*, 189–193.

Foa, E. B., Liebowitz, M. R. Kozak, M. J., Davies, S., Campeas, R., Franklin, M. E., Huppert, J. D., Kjemisted, K., Rowan, V., Schmidt, A. B., Simpson, H. B., & Tux, X. (2005). Randomized, placebo-controlled trial of exposure and ritual prevention, clomipramine, and their combination in the treatment of obsessive–compulsive disorder. *American Journal of Psychiatry, 162*, 151–161.

Foa, E. B., Steketee, G., & Milby, J. B. (1980). Differential effects of exposure and response prevention in obsessive–compulsive washers. *Journal of Consulting and Clinical Psychology, 48*, 71–79.

Franklin, M. E., Abramowitz, J. S., Kozak, M. J., Levitt, J. T., & Foa, E. B. (2000). Effectiveness of exposure and ritual prevention for obsessive–compulsive disorder:

Randomized compared with nonrandomized samples. *Journal of Consulting and Clinical Psychology, 68*, 594–602.

Franklin, M. E., & Foa, E. B. (1998). Cognitive–behavioral treatments for obsessive–compulsive disorder. In P. E. Nathan & J. M. Gorman (Eds.), *A guide to treatments that work* (2nd ed., pp. 367–386). New York: Oxford University Press.

Freeston, M. H., & Ladouceur, R. (1997). What do people do with their obsessive thoughts? *Behaviour Research and Therapy, 35*, 335–348.

Freeston, M. H., Ladouceur, R., Gagnon, F., Thibodeau, N., Rheaume, J., Letarte, H., et al. (1997). Cognitive–behavioral treatment of obsessive thoughts: A controlled study. *Journal of Consulting and Clinical Psychology, 65*, 405–413.

Freiheit, S. R., Vye, C., Swan, R., & Cady, M. (2004). Cognitive–behavioral therapy for anxiety: Is dissemination working? *The Behavior Therapist, 27*, 25–32.

Frost, R. O., & Steketee, G. (Eds.). (2002). *Cognitive approaches to obsessions and compulsions: Theory, assessment, and treatment.* New York: Pergamon Press.

Gallup Organization Inc. (1990). *A Gallup study of obsessive–compulsive sufferers.* Princeton, NJ: Author.

Goisman, R. M., Rogers, M. P., Steketee, G. S., Warshaw, M. G., Cuneo, P., & Keller, M. B. (1993). Utilization of behavioral methods in a multicenter anxiety disorders study. *Journal of Clinical Psychiatry, 54*, 213–218.

Greist, J. H., Marks, I. M., Baer, L., Kobak, K. A., Wenzel, K. W., Hirsch, M. J., et al. (2002). Behavior therapy for obsessive–compulsive disorder guided by a computer or by a clinician compared with relaxation as a control. *Journal of Clinical Psychiatry, 63*, 138–145.

Haugen, G. B., Dixon, H. H., & Dickel, H. A. (1963). *A therapy for anxiety tension reactions.* New York: Macmillan.

Hayes, S. C., Wilson, K. G., Gifford, E. V., Follette, V. M., & Strosahl, K. G. (1996). Experiential avoidance and behavioral disorders: A functional dimensional approach to diagnosis and treatment. *Journal of Consulting and Clinical Psychology, 64*, 1152–1168.

Hayes, S. C., Strosahl, K. D., & Wilson, K. G. (1999). *Acceptance and commitment therapy: An experiential approach to behavior change.* New York: Guilford Press.

Jacobson, E. (1929). *Progressive relaxation.* Chicago: University of Chicago Press.

Jacobson, N. S., Dobson, K. S., Truax, P. A., Addis, M. E., Koerner, K., Gollan, J. K., et al. (1996). A component analysis of cognitive–behavioral treatment for depression. *Journal of Consulting and Clinical Psychology, 64*, 295–304.

Koran, L. M., Thienemann, M. L., & Davenport, R. (1996). Quality of life for patients with obsessive–compulsive disorder. *American Journal of Psychiatry, 153*, 783–788.

Kozak, M. J., & Foa, E. B. (1997). *Mastery of obsessive–compulsive disorder: A cognitive–behavioral approach.* San Antonio, TX: The Psychological Corporation.

Krochmalik, A., Jones, M. K., & Menzies, R. G. (2001). Danger ideation reduction therapy (DIRT) for treatment-resistant compulsive washing. *Behaviour Research and Therapy, 39*, 897–912.

Leon, A. C., Portera, L., & Weissman, M. M. (1995). The social costs of anxiety disorders. *British Journal of Psychiatry, 166*(Suppl. 27), 19–22.

Lindsay, M., Crino, R., & Andrews, G. (1997). Controlled trial of exposure and response prevention in obsessive–compulsive disorder. *British Journal of Psychiatry, 171*, 135–139.

Linehan, M. M., Armstrong, H. E., Suarez, A., Allmon, D., & Heard, H. L. (1993). Dialectical behavior therapy for borderline personality disorder. In D. H. Barlow (Ed.), *Clinical handbook of psychological disorders: A step-by-step treatment manual* (3rd ed., pp. 470–522). New York: Guilford.

March, J. S., & Mulle, K. (1998). *OCD in children and adolescents: A cognitive–behavioral treatment manual.* New York: Guilford Press.

Marks, I. (1987). *Fears, phobias, and rituals.* New York: Oxford University Press.

McLean, P. D., Whittal, M. L., Thordarson, D. S., Taylor, S., Sochting, I., Koch, W. J., et al. (2001). Cognitive versus behavior therapy in the group treatment of obsessive–compulsive disorder. *Journal of Consulting and Clinical Psychology, 69*, 205–214.

Michelson, L., Mavissakalian, M., & Marchione, K. (1985). Cognitive and behavioral treatments of agoraphobia: Clinical, behavioral, and psychophysiological outcomes. *Journal of Consulting and Clinical Psychology, 53*, 913–925.

Murphy, M. T., Michelson, L. K., Marchione, K., Marchione, N., & Testa, S. (1998). The role of self-directed in vivo exposure in combination with cognitive therapy, relaxation training, or therapist-assisted exposure in the treatment of panic disorder with agoraphobia. *Journal of Anxiety Disorders, 12*, 117–138.

Myers, J. K., Weissman, M. M., Tischler, G. L., Holzer, C. E., III, Leaf, P. J., Orvaschel, H., et al. (1984). Six-month prevalence of psychiatric disorders in three communities 1980 to 1982. *Archives of General Psychiatry, 41*, 959–967.

Obsessive Compulsive Cognitions Working Group. (1997). Cognitive assessment of obsessive–compulsive disorder. *Behaviour Research and Therapy, 35*, 667–681.

Obsessive Compulsive Cognitions Working Group. (2001). Development and initial validation of the Obsessive Beliefs Questionnaire and the Interpretation of Intrusions Inventory. *Behaviour Research and Therapy, 39*, 987–1006.

Rachman, S. (1997). The evolution of cognitive behaviour therapy. In C. G. Fairburn (Ed.), *Science and practice of cognitive behaviour therapy* (pp. 3–26). Oxford: Oxford University Press.

Reed, G. F. (1985). *Obsessional experience and compulsive behavior: A cognitive–structural approach.* London: Academic Press.

Robins, L. N., Helzer, J. E., Weissman, M. M., Orvaschel, H., Gruenberg, E., Burke, J. D., Jr., et al. (1984). Lifetime prevalence of specific psychiatric disorders in three sites. *Archives of General Psychiatry, 41*, 949–958.

Roemer, L., & Orsillo, S. M. (2003). Mindfulness: A promising intervention strategy in need of further study. *Clinical Psychology: Science and Practice, 10*, 172–178.

Salkovskis, P. M., & Westbrook, D. (1989). Behaviour therapy and obsessional ruminations: Can failure be turned into success? *Behaviour Research and Therapy, 27*, 149–160.

Schmidt, N. B., Woolaway-Bickel, K., Trakowski, J., Santiago, H., Storey, J., Koselka, M., et al. (2000). Dismantling cognitive–behavioral treatment for panic disorder: Questioning the utility of breathing retraining. *Journal of Consulting and Clinical Psychology, 68,* 417–424.

Segal, Z. V., Williams, J. M. G., & Teasdale, J. D. (2002). *Mindfulness-based cognitive therapy for depression: A new approach to preventing relapse.* New York: Guilford.

Shafran, R., & Rachman, S. (2004). Thought–action fusion: A review. *Journal of Behavior Therapy and Experimental Psychiatry, 35,* 87–107.

Shafran, R., Thordarson, D. S., & Rachman, S. (1996). Thought–action fusion in obsessive compulsive disorder. *Journal of Anxiety Disorders, 10,* 379–391.

Steketee, G., Grayson, J. B., & Foa, E. B. (1987). A comparison of characteristics of obsessive–compulsive disorder and other anxiety disorders. *Journal of Anxiety Disorders, 1,* 325–335.

Tolin, D. F., Abramowitz, J. S., Hamlin, C., Foa, E. B., & Synodi, D. S. (2002). Attributions for thought suppression failure in obsessive–compulsive disorder. *Cognitive Therapy and Research, 26,* 505–517.

Tolin, D. F., Abramowitz, J. S., Przeworski, A., & Foa, E. B. (2002). Thought suppression in obsessive–compulsive disorder. *Behaviour Research and Therapy, 40,* 1255–1274.

Tolin, D. F., & Hannan, S. E. (in press). The role of the therapist in behavior therapy. In J. S. Abramowitz & A. C. Houts (Eds.), *Handbook of obsessive–compulsive spectrum disorders.* New York: Kluwer Academic Publishers.

Tolin, D. F., Maltby, N., Diefenbach, G. J., Hannan, S. E., & Worhunsky, P. (2004). Cognitive–behavioral therapy for medication nonresponders with obsessive–compulsive disorder: A wait-list-controlled open trial. *Journal of Clinical Psychiatry, 65,* 922–931.

Tolin, D. F., Maltby, N., Diefenbach, G. J., & Worhunsky, P. (2004, November). Motivating treatment-refusing obsessive–compulsive disorder patients. In D. J. Dozois (Chair), *Motivational interviewing and related strategies for the treatment of anxiety and depression.* Symposium presented to the Annual Meeting of the Association for Advancement of Behavior Therapy, New Orleans, LA.

Tolin, D. F., Woods, C. M., & Abramowitz, J. S. (2003). Relationship between obsessive beliefs and obsessive–compulsive symptoms. *Cognitive Therapy and Research, 27,* 657–669.

Tolin, D. F., Worhunsky, P., & Maltby, N. (2003, November). *The relationship between obsessive beliefs and thought control strategies in a clinical sample.* Paper presented at the Annual Meeting of the Association for Advancement of Behavior Therapy, Boston.

Tolin, D. F., Worhunsky, P., & Maltby, N. (2004, March). Are *"obsessive" beliefs specific to OCD?* Paper presented at the Annual Meeting of the Anxiety Disorders Association of America, Miami.

van Balkom, A. J., de Haan, E., van Oppen, P., Spinhoven, P., Hoogduin, K. A., & van Dyck, R. (1998). Cognitive and behavioral therapies alone versus in combination with fluvoxamine in the treatment of obsessive compulsive disorder. *Journal of Nervous and Mental Disease, 186,* 492–499.

van Oppen, P., de Haan, E., van Balkom, A. J., Spinhoven, P., Hoogduin, K., & van Dyck, R. (1995). Cognitive therapy and exposure in vivo in the treatment of obsessive compulsive disorder. *Behaviour Research and Therapy, 33,* 379–390.

Vogel, P. A., Stiles, T. C., & Götestam, K. G. (2004). Adding cognitive therapy el-
    ements to exposure therapy for obsessive compulsive disorder: A controlled
    study. *Behavioural and Cognitive Psychotherapy, 32*, 275–290.
Warren, R., & Thomas, J. C. (2001). Cognitive-behavior therapy of obsessive–
    compulsive disorder in private practice: an effectiveness study. *J Anxiety Dis-
    ord, 15*, 277–285.
Wegner, D. M., Schneider, D. J., Carter, S. R., & White, T. L. (1987). Paradoxical
    effects of thought suppression. *Journal of Personality and Social Psychology, 53*,
    5–13.
Wells, A. (1999). A cognitive model of generalized anxiety disorder. *Behavior Mod-
    ification, 23*, 526–555.
Wells, A., & Papageorgiou, C. (1998). Relationships between worry, obsessive–
    compulsive symptoms and meta-cognitive beliefs. *Behaviour Research and Ther-
    apy, 36*, 899–913.
Wolpe, J. (1990). *The practice of behavior therapy* (4th ed.). New York: Pergamon Press.

INTEGRATING ACCEPTANCE AND MINDFULNESS INTO TREATMENTS FOR CHILD AND ADOLESCENT ANXIETY DISORDERS
ACCEPTANCE AND COMMITMENT THERAPY AS AN EXAMPLE

LAURIE A. GRECO, JOHN T. BLACKLEDGE, LISA W. COYNE, AND JILL EHRENREICH

In cognitive–behavioral therapy (CBT) for child and adolescent anxiety disorders, negatively evaluated thoughts and emotions are viewed as problematic responses to be managed via control-oriented strategies such as distraction, systematic desensitization, self-instruction, or cognitive restructuring. Within this framework, anxiety is conceptualized as "the problem," and symptom reduction is a standard index of treatment success. Acceptance- and mindfulness-based therapies such as acceptance and commitment therapy (ACT; Hayes, Strosahl, & Wilson, 1999) differ from standard CBT primarily in their treatment of private events (e.g., thoughts, emotions, physical–bodily sensations, memories). Guided by its philosophical assumptions and scientifically based principles, ACT integrates acceptance and mindfulness into a values-centered behavior therapy to produce psychological flexibility and pave the way for a fundamental change to occur. In contrast to a standard CBT approach, ACT does not target the form or frequency of privately experienced phenomena. Rather, ACT seeks to alter the *function* of private experiences in order to diminish their behavioral impact.

The efficacy of ACT and related approaches has been demonstrated empirically across a broad range of adult clinical disorders (e.g., Hayes, Masuda, Bissett, Luoma, & Guerrero, 2004). Yet, the value and ideal methodology for balancing acceptance and change remain virtually unexplored within the realm of child and adolescent behavior therapy. In this chapter, we discuss the nature of childhood anxiety and briefly summarize several major components of existing CBT protocols for anxious youth. We then apply basic principles of Relational Frame Theory (RFT; Hayes, Barnes-Holmes, & Roche, 2001) to child anxiety, describe the potential role of two RFT-relevant processes (cognitive fusion and experiential control) in childhood anxiety disorders, and outline several core components of ACT. Finally, we provide suggestions for adapting this approach for young people and offer directions for future clinical and empirical work.

CHILD AND ADOLESCENT ANXIETY

With an estimated prevalence of 10%–20%, child and adolescent anxiety disorders are among the most common forms of psychopathology listed in the fourth edition of the *Diagnostic and Statistical Manual of Mental Disorders* (DSM-IV; American Psychiatric Association, 1994; Costello, Mustillo, Erkanli, Keeler, & Angold, 2003). In children, common overt indicators of anxiety include situational avoidance, withdrawal, and skills deficits, as well as oppositional behavior, "freezing," and/or crying. Cognitive responses such as excessive worry, low estimations of competency to cope, and heightened perceptions of threat are also reported among youth, as are somatic symptoms such as heart palpitations, abdominal pain, nausea, and dizziness (e.g., Beidel, Christ, & Long, 1991; Boegels & Zigterman, 2000; Muris et al., 2000).

Developmental trends have been documented with regard to the nature and content of children's fears. Very young children report numerous fears involving concrete stimuli and events such as physical injury, loud noises, strangers, and separation from caregivers (Spence, Rapee, McDonald, & Ingram, 2001). Throughout grade school and adolescence, fears become increasingly abstract and pervasive and may include fears of losing control, negative social evaluation, rejection and loss, and worry over myriad past and future events (Schniering, Hudson, & Rapee, 2000). Assessment of worry demonstrates a similar trend, with older children describing worries of increasing complexity, a greater variety of worries, and an enhanced ability to elaborate on the content and outcomes of worry (e.g., Chorpita, Tracey, Brown, Collica, & Barlow, 1997). This shift from concrete and specific to abstract and diffuse is thought to reflect children's developing cognitive and language abilities (e.g., Vasey & Daleiden, 1994). Notably, the development of language, including the use of "internal language" (e.g., cognition, self-instruction), has been cited as critical to children's emotional development and coping (Blechman, Prinz, & Dumas, 1995; Vygotsky, 1991).

Interventions used to treat child and adolescent anxiety reflect developmental capacities as well as the nature and scope of children's fears. Behavioral procedures such as exposure and contingency management often are applied to specific phobias and fears in very young children (e.g., Durlak, Fuhrman, & Lampman, 1991). Approaches that integrate cognitive and emotion regulation strategies with exposure and skills training have become the dominant approach for treating anxiety disorders throughout middle childhood and adolescence (e.g., Kendall, 1994). The integration of peers and parent behavior management strategies into existent treatment models for child anxiety has also gained empirical support over the past decade (e.g., Barrett, Dadds, & Rapee, 1996; Greco & Morris, 2001).

COGNITIVE–BEHAVIORAL INTERVENTIONS

CBT is a structured, directive treatment that can be effectively utilized to teach children and adolescents skills for coping with various anxiety-provoking situations. Most CBT treatments for child anxiety are manual-guided and almost uniformly based on social learning principles, with a specific emphasis on operant learning, conditioned responses, and cognitive or attentional processes in the maintenance of anxiety (e.g., Dadds & Barrett, 2001). In practice, these treatments focus on the development of skills such as substituting more realistic or less frightening thoughts for anxiety-provoking ones, relaxation techniques, and graduated exposure to feared stimuli. Education about the nature and normal functions of fear and anxiety is typically provided to the child, along with a treatment framework that emphasizes the interrelated nature of emotion, physiological arousal, cognition, and overt behavior.

In CBT, homework assignments are often used to practice skills learned in session, and parental reinforcement of "brave" or approach-oriented behavior is emphasized. Additional treatment components, including modeling techniques, contingency management, and social skills or problem-solving skills training, may be added to a given protocol, depending on the child's individual needs. Exposure techniques, such as imaginal, interoceptive, and in vivo approaches, are almost uniformly included in the CBT treatment of anxious children, with an emphasis on following clear procedural guidelines in their delivery, such as the use of graded hierarchies to determine ordering of exposure stimuli or situations.

CBT treatments for various anxiety disorders in children and adolescents have demonstrated efficacy in terms of reducing anxiety. Evidence suggests that 60%–90% of participants report clinically significant reductions in anxiety and related symptoms at posttreatment and follow-up points several years later (e.g., Barrett, Duffy, Dadds, & Rapee, 2001; Kendall, Safford, Flannery-Schroeder, & Webb, 2004). These treatments employ various combinations of procedures described above and may be presented in either group or individual format, with roughly equivalent efficacy (e.g., Manassis et al., 2002). With a few notable exceptions, most randomized controlled trials using CBT for child and adolescent anxiety disorders have focused on a narrow band of mixed anxiety disorders, with few trials examining the efficacy of CBT for obsessive–compulsive disorder, posttraumatic stress disorder, panic disorder, and other anxiety-related problems such as school refusal.

Despite its demonstrated efficacy, treatment success in CBT has been narrowly defined with an almost exclusive focus on anxiety management and symptom reduction. In contrast, little or no attention has been devoted to broader outcomes reflecting values-oriented behavior, quality of life across personally meaningfully domains, and children's ability to live effectively *with* naturally occurring private events, including anxiety-related thoughts, emotions, and bodily sensations. ACT's focus on acceptance, mindfulness, defusion, and values represents a notable shift from traditional CBT. This shift necessitates parallel modifications in the types of behaviors and processes we target for change. We next present a simple illustration of basic Relational Frame Theory principles and describe several clinically relevant processes targeted in ACT.

RELATIONAL FRAME THEORY AND CHILD ANXIETY

RFT, the behavior-analytic account of human language and cognition upon which ACT is based, was developed on the basis of empirical data garnered from an extensive body of basic research (see Hayes et al., 2001). RFT assumes that, although direct operant and respondent learning histories play vital roles in shaping the way one behaves, operant processes *apparently unique to language* may have an exponentially greater influence on how we perceive our world and correspondingly behave. This approach suggests that *indirect* operant learning accounts for the remarkably generative nature of language and its ability to transcend and take primacy over direct experience (e.g., Blackledge, 2002; Wilson & Blackledge, 2000). A description of basic RFT principles is well beyond the scope of this chapter; however, a simple application of RFT principles is presented below to illustrate how children may come to learn indirectly through *derived relational responding*.

Eight-year-old Cameron feels intensely anxious and fears embarrassment when he is around older boys. Cameron's older brothers and their friends pick on him repeatedly when he makes mistakes, whereas his same-age peers do not. Thus, Cameron has formed the rule that *Older kids are "meaner" than kids my age*. One day Cameron was playing happily with his new friend, Marcus. While awaiting the arrival of a child he has never met before (Tyler), Cameron discovered that Marcus is 2 years older than both he and Tyler. Even though Cameron has had positive experiences with Marcus and has never met Tyler, he derives the following relations: (1) Marcus is "meaner" than me, (2) Marcus is "meaner" than Tyler, (3) I am nicer than Marcus, and (4) Tyler is nicer than Marcus. After learning the approximate ages of Marcus and Tyler, Cameron is able to derive relations regarding their relative ages and corresponding levels of niceness and meanness.

Once related in this fashion, the properties or (more technically) the *stimulus functions* of Tyler and Marcus can change accordingly, such that Cameron now responds to his peers on the basis of the relative value he has verbally assigned to them. For example, when asked who he would most like to play with, Cameron selected Tyler over Marcus. His selection could not possibly be based on direct experience, as Cameron previously enjoyed playing with Marcus and never met Tyler. Choosing Tyler is a product of *derived* relational responding in which the properties or stimulus functions of Marcus and Tyler were transformed in accordance with their relative ages and Cameron's past negative experiences with older children. Once these relations have been made, it is now possible for the presence of Marcus to elicit anxiety regardless of Cameron's direct history with him. Relations between many, many more stimuli are easily made in the same manner (see Twohig, Masuda, Varra, and Hayes, 2005).

While the description just given is oversimplified and brief, RFT implications for child anxiety may seem more apparent now. Our ability to derive relations among stimuli and incorporate information from our personal history produces efficient learning that unfortunately may lead to inaccurate or harmful ways of viewing the world and corresponding behavior that is insensitive to direct contingencies. Language brings with it the ability to imagine a nearly infinite variety of possible futures and reconstructed memories of the past, as well as the ability to evaluate virtually any aspect of experience. Moreover, the language-based ability to self-evaluate and rigidly adhere to one's verbal formulations may markedly contribute to problematic anxiety, even in children who have directly experienced very few negative consequences for anxiety.

As children become increasingly verbal, they are able to respond figuratively to all varieties of imaginable pasts, presents, and futures. This may help explain empirical observations discussed earlier that children's fears generally become more abstract, complex, and pervasive as they age. For example, while a 4-year-old boy may simply fear that a disapproving adult might spank him or send him to time-out, the same boy at age 10 may fear that adult disapproval translates to personal deficiency or unworthiness. Whereas the toddler's fears center upon rather concrete consequences, the older child is able to generate more complex and global implications of adult disapproval.

Language also confers the ability to construct verbal rules about how one should or must behave (e.g., Barnes-Holmes, Hayes, & Dymond, 2001). As children become more language-able, they begin to derive verbal rules either implicitly or explicitly from their experiences and interactions in and with the social–verbal community (e.g., parents, teachers, peers, siblings). Children may, for instance, implicitly or explicitly learn rules about anxiety within the context of parent–child interactions. Research shows that anxious children are more likely to perceive ambiguous situations as threatening and propose avoidant solutions *after* discussing them with their parents (e.g., Barrett, Rapee, Dadds, & Ryan, 1996; Dadds, Barrett, Rapee, & Ryan, 1996). Socially mediated processes such as modeling and rule governance may contribute to this effect referred to as the "family enhancement of anxious responding" (e.g., Barrett et al., 1996; Dadds & Barrett, 2001; Muris, Steerneman, Merckelbach, & Meesters, 1996).

Similarly, modeling and rule governance may be implicated in the bidirectional relation between child anxiety and overprotective parenting (e.g., Greco & Morris, 2002; Rapee, 1997; Rapee & Melville, 1997). It is possible, for example, that a young girl who experiences a history of parental overprotection and control as well as frequent warnings of caution may derive and subsequently "follow" rules that implicitly or explicitly frame the world as a dangerous place to live in. In the absence of actual threat or experienced harm, she may come to perceive even benign events as threatening and work to avoid risky situations as well as any discomforting thoughts and emotions associated with those situations. From an ACT perspective, rigid rule-governed behavior is one aspect of what makes childhood anxiety "disordered." Clinical methods in ACT seek to undermine unproductive forms of rule following, with deliberate efforts to weaken the culturally supported assumption that, *For our lives to be good, we must first eliminate "bad" thoughts and "bad" feelings such as anxiety.*

CHILD ANXIETY AS "DISORDERS" OF FUSION AND EXPERIENTIAL CONTROL

Normative language processes may drastically increase the capacity for human suffering via two potentially pathogenic processes: cognitive fusion and experiential control (Hayes et al., 1999). From an RFT/ACT perspective, anxiety-related problems can be conceptualized as a combination of fusion and excessive or maladaptive attempts to avoid anxiety-provoking experiences. Within this approach, cognitive fusion gives rise to experiential control, which is a core functional dimension that cuts across all of the *DSM-IV* anxiety disorder categories (e.g., Barlow, 2002; Chorpita, 2001; Hayes & Gifford, 1997).

Cognitive fusion is an RFT-based process that, loosely, involves the assumption that one's private experiences are accurate descriptions of reality (Luoma & Hayes, in press). Language abilities allow us to "fuse" with and become entangled in the content of our mind, such that we subsequently respond to private experiences as if they were literally true. In ACT, distinctions are made between "having" versus "buying into" private experiences. When thoughts and emotions are "bought" instead of experienced as passing internal phenomena, unproductive experiential control efforts may ensue.

Experiential avoidance (referred to more broadly as *experiential control*) refers to an *un*willingness to experience certain private events and attempts to avoid, manage, or otherwise control the frequency or form of these subjective–internal experiences (e.g., Hayes & Gifford, 1997). Experiential avoidance and control are not inherently problematic and may engender behavioral effectiveness in some contexts, such as when distraction is implemented with children to facilitate coping during routine immunizations (e.g., Cohen, Bernard, Greco, & McClellan, 2002). Generally speaking, experiential avoidance is not of particular concern when time-limited, circumscribed, and/or unassociated with significant personal costs. In contrast, research shows that chronic, excessive, or rigid levels of experiential avoidance and control underlie most forms of psychopathology and can produce unworkable and life-narrowing outcomes (e.g., Hayes, Wilson, Gifford, Follette, & Strosahl, 1996).

To illustrate these processes, consider the case of an 11-year-old boy with intense social anxiety who buys into thoughts such as *I'm such an idiot; I can't say or do anything without making a complete fool out of myself.* To prevent the possibility of embarrassment, he never answers questions in class, spends lunch hours in the nurse's office or library, and pretends to be sick or otherwise engaged when invited to social gatherings. When situational avoidance is impossible, he engages in distraction, thought replacement, and other functionally similar control strategies to shield himself from his own experience. When taken literally, the young boy's thoughts and feelings would be threatening for anyone, and attempts to avoid or control these private events seem the logical and safe thing to do. In this way, cognitive fusion gives rise to elevated levels of experiential avoidance and control.

COSTS OF EXPERIENTIAL CONTROL IN CHILDHOOD AND ADOLESCENCE

Rigid or excessive attempts to control private experiences predict adverse physical and mental health outcomes in childhood and adolescence (e.g., Fields & Prinz, 1997; Steiner, Erickson, Hernandez, & Pavelski, 2002). Child-focused research indicates a positive association between experiential control and neuroticism (a construct related to anxiety). Results show that children and adolescents who exhibit avoidant coping strategies such as suppression or disengagement consistently score higher on measures of neuroticism (e.g., Kardum & Krapic, 2001; Medvedova, 1998). In a study specific to childhood anxiety, Dempsey and colleagues found that denial and mental distraction predicted posttraumatic stress symptoms among inner-city youth exposed to high levels of violence. Paradoxically, attempts to control violence-related thoughts and emotions predicted a significant increase in these internal phenomena as well as traumatic reexperiencing, flashbacks, and hallucinations surrounding the "avoided" event (Dempsey, Overstreet, & Moely, 2000). Other trauma-related studies point to substantial long-term costs of excessive experiential avoidance in response to childhood adversity. For example, results of two investigations showed that high levels of cognitive and emotional avoidance mediated the relationship between childhood abuse and poor outcomes in adulthood, including psychological distress (Marx & Sloan, 2002) and substance use (Simons, Ducette, Kirby, Stahler, & Shipley, 2003).

Research on adolescent worry yields findings parallel to reports in the adult literature. In one study, intolerance of uncertainty and thought suppression predicted heightened levels of worry among adolescents aged 14–18 years (Laugesen, Dugas, & Bukowski, 2003). Similarly, studies within pediatric psychology demonstrate positive correlations between suppression, other forms of experiential control, and anxiety in children who have chronic medical conditions (e.g., Moos, 2002) and whose parents have a chronic illness (e.g., Steele, Forehand, & Armistead, 1997). Situational and experiential avoidance also have been documented in clinically diagnosed samples. Barrett and colleagues, for instance, found that children diagnosed with anxiety disorders were more likely to propose avoidant solutions to ambiguous scenarios than diagnosis-free and externalizing disorder groups (Barrett et al., 1996).

ACT WITH CHILDREN AND ADOLESCENTS

GENERAL APPROACH TO USING ACT WITH YOUTH

In ACT, therapists use methods that are inherently *less* logical and literal, including metaphor, paradox, and experiential exercises. These methods present certain advantages and challenges when working with children and adolescents. The use of metaphor in ACT may be particularly well-suited for children and adolescents and it may be used to facilitate rapport building, enhance understanding, and reduce resistance to therapeutic directives (Barker, 1996). Moreover, some evidence suggests that children as young as 3–6 years of age prefer and demonstrate greater compliance with metaphorical versus literal language during progressive muscle relaxation (Heffner, Greco, & Eifert, 2003). Notably, this work did not evaluate children's comprehension and recall of abstract metaphors, a topic clearly in need of further empirical study.

ACT may be particularly well-suited for adolescents, as metaphorical and paradoxical interventions are less instructive and consequently more difficult to obey (or disobey). Adolescence, a period marked by transition and change, may present an ideal window of opportunity to promote psychological flexibility and values-based living (see Greco & Eifert, 2004). Teenagers begin to question socially sanctioned rules and often develop values different from those of their parents. The capacity for abstract thinking emerges during this period, yet the dominance of literal language may not be as fully entrenched as in adulthood. Simply put, adults have a longer history of "living in their minds" than do children and adolescents. As such, applying ACT with young people may be equivalent to the prevention—rather than remediation—of maladaptive rule following, fusion, and experiential control.

One potential concern in using ACT with young children involves problems with the comprehensibility and developmental appropriateness of metaphor and paradox. Therapists can guard against the ineffective use of ACT methods through the careful selection and strategic tailoring of content. For example, metaphors can be adapted in a way that corresponds with children's developmental level, personal interests, and presenting concerns. Indeed, our work with children and teens points to the necessity of altering the content to fit the context while keeping the function of ACT methods the same. In addition to promoting the flexible and functional use of ACT, such an approach underscores the importance for therapists to understand the purposes of clinical methods and treatment-relevant processes that underlie an ACT model of suffering and approach to treatment.

Another suggestion for working with children is to make ACT exercises as interactive and experiential as possible. We have found it useful in our clinical practice to incorporate visual aides, props, role plays, and activities such as stories, artwork/drawing, and card or board games. Such strategies may be helpful in terms of enhancing children's interest, facilitating rapport, and bringing young people into experiential contact with material that may be complicated and more difficult to grasp on a rational–logical level. Therapist creativity will facilitate age-appropriate adaptations of ACT techniques and help children connect with the purposes of clinical exercises (see Murrell, Coyne, & Wilson, 2004). Finally, as with any approach to treating young people, we recommend integrating important social influences such as those of parents, teachers, and peers into treatment whenever possible and appropriate (e.g., Morris & Greco, 2002).

Working with Parents of Anxious Children

Parents are often incorporated into treatments for anxious youth, with younger children requiring more support, structure, modeling, and if necessary, behavior management as they progress through an intervention. When inviting parents to participate in their child's treatment, it is important to take developmental issues into consideration. In the case of young children who are more embedded within their families and who may be actively enlisting parents in their avoidance efforts, there is an increased need for parents to help structure and ensure completion of exposure tasks. In addition, parents may help their child remain focused on his or her values. Older children and adolescents may be more capable of structuring and conducting their own tasks. In this case, it might be useful for parents to monitor from a distance and to provide room for their children to take greater responsibility for their own treatment.

In treatment, it is often difficult for parents to watch their children struggle with anxiety, perhaps even more so for parents who may be engaged in their own unworkable struggle with anxiety. Thus, many of the tactics parents use to "help" their child may be geared toward removing or reducing their child's anxiety and related distress. Another important purpose of parental efforts may be to reduce *the parents'* own discomfort when their child experiences anxiety. Therapists should assess the parent's role in and responses to the child's struggle with anxiety, as even well-intentioned parenting efforts may derail attempts to structure and effectively conduct exposure tasks both within and between sessions.

When incorporating parents into the treatment of anxious children, it is important to remember that parents, being language-able, are subject to the same pitfalls as their children. Most parents have rules about what their child's experience of anxiety is like (*intolerable, damaging, horrific*), about their child's ability to handle or manage anxiety (*it's just too much for him ...*), when they can or cannot intervene (*only when she seems angry, not when she is worried*), and how they might help their child (*soothing, setting limits, dismissing, rationalizing*). Such rules are often unworkable and may lead to excessive psychological control, as well as insensitivity to the immediate contingencies in parents' interactions with their children (see Coyne & Wilson, 2004).

When working with parents, it is important to explore these rules and to assess their functional impact on parents' ability to support their child through treatment. One useful tool involves contracting with parents to allow their child to participate *fully* in treatment (regardless of how difficult, boring, or intense, as these experiences can be expected to vary). Therapists might ask parents to commit to "making room" for difficult experiences and discomfort they or their child might experience throughout the course of treatment. This is done in service of the parents' own valued, meaningful goals for their child *rather* than for the sake of reducing or ameliorating their child's and/or their own symptoms. Likewise, defusion strategies for parents may help loosen their attachment to unproductive rules about their child's and their own anxiety. Moreover, inviting parents to participate in defusion sessions may help create an opportunity for parents to model psychological acceptance.

Just as it is useful with children, metaphor may be useful in describing the course of treatment to parents. For example, therapists might use the metaphor of walking through a smelly swamp to reach a beautiful, mountainous vista from which completely new, unexpected experiences may be appreciated. Or, if using a hierarchical approach in which children are asked to participate in progressively more challenging exposures or learn more sophisticated skills, one might try the metaphor of climbing Everest. A person learning to climb a mountain would never be told "There's Everest! Give it your best shot!" Instead, they would begin hiking in gentle foothills that might well seem difficult in the beginning but, with repeated practice, would seem like a piece of cake. The sake of the journey is *not* to reduce the effort involved in reaching the vista; rather, it is the possibility of experiencing a new horizon.

Because parents—both in and out of sessions—may have a tremendous impact in how children fare during their treatment and beyond, therapists must place at least some emphasis on parent change agendas. In addition, it is crucial to treatment success to explore parents' values, especially with regard to their children. Because parents' goal for bringing their child to therapy may be to reduce anxiety, it is helpful to explore what their own life, as well as their child's life, would "look like" if anxiety disappeared. Facilitating experiences that allow parents to contact their values are central in directing treatment, as well as helping maintain parent motivation and adherence, even in the face of difficult exposure work for their child. In the case of one young girl struggling with obsessive–compulsive disorder, both she and her parents pictured a life in which she would be free to make and keep friends, to be an outstanding student, and simply to experience the beauty in each day without interference from the paralyzing obsessions and rituals. *Working for* such a life, instead of *working to remove* symptoms, dignified the hard work of therapy, inspired both the girl and her parents, and galvanized the family's treatment efforts.

OVERVIEW OF ACT

In this section, we summarize major components of ACT and provide suggestions for child-friendly exercises included in the ACT book (Hayes et al., 1999). It is essential to note that there are hundreds of metaphors and experiential exercises in ACT and more are being created and refined by researchers, therapists, and clients every day. Because of limited space, we describe only a handful of strategies that have been clinically useful in our work with children and adolescents.

CREATIVE HOPELESSNESS

During creative hopelessness, the therapist and child explore the nature of the child's (and family's) struggle with anxiety. In doing so, the child and parent might be asked to describe what efforts he or she and others have taken to improve the "anxiety problem." Children and parents are then asked to evaluate the short- and long-term effectiveness of past and current change efforts as well as any personal costs associated with attempts to alleviate anxiety. A child suffering from frequent panic attacks, for instance, might note that avoiding public venues "works" in terms of escaping unpleasant bodily sensations, at least temporarily. Chronic avoidance of this kind, however, likely leads to significant long-term personal costs, perhaps impeding the child's ability to develop meaningful relationships with peers. This is particularly problematic if the child values his or her peer group and wishes to form close and supportive friendships.

When working with children and adolescents, it may be useful to diagram the "struggle with anxiety" in session such as on a large sheet of paper or dry erase board. Visual aides and diagrams may help children and adolescents learn to discriminate between internal and external events as well as among various privately experienced phenomena (e.g., thoughts, emotions, and bodily sensations). One simple suggestion is to draw a large circle and ask the child to describe everything he or she has been struggling with (e.g., "What do you see as standing between you and the life you want or would choose if anything were possible?"). Therapists can then write problematic private events such as "thoughts about dying," "fear of failure," and "pounding heart" inside of the circle while verbally labeling each experience as a thought, emotion, or bodily sensation, respectively. Overt behavior and external events named as part of the struggle can be written outside of the circle as a way to distinguish the word *inside* from the word *outside* the child's skin. A variant of this exercise for younger children involves using a full-sized cutout of a person and having the child write painful thoughts and emotions in the person's mind and near the person's heart, respectively. Physical sensations such as "butterflies in my stomach" can be written near the corresponding body part (e.g., abdomen), and overt actions, such as "leaving school early" or "taking medicine," can be written on the cutout of child's arms or legs (see Murrell et al., 2004).

CONTROL IS THE PROBLEM/WILLINGNESS AS ALTERNATIVE

After children experience the unworkability of their current situation, the struggle with anxiety is given a name: *Control*. The Chinese Handcuff metaphor described by Hayes et al. (1999) is a child-friendly exercise that can be used with youth to demonstrate the paradox of control. We recommend doing this exercise experientially with an actual finger trap (a woven straw tube approximately 15 cm long and 1 cm in diameter). In this exercise, the child slides his or her index fingers into both sides of the straw tube and is asked to imagine that the situation of being trapped in this tube is similar to his or her experience with anxiety. The therapist might point out that the child is stuck and that living with anxiety can be very restricting and uncomfortable. Historically, the child's efforts have been aimed at getting out of the "anxiety trap" by doing what intuitively makes sense—pulling out. At this point, the child typically attempts to escape from the trap by pulling hard with both fingers. However, this intuitive action causes the tube to catch and tighten, thereby creating more discomfort and less room to move. The only way to reduce the struggle is to do something completely different and counterintuitive: the child must *lean into* the trap by pushing his or her fingers *in* rather than trying to pull out. The goal of this exercise is to illustrate experientially that attempting to get out of the trap by doing the seemingly logical and obvious thing (pulling hard) creates only more tension and perpetuates the struggle. In contrast, pushing the fingers in rather than out creates more room to move, possibly allowing for something new to happen. Exercises in this early phase of treatment are used to help children loosen their grip on counterproductive control agendas so that a fundamentally different approach to living constructively with anxiety can be introduced. Instead of presenting children with more anxiety management or control strategy (e.g., cognitive restructuring, progressive muscle relaxation, imagery), ACT promotes a thoroughgoing willingness to experience private events *as they are*.

Defusion/Deliteralization

Defusion or deliteralization exercises are used to undermine excessive fusion by weakening the literal and evaluative functions of language, challenging well-worn verbal conventions that interfere with willingness, and reducing the believability and behavioral impact of verbally mediated private events (e.g., Luoma & Hayes, 2003). Titchener's (1916) *Milk, Milk, Milk* exercise can be used with children to demonstrate experientially how the psychological meaning attached to a word can be weakened as other more direct properties are noticed. In this exercise, the child and therapist rapidly repeat the word *milk* over and over until its literal meaning (e.g., "White, creamy breakfast drink that comes from cows") quickly dissolves, and the direct stimulus functions of "milk" become more salient. For example, the child might begin to experience "milk" as a string of letters that produces a strange sound similar to noises made by birds. The child might also notice how her mouth feels and the way her lips press together when saying this funny word. This exercise is then be repeated with personally relevant words and phrases (e.g., "Loser," "Ugly," "Bullies," "Test") that elicit anxiety and related emotional distress (Hayes et al., 1999).

Variations of the *Tin Can Monster* exercise (Hayes et al., 1999) can also be adapted for children and teens. Using an assortment of craft supplies (e.g., construction paper, markers, magazines, pipe cleaners, blocks, Play-Doh), children might be asked to be creative in constructing the "anxiety monster" with which they are struggling. A 9-year-old girl who participated in this exercise included staples found on the floor as part of her creation, stating that the anxiety monster is scary and bullies her around as if it had knives for hands. Once the anxiety monster was created, she was asked to deconstruct it piece by piece, holding and describing each piece before placing it on the table in front of her. While doing this exercise, the 9-year-old girl spontaneously noted that "the monster isn't so scary anymore—it just looks like a pile of junk now." The *Tin Can Monster* can be repeated as an eyes-closed mindfulness exercise in which each component of the child's anxiety (e.g., bodily sensations, thoughts, and memories) is elicited in turn and experienced fully in session. Children and adolescents might also use craft supplies to construct the "shield" they carry throughout life to keep away or minimize contact with the anxiety monster. A 15-year-old adolescent participating in this exercise used clippings from teen magazines to create a collage depicting her "anxiety shield." The teen indicated that a massive shield was needed to fend off the seemingly large and scary anxiety monsters. During this exercise, she commented on how heavy the shield had become and how carrying this heavy burden was interfering with various aspects of her life.

SELF-AS-CONTEXT AND MINDFULNESS

In this phase of therapy, clients are taught to experience the transient and ongoing nature of private events from an "observer perspective" that is constant, safe, and beyond evaluation (Hayes et al., 1999). To facilitate mindfulness training, children might be instructed to experience thoughts and emotions as a continuous flow of bubbles floating in front of their face. When thoughts and emotions come up, they are placed in a bubble and observed with a gentle curiosity. The goal is for children simply to notice their private content without popping the bubbles. Grabbing at or attempting to hold onto desirable content will result in popping, as will attempting to push or blow away unwanted content. For school-aged children, it might further be useful to liken mindfulness exercises to that of a scientist observing an amoeba under a microscope. There is a healthy distance between the scientist and the amoeba and, even though the specimen is important to the scientist, he or she is able to observe and describe its properties with a nonattached curiosity. Children can be asked to notice their experiences from an "observer perspective," much as a scientist would observe an amoeba with curiosity through a microscope. Similar to a scientist becoming an expert of his or her subject matter, children work toward becoming their very own "experience experts."

Valuing and Committed Action

In ACT, goal-setting and behavioral tasks are guided by the client's most deeply held personal values and life goals. Throughout therapy, children and therapists work collaboratively to explore what *really* matters to the child and how rigid efforts to control anxiety have interfered with personal values across meaningful life domains (e.g., family, school, friendships, and health). With children and teens, it may be helpful to initiate values work early in therapy to establish a course for treatment and dignify the hard work of therapy (Wilson & Murrell, 2004). Values work with teens may be particularly effective given the developmental importance of values clarification during this period (Peterson, 1993). In our experience, most children and teens enjoy talking about what matters to them and are very receptive to ACT interventions that promote the pursuit of personally chosen values.

The final phases of ACT help clients identify barriers and remain committed to traveling in their valued directions. Defusion, mindfulness, and other acceptance methods may be revisited at this point to enhance children's willingness to experience internal barriers that interfere with values-based living. In addition, problem-solving and other more traditional change-oriented approaches might be implemented to promote responsibility and values-oriented action in response to external barriers that are amenable to change.

Conceptual and Empirical Research

Clinical and empirical advances in recent years suggest that ACT and its components can be tailored to meet the unique developmental and psychosocial needs of children, adolescents, and families. Some researchers point to the role of maladaptive fusion and experiential avoidance in the development of impaired parenting practices and offer suggestions for integrating ACT into empirically supported treatments for childhood behavior disorders (e.g., Blackledge, 2004; Coyne & Wilson, 2004; Twohig & Hayes, in press). Greco and Eifert (2004) similarly considered the utility of balancing acceptance and change into an integrative family therapy for parent–adolescent conflict. Results of a case study suggested that an ACT approach may lead to notable reductions in parent–adolescent conflict and increases in values-oriented behavior among family members (Greco, 2003). In addition, there is preliminary evidence supporting the use of ACT with youth experiencing chronic pain (Wicksell, Olsson, Dahl, & Melin, 2004) and adolescents at risk for school dropout (Moore et al., 2003).

We know of only two unpublished case reports examining the use of ACT with childhood anxiety disorders. In the first case, ACT was used to treat anxiety-based school refusal behavior in an 11-year-old boy, with gains maintained over a 2-year follow-up period (Wilson & Coyne, 2003). In a second report, ACT was used with a 10-year-old girl with social phobia and generalized anxiety disorder (Greco, 2002). Core components of ACT were implemented in a 12-week outpatient protocol composed of eight individual and four family sessions. Throughout treatment, the young girl demonstrated improved school attendance. Furthermore, she reported decreases in social anxiety and increases in acceptance and values-consistent behavior at posttreatment and 4-week follow-up. Collectively, clinical and empirical work suggests that ACT can be adapted for children and adolescents experiencing a range of presenting concerns. It is clear, however, that continued treatment development and rigorous empirical evaluation are needed to document the short- and long-term effects of ACT relative to other treatment approaches.

As mentioned earlier, ACT's focus on acceptance and values represents a shift from traditional CBT targets and goals. This shift necessitates parallel modifications in the types of instruments we use to measure treatment outcome and processes. As we continue to develop and refine measures for children and teens, it will be important to include indices of healthy adaptation, life quality, and values-consistent behavior. Moreover, there are currently no published measures of acceptance for youth, perhaps contributing to the limited research in this area. As an initial step, Greco, Murrell, and Coyne (2004) developed the *Willingness and Action Measure for Children and Adolescents* (WAM-C/A), a 50-item scale that assesses willingness to experience private events, values-oriented action, and cognitive fusion. Greco and colleagues are currently collecting data in large community and clinic samples to test the factor structure and psychometric properties of a revised version of this measure.

SUMMARY AND CONCLUSIONS

We briefly described standard cognitive–behavioral interventions for childhood anxiety and presented an alternative approach to the conceptualization and treatment of this class of disorders. Basic RFT principles were applied to child anxiety and linked with clinically relevant processes such as rigid rule governance, cognitive fusion, and experiential control. Core components of ACT were then outlined, and suggestions were provided for adapting this approach for children and adolescents struggling with anxiety.

In summary, ACT utilizes acceptance- and mindfulness-based methods to promote psychological flexibility and values-based living. From an ACT perspective, willingness to experience private events and values-guided action are the primary markers of therapeutic success, whereas symptom alleviation is ancillary and may or may not be achieved. Taken together, recent conceptual and empirical advances suggest that ACT is a viable treatment for adults. Moreover, preliminary evidence and clinical experience suggest that ACT can be adapted for various child and adolescent populations. It is important to emphasize that research on ACT and other acceptance-based approaches is still in its infancy. Much remains to be done, particularly within the realm of child and adolescent disorders. Thus, it is essential for clinical researchers to develop age-appropriate protocols and to evaluate their efficacy and clinical effectiveness in well-designed clinical trials. We hope that our chapter stimulates treatment innovations and empirical scrutiny of exactly this kind.

REFERENCES

American Psychiatric Association. (1994). *Diagnostic and statistical manual of mental disorders* (4th ed. text Rev.). Washington, DC: Author.

Barker, P. (1996). *Psychotherapeutic metaphors: A guide to theory and practice.* Philadelphia: Brunner/Mazel, Inc.

Barlow, D. H. (2002). *Anxiety and its disorders: The nature and treatment of anxiety and panic* (2nd ed.). New York: Guilford Press.

Barnes-Holmes, D., Hayes, S. C., & Dymond, S. (2001). Self and self-directed rules. In S. C. Hayes, D. Barnes-Holmes, S. C. Hayes, & B. Roche (Eds.), *Relational frame theory; A post-Skinnerian account of human language and cognition* (pp. 119–139). New York: Kluwer Academic/Plenum.

Barrett, P. M., Dadds, M. R., & Rapee, R. M. (1996). Family treatment of childhood anxiety: A controlled trial. *Journal of Consulting and Clinical Psychology, 64,* 333–342.

Barrett, P. M., Duffy, A. L., Dadds, M. R., & Rapee, R. M. (2001). Cognitive–behavioral treatment of anxiety disorders in children: Longer-term (6-year) follow-up. *Journal of Consulting and Clinical Psychology, 69,* 135–141.

Barrett, P. M., Rapee, R. M., Dadds, M. R., & Ryan, S. (1996). Family enhancement of cognitive styles in anxious and aggressive children: The FEAR effect. *Journal of Abnormal Child Psychology, 24,* 187–203.

Beidal, D. C., Christ, M. A., & Long, P. J. (1991). Somatic complaints in anxious children. *Journal of Abnormal Child Psychology, 19,* 659–670.

Blackledge, J. T. (2002). An introduction to Relational Frame Theory: Basics and applications. *The Behavior Analyst Today, 3,* 421–433.

Blackledge, J. T. (2004). *Using acceptance and commitment therapy to support parents of children diagnosed with autism.* Unpublished doctoral dissertation, University of Nevada, Reno.

Blechman, E. A., Prinz, R. J., & Dumas, J. E. (1995). Coping, competence, and aggression prevention : Developmental model. *Applied & Preventive Psychology,* 4, 211–232.

Boegels, S. M., & Zigterman, D. (2000). Dysfunctional cognitions in children with social phobia, separation anxiety disorder, and generalized anxiety disorder. *Journal of Abnormal Child Psychology, 28,* 205–211.

Chorpita, B. F. (2001). Control and the development of negative emotion. In M. W. Vasey & M. R. Dadds (Eds.), *The developmental psychopathology of anxiety* (pp. 112–142). Oxford: University Press.

Chorpita, B. F., Tracey, S. A., Brown, T. A., Collica, T. J., & Barlow, D. H. (1997). Assessment of worry in children and adolescents: An adaptation of the Penn State Worry Questionnaire. *Behaviour Research and Therapy, 35,* 569–581.

Cohen, L. L., Bernard, R. S., Greco, L. A., & C. McClellan. (2002). Using a child-focused intervention to manage procedural pain: Are parent and nurse coaches necessary? *Journal of Pediatric Psychology, 27,* 749–757.

Costello, J. E., Mustillo, S., Erkanli, A., Keeler, G., & Angold, A. (2003). Prevalence and development of psychiatric disorders in childhood and adolescence. *Archives of General Psychiatry, 60,* 837–844.

Coyne, L. W., & Wilson, K. W. (2004). The role of cognitive fusion in impaired parenting: An RFT analysis. *International Journal of Psychology and Psychological Therapy, 4,* 469–486.

Dadds, M. R., & Barrett, P. M. (1996). Family processes in child and adolescent anxiety and depression. *Behaviour Change, 13,* 231–239.

Dadds, M. R., & Barrett, P. M. (2001). Psychological management of anxiety disorders in childhood. *Journal of Child Psychology and Psychiatry and Allied Disciplines, 42,* 999–1011.

Dadds, M. R., Barrett, P. M., Rapee, R. M., & Ryan, S. (1996). Family process and child anxiety and aggression: An observational analysis. *Journal of Abnormal Child Psychology, 24,* 715–734.

Dempsey, M., Overstreet, S., & Moely, B. (2000). "Approach" and "avoidance" coping and PTSD symptoms in inner-city youth. *Current Psychology: Developmental–Learning–Personality–Social, 19,* 28–45.

Durlak, J. A., Fuhrman, T., & Lampman, C. (1991). Effectiveness of cognitive–behavior therapy for maladapting children: A meta-analysis. *Psychological Bulletin, 110,* 204–214.

Fields, L., & Prinz, R. J. (1997). Coping and adjustment during childhood and adolescence. *Clinical Psychology Review, 17,* 937–976.

Greco, L. A. (2002, November). Creating a context of acceptance in child clinical and pediatric settings. In G. H. Eifert (Chair), *Balancing acceptance and change in the treatment of anxiety disorders.* Symposium presented at the Association for the Advancement of Behavior Therapy, Reno, NV.

Greco, L. A. (2003, August). Balancing acceptance and change in a family-based behavior therapy for teens. In L. A. Greco (Chair), *Acceptance and change in adolescence: understanding and applying RFT/ACT through a developmental Lens.* Symposium conducted at the World Conference on ACT, RFT, and the New Wave Behavioral Therapies, Linkoping, Sweden.

Greco, L. A., & Eifert, G. H. (2004). Treating parent–adolescent conflict: Is acceptance the missing link for an integrative family therapy? *Cognitive and Behavioral Practice, 11,* 305–314.

Greco, L. A., & Morris, T. L. (2001). Treating childhood shyness and related behavior: Empirically investigated approaches used to promote positive social interactions. *Clinical Child and Family Psychology Review, 4,* 299–318.

Greco, L. A., & Morris, T. L. (2002). Paternal child-rearing style and child social anxiety: Investigation of child perceptions and actual father behavior. *Journal of Psychopathology and Behavioral Assessment, 24,* 259–267.

Greco, L. A., Murrell, A. M., & Coyne, L. W. (2004). *Willingness and acceptance measure for children and adolescents (WAM-C/A).* Available from Laurie Greco, Division of Adolescent Medicine and Behavioral Science, Vanderbilt University Medical Center, Nashville, TN.

Hayes, S. C., Barnes-Holmes, D., & Roche, B. (2001). Relational frame theory: A precis. In S. C. Hayes, D. Barnes-Holmes, S. C. Hayes, & B. Roche (Eds.), *Relational frame theory: A post-Skinnerian account of human language and cognition* (pp. 141–154). New York: Kluwer Academic/Plenum.

Hayes, S. C., & Gifford, E. V. (1997). The trouble with language: Experiential avoidance, rules, and the nature of verbal events. *Psychological Science, 8,* 170–173.

Hayes, S. C., Masuda, A., Bissett, R., Luoma, J., & Guerrero, L. F. (2004). DBT, FAP, and ACT: How empirically oriented are the new behavior therapy technologies? *Behavior Therapy, 35,* 35–54.

Hayes, S. C., Strosahl, K. D., & Wilson, K. G. (1999). *Acceptance and commitment therapy: An experiential approach to behavior change.* New York: The Guilford Press.

Hayes, S. C., Wilson, K. G., Gifford, E. V., Follette, V. M., & Strosahl, K. (1996). Experiential avoidance and behavioral disorders: A functional dimensional approach to diagnosis and treatment. *Journal of Consulting and Clinical Psychology, 64,* 1152–1168.

Heffner, M., Greco, L. A., & Eifert, G. H. (2003). Pretend you are a turtle: Children's responses to metaphorical and literal instructions during progressive muscle relaxation. *Child and Family Behavior Therapy, 25,* 19–33.

Kardum, I., & Krapic, N. (2001). Personality traits, stressful life events, and coping styles in early adolescence. *Personality and Individual Differences, 30,* 503–515.

Kendall, P. C. (1994). Treating anxiety disorders in children: Results of a randomized clinical trial. *Journal of Consulting and Clinical Psychology, 62,* 100–110.

Kendall, P. C., Safford, S., Flannery-Schroeder, E., & Webb, A. (2004). Child anxiety treatment: Outcomes in adolescence and impact on substance use and depression at 7.4-year follow-up. *Journal of Consulting and Clinical Psychology, 72,* 276–287.

Laugesen, N., Dugas, M. J., & Bukowski, W. M. (2003). Understanding adolescent worry: The application of a cognitive model. *Journal of Abnormal Child Psychology, 31*, 55–64.

Luoma, J., & Hayes, S. C. (2003). Cognitive defusion. In W. T. Donohue, J. E. Fisher, & S. C. Hayes (Eds.), *Empirically supported techniques for cognitive behavior therapy: A step by step guide for clinicians* (pp. 71–78). New York: Wiley.

Manassis, K., Mendlowitz, S. L., Scapillato, D., Avery, D., Fiksenbaum, L., Freire, M., et al. (2002). Group and individual cognitive–behavioral therapy for childhood anxiety disorders: A randomized trial. *Journal of the American Academy of Child and Adolescent Psychiatry, 41*, 1423–1430.

Marx, B. P., & Sloan, D. M. (2002). The role of emotion in the psychological functioning of adult survivors of childhood sexual abuse. *Behavior Therapy, 33*, 563–577.

Medvedova, L. (1998). Personality dimensions—"Little Five"—and their relationship with coping strategies in early adolescence. *Studia Psychologica, 40*, 261–265.

Moore, D., Wilson, K. G., Wilson, D. M., Murrell, A. R., Roberts, M., Merwin, R., et al. (2003, May). *Treating at-risk youth with an in-school acceptance and commitment training program.* Paper presented at the 2003 meeting of Association for Behavior Analysis, San Francisco.

Morris, T. L., & Greco, L. A. (2002). Assessment and treatment of childhood anxiety disorders. In L. VandeCreek (Ed.), *Innovations in clinical practice: A source book* (Vol. 20, pp. 76–86). Sarasota, FL: Professional Resource Press.

Muris, P., Kindt, M., Boegels, S., Merckelbach, H., Gadget, B., & Moulaert, V. (2000). Anxiety and threat perception abnormalities in normal children. *Journal of Psychopathology and Behavioral Assessment, 22*, 183–199.

Muris, P., Steerneman, P., Merckelbach, H., & Meesters, C. (1996). The role of parental fearfulness and modeling in children's fear. *Behavioural Research and Therapy, 34*, 265–268.

Murrell, A. R., Coyne, L. W., & Wilson, K. G. (2004). Acceptance and commitment therapy with children, adolescents, and their parents. In S. C. Hayes & K. Strosahl (Eds.), *A practical guide to acceptance and commitment therapy* (pp. 249–273). New York: Springer.

Peterson, A. C. (1993). Presidential address: Creating adolescents: The role of context and process in developmental trajectories. *Journal of Research on Adolescence, 3*, 1–18.

Rapee, R. M. (1997). Potential role of childrearing practices in the development of anxiety and depression. *Clinical Psychology Review, 17*, 47–67.

Rapee, R. M., & Melville, L. F. (1997). Recall of family factors in social phobia and panic disorder: Comparison of mother and offspring reports. *Depression and Anxiety, 5*, 7–11.

Schniering, C. A., Hudson, J. L., & Rapee, R. M. (2000). Issues in the diagnosis and assessment of anxiety disorders in children and adolescents. *Clinical Psychology Review, 20*, 453–478.

Simons, L., Ducette, J., Kirby, K. C., Stahler, G., & Shipley, T. E. (2003). Childhood trauma, avoidance coping, and alcohol and other drug use among women in residential and outpatient treatment programs. *Alcoholism Treatment Quarterly, 21*, 37–54.

Spence, S. H., Rapee, R., McDonald, C., & Ingram, M. (2001). The structure of anxiety symptoms among preschoolers. *Behavior Research and Therapy, 39*, 1293–1316.

Steele, R. G., Forehand, R., & Armistead, L. (1997). The role of family processes and coping strategies in the relationship between parental chronic illness and childhood internalizing problems. *Journal of Abnormal Child Psychology, 25*, 83–94.

Steiner, H., Erickson, S. J., Hernandez, N. L., & Pavelski, R. (2002). Coping styles as correlates of health in high school students. *Journal of Adolescent Health, 30*, 326–335.

Titchener, E. B. (1916). *A text-book of psychology*. New York: MacMillan.

Twohig, M. P., & Hayes, S. C. (in press). Implications of verbal processes for childhood disorders: Tourette's disorder, attention deficit hyperactivity disorder, and autism. In D.W. Woods & J. Kantor (Eds.), *Understanding behavior disorders: A contemporary behavioral perspective*. Reno, NV: Context Press.

Twohig, M. P., Masuda, A., Varra, A. A., & Hayes, S. C. (2005). Acceptance and commitment therapy as a treatment for anxiety disorders. In S. Orsillo & L. Roemer (Eds.), *Acceptance- and mindfulness-based approaches to anxiety* (pp. 101–129). New York: Springer.

Vasey, M. W., & Daleiden, E. L. (1994). Worry in children. In G. Davey & F. Tallis (Eds.), *Worrying: Perspectives on theory, assessment, and treatment* (pp. 185–207). New York: Wiley.

Vygotsky, L. S. (1991). Genesis of the higher mental functions. In P. Light & S. Sheldon (Eds.), *Learning to think. Child development in social context* (Vol. 2, pp. 32–41). Florence, KY: Taylor & Francis/Routledge.

Wicksell, R. K., Olsson, G. L., Dahl, J., & Melin, L. (2004, November). Using ACT to promote rehabilitation among children and adolescents with chronic pain. In L. A. Greco & G. H. Eifert (Cochairs), *Using acceptance and commitment therapy (ACT) with children and adolescents: Applications and empirical findings across school, family, and medical settings*. Symposium to be conducted at the Association for Advancement of Behavior Therapy, New Orleans, LA.

Wilson, K. G., & Blackledge, J. T. (2000). Recent developments in the behavioural analysis of language: Making sense of clinical phenomena. In M. J. Dougher (Ed.), *Clinical behavior analysis* (pp. 27–46). Reno, NV: Context Press.

Wilson, K. G., and Coyne, L. W. (2003, May). *Treatment of refractory school refusal using a values-centered ACT approach*. Paper presented at the Applied Behavioral Analysis Conference, San Francisco, CA.

Wilson, K. G., & Murrell, A. R. (2004). Values-centered interventions: Setting a course for behavioral treatment. In S. C. Hayes, V. M. Follette, & M. Linehan (Eds.), *The new behavior therapies: Expanding the cognitive behavioral tradition*. New York: Guilford.

Part IV

FUTURE DIRECTIONS

Chapter 13

EXPLORING BASIC PROCESSES UNDERLYING ACCEPTANCE AND MINDFULNESS

Michael J. Zvolensky, Matthew T. Feldner,
Ellen W. Leen-Feldner, and Andrew R. Yartz

There is little doubt that the ability to adapt to anxiety-related states and the aversive life events that traditionally accompany them is a critical component of psychological health and emotional adjustment. Indeed, theoretical and empirical work has focused on such processes since the emergence of psychology as a unique discipline. Testifying to the general recognition of the importance of this domain, processes involved in the adaptation to emotionally evocative events have historically been studied from a variety of theoretical frameworks and methodological perspectives that cut across disciplines, as well as literatures within the same discipline. The central integrative theme across such work has been, and continues to be, that the organism responds to anxiety-eliciting interoceptive and exteroceptive events in a meaningful way, and those responses, in turn, are associated with greater or lesser degrees of psychological health. The present book, *Acceptance and Mindfulness-Based Approaches to Anxiety: Conceptualization and Treatment*, represents an explicit recognition that adaptation processes continue to be of central importance to anxiety-related phenomena, including the etiology, maintenance, and relapse of anxiety psychopathology.

The specific focus on acceptance and mindfulness processes, relative to other adaptation variables, suggests that there is growing consensus that these two factors may be particularly relevant to better understanding the nature of anxiety and its disorders. In fact, there has been a dramatic increase in empirical attention devoted to understanding acceptance and mindfulness in recent years, as evidenced by recent books on the topic (e.g., Hayes, Strosahl, & Wilson, 1999; Kabat-Zinn, 1990), special series in leading journals in clinical science addressing the operationalization and conceptual underpinnings of these variables (e.g., Baer, 2003; Dimidjian & Linehan, 2003; Kabat-Zinn, 2003), and treatment programs targeting acceptance and mindfulness processes (e.g., Kabat-Zinn, Lipworth, Burney, & Sellers, 1987; Orsillo, Roemer, & Barlow, 2003; Ramel, Goldin, Carmona, & McQuaid, 2004; Roemer & Orsillo, 2002; Williams, Teasdale, Segal, & Soulsby, 2000). It is clear that clinical scientists from disparate theoretical orientations believe that acceptance and mindfulness, and perhaps affect regulatory processes more generally, may be critical components in anxiety vulnerability (Hayes & Feldman, 2004; Mennin, Heimberg, Turk, & Fresco, 2002). There is far less consensus, however, in regard to the best way to conceptualize, define, assess, and study them (Brown & Ryan, 2003). In the present chapter, we discuss issues relevant to basic research on acceptance and mindfulness in the study of anxiety and its disorders. In the first section of the chapter, we briefly summarize three broad-based areas in the study of acceptance and mindfulness in need of further work. In the second section of the paper, we provide a critical analysis of extant anxiety-relevant experimental psychopathology work on acceptance and mindfulness processes. We conclude in the third portion of the chapter by outlining particular domains of the study that we believe will be important to address in future basic research on acceptance and mindfulness.

BROAD-BASED ISSUES IN THE STUDY OF ACCEPTANCE AND MINDFULNESS FOR ANXIETY AND ITS DISORDERS: FURTHER STRENGTHENING THE FOUNDATION FOR BASIC RESEARCH

A number of overarching conceptual, definitional, and measurement issues are relevant to the study of acceptance and mindfulness processes. Although scholars have considered these issues for many years (see, e.g., Deikman, 1983; Wilber, 2000), there is, as of yet, no far-reaching consensus about them (Brown & Ryan, 2004; Strauman & Merrill, 2004). We believe, therefore, that it is fruitful to briefly outline some cornerstone issues in this domain as a general foundation for more specific directions in basic research on the topic. Indeed, progress in these "meta-domains" likely will be directly proportional to the relative degree of progress in specific areas of experimental psychopathology addressing these factors.

Clarify Conceptual Basis and Integrate Models Used in the Study of Acceptance and Mindfulness

The natural starting point for any discussion of the role of acceptance and mindfulness processes in anxiety psychopathology is clarifying the conceptual basis for these factors. Much has been written on issues related to gaining a precise theoretical perspective on these factors, as outlined in many recent scholarly works on the topic (Bishop et al., 2004; Hayes & Shenk, 2004). One clear concluding observation from these works is that there is as of yet no operational definition for acceptance or mindfulness that scholars uniformly agree upon (Brown & Ryan, 2004). In this context, it is noteworthy that some scientists have argued that these are distinct constructs relative to other factors and therefore offered theory-driven definitions for these variables (Bishop et al., 2004; Hayes, Wilson, Gifford, Follette, & Strosahl, 1996). Others have suggested that the field may perhaps be using new labels to denote particular types of coping processes involved in the engagement with emotions (Feldner, Zvolensky, & Leen-Feldner, 2004; Salovey, Rothman, Detweiler, & Steward, 2000). And still others have observed that acceptance and mindfulness terminology has been increasingly incorporated into clinical intervention work with little supporting basic theory, operationalization, adequate measurement, or data in support of the core processes involved (Strauman & Merrill, 2004). Despite the disparate views represented, one emerging trend from these scholarly discussions has been an emphasis on recognizing that these processes appear to be fundamentally related to self or affect regulation (A. M. Hayes & Feldman, 2004). As one illusrtative example, Bishop et al. (2004) recently proposed a definition of mindfulness that suggests it represents the *self-regulation* of attention in an effort to achieve a nonelaborative awareness of current experience and how one relates to that experience (see also Brown & Ryan, 2003, for a related operationalization that defines this process from a self-regulatory perspective). In a similar way, emotional acceptance has been suggested to be a particular way of *reacting* to affective and other life events, where persons remain open to such experiences rather than attempting to alter them via downregulation (Roemer & Orsillo, 2002). As Baumeister, Heatherton, and Tice (1994) suggest in a review of the literature, this type of response is implicitly *affect regulatory* in nature when it is applied to affective events; specifically, emotion acceptance, as a theoretically defined alternative to predominant types of "downregulation," represents a type of response to an affective event, presumably altering its sequelae (i.e., it maintains affect regulatory functions). Moreover, if this type of response did not have unique functional (emotional) consequences, it would be challenging to understand why it would be maintained over time or be discussed in relation to affective processes at all.

Given the nascent level of scientific attention focused on acceptance and mindfulness, in conjunction with the fact that scientists working on these factors have historically come from different theoretical orientations, it is not surprising that researchers have thus far tended to focus work on different issues emanating from their different conceptualizations. To briefly illustrate the distinct contemporary conceptualizations currently employed, it is interesting to examine examples drawn from current work on emotion acceptance in clinical science. Some researchers have couched this work in theory and basic research on emotion, self-regulation, and developmental outcomes, leading to a coping-oriented perspective on this process variable (Eisenberg, Fabes, & Guthrie, 1997; Davidson, 2000; Gross, 1999; Hayes & Feldman, 2004; Rothbart, Ziaie, & O'Boyle, 1992). This perspective is bolstered by increasingly well-developed empirical data. For instance, factor-analytic research across developmentally and ethnically diverse populations suggests that acceptance processes are specific types of voluntary coping responses that reflect "engagement" with one's own responses to a life event (Connor-Smith, Compas, Wadsworth, Thomsen, & Saltzman, 2000). Other researchers have become interested in acceptance by virtue of the nature of psychopathology more broadly and its origin and consequences (Bach & Hayes, 2002; Hayes, 2002). Work in this domain has suggested that emotion acceptance may be related to the function and utilization of language (Friman, Wilson, & Hayes, 1998; Hayes, Barnes-Holmes, & Roche, 2001; Hayes & Wilson, 2003). This perspective has led to an approach that tends to emphasize the function of responses to internal and external events and using such work to inform efforts to improve clinical interventions (Roemer & Orsillo, 2002). Still other work has examined issues of emotion acceptance in the context of regulating specific types of aversive internal states related to drug use (e.g., urges). Recent work in this substance use arena has begun to address these factors within the broader context of managing emotional vulnerability (see Brown, Lejuez, Kahler, Strong, & Zvolensky, in press, for a review). Finally, certain clinical scientists have built models of symptom management around the idea of helping clients learn to manage their mood states via emotion regulation tactics (Telch et al., 1993). This work has included psychological-based lessons that help clients understand from a theoretical and experiential perspective that certain negative mood states are not something that can be successfully avoided.

Although there may be complementary points of intersection between different approaches used in the study of acceptance and mindfulness in clinical science, it is noteworthy they have thus far seemed to operate at a general level of isolation from one another. We believe that this relative isolation perhaps contributes to a lack of focused integration of theory and research across subdisciplines in clinical science. As one example, findings from coping research suggest that it is important to understand affect regulatory processes in relation to the proportional use of other regulatory strategies used to deal with mood states (e.g., Vitaliano, Maiuro, Russo, & Becker, 1987). This approach avoids the potential "overinflation" of one response by explicitly noting the frequency of utilization of other response strategies that serve similar functions, and hence, the broader context of affect regulatory processes (Compas, Connor-Smith, Saltzman, Thomsen, & Wadsworth, 2001). Although arguably this is a very important issue from both analytic and clinical relevance perspectives, other research areas have not as of yet incorporated this assessment approach. This issue illustrates that various scientists interested in presumably the same process variable are not necessarily using information learned in one area and applying it to another domain. Given the research developments on acceptance and mindfulness processes across literatures, it is important that a more concerted effort be placed into utilizing the information that has been learned from these domains across various subdisciplines in the field. By incorporating and clarifying similar process-based issues in such work, it should be possible to make a more concerted effort toward clarifying their conceptual basis, forwarding systematic research on them, and increasing professional consensus as to their fundamental nature. *Thus, our first general recommendation is to call attention to the work being conducted on acceptance and mindfulness processes across literatures, and encourage anxiety researchers interested in these issues to be more cognizant of, and cast their work in, a broader and perhaps more integrated nomological net of evidence.*

DISTINGUISH ACCEPTANCE AND MINDFULNESS EFFECTS FROM THEORETICALLY RELEVANT PROCESSES

Inspection of the empirical and theoretical literatures on acceptance and mindfulness across various domains in clinical science highlights that it is not yet clear that these factors are empirically distinguishable from other responses to anxiety-related states (e.g., a tendency to be intolerant of emotional states), or other vulnerability factors for anxiety (e.g., general propensity to experience negative affect). We believe it is important that anxiety researchers be more appreciative of the fact that there are a multitude of constructs that have been identified and empirically evaluated in relation to anxiety vulnerability. Yet, in the absence of clarity with regard to relations between acceptance/mindfulness and these factors, it will remain empirically unclear whether acceptance or mindfulness offers unique explanatory power in models of anxiety vulnerability. Indeed, an important first step in a program of work on acceptance and mindfulness is to test whether they have incremental explanatory utility relative to other theoretically relevant factors (Sechrest, 1963). Moreover, consideration of whether a particular index of acceptance or mindfulness provides something above and beyond other instruments tapping already established factors ultimately becomes central in the rationalization of its inclusion as a clinically meaningful assessment tool.

As one illustrative example, nearly all major theories of anxiety psychopathology suggest that temperamental factors indexing a generalized emotional vulnerability (i.e., negative affectivity) are an initial formative basis for anxiety problems (e.g., Barlow, 2002; Craske, 1999, 2003; Fowles, 1995; Joiner & Lonigan, 2000). Importantly, negative affectivity and closely related yet theoretically distinct temperaments (e.g., behavioral inhibition sensitivity) are important in the foundation of coping and self-regulation processes (e.g., attentional control; Rothbart, Ahadi, & Evans, 2000). Specifically, research suggests that these anxiety-relevant temperaments are related to *both* (1) anxiety states and (2) regulatory processes related to anxiety (Gray & McNaughton, 1996). It is therefore important to ensure that acceptance and mindfulness offer unique explanatory power in regard to anxiety outcomes beyond measures of negative affectivity and related temperamental constructs (e.g., behavioral inhibition sensitivity). If empirical evidence is found for acceptance and mindfulness in relation to anxiety outcomes compared to these other theoretically relevant factors, support for their import—theoretically and clinically—would be substantially strengthened. Without such supporting empirical evidence, it will be more challenging to convincingly argue for their unique explanatory relevance in models of anxiety vulnerability. Of course, these tests will be the most compelling when they are guided by clear theory linking one variable, relative to another, in explaining a particular aspect of an anxiety phenomenon.

Thus far, there has been relatively little scientific attention devoted to the issue of incremental validity in the study of acceptance and mindfulness as it relates to anxiety outcomes. Moreover, of the work that has been completed, there is not necessarily compelling empirical evidence at the current stage of research development that supports the unique explanatory value of these constructs. As one specific example, Brown and Ryan (2003) have developed a promising self-report device to tap the mindfulness construct from a self-regulatory perspective; the Mindful Attention and Awareness

Scale (MAAS) measures awareness and attention to present events and experiences (example item: "I tend not to notice feelings of physical tension or discomfort until they really grab my attention"). Here, cross-sectional incremental validity data pertaining to mindfulness in relation to anxiety symptoms were markedly attenuated when the effects of neuroticism were covaried (Brown & Ryan, 2003, see Table 5). These findings empirically underscore that it will be important to understand acceptance and mindfulness processes in relation to negative affectivity in future work. *Thus, our second general recommendation is that future anxiety-related work on acceptance and mindfulness unambiguously specify the theoretical distinctions between such processes and other established factors tied to similar outcomes (e.g., negative affectivity) and empirically evaluate their explanatory power relative to these variables.*

Assessment of Acceptance and Mindfulness Processes

Naturally, it is important to develop and utilize assessment tools that tap acceptance and mindfulness in a reliable and valid manner. With only a relatively limited level of focused research to date, a key domain for future study pertains to the quality of existing measures and their ability to tap the core constructs of interest. Here, it is worth noting from the outset that the principal method for assessing acceptance and mindfulness processes has thus far largely been self-report devices. A complete reliance on self-report instruments may challenge work in this domain for at least two key reasons. First, models of acceptance and mindfulness suggest that these factors (a) have many automotized functions and (b) involve processes not fully accessible to conscious awareness (e.g., attention; Kabat-Zinn, 1990). Thus, it is possible that individuals may not be capable of being aware of all aspects of these factors and therefore encounter marked difficulties reporting on them. Second, solely using self-report devices of acceptance and mindfulness will increase method variance; that is, variability in acceptance or mindfulness may be resulting from something other than these processes (Campbell & Fiske, 1959). Previous work has found that method variance artifactually affects study outcomes in a variety of important ways (see Sechrest, Davis, Stickle, & McKnight, 2000, for a discussion). This issue will surely become more prominent in future efforts to understand the temporal stability of these constructs as well as their relations with anxiety outcome variables.

Inspection of existing assessment tools also suggests that many existing measures of acceptance and mindfulness may not yet be fully teasing apart these factors from indices of psychological distress or related constructs of interest. The lack of disentanglement of the construct of interest from the outcome to which it is theoretically related, or other (associated) constructs, can directly threaten the internal validity of this research and impede future progress. As one illustrative example, an initial version of the Acceptance and Action Questionnaire (AAQ; Hayes et al., 2004), tapping emotion acceptance, is commonly used in anxiety disorder research and practice (Eifert & Heffner, 2003; Feldner, Zvolensky, Eifert, & Spira, 2003; Forsyth, Parker, & Finlay, 2003; Sloan, 2004; Zvolensky & Forsyth, 2002). Yet, sample items of the nine-item version of the measure reflect processes that may be tied to emotion sensitivity (e.g., "I'm not afraid of my feelings"), attitudes about affect (e.g., "Anxiety is bad"), problem solving (e.g., "I am able to take action on a problem even if I am uncertain what is the right thing to do"), wishful thinking (e.g., "If I could magically remove all the painful experiences I've had in my life, I would do so"), comparative judgments (e.g., "When I compare myself to other people, it seems that most of them are handling their lives better than I do"), and so on. Although this measure has clearly helped forward work on acceptance processes, with this type of diversity in item content on a nine-item assessment instrument, it may be difficult to index emotion acceptance in a relatively "pure" way and distinguish it from related constructs. Indeed, researchers have not surprisingly reported very low levels of internal consistency for the nine-item AAQ (e.g., Cronbach's α < .50).

Improving the quality of assessment devices in the field has been increasingly recognized by clinical scientists. For example, a number of researchers have been developing new self-report instruments for acceptance and mindfulness (e.g., Brown & Ryan, 2003; Gratz & Roemer, 2004; Hayes & Feldman, 2004). Others have begun to implement behavioral and psychophysiological indices of response strategies broadly related to acceptance and mindfulness (e.g., willingness to undergo an anxiety-relevant task in the future; Levitt, Brown, Orsillo, & Barlow, 2004). Theoretically, there has been a recent movement to conceptualize emotion tolerance as an overarching construct for specific processes related to acceptance and mindfulness (Brown, et al., in press). For example, Otto, Powers, and Fischmann (in press) have called attention to the idea that many affect vulnerability constructs may be indexing an *intolerance* for emotional states. Continued empirical development of this domain may prove fruitful in that it could offer a hierarchical conceptualization of these factors. This focus on measurement, methodologically and conceptually, is an important, formative step in the emerging science of acceptance and mindfulness. *For this reason, our third general recommendation is that continued focused effort needs to be placed in developing measures that can isolate acceptance and mindfulness from psychological distress and other constructs related to the theoretical processes of interest.*

SUMMARY

Together, there is a need for continued efforts to improve work on acceptance and mindfulness in a number of general domains. Specifically, we believe substantial progress can be made by (1) drawing from the available empirical literatures that speak to these issues and work toward developing (a) operational definitions that are used across studies and (b) more integrated theoretical models; (2) conducting tests of incremental validity relative to other theoretically relevant and established constructs known to be associated with anxiety and self-regulatory processes; and (3) further improving upon existing assessment tools. Indeed, forward movement in these three areas alone would greatly benefit the area by providing an even stronger foundation for basic research on the topic.

EXPERIMENTAL PSYCHOPATHOLOGY RESEARCH ON ACCEPTANCE AND MINDFULNESS

We now review some cornerstone basic laboratory-based research on acceptance and mindfulness in relation to anxiety and its disorders. It should be noted from the outset that this review is intended to *illustrate some recent developments in one key branch of laboratory work, rather than draw from all possible empirical sources that speak to such issues (e.g., emotional disclosure, attentional bias, metacognition literatures).* This analysis, although not fully comprehensive, will help illustrate what we currently know about these processes, the complexities involved, and where future work can be directed using similar laboratory paradigms. In this review, we have specifically restricted our discussion to studies that fall within the purview of *experimental psychopathology focused on anxiety-related processes,* defined as laboratory-based research involving human participants (see Forsyth & Zvolensky, 2002; Zvolensky, Lejuez, Stuart, & Curtin, 2001, for expanded discussions of the history and nature of various experimental psychopathology perspectives). Although there are merits and challenges to restricting our review to laboratory-based studies (see McNally, 1999, for an interesting discussion), given that many of the chapters in the present book focus on clinical research issues, we are hopeful that our focus will offer a unique contribution that culls out issues involved in understanding the study of basic processes. Throughout our review, we focus only on those studies that have explicitly used anxiety-related outcomes. This focus serves to help make more precise statements regarding acceptance and mindfulness processes and anxiety states, given the well-established structural and functional differences between different emotional states (see Lang, 1984, for an expanded discussion of this emotion specificity issue).

Prior to reviewing research on acceptance and mindfulness, it is important to note that researchers have only recently begun anxiety-relevant laboratory work on these process variables. Moreover, the vast majority of this work has interestingly focused on emotion regulatory processes that presumably reflect the *opposite* functions of acceptance and mindfulness. For example, researchers have utilized paradigms that have participants suppress an ongoing anxious emotional state compared to observing that state. It is noteworthy in this context that this work often is discussed as supporting evidence for studying acceptance and mindfulness processes (cf. negative effects associated with escape and avoidance strategies). In all cases, the rationale for using this approach is threefold. First, escape and avoidance of aversive events presumably represents a prototypical illustration of "nonacceptance" most likely to be related to increased anxiety vulnerability (Zvolensky, Lejuez, & Eifert, 2000). Interestingly, to the best of our knowledge, this assumption has not been empirically tested and, again, underscores the need for more work to be done at a theoretical and assessment level (see "Broad-Based Issues" section). Specifically, it is not empirically evident that acceptance and avoidance are, in fact, end points on the same latent continuum or even best understood from a dimensional perspective at all (see Bernstein, Zvolensky, Weems, Stickle, & Leen-Feldner, in press, for an expanded discussion of this type of measurement model issue). Second, escape and avoidance processes seem to be easier to experimentally manipulate than acceptance processes and therefore a potentially more prudent starting point for research in this domain. Third, this work has historically been preceded by work on thought suppression, which has successfully used suppression manipulations in the laboratory. Although thought suppression is a closely related behavioral process (cf. emotion suppression), we do not review this literature for two reasons. First, there are many recent summaries and critical reviews of this area readily available (see, e.g., Abramowitz, Tolin, & Street, 2001; Rassin, Merckelbach, & Muris, 2001; Wenzlaff & Wegner, 2000, for reviews). Second, cognitive processes are just one component of an emotional response (Lang, 1984), making these investigations less directly applicable to the focus of the current chapter.

Anxiety-Related Experimental Laboratory Investigations

The predominant route laboratory-based researchers have taken to study processes related to emotion acceptance is examining strategies that theoretically represent the extreme end of *nonacceptance*. In this paradigm, participants are exposed to some evocative anxiety-relevant stimulus and instructed to regulate their response to it in a theoretically relevant way (e.g., suppress, distract). By definition, these studies represent investigations focused on the *acute effects* of emotion regulation for anxiety-eliciting events. They are powerful sources of information in that they help reduce problems associated with reporting errors common to anxiety-related states and disorders (e.g., recall bias or memory distortion) as well as typically provide data across and between levels of analysis. These studies also are valuable in the sense that they offer *directional* tests of theoretically derived hypotheses, a currently underrepresented domain of work on acceptance and mindfulness.

Anxiety and Fear Studies

In one of the first studies to examine emotion suppression in relation to anxiety-relevant responding, Jackson, Malmstadt, Larson, and Davidson (2000) exposed 48 college students to 90 unpleasant and 30 neutral slides from the International Affective Picture Set (IAPS; Center for the Study of Emotion and Attention [CSEA-NIMH], 1996). Participants were instructed to either suppress or enhance their emotional response to the stimuli; dependent variables were startle eyeblink magnitude and corrugator activity. Consistent with hypotheses, results indicated that relative to participants instructed to enhance, subjects in the suppression condition evidenced smaller startle eyeblink magnitudes and decreased corrugator activity, suggesting that, when experimentally directed, subjects can effectively suppress negative emotion and that decreases in these specific indices of physiological arousal are commensurate with the degree of inhibition of emotional expression. This study suggests that emotion suppression is an effective affect regulatory response in that it may offer short-term "relief" from emotional states.

Using a similar methodology, Leen-Feldner, Zvolensky, and Feldner (2004) examined the moderating effect of behavioral inhibition sensitivity on emotion suppression in response to fear-relevant slides. Ninety-five nonclinical adolescents (aged 12 to 17 years) were randomly assigned to either a suppression or an observation condition and asked to view 20 color images from the IAPS (CSEA-NIMH, 1995). Unexpectedly, results indicated that, compared to participants in the emotion suppression condition, subjects in the *observation* group evidenced increased postchallenge anxiety. Although main effects of behavioral inhibition sensitivity were observed for postchallenge anxiety, valence, and control, this variable did not moderate the effects of condition. Finally, none of the predictor variables were related to postchallenge psychophysiological responding. Overall, these findings are interesting in that emotion suppression, either as a main effect or as an interactive effect with behavioral inhibition sensitivity, was not associated with increased emotional distress or physiological reactivity. Such null results cannot be attributed to the efficacy of the experimental manipulation, as analyses indicated participants were successful in understanding and following the directional set. These data are inconsistent with contemporary perspectives that suggest the active inhibition of negatively valenced (ongoing) emotional responding exacerbates emotional distress. Given that the sample was screened for psychopathology, future work may seek to evaluate the same predictions using a sample that includes youth with anxiety psychopathology. That is, the null suppression effects may be related to truncated upper-end variability in psychological vulnerability.

Other investigations have examined the effects of suppressing responses to carbon dioxide–enriched air (CO_2), a salient panic-relevant biological challenge (Zvolensky & Eifert, 2000). In the first study to employ this methodology, Feldner et al. (2003) examined the relations among emotion suppression, emotional avoidance, and anxious responding to four inhalations of 20% CO_2. Participants were 48 psychologically healthy young adults selected on the basis of preexperimental differences (high vs low) in self-reported experiential avoidance, as measured by the nine-item AAQ (Hayes et al., 2004). Participants were instructed to either suppress or observe their emotional response to CO_2. Results suggested that for persons high in emotional avoidance, suppressing emotional responses to the CO_2 resulted in greater anxious responding than observing such responses. In terms of psychophysiological responding, compared to participants in the emotion observation group, individuals in the suppression group evidenced lesser heart rate reactivity. Given that participants were selected on the basis of the nine-item AAQ, it is unclear if the suppression effects are specific to emotional avoidance per se (cf. negative affectivity). Nonetheless, it appears that these findings suggest the consequences of emotion suppression may vary as a function of other individual differences (i.e., moderating effect).

In a follow-up study, Feldner, Zvolensky, Stickle, Bonn-Miller, and Leen-Feldner (in press) examined anxiety-related responding to, and recovery from, a 5-min 10% CO_2 presentation among 80 nonclinical young adults. As before, participants were instructed to either suppress or observe their response to the challenge. Additionally, a key objective of this study was to examine the moderating effects of the Physical Concerns facet of the Anxiety Sensitivity Index (AS-PC; Reiss, Peterson, Gursky, & McNally, 1986) on the association between emotion suppression and responding to the biological challenge. Results indicated there was a main effect for AS-PC on postchallenge self-reported anxiety; condition approached but did not reach traditional levels of statistical significance. Additionally, AS-PC moderated the effect of suppression on emotion valence during

recovery, suggesting suppression has differential psychological consequences as a function of individual differences in AS-PC. In terms of physiological responding, relative to participants in the observation group, subjects instructed to suppress evidenced a cardiovascular "rebound" effect;
heart rate steadily increased during the 10-min recovery period. Overall,
these results were only partially consistent with original prediction and
underscored the subtleties involved with studying affective processes outside of the immediate challenge.

Using a similar design to that of Felder et al. (2003), Levitt et al. (2004)
examined emotion suppression in response to a 15-min 5.5% CO_2 challenge among 60 persons diagnosed with panic disorder. Participants were
assigned to a suppression, acceptance, or control group. Compared to the
suppression and control groups, participants in the emotion acceptance
condition reported significantly less anxiety and greater willingness to participate in a second CO_2 trial; there were no differences among the groups
in terms of panic symptoms or psychophysiological responding, nor were
there any differences between the control and suppression groups on any
criterion variables. It is noteworthy that the assessment of emotional responding was limited to one immediate postchallenge data point; it would
be interesting and theoretically important to know whether emotion suppression affected recovery from the emotion induction among this clinical
population.

In another biological challenge study, Eifert and Heffner (2003) compared the effects of acceptance versus control strategies on the avoidance
of panic-relevant interoceptive stimulation elicited by two 10-min trials of
10% carbon dioxide–enriched air among 60 high-anxiety–sensitive women.
Specifically, participants were assigned to either (1) a control condition
(i.e., instructed to engage in diaphragmatic breathing in an effort to control the experience), (2) an acceptance condition (i.e., practice the Chinese
finger trap metaphor; see Hayes et al., 1999) or (3) no-instruction condition. Results indicated that, compared to participants in the control and
no-instruction conditions, participants in the acceptance condition were
less behaviorally avoidant (e.g., shorter latency to commence second trial;
willingness to participate in another CO_2 study), reported less intense fear,
and fewer catastrophic thoughts during the trials. As no independent evaluations were completed in regard to the nature of the training, one important interpretative caveat to this investigation pertains to the efficacy of the
training for the various conditions. Specifically, it is unclear if experimenter
effects (e.g., biases in interaction style, differential time in training participants) influenced, in part, the study results. This is perhaps especially noteworthy in this study because of the higher-than-average rates of dropout
reported. Additionally, utilization of a breathing retraining condition as

an index of a control strategy may be problematic in a CO_2 paradigm. Specifically, it might have been difficult for participants to complete diaphragmatic breathing while simultaneously inhaling CO_2, rendering at least one of the comparisons less than ideal. Independent replication of the study will therefore be an important next research step.

In an interesting study using film clips as the provocation strategy, Campbell-Sills, Barlow, Brown, and Hofmann (in press) examined emotion regulation, using two separate emotion inductions. In the first induction, 60 young adult participants with anxiety and mood diagnoses and 30 control participants responded spontaneously to a film clip from the "Deer Hunter." Results indicated that, compared to controls, clinical participants engaged in more emotion suppression and that this strategy was associated with poorer mood recovery, increased sympathetic arousal, and decreased self-efficacy. Only clinical subjects participated in the second induction, which was another clip from the same film. Here, participants were instructed to either suppress or accept their emotional response to the film. Compared to participants in the acceptance condition, participants in the suppression condition evidenced increased cardiac arousal and inhibited mood recovery. One potential limitation of this study with regard to the current chapter pertains to the film clip employed; specifically, it is unclear to what extent the "Deer Hunter" elicits anxiety specifically, or negative affectivity generally (cf. CO_2). Thus, conclusions about whether the strategies studied herein are specific to anxiety-related problems are unclear. Additionally, findings pertain to maintenance, rather than etiological, effects of emotion suppression and acceptance.

Disgust Studies

Disgust recently has been examined in laboratory studies of emotion suppression for a variety of clinical and methodological reasons. With respect to its clinical relevance, disgust is increasingly recognized for its role in the development and maintenance of several forms of psychopathology (see Woody & Teachman, 2000, for a review), particularly among anxiety disorders including blood–injury phobia (Page, 1994), specific phobia (de Jong & Merckelbach, 1998), and obsessive–compulsive disorder (Mancini, Gragnani, & D'Olimpio, 2001). Moreover, individuals with these diagnoses often measure high in sensitivity to disgusting materials (Sawchuk, Lohr, Tolin, Lee, & Kleinknecht, 2000; see also the *Journal of Anxiety Disorders*, special issue, 2002), suggesting that clinical avoidance behaviors are related to disgust.

In an interesting laboratory study, Gross and Levenson (1993) examined the effects of emotion suppression across subjective, behavioral, and physiological modalities. Unselected student participants (43 men and 42 women) watched two short (approximately 1 min) disgust-eliciting films—one depicting an amputation surgery and the other treatment of a burn victim—either as they normally would (no suppression condition) or while behaving "in such a way that a person watching you would not know you were feeling anything" (suppression condition). Results indicated that suppression had no effect on participants' subjective experience of disgust, but it did reduce overt behavioral indicators of emotion (facial expressivity). In contrast to the author's expectations, suppression did not result in decreased physiological responding overall, but rather led to increased physiological responding among autonomic indices (Gross & Levenson, 1993).

In a follow-up investigation, Gross and Levenson (1997) conducted a similar study examining the effects of inhibiting emotion across a broader range of affective valence. Unselected female participants ($n = 180$) were asked to view sad, neutral, and amusing films under conditions of either suppression or no-suppression. Results indicated that suppression was again associated with reduced expressive behavior across affective conditions, but had no effect on subjective ratings of sadness relative to the no-suppression condition (interestingly, amusement ratings were reduced during suppression of the amusement film). Importantly, suppression had no effect on physiological measures during the neutral film, but resulted in increased responding across autonomic indices during both sad and amusing films, suggesting that the inhibition of emotion is associated with an increase in physiological activation regardless of whether the emotion being suppressed is positively or negatively valenced.

These findings led Gross (1998) to posit a process model of emotion regulation that suggests that regulating emotion at different points in the emotion-generative process will have differential effects on subsequent emotion development and emotional responding. A central tenet to the model is that strategies used to regulate responding relatively later in the emotion developmental process (such as suppression) require additional effort, presumably due to the increased attentional resources needed to compare the current state of a system (e.g., one's facial expression) with a desired state for that system (e.g., facial nonexpression), and make appropriate behavioral adjustments to minimize the difference between the two (Richards & Gross, 1999). Additional support for this idea is provided by data demonstrating that suppression, but not reappraisal, is associated with decreased cognitive performance, as measured by memory tasks requiring participants to recall stimulus details, during an emotion suppression attempt (Richards & Gross, 2000). These greater cognitive and physiological resource requirements suggest that relative to reappraisal, suppression may be more effortful.

Perhaps most central to the present discussion, this work consistently demonstrates that the suppression of ongoing emotional experience reduces observable expressive facets of the emotion, but does not alter the subjective experience of the emotion (cf. Jackson et al., 2000). This finding was corroborated by a recent study (Yartz & Hawk, 2004) in which 60 unselected undergraduate participants (36 men and 24 women) were asked to view a mixed series of pleasant and disgust pictorial stimuli under varying conditions of emotion regulation. Specifically, participants were provided with extensive training in suppression, reappraisal, and enhancement techniques, and then instructed to view affective stimuli either as they normally would ("just watch" control condition) or using one of the regulatory techniques on a trial-by-trial basis (all conditions were counterbalanced and matched across affective stimuli). Dependent measures included subjective ratings of valence, arousal, and disgust, as well as facial EMG measures of levator labii (which is reactive and specific to disgust; Yartz & Hawk, 2002) and zygomaticus major (which is reactive to positive emotion; Vrana, 1993), which were employed as expressive–behavioral indices of disgust and pleasantness, respectively.

Results indicated that relative to the "just watch" control condition, levator EMG responses to disgust pictures were attenuated during both reappraisal and suppression, but were not augmented during enhancement. Zygomatic EMG responses to pleasant pictures also were attenuated during both reappraisal and suppression, but were augmented during enhancement. For disgust stimuli, subjective ratings of disgust decreased during reappraisal and increased during enhancement, but did not differ during suppression relative to the control condition. For positive stimuli, subjective ratings of pleasantness decreased during reappraisal and increased during enhancement, as expected, but suppression of positive emotional states was interestingly associated with a reduction in experiential pleasantness, a result also reported by Gross and Levenson (1997). Overall, these findings support the notion that suppressing or inhibiting affect may not reduce experiential aspects of emotion, particularly among negatively valenced states.

Anxiety-Related Correlational Laboratory Investigations

Aside from experimental work, it is noteworthy that there are number of correlational laboratory investigations that have addressed acceptance, mindfulness, and related constructs (e.g., emotion avoidance). Relative to experimental work on the topic, there are a smaller overall number of investigations in this domain, although many more have been completed outside of laboratory settings (e.g., Forsyth et al., 2003; Lynch, Robins, Morse, & Krause, 2001; Plumb, Orsillo, & Luterek, 2004; Zvolensky & Forsyth, 2002).

In an early study in this domain, Spira, Zvolensky, Eifert, and Feldner (2004) examined to what extent preexperimental levels of avoidance-oriented coping, relative to other theoretically relevant variables (e.g., anxiety sensitivity), predicted anxious and fearful responding to 10% CO_2. Participants were psychologically healthy young adults. A composite index of avoidance coping using subscales from the COPE (Carver, Scheier, & Weintraub, 1989) questionnaire was utilized ($\alpha = .81$); it indexes strategies individuals use in response to general stressors (cf. anxiety-specific events). The coping strategies represented by the Denial, Mental Disengagement, and Alcohol–Drug Disengagement subscales of the COPE were conceptualized as "avoidance" strategies because they include items describing behavior aimed at decreasing the probability that an individual will experience emotional distress. Results indicated that avoidance-oriented coping was the single best (significant) predictor of increased physical panic symptoms and self-reported anxiety elicited by the biological challenge. In this study, avoidant coping did not have any association with physiological responsiveness. One important methodological caveat of this investigation is the use of a composite index of avoidance that, although relatively internally consistent, has not been more extensively empirically evaluated. Nonetheless, the findings suggest avoidance coping is a premorbid predictor of self-reported anxious and fearful responding to bodily sensations.

In a subsequent investigation, Sloan (2004) examined the association between emotional reactivity to pleasant, unpleasant, and neutral stimuli as a function of preexperimental differences in emotion avoidance. In this study, emotion avoidance was indexed by the nine-item AAQ. Participants included 62 young adults who were not screened for psychopathology, but were excluded on the basis of current psychotropic medication use. Results indicated that individuals with high, compared to low, AAQ scores reported greater emotional experience to both unpleasant and pleasant stimuli. At the same time, persons with high, compared to low, AAQ scores demonstrated attenuated heart rate reactivity to only the unpleasant stimuli. The fact that participants with high AAQ scores responded to both pleasant and unpleasant stimuli may indicate that the consequences of relying on emotion avoidance strategies in terms of acute emotional responding may be invariant across affective state. However, given that the nine-item AAQ may be saturated with variance related to emotionality, as described earlier, it will be necessary to replicate and extend these results with another measure of emotion avoidance prior to drawing more firm conclusions.

Karekla, Forsyth, and Kelly (2004) examined differences between nonclinical young adults high ($n = 27$) and low ($n = 27$) in emotion avoidance (as indexed via the nine-item AAQ; Hayes et al., 2004) in terms of responding to twelve 20-s inhalations of 20% CO_2. Results suggested persons high, relative to low, in emotion avoidance responded to the CO_2 inhalations with more panic symptoms, more severe cognitive symptoms, and more fear, panic, and uncontrollability. No differences in psychophysiological responding were observed. These findings are in accord with other related examinations (e.g., Feldner et al., 2003) in that they suggest persons who score high on the AAQ (Hayes et al., 2004) demonstrate greater panic-relevant reactivity to biological challenge. Unfortunately, these researchers' assessment was not designed to examine recovery from the CO_2 inhalations, thereby not allowing for statements regarding possible differential recovery as a function of emotion avoidance. Additionally, as with our studies that have used the nine-item AAQ, it is unclear if prechallenge variability in this measure is indicative of emotional avoidance or negative affectivity.

Synthesis of Observations

The experimental psychopathology literature on acceptance and mindfulness and related processes is indeed growing. These studies have begun to provide clues as to the nature of these factors and their possible role in anxiety vulnerability. At this stage of research development, there appear to be a number of tentative observations that can be drawn and specific points for future work.

One central observation is that investigations thus far have principally examined suppression of an ongoing affective response or the extent to which indices of avoidant affect regulatory styles relate to anxiety symptoms. This work is beginning to lay an empirical foundation to approaches that can be used to study acceptance and mindfulness. However, it is important to note that these studies do not necessarily fully apply to acceptance and mindfulness processes. For example, as of yet, it is not empirically evident that suppression of an affective response is, in fact, an opposite of emotional acceptance. Additionally, although some investigators may view acceptance as an aspect of mindfulness (Bishop et al., 2004), research parceling mindfulness effects from acceptance effects, or vice versa, has not been specifically conducted. We believe that part of the explanation for this focus is due to the issues raised in the early portions of this chapter; namely, an overarching lack of conceptual, operational, and measurement consensus as to the nature of these factors. Future progress in experimental psychopathology approaches to acceptance and mindfulness will therefore need to be commensurate with advances in these broader domains.

A second observation indicates that effects related to emotion suppression are not as uniform as would be initially expected by some prevailing theoretical models (e.g., Hayes et al., 1996). Indeed, there is clear empirical evidence from extant work that emotion suppression has different effects across response parameters, nature of regulation strategy (e.g., inhibition of expression of response or emotional response itself), and stimulus types (e.g., valence of target emotion). For example, in terms of disgust stimuli, self-reported ratings do not differ during suppression relative to a control condition (Yartz & Hawk, 2004). Similarly, there is evidence of null effects for emotion suppression despite evidence of experimental manipulations being successful (Leen-Feldner et al., 2004). Moreover, the effects of emotion suppression appear to be, at least in part, moderated by other factors related to emotion sensitivity (anxiety sensitivity; Feldner et al., 2004). These findings suggest that replication and extension of extant work will be particularly important in the near future as will studies that include tests of emotion specificity and intensity. Current models addressing these factors do not predict such effects and therefore will need to adapt in the future to better account for the observed phenomena. By building a larger and more integrated base of experimental psychopathology work, we will be in a better position to understand the role of such factors in models of anxiety vulnerability.

A related observation is that only one study to date has examined parameters of emotional responding related to suppression or acceptance other than maximum distress experienced during or after a laboratory-based challenge (i.e., Feldner et al., in press). Davidson and colleagues have emphasized the importance of examining less commonly studied facets of emotional responding, including but not limited to, recovery (Davidson, 2000; Davidson, Jackson, & Kalin, 2000). These researchers and others have noted that powerful emotional stressors (e.g., CO_2) may result in "normative physiological responses" characterized by high levels of reactivity, thus potentially masking group differences (ceiling effect; Zvolensky, Feldner, Eifert, & Brown, 2001). Such an explanation could account for the observation that suppressing (Levitt et al., 2004) and high levels of emotion avoidance (Karekla et al., 2004) do not result in greater overall magnitude of psychophysiological response to CO_2. To more finely analyze the relation between emotional reactivity and emotion regulatory processes, such as acceptance and mindfulness, within the context of a laboratory-based paradigm, it would be useful to examine other parameters of emotion responding (e.g., recovery; Feldner et al., in press).

A fourth observation is that there is a striking lack of focused work on children and adolescents, with only one investigation being focused on this segment of the lifespan (Leen-Feldner et al., 2004). We believe much could be gained by taking a more proactive stance toward addressing developmental factors in the study of these processes, rather than simply "downward extending" adult findings to youth. Indeed, the "developmental relevance" of these processes should not be underestimated, as it is unlikely that the structure and function of self-regulatory processes are similar across development. Specifically, an individual's developmental stage or level is likely to be related to, and defined by, the cognitive, behavioral, physiological, and affective resources available for enacting a response to evocative events; they place, in essence, boundaries on resources for affect regulation and probably the specific types of responses that can be employed (Grant et al., 2003). Thus, future work should work on crafting theories of acceptance and mindfulness processes with explicit attention to developmental effects to enhance explanatory precision in regard to models of anxiety vulnerability.

FUTURE STUDY

In the final section, we outline particular domains of study that we believe will be important to address in basic research on acceptance and mindfulness processes relevant to anxiety and its disorders. From the outset, it is important to note that progress in addressing the domains presented below necessarily rests, to a large degree, on the ability to (1) precisely clarify theoretical underpinnings and (2) reliably and validly assess acceptance and mindfulness processes. Additionally, this work builds from existing studies of emotional suppression previously reviewed.

DOMAIN 1: ISOLATING DIRECTIONAL EFFECTS IN THE RELATION BETWEEN ACCEPTANCE AND MINDFULNESS PROCESSES AND ANXIETY PROCESSES

One domain warranting scientific attention is the relation between specific acceptance and mindfulness and anxiety processes as they pertain to the etiology and maintenance of anxiety psychopathology. As illustrated by the exciting chapters of this book, it is clear that many central questions about the relations between acceptance and mindfulness processes and anxiety vulnerability remain unanswered. For example, are various forms of functionally defined emotion avoidance of anxiety-related events causes, consequences, both, or neither for developing an anxiety disorder? Most theories predict certain regulatory processes lessen psychological vulnerability, but it is equally plausible that as specific psychological symptoms decrease, persons utilize different regulation strategies (i.e., regulation strategy is a consequence of anxiety). Evaluating such questions, with explicit attention to these potential bidirectional issues, will require the complementary use of experimental and prospective designs to tease apart timing effects (e.g., manipulations of a regulation process compared to no manipulation) as well as the stability of those effects in reference to concurrent and longer term outcomes. It is worth noting that some forms of affect regulation may be capable of being currently studied only in certain settings (e.g., automatic regulation processes and responses to evocative events may be possible to isolate only in the laboratory). Thus, recurrent testing as a function of experimental and control groups across time will be an important methodological tactic. Additionally, addressing such directional questions will offer the most utility when asked in a manner that is specific to the natural history of an anxiety disorder (i.e., etiology, maintenance, and relapse phases, respectively).

DOMAIN 2: EXPLICATING MEDIATING AND MODERATING EFFECTS

A second key domain in need of further study pertains to clarifying the mediational and moderational processes linking acceptance and mindfulness processes to specific anxiety-related characteristics (or vice versa). To date, the vast majority of research on self-regulation has focused on main effects, that is, "does it" versus "does it not" types of questions.

In regard to mediational effects, there is now a large theoretical and empirical psychopathology literature, as well as recent "calls to action" at the national level (e.g., National Institute of Drug Abuse, 2004), that emphasizes the importance of clarifying the precise mechanisms of action involved in associations between variables of interest (Baron & Kenny, 1986). Although we will not reiterate the many reasons for addressing mediators here, we believe it is important to note that identification of these factors is relevant to basic and applied questions because they help identify *mechanisms* through which affect regulatory processes may achieve their effects on anxiety-related adjustment. In theory, these mechanisms represent the causal connections among affect regulatory processes and anxiety-related factors (Kazdin & Weisz, 1998). Identifying mediators and moderators is important to begin to specify the factors that determine for whom and under what conditions anxiety-related problems develop. Thus, by explicating the mechanisms involved in these important linkages, researchers will be in a sound position to enhance the impact of interventions that target the regulatory process (e.g., acceptance), presumably leading to larger effect sizes or the delivery of the intervention in shorter amounts of time, both of which translate to increased clinical cost-effectiveness. Of course, clarifying the mechanism(s) of action in a particular regulatory process also will further substantiate that process in the etiology and/or maintenance of a particular anxiety disorder.

For reasons discussed earlier, it is indeed noteworthy that existing models and theories of acceptance and mindfulness have largely not dealt with explicating possible mediators, even at the theoretical level. Some anxiety-relevant theories suggest that individuals may develop anxiety psychopathology, in part, because they attempt to rigidly escape or avoid anxiety-related states (Hayes et al., 1996). Yet, little is known about how this process unfolds and what connects the behavior to the outcome. As an example of how work may focus on identifying mediators, we have drawn on this perspective in examining the comorbidity of smoking and panic disorder by exploring cognitive narrowing processes related to attention (see Zvolensky, Feldner, Leen-Feldner, & McLeish, in press; Zvolensky, Schmidt, & Stewart, 2003, for reviews). To escape from anxiety-related symptoms due, for instance, to tobacco withdrawal, an individual may narrow his or her attention span focusing only on the present "affective event." In such a cognitive state, there may be a greater opportunity for behavioral disinhibition (e.g., smoking) and vulnerability to irrational thought (e.g., "If I don't have a cigarette, I'm going to go crazy"; Zvolensky, 2004). From this perspective, smoking behavior under these conditions occurs in response to thinking that does not permit attention to the meanings of such action. Additionally, catastrophic or irrational thinking may occur because high-level reasoning is relatively nonoperational, precluding the critical assessment of more adaptive problem-solving tactics related to abstinence. Future work could usefully address the role of "deconstructed thought processes" in the mediation of associations between anxiety states and smoking-related coping responses.

Understanding moderating factors in the development of anxiety psychopathology is necessary and clinically important for numerous reasons, including (1) they may help identify subpopulations with potentially different causal mechanisms or courses of illness; (2) they can be used to help identify which high-risk individuals might be most appropriate for specialized preventive interventions; and (3) they help elucidate relations among key risk factors (Kraemer et al., 1997). Thus, identification of factors that moderate the effects of acceptance and mindfulness relevant to anxiety psychopathology will alter the empirical and theoretical landscape pertaining to how these problems develop, are maintained, and potentially targeted for intervention (including both prevention and treatment). Although a review of all of the promising moderators for specific theoretically relevant affect regulation processes is beyond the scope of the current chapter, it is worth noting that contexts, including sociocultural environments, trait variables (individual differences), and specific environmental features (e.g., cues tied to positive and negative affect) all are likely candidates for anxiety disorder research and practice. Here, it is perhaps useful to recall one of Cannon's (1927) lasting influences on anxiety disorder research and practice, whereby he argued strongly that affect states frequently do not begin with conscious awareness. Although the details of Cannon's original position have not necessarily been substantiated, it is indeed evident that automatic aspects of emotional states do, in fact, differ by contextual factors related to the elicitation of the emotion (Lacey, 1967). These data empirically underscore the "context matters" in anxiety-related research.

With this background, it is clear that psychopathologists need to explicitly incorporate theoretically relevant contexts into their models of, and research on, acceptance and mindfulness. There are numerous important avenues to pursue in this domain. As one illustrative example, emotion acceptance of anxiety-related states may have fundamentally different consequences on the subsequent development of posttraumatic memories for children living in environments where they are currently being maltreated compared to environments where they are not being maltreated. Here, avoidance responses in the maltreatment environment may prove relatively *more* personally adaptive and inspire a sense of mastery, whereas avoidance in the opposite situation may hinder personal emotional development and a sense of control. Here, the same regulatory response implemented in two different environmental contexts may lead to the development and availability of, for instance, different emotional–cognitive resources, associated subsequent social learning, and so on. Basic research provides empirical support for this type of account, as being able to control aversive events via a number of different ways (e.g., attentional control, behavioral response) compared to when one cannot exert such control yields a greater degree of positive psychological outcomes (e.g., Zvolensky, Eifert, Lejuez, & McNeil, 1999). In addition to the implications of emotion regulation on the experience of control, it may be that such regulatory responses for aversive events may make the experience more predictable and thereby less emotionally distressing. Overall, extant theory and evidence seems to suggest that contextual factors may influence the development of anxiety-related emotions and associated affect regulation responses to them.

Domain 3: Increased Utilization of "Real Time" Emotion-Specific Elicitation Paradigms

Although there are many promising questions to pursue, certain methodological tactics may hold particular merit in future work on affect regulation involved with anxiety and its disorders. A central problem to the study of acceptance and mindfulness processes used in response to anxiety in real-world settings is that the processes being studied may be measured primarily via self-report strategies. Although there is much to be gained from self-reported accounts, it is unlikely to provide a fully comprehensive or integrated account. For example, numerous studies of emotion have indicated that there often are only very modest relations between certain physiological processes and self-reported anxiety states. Thus, emotion–excitation paradigms have been suggested as a powerful tactic that enables the complementary use of self-report devices with other measurement tools that reflect aspects of the emotional experience not attainable by self-report (e.g., physiological reactivity).

Aside from measuring responses across systems in real time and thereby reducing recall biases, reporting errors, and so on, emotion excitation tactics also should help provide more powerful tests of specific affect regulation strategies related to different (specific) emotional states. Currently, it is entirely unclear whether observed effects of acceptance and mindfulness strategies are general or specific to emotional states. When conducting such work, it will be important not to assume that the same paradigm will be uniformly applicable to individuals at different age ranges. Indeed, there are critically important experience-related and maturational-related factors that affect the physiological substrates and emotion regulation capacities across the lifespan (Davidson et al., 2000). In short, differences in such emotional capacities may require different methodological tactics to accurately titrate the nature and function of emotional processing across development.

DOMAIN 4: BROADENING THE ASSESSMENT OF ANXIETY VULNERABILITY PROCESSES

A fourth issue we wish to consider for future work pertains to the parameters of emotional responsivity. To date, the vast majority of research on acceptance and mindfulness processes for anxiety and its disorders addressed questions pertaining to the "average level of emotional distress" in a certain window of time. This issue appears to be a by-product of methodological factors and limits of integrated theoretical conceptualizations of core processes. If we maintain such a viewpoint on the nature of emotional processing, progress may be hindered relative to if we extend analyses to other parameters. This observation may be improved upon by simply extending existing work that has utilized largely cross-sectional designs to prospective tests. However, as we describe below, this change alone likely will be insufficient in the sense that it does not address the *range* of theoretically relevant domains potentially applicable to anxiety vulnerability.

To better capture the parameters of emotional responsivity, Davidson and his colleagues have offered the term *affective style*. We find utility in this heuristic in that it explicitly calls attention to the fact that emotional responding unfolds over time, usually in a dynamic fashion. According to Davidson et al. (2000), affective style can include such features as (1) threshold to respond, (2) magnitude of response, (3) rise time to the peak of response, (4) recovery function of response, and (5) duration of response. Of course, any of these features can be mapped via multimethod assessments, integrating it into a web of cross-system evidence. We anticipate that, given existing empirical work on regulation processes related to anxiety, certain aspects of these affective patterns will hold particular merit. For instance, the affect recovery period may be more theoretically and clinically relevant than maximal degree of distress when the context itself calls for a normative response (e.g., CO_2 challenge paradigm; Zvolensky & Eifert, 2000).

DOMAIN 5: TYING ACCEPTANCE AND MINDFULNESS TO ANXIETY-RELEVANT LEARNING PROCESSES AND PHYSIOLOGICAL SUBSTRATES

It is noteworthy that there is a paucity of empirical work linking acceptance and mindfulness processes to theoretically relevant types of learning involved with anxiety and its disorders. Experimental psychopathology approaches will have much to offer in this domain. In regard to associative learning, for instance, there is a long history of research and theory suggesting that fear conditioning plays a role in anxiety psychopathology (see Bouton, Mineka, & Barlow, 2001). Most contemporary models of posttraumatic stress disorder, as a second illustrative example, suggest that individuals learn to associate stimuli with anxiety and fear reactions related to traumatic events. At present, little is known about to what extent different affect regulatory responses modulate fear conditioning. Future laboratory-based work could usefully test theoretically relevant predictions regarding acceptance and its role in fear conditioning. For example, active attempts to suppress anxiety compared to acceptance may increase associations to an anxiety-eliciting event and perhaps resistance to extinction. This type of work would offer a learning-based explanatory linkage between affect regulatory responses and the etiology and maintenance of anxiety problems. As extinction presumably plays a major role in exposure-based therapies for anxiety disorders, this work also could inform fear reduction strategies. Of course, it is important to note that similar work could be conducted in relation to operant conditioning and modeling.

There also is work needed in regard to developing a better understanding between acceptance and mindfulness and associations with physiological substrates relevant to anxiety problems. The vast majority of laboratory research on these factors has examined peripheral indices of physiological responsiveness (e.g., heart rate reactivity). Extending research to examining associations between these factors and neurobiological variables will be a useful research step in elucidating physiological pathways and points of "activation." Davidson et al. (2003) provide an interesting illustration of how work in this domain can be successfully carried out. In this investigation, neurobiological activity was assessed before, after, and then at 4-month follow-up after an 8-week training program in mindfulness meditation. Results indicated that, compared to wait-list control, participants in the mindfulness meditation condition recorded significant increases in left-sided anterior activation, a pattern associated with positive affect. Moreover, individuals in the mindfulness condition demonstrated enhanced immune system function. Although this study did not have an active control comparison group, it illustrates a potential physiological localization of mindfulness-based meditation effects. Future study will benefit from replicating and extending these findings to psychologically relevant challenges (e.g., emotion–elicitation paradigms). It also may prove useful to use dismantling types of design to explicate the components involved with the meditation program that were responsible for the observed changes in outcome variables. This type of work, particularly when coupled with basic research on these topics, will elucidate the nature of mindfulness-based mediation effects.

SUMMARY

The present book highlights the importance of, and growing work on, acceptance and mindfulness in anxiety disorders research and practice. There is progress being made in the study of these factors, although much work still needs to be done across conceptual, definitional, and research fronts. Experimental psychopathology investigations, in particular, should serve a unique and important role in future work on these topics by focusing analyses on core processes in a controlled environment. Indeed, this type of research paradigm will help explicate the mechanisms of observed effects, reduce confounds common to nonlaboratory environments, and address the relative degree of convergence across and between levels of analysis. Existing work on emotional suppression is evidence of the progress that can be made in this domain. Building from extant work, it is our hope that researchers examining acceptance and mindfulness processes in the laboratory and beyond will benefit by attending to the points raised in this chapter.

REFERENCES

Abramowitz, J. S., Tolin, D. F., & Street, G. P. (2001). Paradoxical effects of thought suppression: A meta-analysis of controlled studies. *Clinical Psychology Review, 21*, 683–703.

Bach, P., & Hayes, S. C. (2002). The use of acceptance and commitment therapy to prevent the rehospitalization of psychotic patients: A randomized controlled trial. *Journal of Consulting & Clinical Psychology, 70*, 1129–1139.

Baer, R. A. (2003). Mindfulness training as a clinical intervention: A conceptual and empirical review. *Clinical Psychology: Science & Practice, 10*, 125–143.

Barlow, D. H. (2002). *Anxiety and its disorders* (2nd ed.). New York: Guilford.

Baron, R. M., & Kenny, D. A. (1986). The moderator–mediator variable distinction in social psychological research: Conceptual, strategic, and statistical considerations. *Journal of Personality & Social Psychology, 51*, 1173–1182.

Baumeister, R. F., Heatherton, T. F., & Tice, D. M. (1994). *Losing control: How and why people fail at self-regulation.* San Diego, CA: Academic Press.

Bernstein, A., Zvolensky, M. J., Weems, C., Stickle, T., & Leen-Feldner, E. (in press). Taxonicity of anxiety sensitivity: An empirical test among youth. *Behaviour Research and Therapy.*

Bishop, S. R., Lau, M., Shapiro, S., Carlson, L., Anderson, N. D., Carmody, J., et al. (2004). Mindfulness: A proposed operational definition. *Clinical Psychology: Science and Practice, 11*, 230–241.

Bouton, M. E., Mineka, S., & Barlow, D. H. (2001). A modern learning theory perspective on the etiology of panic disorder. *Psychological Review, 108*, 4–32.

Brown, K. W., & Ryan, R. M. (2003). The benefits of being present: Mindfulness and its role in psychological well-being. *Journal of Personality and Social Psychology, 84*, 822–848.

Brown, K. W., & Ryan, R. M. (2004). Perils and promise in defining and measuring mindfulness: Observations from experience. *Clinical Psychology: Science and Practice, 11*, 243–248.

Brown, R. A., Lejuez, C. W., Kahler, C. W., Strong, D. R., & Zvolensky, M. J. (in press). Distress tolerance and early smoking lapse. *Clinical Psychology Review.*

Campbell, D. T., & Fiske, D. W. (1959). Convergent and discriminant validation by the multitrait–multimethod matrix. *Psychological Bulletin, 56*, 81–105.

Campbell-Sills, L., Barlow, D. H., Brown, T. A., & Hofmann, S. G. (in press). Effects of emotional suppression and acceptance in individuals with anxiety and mood disorders. *Behaviour Research and Therapy.*

Cannon, W. B. (1927). The James-Lange Theory of emotion: A critical examination and alternative theory. *American Journal of Psychology, 39*, 106–124.

Carver, C. S., Scheier, M. F., & Weintraub, J. K. (1989). Assessing coping strategies: A theoretically based approach. *Journal of Personality and Social Psychology, 64*, 94–103.

Center for the Study of Emotion and Attention. (1995). *The international affective picture system* [IAPS; photographic slides]. Gainesville: University of Florida, the Center for Research in Psychophysiology.

Compas, B. E., Connor-Smith, J. K., Saltzman, H., Thomsen, A. H., & Wadsworth, M. E. (2001). Coping with stress during childhood and adolescence: Problems, progress, and potential in theory and research. *Psychological Bulletin, 127,* 87–127.

Connor-Smith, J. K., Compas, B. E., Wadsworth, M. E., Thomsen, A. H., & Saltzman, H. (2000). Responses to stress in adolescence: measurement of coping and involuntary stress responses. *Journal of Consulting and Clinical Psychology, 68,* 976–692.

Craske, M. G. (1999). *Anxiety disorders: Psychological approaches to theory and treatment.* Boulder, CO: Westview Press.

Craske, M. G. (2003). *Origins of phobias and anxiety disorders: Why more women than men?* New York: Elsevier.

Davidson, R. J. (2000). Affective style, psychopathology, and resilience: Brain mechanisms and plasticity. *American Psychologist, 55,* 1196–1214.

Davidson, R. J., Kabat-Zinn, J., Schumacher, J., Rosenkranz, M., Muller, D. Santorelli, S. F., et al. (2003). Alterations in brain and immune function produced by mindfulness meditation. *Psychosomatic Medicine, 65,* 564–570.

Davidson, R. J., Jackson, D. C., & Kalin, N. H. (2000). Emotion, plasticity, context and regulation: Perspectives from affective neuroscience. *Psychological Bulletin, 126,* 890–906.

de Jong, P. J., & Merckelbach, H. (1998). Blood–injection–injury phobia and fear of spiders: Domain specific individual differences in disgust sensitivity. *Personality & Individual Differences, 24,* 153–158.

Deikman, A. J. (1983). The evaluation of spiritual and utopian groups. *Journal of Humanistic Psychology, 23,* 8–18.

Dimidjian, S., & Linehan, M. M. (2003). Defining an agenda for future research on the clinical application of mindfulness practice. *Clinical Psychology: Science & Practice, 10,* 166–171.

Eifert, G. H., & Heffner, M. (2003). The effects of acceptance versus control contexts on avoidance of panic-related symptoms. *Journal of Behavior Therapy & Experimental Psychiatry, 34,* 293–312.

Eisenberg, N., Fabes, R. A., & Guthrie, I. (1997). Coping with stress: The roles of regulation and development. In J. N. Sandler & S. A. Wolchik (Eds.), *Handbook of children's coping with common stressors: Linking theory, research, and intervention* (pp. 41–70). New York: Plenum.

Feldner, M. T., Zvolensky, M. J., Eifert, G. H., & Spira, A. P. (2003). An experimental manipulation of experiential avoidance of emotional responses to a carbon dioxide–enriched air biological challenge. *Behaviour Research and Therapy, 41,* 403–411.

Feldner, M. T., Zvolensky, M. J., & Leen-Feldner, E. (2004). A critical review of the literature on coping and panic disorder. *Clinical Psychology Review, 24,* 123–148.

Feldner, M. T., Zvolensky, M. J., Stickle, T. R., Bonn-Miller, M. O., & Leen-Feldner, E. W. (in press). Anxiety Sensitivity—Physical Concerns as a moderator of the emotional consequences of emotion suppression during biological challenge: An experimental test using individual growth curve analysis. *Behaviour Research and Therapy.*

Forsyth, J. P., & Zvolensky, M. J. (2002). Experimental psychopathology, clinical science, and practice: An irrelevant or indispensable alliance? *Applied and Preventive Psychology: Current Scientific Perspectives, 10,* 243–264.

Forsyth, J. P., Parker, J. D., & Finlay, C. G. (2003). Anxiety sensitivity, controllability and experiential avoidance and their relation to drug of choice and addiction severity in a residential sample of substance-abusing veterans. *Addictive Behaviors, 28,* 851–870.

Fowles, D. C. (1995). A motivational theory of psychopathology. In W. Spaulding (Ed.), *Nebraska Symposium on Motivation: Integrated views of motivation, cognition, and emotion* (Vol. 41). Lincoln: University of Nebraska Press.

Friman, P. C., Wilson, K. G., & Hayes, S. C. (1998). Behavior analysis of private events is possible, progressive, and nondualistic: A response to Lamal. *Journal of Applied Behavior Analysis, 31,* 707–708.

Grant, K. E., Compas, B. E., Stuhlmacher, A. F., Thurm, A. E., McMahon, S. D., & Halpert, J. A. (2003). Stressors and child and adolescent psychopathology: Moving from markers to mechanisms of risk. *Psychological Bulletin, 129,* 447–466.

Gratz, K. L., & Roemer, L. (2004). Multidimensional assessment of emotion regulation and dysregulation: Development, factor structure, and initial validation of the Difficulties in Emotion Regulation Scale. *Journal of Psychopathology and Behavioral Assessment, 26,* 41–54.

Gray, J. A., & McNaughton, N. (1996). The neuropsychology of anxiety: A reprise. In D. A. Hope (Ed.), *Nebraska Symposium on Motivation: Perspectives on anxiety, panic, and fear* (Vol. 43, pp. 61–134). Lincoln: University of Nebraska Press.

Gross, J. J. (1998). Antecedent- and response-focused emotion regulation: Divergent consequences for experience, expression, and physiology. *Journal of Personality and Social Psychology, 74,* 224–237.

Gross, J. J. (1999). Emotion regulation: Past, present, future. *Cognition and Emotion, 13,* 551–573.

Gross, J. J., & Levenson, R. W. (1993). Emotional suppression: Physiology, self-report, and expressive behavior. *Journal of Personality and Social Psychology, 64,* 970–986.

Gross, J. J., & Levenson, R. W. (1997). Hiding feelings: The acute effects of inhibiting negative and positive emotion. *Journal of Abnormal Psychology, 106,* 95–103.

Hayes, S. C. (2002). Acceptance, mindfulness, and science. *Clinical Psychology: Science & Practice, 9,* 101–106.

Hayes, S. C., Barnes-Holmes, D., & Roche, B. (2001). Relational frame theory: A precis. In S. C. Hayes & D. Barnes-Holmes (Eds.), *Relational frame theory: A post-Skinnerian account of human language and cognition.* New York: Kluwer Academic/Plenum Publishers.

Hayes, A. M., & Feldman, G. (2004). Clarifying the construct of mindfulness in the context of emotion regulation and the process of change in therapy. *Clinical Psychology: Science and Practice, 11,* 255–262.

Hayes, S. C., & Shenk, C. (2004). Operationalizing mindfulness without unnecessary attachments. *Clinical Psychology: Science and Practice, 11,* 249–254.

Hayes, S. C., Strosahl, K. D., & Wilson, K. G. (1999). *Acceptance and Commitment Therapy*. New York: Guilford.

Hayes, S. C., Strosahl, K. D., Wilson, K. G., Bissett, R. T., Pistorello, J., Toarmino, et al. (2004). Measuring experiential avoidance: A preliminary test of a working model. *Psychological Record, 54,* 553–578.

Hayes, S. C., & Wilson, K. G. (2003). Mindfulness as method and process. *Clinical Psychology: Science and Practice, 10,* 161–165.

Hayes, S. C., Wilson, K. G., Gifford, E. V., Follette, V. M., & Strosahl, K. (1996). Experiential avoidance and behavioral disorders: A functional dimensional approach to diagnosis and treatment. *Journal of Consulting and Clinical Psychology, 64,* 1152–1168.

Jackson, D. C., Malmstadt, J. R., Larson, C. L., & Davidson, R. J. (2000). Suppression and enhancement of emotional responses to unpleasant pictures. *Psychophysiology, 37,* 515–522.

Joiner, T. E., Jr., & Lonigan, C. J. (2000). Tripartite model of depression and anxiety in youth psychiatric inpatients: Relations with diagnostic status and future symptoms. *Journal of Clinical Child Psychology, 29,* 372–382.

Kabat-Zinn, J. (2003). Mindfulness-based interventions in context: Past, present, and future. *Clinical Psychology: Science & Practice, 10,* 144–156.

Kabat-Zinn, J. (1990). *Full catastrophe living: Using the wisdom of your body and mind to face stress, pain, and illness*. New York: Dell.

Kabat-Zinn, J. L., Lipworth, L., Burney, R., & Sellers, W. (1987). Four-year follow-up of a medication-based program for the self-regulation of chronic pain: Treatment outcome and compliance. *Clinical Journal of Pain, 2,* 159–173.

Karekla, M., Forsyth, J. P., & Kelly, M. M. (2004). Emotional avoidance and panicogenic responding to a biological challenge procedure. *Behavior Therapy, 35,* 725–746.

Kazdin, A. E., & Weisz, J. R. (1998). Identifying and developing empirically supported child and adolescent treatments. *Journal of Consulting and Clinical Psychology, 66,* 19–36.

Kraemer, H., Kazdin, A., Offord, D., Kessler, R., Jensen, P., & Kupfer, D. (1997). Coming to terms with the terms of risk. *Archives of General Psychiatry, 54,* 337–343.

Lacey, J. (1967). Somatic response patterning and stress: Some revisions of activation theory. In M. H. Appley & R. Trumbell (Eds.), *Psychological stress*. New York: Appleton-Century-Crofts.

Lang, P. J. (1984). Cognition in emotion: Concept and action. In C. E. Izard, J. Kagan, & R. B. Zajonc (Eds.), *Emotions, cognition, and behavior* (pp. 192–228). New York: Cambridge University Press.

Leen-Feldner, E. W., Zvolensky, M. J., & Feldner, M. T. (2004). Adolescent behavioral inhibition and response suppression: An experimental examination. *Journal of Clinical Child and Adolescent Psychology, 33,* 783–791.

Levitt, J. T., Brown, T. A., Orsillo, S. M., & Barlow, D. H. (2004). The effects of acceptance versus suppression of emotion on subjective and psychophysiological response to carbon dioxide challenge in patients with panic disorder. *Behavior Therapy, 35,* 747–766.

Lynch, T. R., Robins, C. J., Morse, J. Q., & Krause, E. D. (2001). A mediational model relating affect intensity, emotion inhibition, and psychological distress. *Behavior Therapy, 32*, 519–536.

Mancini, F., Gragnani, A., & D'Olimpio, F. (2001). The connection between disgust and obsessions and compulsions in a non-clinical sample. *Personality & Individual Differences, 31*, 1173–1180.

McNally, R. J. (1999). Panic induction: A critical appraisal. *Behavior Therapy, 30*, 245–261.

Mennin, D. S., Heimberg, R. G., Turk, C. L., & Fresco, D. M. (2002). Applying an emotion regulation framework to integrative approaches to generalized anxiety disorder. *Clinical Psychology: Science and Practice, 9*, 85–90.

National Institute of Drug Abuse. (2004). *Identifying the Mechanisms of Action (MOA) of behavioral treatment: Setting the stage for dissemination.* NIDA-sponsored workgroup meeting, Gaithersburg, MD.

Orsillo, S. M., Roemer, L., & Barlow, D. H. (2003). Integrating acceptance and mindfulness into existing cognitive–behavioral treatment for GAD: A case study. *Cognitive & Behavioral Practice, 10*, 222–230.

Page, A. C. (1994). Blood–injury phobia. *Clinical Psychology Review, 14*, 443–461.

Plumb, J. C., Orsillo, S. M., & Luterek, J. A. (2004). A preliminary test of the role of experiential avoidance in post-event functioning. *Journal of Behavior Therapy & Experimental Psychiatry, 35*, 245–257.

Ramel, W., Goldin, P. R., Carmona, P. E., & McQuaid, J. R. (2004). The effects of mindfulness meditation on cognitive processes and affect in patients with past depression. *Cognitive Therapy & Research, 28*, 433–455.

Rassin, E., Merckelbach, H., & Muris, P. (2001). Thought suppression and traumatic intrusions in undergraduate students: A correlational study. *Personality & Individual Differences, 31*, 485–493.

Reiss, S., Peterson, R. A., Gursky, M., & McNally, R. J. (1986). Anxiety, sensitivity, anxiety frequency, and the prediction of fearfulness. *Behaviour Research and Therapy, 24*, 1–8.

Richards, J. M., & Gross, J. J. (1999). Composure at any cost? The cognitive consequences of emotion suppression. *Personality & Social Psychology Bulletin, 25*, 1033–1044.

Richards, J. M., & Gross, J. J. (2000). Emotion regulation and memory: The cognitive costs of keeping one's cool. *Journal of Personality and Social Psychology, 79*, 410–424.

Roemer, L., & Orsillo, S. M. (2002). Expanding our conceptualization of and treatment for generalized anxiety disorder: Integrating mindfulness/acceptance-based approaches with existing cognitive–behavioral models. *Clinical Psychology: Science and Practice, 9*, 54–68.

Rothbart, M. K., Ahadi, S. A., & Evans, D. E. (2000). Temperament and personality: Origins and outcomes. *Journal of Personality and Social Psychology, 78*, 122–135.

Rothbart, M. K., Ziaie, H., & O'Boyle, C. G. (1992). Self-regulation and emotion in infancy. In N. Eisenberg & R. A. Fabes (Eds.), *Emotion and its regulation in early development: New directions for child development* (pp. 7–23). San Francisco: Jossey-Bass.

Salovey, P., Rothman, A. J., Detweiler, J. B., & Steward, W. T. (2000). Emotional states and physical health. *American Psychologist, 55*, 110–121.

Sawchuk, C. N., Lohr, J. M., Tolin, D. F., Lee, T. C., & Kleinknecht, R. A. (2000). Disgust sensitivity and contamination fears in spider and blood–injection–injury phobias. *Behaviour Research & Therapy, 38*, 753–762.

Sechrest, L. (1963). Incremental validity: A recommendation. *Educational & Psychological Measurement, 23*, 153–158.

Sechrest, L., Davis, M. F., Stickle, T. R., & McKnight, K. M. (2000). Understanding method variance. In Bickman, L. (Ed.), *Essays in honor of Donald Campbell*. Newbury Park, CA: Sage Publications.

Sloan, D. M. (2004). Emotion regulation in action: Emotional reactivity in experiential avoidance. *Behaviour Research and Therapy, 42*, 1257–1270.

Spira, A. P., Zvolensky, M. J., Eifert, G. E., & Feldner, M. T. (2004). The relation of anxiety sensitivity and coping strategy to CO_2-induced anxious and fearful responding. *Journal of Anxiety Disorders, 18*, 309–323.

Strauman, T., & Merrill, K. A. (2004). The basic science/clinical science interface and treatment development. *Clinical Psychology: Science and Practice, 11*, 263–266.

Telch, M. J., Lucas, J. A., Schmidt, N. B., Hanna, H. H., Jaimez, T. N., & Lucas, R. A. (1993). Group cognitive–behavioral treatment of panic disorder. *Behaviour Research and Therapy, 31*, 279–287.

Vitaliano, P. P., Maiuro, R. D., Russo, J., & Becker, J. (1987). Raw versus relative scores in the assessment of coping strategies. *Journal of Behavioral Medicine, 10*, 1–18.

Vrana, S. R. (1993). The psychophysiology of disgust: Differentiating negative emotional contexts with facial EMG. *Psychophysiology, 30*, 279–286.

Wenzlaff, R. M., & Wegner, D. M. (2000). Thought suppression. *Annual Review of Psychology, 51*, 59–91.

Wilber, K. (2000). *Integral psychology: Consciousness, spirit, psychology, therapy*. Boston: Shambhala Publications.

Williams, J., Teasdale, J. D., Segal, Z. V., & Soulsby, J. (2000). Mindfulness-based cognitive therapy reduces overgeneral autobiographical memory in formerly depressed patients. *Journal of Abnormal Psychology, 109*, 150–155.

Woody, S. R., & Teachman, B. A. (2000). Intersection of disgust and fear: Normative and pathological views. *Clinical Psychology: Science & Practice, 7*, 291–311.

Yartz, A. R., & Hawk, L. W., Jr. (2002). Addressing the specificity of affective startle modulation: Fear versus disgust. *Biological Psychology, 59*, 55–68.

Yartz, A. R., & Hawk, L. W., Jr. (2004). Individual differences in disgust sensitivity and voluntary emotion regulation: Subjective, physiological, and behavioral responses to disgust and pleasant pictures. Manuscript submitted for publication.

Zvolensky, M. J., & Eifert, G. H. (2000). A review of psychological factors/processes affecting anxious responding during voluntary hyperventilation and inhalations of carbon dioxide–enriched air. *Clinical Psychology Review, 21*, 375–400.

Zvolensky, M. J., Eifert, G. H., Lejuez, C. W., & McNeil, D. W. (1999). The effects of offset control over 20% carbon dioxide–enriched air on anxious responding. *Journal of Abnormal Psychology, 108,* 624–632.

Zvolensky, M. J., Feldner, M. T., Eifert, G. H., & Brown, R. A. (2001). Affective style among smokers: Understanding anxiety sensitivity, emotional reactivity, and distress tolerance using biological challenge. *Addictive Behaviors, 26,* 901–915.

Zvolensky, M. J., Feldner, M. T., Leen-Feldner, E., Bonn-Miller, M. O., McLeish, A. C., et al. (2004). Evaluating the role of anxiety sensitivity in smoking outcome expectancies among regular smokers. *Cognitive Therapy and Research, 28,* 473–486.

Zvolensky, M. J., Feldner, M. T., Leen-Feldner, E. W., & McLeish, A. (in press). Smoking and panic attacks, panic disorder, and agoraphobia: A review of the empirical literature. *Clinical Psychology Review.*

Zvolensky, M. J., & Forsyth, J. P. (2002). Anxiety sensitivity dimensions in the prediction of body vigilance and emotional avoidance. *Cognitive Therapy and Research, 26,* 449–460.

Zvolensky, M. J., Lejuez, C. W., & Eifert, G. H. (2000). Prediction and control: Operational definitions for the experimental analysis of anxiety. *Behaviour Research & Therapy, 38,* 653–663.

Zvolensky, M. J., Lejuez, C. W., Stuart, G. L., & Curtin, J. J. (2001). Experimental psychopathology in psychological science. *Review of General Psychology, 5,* 371–381.

Zvolensky, M. J., Schmidt, N. B., & Stewart, S. H. (2003). Panic disorder and smoking. *Clinical Psychology: Science and Practice, 10,* 29–51.

INDEX